Thirty Years of
BEST SPORTS STORIES

Thirty Years
of
BEST SPORTS
STORIES

Edited by
Irving T. Marsh and Edward Ehre

With Thirty Top Sports Photographs

E. P. DUTTON & CO., INC.   /   NEW YORK   /   1975

Library of Congress Cataloging in Publication Data

Marsh, Irving T   comp.
Thirty years of Best sports stories.

1. Sports stories.   I. Ehre, Edward, joint comp.
    II. Best sports stories.   III. Title.
GV707.M28   796'.08   74-12045

Published simultaneously in Canada by Clarke, Irwin & Company Limited,
Toronto and Vancouver
ISBN: 0-525-21767-3
Designed by The Etheredges

CONTENTS

WHO'S WHO IN
THIRTY YEARS OF *BEST SPORTS STORIES*

PHOTOGRAPHS

PREFACE

It was early in the year of 1944 that your editors approached Mr. Elliott Macrae, then president of E. P. Dutton & Co., with an idea. Sitting in his comfortable office, the walls lined with the works of Dutton writers, they broached the thought of an annual compendium of sports stories that would, in effect, be a history of each year in sport as set down by the top stories and pictures of the events of that year.

The editors suggested that the book take the form of a prize competition, with the top story, as voted on by a group of three judges, awarded $500, the top pictures $100 (that was money in them days).

Although Dutton had not published many books on sports before that, Mr. Macrae was immediately receptive. He met with his editorial board and the green light was given within a very few days.

Thus was born the *Best Sports Stories* series. Since the original volume in 1944 (which was also published in paperback by the Armed Forces for American troops overseas) the format has changed little. Instead of one prize of $500 for a single story, the editors established three categories—best magazine, best news-feature and best news-coverage—awarding $250 for the best in each of these classes, again based on the votes of a panel of judges. The prize-photo competition was divided into two—action and feature.

A system of voting was established. The judges received the entries not knowing who wrote them or where they appeared. They were disguised under what is known in newspaperese as a "slug," or an identification mark of a word or two. The judges indicated their choices by a point system: 3 for a first-place choice, 2 for a second, 1 for a third.

The reception by sports writers and photographers was enthusiastic. The first competition drew in the neighborhood of 500 story entries from all parts of the nation. It was an extremely difficult task to select the 50 stories that would go to the judges, as it was to choose 30 photographs from the nearly 200 submitted.

The press was kind in its reviews, the public equally kind in its purchases, and we were on our way.

For the 30 years since the beginning, 1,500 stories and about 800 photos have been included in the *Best Sports Stories* anthologies. The prizewinning stories and pictures of the first 20 years were reprinted in 1964 in an omnibus volume called *Best of the Best Sports Stories*. Now, after 30 years, comes the second omnibus volume, containing top stories not reprinted in the earlier volume, with two exceptions, and many of the last ten years' prizewinners. There are a story and a photo for each of the 30 years.

In those years there have been many changes in sports and sports writing. Not the least of the changes in sports as a whole has been the shift in emphasis from amateur sport to professional sport, to the point where professional football has gained the No. 1 spot in popularity among the fans of the nation. Moreover, there has been a tremendous growth in pro golf, tennis, hockey, baseball (the previous leader in popularity), and basketball.

The change in sports writing is reflected in the shift from what is known as the "Gee Whiz" school to the "Aw, Nuts" school, or from the hero-worship type of writing to the cynical and even critical type. Televised sports has been a great factor in this change. More sophisticated fandom has been another. More people know more about sports now than ever.

It is fitting at this point to give recognition and sincere thanks to some people who have helped in the production of these 30 annuals and two omnibuses:

To our judges—the late Franklin P. Adams, Bob Harron, Quentin Reynolds and Frank Graham—as well as to John Chamberlain, John Hutchens, Red Smith, and Bob Considine, sports enthusiasts all. Chamberlain has served the full 30 years.

To our editors—John Tebbel, who later turned from editing to teaching at New York University's Journalism Department and to freelance writing; Ms. Jeanne Frank Bernkopf and Bill Doerflinger, all three of whom have been of immense help with the series.

To the chroniclers of sport, both with typewriter and camera, who have contributed their efforts in ever-increasing numbers over the years so that the entries for *Best Sports Stories—1974* totaled well over 1,000.

And, of course, to the sports-loving public, which has enabled us, by their interest, to continue this series for 30 years.

We hope the current volume will lend luster to the events described, as well as enjoyment and perhaps even nostalgia to all of you.

IRVING T. MARSH
EDWARD EHRE

THE STORIES

1944

GAELIC DISASTER
By Walter (Red) Smith

FROM THE PHILADELPHIA RECORD

*Red Smith made his debut in the first volume, in 1944,
with these opening lines, "Quiet country churchyards from
Killarney to Kimberly gave off a strange whirring sound
this afternoon as departed Irish wheeled and spun and did
flipflops under the sod." Red was describing the debacle of
the Army win over the Irish, 59–0, after 13 years of
futility, and those who never saw Army's Davis and
Blanchard (Mr. Inside and Mr. Outside) function will
read of their feats described with the humor and percep-
tiveness of a fine reporter.*

Quiet country churchyards from Killarney to Kimberly gave off a
strange, whirring sound this afternoon as departed Irish whirled
and spun and did flipflops under the sod.

In the most horrendous Gaelic disaster since the Battle of
the Boyne, the Celtic Szymanskis and Dancewiczes of Notre
Dame were ravaged, routed and demolished by Army's football
team by the most garish score in history—59 to 0.

Billed as the classiest spectacle in sports, the gridiron's
equivalent of the Kentucky Derby, the World Series, and the
Philadelphia Assembly, it was a travesty engineered by the joint
efforts of the best of all West Point's teams and one of South
Bend's weakest.

Yankee Stadium's plus-capacity crowd of 74,430 witnesses—
some of whom paid scalpers as much as $25 for a seat behind a
steel stanchion or a backless bench built up against the rafters or
a funeral-parlor chair on the sideline—watched the dreadful
destruction with mixed feelings, in which numbed disbelief
predominated.

It was Army's first triumph over Notre Dame since way back before the Roosevelt administration—the Cadets' last was achieved in 1931—and if it had happened a week earlier it probably would have cost the New Deal the Irish vote.

But if it seemed a low-comedy burlesque to Notre Dame's famed "subway alumni," its reception was something else again in the left-field stands populated by the gray-coated corps of the Military Academy.

From the early moments of the opening quarter, when Army stormed 44 yards to its first touchdown, until the red hand of the clock completed its last revolution, these young characters whooped and gloated and screamed for more of the same.

Not one of them ever saw an Army team score against Notre Dame. (Neither did anyone else since 1938.) Now they were seeing it happen almost every time they lifted their eyes. When the score was 46 to 0 they set up a hungry chant:

"More yet! More yet! More yet!"

When the count was 58 to 0—matching the score Wisconsin made in 1904 in Notre Dame's worst previous hiding—the chorus still resounded: "We want more! We want more!"

And Army's coach, Lieutenant Colonel Red Blaik, is not the sort to go soft and disappoint his constituents. He rushed his place-kicking specialist, Dick Walterhouse, in to convert the 59th point.

The mission briefed for unbeaten Army this day was threefold. The Cadets had to spread salve on wounds that Notre Dame has kept raw by winning 22 of 30 earlier engagements; they had to strike terror into the hearts of Penn, their next victims; they had to make this the first season that ever saw Navy and Army triumphant over the Irish, and in doing so, improve on the Midshipmen's 32–13 margin of victory last week.

They had what it took and to spare. They unwrapped a backfield far more versatile than Navy's, although perhaps not quite so loaded with crushing power, in which Doug Kenna and Glenn Davis and Max Minor and Dale Hall and Felix Blanchard vied at uncorking ever more blinding speed.

They needed no help to win as they pleased. But help they got nevertheless, in job lots. Notre Dame persistently furnished aid by resorting again and again to a passing game, which was Army's most devastating weapon.

Army intercepted eight passes—Notre Dame completed only ten—and five touchdowns stemmed from these thefts, one of the interceptors scoring as he made his catch.

Two other touchdowns resulted from blazing punt runbacks, one of 60 yards by Minor, which went over the goal line, and one that took Kenna 37 yards to the Notre Dame 20.

Another was accomplished by the dazzling Davis on a 56-yard sprint from scrimmage. Still another was made possible by recovery of a fumbled Notre Dame lateral. And finally there was one built on plain power.

Thus, although the Irish were bound to lose whatever they tried, the fact is they dug their own grave deeper by insistent gambling with an air game against a defense whose members all field like the St. Louis Cardinals' Slats Marion.

Davis scored three touchdowns, Minor two, Kenna one, a pair of ends, named Ed Rafalko and Dick Pitzer, one each, and a tackle named Harold Tavzel, one. Here's how:

1. Receiving Notre Dame's first punt, Army drove 43 yards to the 1-yard line on straight T-formation plunges, plus one pass. On third down, Center Frank Szymanski smashed Minor for a five-yard loss, and on fourth down Kenna missed Rafalko with a pass.

However, both teams were offsides on this play, so instead of losing the ball, Army got another chance. This time Kenna fled wide around his right end as one tackler after another hurled himself against his blocking screen and bounced off.

Kenna scored, as did all the others, standing upright and hermetically sealed away from prying hands.

Walterhouse converted from placement. He made good five times in nine chances, once from the 26-yard line after Army drew a holding penalty. Two kicks were blocked. Once the pass from center was wild, and he made a hurried, futile effort at a drop kick.

2. Almost immediately after the ensuing kickoff Kenna intercepted a pass by Frank Dancewicz and ran to Notre Dame's 26. Here, on a magnificently faked reverse to the left, Minor broke into the clear.

3. Notre Dame's next play was a pass which Blanchard leaped high to grab, coming down on the Irish 35. Kenna faded and fired a strike to Rafalko, who had slipped past Bill Chandler at the goal line.

4. Davis snatched a pass by Dancewicz from under Bob Kelly's nose and leaped along a curling 41-yard course to the 7-yard line, where Dancewicz, the passer and last defender, spilled him. Then he circled his right end.

5. Catching a punt on his 43, Kenna started to his right but

was trapped near the sideline by Bill O'Connor, who had fought off two blockers. Reversing his field, he dashed toward the left boundary, was eased around the corner by George Poole's cruel block, and ripped down to Notre Dame's 20. When the ball reached the 5-yard stripe, Davis slipped around end on a bootleg reverse.

6. Two minutes after the second half opened, Kenna caught a punt, darted to his right, and handed the ball to Minor, who met him at top speed. Flashing 60 yards down the left sideline, Minor met only Kelly, whom Blanchard bounced aside.

7. After Pitzer grabbed a lateral muffed by Kelly, he caught a touchdown pass from Kenna.

8. Taking a direct pass from center on his 44-yard line, Davis faked a pass, tucked the ball under his arm, slanted off to the left of center, and broke out of the pack, completing the trip alone.

9. Still gambling for a score with less than three minutes to go, Notre Dame tried a screen pass, with the passer in his end zone. Joe Gasparella's toss went to the astonished Tavzel, who collapsed from sheer glee. He had the foresight to collapse across the goal line.

1945

RETURN OF THE "VERCE"

By Harold Rosenthal

FROM PAGEANT

Copyright © 1945, Pageant

This is a short sketch of the original and respected Harry Balogh, who won national radio fame for his Madison Square Garden announcements and who was in most cases more popular than the bouts themselves. It is a gem of a piece that recalls the days when boxing was much more than a money-mad TV spectacle. With his evening clothes and malapropisms, Balogh became to the ring what Casey Stengel was to the Yankees.

Some folks don't like Harry Balogh. They say that his accents are at one and the same time an exotic blend of Oxford, Back Bay, and Greenpernt; also, that he wears ultra-formal tails with black tie and bags under his eyes to match. But like him or not, everyone was glad when Harry came out of retirement at the start of the year to resume his place as the world's foremost prizefight announcer.

For two solid years, fight fans in Madison Square Garden, New York, filed their nails, fidgeted, yawned, and were otherwise preoccupied when sundry nondescript characters intoned pre-fight names, weights etc., and equally as colorlessly announced the winner. Then one magical night Mike Jacobs, boxing's No. 1 entrepreneur, smiled—the "Verce" came back.

The secret of the "Verce's" charm lies in his ability to say the right thing at least twice and, if he's feeling good, three times. F'r instance, "I crave your indulgence, laydeez and gennelmen, and beg leave to trespass on your time and good nature to the extent of asking your forbearance while I make a few announcements

7

and pass along a few facts relative to and connected with boxing and the sport of pugilism." These were the first words uttered in his comeback.

Harry Balogh (pronounced "Ba-low") has been tops as a fight announcer for the past decade, or ever since Joe Humphreys died. A native New Yorker, Balogh was Humphreys' protégé. After a short whirl as a pugilist, Balogh decided that his place was at the start and finish of each fight on the program.

Harry conceived the idea that someone should be well dressed in a prizefight ring—you can't depend on the fighters or the referee—so evening clothes became part of his stock in trade. His delivery style was natural enough until the various arenas began to install public-address systems, and then he had to bow to progress.

Harry's an expert in the fine old art of chauvinism and will allude, point to, and refer to a boxer's East Side or West Side heritage half a dozen times. It's supposed to have a salubrious effect on the box office.

In less palmy days Harry had to take his jobs where he found them and often as not it would be in some smoke-filled, frowzy barn with perhaps a two-to-one cop-customer ratio. It was in places like these that Harry, handling fights involving boxers of different hues, had a chance to work up a speech calling for "no display of prejudism, please!"

He was doing a fight show at St. Nick's when he broke his names-weights-color-of-tights routine to make a March of Dimes plea.

"And now," he concluded, "the pretty little girls will pass among you with their little cans. Please give until it hurts!"

The sports department of the *New York Herald Tribune* obtained Harold Rosenthal in June, 1941, in a straight-cash, no-trade deal for an undisclosed amount. In October, 1942, Our Boy was waived to the Army of the United States, where he subsequently played a spotty left field for the Army Air Force.

He served, with distinction and otherwise, in such organizations as Headquarters Squadron, Army Air Forces; Assistant Chief of Air Staff, A-4, etc.; and learned that, if you can't win a war with 3-by-5 index cards (ruled), you can usually do it with 5-by-8's. Incidentally, he rocketed to buck sergeant in three short years. It was during this period that he tried his hand at magazine writing. "The Return of the 'Verce'" is the result of one of these tries.

The ex-sergeant is now back on the sports staff of the *New York Herald Tribune*. He is married, lives a stone's throw from the office, and does *not* have two children.

1946

HOT TAMALE CIRCUIT

By Kyle Crichton

FROM COLLIER'S

Copyright ©1946, Kyle Crichton

In 1946 the American baseball player was still in serfdom to the reserve clause and all the attendant evils that a standard baseball contract offered. Playing ball in Mexico during the off season was an attractive moonlight occupation which American owners resented and fought. The author comes to grips with the whole issue of the relationship between management and employees that even today is besmirching the sport of baseball. Originally this piece was two different articles, but they are here combined.

I

In Mexico City Mickey Owen was on second base when the next hitter drove a fly into right field. Mickey tagged up and set sail for third as soon as the ball was caught. He made it safely by one of the famous belly-buster slides specialized in by Pepper Martin of the St. Louis Cardinals.

This was Mr. Owen's first game in Mexico City and he had been on Mexican soil only a week. The altitude in Mexico City is 7,325 feet and most visitors not only refrain from belly-busting but take to their beds immediately on arrival. Mickey is obviously a brave man, but as he lay on the ground at Delta Parque there were varying thoughts about him in the capacity crowd. Had it not been for the stern and challenging eye of Señor Jorge Pasquel, president of the American League, it is quite possible that sporting bloods among the spectators would willingly have ventured a few centavos on the proposition that Señor Owen would never get up alive. Mr. Owen arose, dusted particles of sacred Aztec soil from his uniform, and was left there on third when Chili Gomez hit into a double play and killed the rally.

We mention this excruciatingly unimportant detail because it represents one of the minor hazards to be faced by American players crossing the border. Now that the original tumult and shouting have died, it is possible to estimate Mexican baseball and see what it means to the blacklisted American players who have temporarily departed the homeland for a sample of Señor Pasquel's gold.

It may seem farfetched to say it, but that arrival of Mickey Owen in Mexico City was an event of considerable international importance. It followed close on the departure of Vernon Stephens, who had fled to the States across the border at Laredo as if he were escaping from a concentration camp. This was bad enough, but subsequent interviews with Stephens produced varying reflections about Mexico which were considered insults by the Mexicans. When a spokesman for the State Department in Washington hinted that it might be well for the American leagues and the Mexican League to get together, he was obviously speaking from information not available to the public.

In the interests of mutual amity, we shall not recount the entire Stephens story, but it can be said that Jack Fournier, of the St. Louis Browns, met Stephens at Monterrey, and other mysterious Americans went over the border with the intent of facilitating Stephens's release. An explosion could easily have occurred there which would have had tragic consequences for our relations with Mexico. We can get an idea of how the Mexicans felt by envisioning a situation in which Mexican agents filtered into Chicago by nightfall and spirited away a Mexican player on the ground that he was in danger from gangsters.

Owen and his wife had reached San Antonio on their way to Mexico when the Stephens incident occurred. It gave them pause, and they were further harassed by pressure from the American side. The general tenor of the remarks was that the Mexican League would blow up and Owen wouldn't get his money; also he would be mixed up with a gambling racket, would sacrifice a good career in the States, and might even end up shot by tough Mexican hombres who didn't like his style of catching. The phone in the Owen hotel room rang all night long, and after a few days it was plain that they either had to get away or collapse.

A phone call with Branch Rickey had brought merely the suggestion that Mickey come back and be a good boy and Brooklyn would look into his case. Rickey promised further that in fifteen days he would dig up the money so Owen could repay the $20,000 already received from Pasquel. The Owens then got in their car and started to roam. When they reached Vicksburg, Mississippi, they read a newspaper story saying that Rickey was adamant in his determination that Owen would never again play for Brooklyn but would be traded. That was the finisher. Mickey got in touch with Alfonso Pasquel in Houston and later joined him in Laredo. What Mickey wanted was proof that his five-year contract would be carried out.

"Name any proposition you want and you'll get it," said Alfonso.

Jorge Pasquel has stated privately that Owen was paid $50,000 in advance on his contract; Mickey says he was paid a bonus of $12,500 and was given his fifth year's salary of $15,000 in advance. In all, he got $27,500, says Mickey, and is being paid for this year's work as he goes along. He explains the difference between his own and Pasquel's figures by the amount that Pasquel will pay out for Owen's living expenses. It seems impossible that Mickey could live that sumptuously but the point need not be stressed; it is certain that Owen has $27,500 at least and ample assurance for the rest.

What is most immediately apparent in interviewing the ball players in Mexico is that Pasquel would have had no luck whatever in his recruiting if the players had not been dissatisfied with conditions in the States.

The landscape of Mexico is dotted, for example, with ex-New York Giant players. Down at Puebla you will see a familiar figure waddle his way out of the coaching box and will recognize him immediately as Dolf Luque, former pitcher and coach of the Giants. With him at Puebla are Napoleon Reyes, Adrian Zabala, and Salvatore Maglie. Up at Laredo are Roy Zimmerman and Tommy Gorman; Danny Gardella and Charley Mead are with the Vera Cruz team in Mexico City. George Hausmann is up at Torreón with Red Hayworth, former St. Louis Browns catcher. Ace Adams and Harry Feldman are new arrivals.

"I did good with Cincinnati and Brooklyn," said Luque, "but those Giants . . ." He stopped and waved a hand. "They don't want to pay nobody no money."

"Don't forget those two autographed balls they sent us as a bonus last winter," laughed Maglie.

It is difficult to reconcile the opinion the public has of Mel Ott and the resentment the Mexican ex-Giant contingent has against him. Quite aside from the salary differences, they maintain that there is no team spirit on the Giants because Ott suppresses it. At least half a dozen of the men said to us: "Ott never even looked at us away from the ball park. He doesn't mean to do it but he beats you down until you haven't any spirit left as a player."

The players particularly resented the treatment given to Nap Reyes, Danny Gardella, and Ace Adams.

"Maybe Reyes isn't a great player, but he worked his head off for the Giants last year. He played third base and first base and kept going even when he had a leg injury that would have put anybody else on the bench. Then when he couldn't get what he wanted with New York and signed with the Mexican League, the newspapers said it was good riddance and he was a bum anyhow. You can say what you want, but Gardella was the only drawing card the Giants had last year. Ace Adams pitched in over 60 games for two years in a row, and when he left New York, one paper said it was the best break the Giants ever had. The Giants broke their record for home attendance last year, with a low-salaried team—and that's what they say about the players that helped them make a fortune."

But the financial details are less important than the human element. How are the Americans going to get along in Mexico? What chance has the Mexican League to last? What sort of a man is Jorge Pasquel (pronounced "Pass-kell")? How will the Americans be affected by the living conditions, the food, the water, the necessity of learning a foreign tongue? To get the answers, we visited the homes of as many American players as we could reach and talked also with Cuban, Puerto Rican, and Mexican players. We have found out a great deal about Mexican baseball and almost as much about American baseball.

Take the case of Tommy De La Cruz, formerly a very good pitcher for the Cincinnati Reds. Tommy was setting the league on fire last year for the Mexico City team (working on a five-year contract at a salary almost twice that of Cincinnati) when he tore a muscle in his leg. He collected his salary for the remaining two months of the year and then Pasquel paid all expenses for a major operation last winter in Havana. When De La Cruz returned to Mexico City this spring, Pasquel refused to let him pitch until it was certain he was in shape. He still wasn't pitching a month after the season opened.

"Jorge said it didn't matter if I ever pitched again," said De La Cruz. "He said I was with him for life and could be a manager or coach if I couldn't pitch."

The De La Cruzes were established in an expensive apartment in the Washington Apartments with their rent paid and their living expenses assured by the club. The Owens were around the corner in another nice apartment, and down the block were the Frank Scalzis. Scalzi, the former New York Giant player, is known in Mexico as Rizzuti because he played in Mexico under that assumed name in 1940. A short distance away are the Bobby Estalellas in the Latino-Americano apartments. Danny Gardella, late of the New York Giants, is set up in style in an apartment near Hamburgo Street, where Jorge Pasquel lives. Luis Olmo, the former Brooklyn star, is also living in Mexico City, and Charley Mead of the Giants is a new arrival.

The apartments are rent-free and last year the players were given six hundred pesos a month for living expenses (approximately $120 at the current rate of exchange). But this means nothing under the Pasquel system. If groceries come higher, the players let Pasquel know and he puts up the difference. Without doubt, it is the most amazing thing ever known in the history of sports. The players practically get their salaries clear.

George Hausmann has his wife and children at Torreón, where they enjoy the privileges of the country club and have a swimming pool for the children. Red Hayworth is also at Torreón and likes it so well that he has sent for his family. Mickey Owen reports that Roy Zimmerman is happy at Nuevo Laredo, and we can testify that the Mexico City contingent feel they are sitting on top of the world. They were worried about Murray Franklin, the ex-Detroit player, at Tampico, where it is hot and not too attractive, but Franklin has stated that he is quite content there. He feels he got a raw deal from Detroit in being dropped after a month of spring training, and is one of the greatest boosters for Mexican baseball.

Pasquel treats the players with such prodigality that they go about with their eyes popping. In addition to the salaries, bonuses, free apartments, and allowances for living expenses, he pays all doctor and dentist bills and is so free with his largesse that all the players' wives have gold bracelets as gifts from him and many of the players have clothes, watches, and rings as presents. Ramon Bragana, Cuban Negro pitcher and manager of the Vera Cruz team, is wearing a diamond ring presented by Jorge and said to be worth $6,000. Dolf Luque down at Puebla has a new car as a gift from the club.

Thinking that this might only be true for the higher-priced athletes, we talked with Raymond Dandridge, American Negro second baseman for Mexico City. He assured us that conditions

are exactly alike for all players. Since he has been coming to
Mexico for many years, he knows the situation well and other
players told us with envy that Dandridge was installed in one of
the finest houses in town. At forty-two, Dandridge is a wonder as
a fielder and hitter. He plays baseball 11 months a year (Panama,
Cuba, and Mexico), and there is general agreement that he
would be a star on any big-league club in America.

However, Mexico is not the United States and there are
handicaps that are inclined to irk the visitor. It is a country
without water, and Mexico City, modern as it may be, is no
exception. In some apartments the water is turned off at noon
and unless the housewife learns to keep a reserve supply in the
bathtub, the family may have a tough time during the day.
However, the 6,000 other Americans who make Mexico City their
permanent home get used to such difficulties and also accustom
themselves to the differences in food.

The Mexico City ball park looks like a run-down minor-
league plant in this country. It seats around 20,000 but is a
rickety job with no lavatory conveniences, no clubhouse, and no
showers for the players. They dress at home and go back home to
change. Even President Pasquel's box has no chairs; you sit on
the flat boards with no backrest. There is a line of boxes in front
holding four patrons sitting on small wire chairs such as we see in
drugstores. The Puebla ball park holds around 10,000 and the
boxes there consist of one row of grandstand seats protected by a
railing.

However, the league will spend $6,000,000 next year for new
parks. Pasquel now has two architects in the States inspecting our
plants, and ground will be broken in January for a $2,000,000
Baseball City in Mexico City, with an apartment house for the
ball players, space under the stadium for 2,000 cars, and theater
seats for the paying guests. Puebla is even now extending its
grandstand to care for this season's crowds and will have a new
park next year. At Tampico a spur of railroad track runs through
right field but that also will soon be corrected.

Night ball is played only in Torreón and Laredo. Formerly
the league played three games a week, Thursday, Saturday, and
Sunday morning at 11:30. A fourth game was added, starting in
May, and this met with the players' approval because they
complain about getting out of shape from too much lying around.
But they are frankly relieved at getting away from the seven-day
grind in the States.

"Hell!" said one of the Americans disgustedly. "If we ever

had an off day, they'd book an exhibition game. On this system
down here a guy should be good to fifty."

Pasquel owns two clubs in Mexico City (Mexico and Vera
Cruz), controls every park in the league, and is said also to own
San Luis Potosí and Torreón. The Tampico is owned by the
American Coca-Cola representative, Fleischmann, who is said to
net $100,000 a month from the franchise. Laredo is backed by
men worth $40,000,000. Monterrey is a rich city and is completely
nuts about baseball, and this is true of the whole country.
Monterrey, with no American players on its roster, was leading
the league in early May. Pasquel's own pet team, Vera Cruz (he
was born there and still keeps a residence there), was in last
place, and Jorge was suffering audibly. He acts for the good of
the league, but when Vera Cruz loses goes into mourning. If he is
a dictator, he is having little luck with his dictating.

Pasquel's personality is all-important in any discussion of
Mexican baseball, and it can be said immediately that he is an
amazing man. He conducts an importing and exporting business
with his brothers (Alfonso, Bernardo, Gerardo, and Mario) but
his fingers are in dozens of pies. He owns a ranch near San Luis
Obispo and his brother Gerardo owns another near Torreón.
Bernardo and Alfonso are installed at Laredo, and Mario, the
youngest, is a lawyer in Mexico City. Nobody in Mexico City has
any idea what Jorge is worth; it is a matter of as much heated
discussion there as it is in some circles here. The first surmise is
that Pasquel is confusing pesos and dollars when he speaks of a
$60,000,000 fortune, but Pasquel replies that he is well aware of
the difference, and it is dollars he is mentioning.

All we know is that Pasquel seems to be connected with
almost every line of activity in Mexico. It is rather well established that he controls a Mexico City bank, although this is not
publicly known. His mother owns a cigar factory in Vera Cruz.

Whether Pasquel has 18 pesos or $60,000,000, he is a red-hot
baseball fan and he is also a proud Mexican and there is no
possibility whatever that he will give up the fight against American baseball (the baseball monopoly, he calls it) or that he will
renege on his contracts. When Branch Rickey followed Luis
Olmo's defection with harsh words against Mexican baseball, the
die was cast.

"That hurt me, that hurt my pride," says Jorge, with his hand
on his heart. "It hurts the pride of all Mexicans. If American
baseball wants peace with us, I will not go to them. They will get
peace only when Commissioner Chandler comes here to this

office and sits in this chair and explains what he has meant by his words about Mexico."

His feelings were not assuaged in the slightest by the injunction taken by Colonel Larry MacPhail and Branch Rickey in American courts to prevent Pasquel's agents from tampering with their players. This would certainly be accounted another provocation by Jorge.

Pasquel's acquaintance with the Americans came in a rough way. As a boy of six, he cowered in a cellar in Vera Cruz while American warships blasted the town and killed hundreds of citizens of the little port town. Relations with Mexico were so bad in the First World War it was estimated that the country was almost unanimous in desiring a German victory.

The episode has been forgotten now, and Jorge Pasquel forgot it to the point where he began making yearly trips to this country in 1931. He knows more about the United States, its roads, its industries, its farms, than most Americans. He thinks the United States is the greatest country ever created by God and destined to rule the world for the next thousand years.

On the personal side, Pasquel is a fanatic on good health and sports. He neither smokes nor drinks, and when Danny Gardella arrived in Mexico, they rigged up a gymnasium in the patio of Pasquel's Mexico City house (a lavish affair on all counts) where they have daily workouts with Jorge's American trainer, Robert Janis. On Sunday afternoons after the ball game, they go out to Chapultepec Heights and play a variety of squash tennis on a jai alai court. During the week Jorge sneaks away from his work and turns up at Delta Parque to throw a few with the ball players. He was an amateur player and got deeply interested in the sport in 1940, when he managed Vera Cruz into the pennant. He may not be an expert, but he knows the game thoroughly.

What is not generally understood in the States is that Mexico is baseball mad. On the train coming down from Laredo, we saw dozens of games going on in backlots; in Puebla the grocery boys wore baseball caps with the peaks turned up, like kids all over America; the waiters in the Ritz Hotel were more concerned about how the game came out than in getting the soup on the table hot. Bobby Estalella and Tommy De La Cruz tell us that Cuba is even wilder about the sport.

Lefty Gomez is managing a team in Venezuela and it seems only a short time till baseball captures all Latin America.

Which is to say that Jorge Pasquel is no fool. He likes baseball, but he is also a businessman. We saw seven games in

Mexico and all but one (Easter Sunday) was a complete sellout, with the gates closed at game time and crowds around the outfield and sitting in front of the stands (at Puebla).

Jorge Pasquel expects the league to gross between $2,000,000 and $2,250,000 this year, which will allow it to break even, despite the high salaries being paid. Fifty-five percent of all receipts are turned into the league treasury and divided among the teams at the end of the year. This means that Mexico City (and Pasquel) carries the league; that is why other owners are quite content to let him run things.

Next year, with the new parks built, Mexican baseball is going to be a gold mine. The prices range from two and a half pesos (50 cents) to 10 pesos (two dollars) for box seats. Pasquel figures that next year his games at the new Mexico City Park will bring average daily receipts of $30,000. This is money in any language, but the enthusiasm of the Mexicans for baseball seems to warrant Pasquel's expectations. In view of this, his three- and five-year contracts to American players appear less startling. The man knows exactly what he is doing, and things that strike outsiders as fantastic may turn out to be sound business deals. Mickey Owen would probably have brought Brooklyn $75,000 in a trade; Pasquel gets him for a $12,500 bonus. Mickey makes a good deal for himself, Pasquel gets a valuable player; everybody's happy except Brooklyn.

The Mexico and Vera Cruz teams travel either by air or by Pullman on their trips. Tampico, Laredo, and Torreón also travel by air and train. Monterrey has its own bus; San Luis Potosí uses bus, train, and plane on other trips. We mention this because of reports in the States that Mexican players travel like a class-C American outfit, taking their chances in rickety charabancs with *paisanos*, chickens, goats, and odors.

The players feel that the American baseball contract is inequitable and harsh in its terms. It contains a clause whereby a player may be discharged with ten days' notice and an even more famous clause (the reverse clause) which permits the club to retain possession of the player from one season to the next. Because of this he is always the property of some club in organized baseball and is prevented from making a deal for his services.

It is plain from speaking to players on both sides of the border that the Pasquel threat is the finest thing that ever happened to them. Even if they don't jump to the Mexican League, their salaries are being hiked here. Instead of being at the mercy of the American club owners, they now have a leverage that makes life infinitely sweeter for them. It seems inevitable that if Pasquel persists in his campaign, changes will be made in the American system that will greatly better the status of the players.

All reports to the contrary, the players down below consider it a Mexican hay ride. If they are eating their hearts out with regret, they are dissembling in a most amiable manner. It doesn't show.

II

Mexican baseball is exactly like American baseball, except for the extraneous embellishments. They work the hit-and-run and make the double play, but they don't sell the hot dog. The Mexico City ball park (Delta Parque) looks like something discarded in Oskaloosa, Iowa, in 1915, but the bleacher fans are a spitting image of the horny-handed sons of toil from downstate Missouri who crowd the stands in St. Louis for a Sunday doubleheader. In spirit, however, they are much like a New York crowd. Which is to say, they are impartial and often on the side of the visiting team.

Games in Mexico are really a spectacle for the gods. The bleacher aficionados (fans) are rattling the gates for admittance long before the ball players arrive. Outside the concessionaires are lining up their wares. A young man stands on a table busily mixing huge bowls of what seem to be soft drinks. In little booths outside the park, frijoles, tamales, and tortillas are steaming on the stoves. In the grandstand early arrivals are having their shoes shined by bootblacks.

After the game starts, the vendors begin selling oyster cocktails, tall glasses in which the oysters are embedded in tomato sauce. Another delicacy is chicken, of which you buy a very full plate with a mixture of white and dark meat. Despite what the young man is selling outside, the vendors inside are getting rid of vast quantities of soft drinks.

It's an American game, right down to the nomenclature. On the scoreboard are places for Strikes, *Bolas,* Runs.

Out on the field the players are proving that *beisbol* has an excellent chance of becoming an international sport. The teams are made up of Mexicans, Cubans, Puerto Ricans, South Americans, and recruits from the States. They handle themselves with every mannerism known to American players. And don't let anybody fool you with the theory that Mexican baseball is amateurish. They play fast, hard, and very good ball. The Americans playing down there feel it ranks up with AA baseball in the States. If the seven we watched were a fair test, the Mexican League has major-league class in defensive play, at least.

In the Vera Cruz–Monterrey game, Colas for Vera Cruz made a sensational catch of a screaming low drive into center field with the bases full and two out. In the San Luis Potosí–Puebla game, the Puebla third baseman made a fantastic play on a ball over the bag, converting it into a double play in the ninth with the bases full and none out.

What will be harder to believe is that the best ball we saw played in Mexico was by Danny Gardella, who was noted in New York for his awkwardness as an outfielder. Gardella happens to be a physical-culture fanatic who can do flying splits and tie himself into a knot with ease. Vera Cruz had him on first base, which is where he perhaps should always have been. He made three unbelievable plays in a game with Monterrey, on the last play throwing himself full length on the ground to the left, keeping his foot on the bag and making a backhanded pickup of a wild throw. Hal Chase in his palmiest days never did better.

But what about the pistol-toting Mexicans from whom Vernon Stephens of the St. Louis Browns fled in terror? Stephens signed a Mexican League contract with Jorge Pasquel, played two games to the frantic approbation of the Mexican fans, and then decamped. Do the Mexicans carry guns? Ladies and gentlemen, they most certainly do! Sitting in a box with Pasquel, you will discern the glint of something at his feet and there the revolver will be. The gentleman next to him may have taken his out of his holster in the hot weather and have it resting easily under his seat cushion.

We offer no explanation of this, but can report no instances where ball players were pinked in the anatomy for ineptitude. The revolution may still be in action in Mexico or it may merely be a frontier country, but the gentry wear their gats at social events and there is no denying it.

And how about gambling? There are persistent reports in the States that baseball in Mexico is merely an excuse for gambling and that games are run accordingly. This suggests that gambling coups are possible with games being thrown, which naturally is repugnant to all loyal Americans. From what we could see—and we looked with gimlet eye and made every investigation possible—this is a lot of nonsense. There is absolutely no open gambling at the ball parks and certainly no animated group of swindlers such as are seen behind third base in every ball park in this country.

There is the further charge that baseball in Mexico is a syndicate affair because Jorge Pasquel owns or is interested in every club in the league, but this also blows up on interviewing the owners of the various teams. They are fanatically proud of their organizations and determined to win the pennant. Pasquel takes the greatest care not to overload his favorite team, Vera Cruz, with the best players. The Mexicans look with horror at the very thought of anything irregular in their sports.

"You've never heard of a bullfight or soccer or prizefighting scandal down here, have you?" they ask, with flashing eyes. They take this inquiry about syndicate ball very hard, as if it were a reflection on their integrity, and we can only surmise that Pasquel would be in grave danger if any hint of manipulation ever arose.

The crux of the whole situation is Jorge Pasquel, who is an amazing character. At thirty-eight he is a well-set-up, vigorous man with very definite ideas on the future of baseball in Mexico. At his elaborate home on Hamburgo Street there is a statuette of Napoleon prominently placed in the reception hall. Pasquel admits to having read 25 books on Napoleon and being an authority on his life. This may account for a lot in his career.

Although he is not the oldest, he is the head of the Pasquel family. Living at home with him are his mother, his brother Mario and sister Rosarie, his married sister and her husband and two children. Another sister is married and lives in Puebla in another fabulous Pasquel mansion. The old family home is kept up in Vera Cruz, and there is another Pasquel establishment in Nuevo Laredo, where brothers Bernardo and Alfonso live. Gerardo runs a huge ranch near Torreón.

The Vernon Stephens affair was particularly painful to Jorge (pronounced "Hor-gay" in Spanish but now "George" by common consent) because Stephens had been taken into the Pasquel home as a guest, a distinctive honor. This accounts for Pasquel's determination to sue Stephens for breach of contract. "I will sue him as long as he lives," Jorge kept saying over the phone to New York, when reporters called him during the excitement about Mickey Owen's arrival.

This suit could easily be a disaster for American baseball, and it ties in with much of the resentment among American players against American club owners. The baseball contract is admittedly a one-sided affair. The player is tied to organized baseball for life, but he can be discharged at will. The player either works for what the club owner offers or he doesn't work at all, for no club is allowed to tamper with the players of any other club.

It must be admitted at once that without this type of contract, baseball might be impossible. If the players were free after each season to make new deals for themselves, the best players would naturally gravitate to the best-heeled clubs and no team would know from year to year where it stood.

However, there is a possibility that the courts would find the present contract a form of peonage, since the player has no legal rights whatever. This has been known to the owners for a long time and accounts for their reluctance to tangle with the law. It is most ironically possible that Pasquel could lose the suit against Stephens for damages (even though Pasquel reported in the middle of May that Stephens had not returned any of the money advanced to him by Pasquel) and yet blow up the whole structure of baseball by getting the present standard contract held invalid.

Since Pasquel's raids on our leagues, facts about American salaries have become public and shocked the fans. Luis Olmo knocked in 110 runs for Brooklyn last year and was offered a contract this season for $7,500. Hal Gregg won 18 games for the same team and was given $8,000 after a hard fight. We were told by American players in Mexico that the St. Louis Cardinals pay their new men $400 a month, raising the ante to $600 after May 15, if they stick. The season is five and a half months.

There was a report in New York that Ralph Branca of the Dodgers had signed a three-year contract calling for a total salary of $4,900. It is alleged that men on the Philadelphia Nationals have played for as little as $1,750 a year. The newspapers reported that Branch Rickey had offered Joe Hatten, the spectacular southpaw, a salary of $500 a month this spring. Hatten held out and got more.

"If a player is good enough to make a big-league team," said Sal Maglie when he left the Giants, "he should be worth at least $10,000 a year."

We talked with Maglie in Puebla, where he and his wife are installed in a suite in the best hotel in town and very contented with their fate.

"I'm twenty-nine years old and had a hard time making the big leagues. I won five straight games for them when I came in late last year, but that didn't seem to mean anything to them this spring. They didn't answer my letters when I wrote them about a new contract and then finally offered me one with a small raise. When they heard I had been approached by the Mexican League, they boosted it to $8,000. I'm working on a three-year contract down here and even if I'm no good and am dropped after the first season, I'll still be better off than if I'd stayed three or four years with the Giants."

Pasquel has been swamped with letters from players in this country since starting his raiding campaign. Many of them are from amateurs and minor-leaguers with no chance in Mexico, but we can testify to being startled by some of the big names involved. The players seem to feel that they play baseball for a living and are entitled to make the best deal for their services. If an engineer can run off to Egypt or Russia or India to build a bridge, they don't see the disloyalty in making the best of their talents in Mexico.

The Mexicans are unable to understand our psychology in the battle between Pasquel and the big leagues. Baseball is our national sport and it seems to the Mexicans we should be the proudest people in the world at the thought that others are taking it up. With the war over and big-league rosters crammed with players, the Mexicans think it would have been a smart thing for us to offer Pasquel some of our overflow talent. Instead, we have practically waged a vendetta against them, they claim, replete with insults, recriminations, and boycotts.

"The manufacturers took our order for 2,000 dozen baseballs," says Pasquel, "and then refused to fill it. We have to get baseballs and bats from retail stores in the States, just as if we were bootlegging them. Every foul ball that goes over the fence costs us fourteen pesos [approximately $2.80]."

That pettiness was not lost on the Mexican fans, who are aware of everything going on over here. The big Mexico City dailies (*Excelsior, Universal*) carry more baseball news than any paper in this country. *La Afición* is said to be the only daily sports paper in the world.

The madness for baseball in Mexico will probably soon produce many fine Mexican players. At the present time the core of the league are the Negro players from Cuba, Puerto Rico, and the United States. There are some great players in this group, but the Mexicans are coming fast with such talented young fellows as Vecino and Magallon of San Luis Potosí and Bache, a fine short-

stop, and Torres, a great outfielder of Monterrey. Torres is a
natural hitter and is said to have the best arm in the league.

When we asked if the Mexicans might not resent the influx
of American players, the Mexicans answered with astonishment:
"The Mexican players are entirely satisfied because the success of
baseball here has raised their salaries about 400 percent. Hockey
is a popular game in your country and yet all the players are
Canadians. Do you resent that?"

The raiding has not all been on one side. For years Joe
Cambria, scout for Washington, has been luring prospects north.
The Mexicans feel that Commissioner Chandler is slightly less
than logical when he objects to Mexico seeking our players and
yet welcomed Vernon Stephens back with open arms, although
he had repudiated a Mexican contract; but their chief resentment
is against Clark Griffith of Washington, who for years has had
almost a monopoly on Latin-American players.

When Griffith welcomed the flurry of injunctions against
Mexican tampering with American players by saying that the
Mexican officials "can be prosecuted for trying to persuade Amer-
can players to jump their contracts, since this is clearly outside
the law," the Mexican laughter rose to hysterical heights. They
pointed out that Griffith, Connie Mack, and Ban Johnson formed
the American League by raiding the National League, a battle in
which contracts were repudiated right and left. They also recalled how contracts were flouted in the famous Federal League
war of 20 years ago and noted that in the present conflict
between American professional football leagues many strange
things are happening to the sanctity of the contracts.

The cardinal point in the discussion is that baseball is in
Mexico to stay. They call their home runs *jonróns* or *cuadralangu-
lares,* but the crowd gets into hysterics over them just as they do
at the Yankee Stadium, and the happy team rushes out en masse
to meet the hitter when he arrives at home plate. We observed
the umpiring down there and were convinced that it was honest.

Two of the best umpires are Atan, a Chinese Cuban, and
Maestri of Cuba. Maestri made his reputation years ago by
ignoring insults on the field but meeting the offender after the
game under the stands and fighting it out.

From a ball player's point of view, Mexico is not all peaches
and cream. The altitude at Mexico City and Puebla has a bad
effect on some players and this is especially felt among the wives.

Most visitors to Mexico get a touch (sometimes a serious

touch) of dysentery from being careless about eating fresh vege-
tables and drinking impure water. The ball parks are primitive
and the playing fields rough specimens compared with our big-
league layouts. The pitchers find that their curve ball doesn't
break at high altitudes (Tampico, at sea level and with a muggy
climate, is said to be a pitcher's idea of heaven), but the hitters
admire the way a ball travels in the thin air at 7,000 feet.

The players we interviewed in Mexico all felt they had
landed in the middle of a gold mine and could easily put up with
the hardships.

Mickey Owen is considering offers from Cuba and South
America for the winter months. He has paid off his farm at
Springfield, Missouri, and is dickering for another one.

"The way I was going in the big leagues, I couldn't have
done that in ten years, if ever," he says.

According to J. K. Lasser's authoritative book *Your Income
Tax* (1946 edition), American players will not have to pay an
income tax here if they get their "compensation for services
outside the country for the entire year." In that period they can
make business and vacation trips to this country without changing their status. This is not to say that any of the players looks
down his nose at American baseball and certainly none will risk
his American citizenship, no matter how much pelf is involved.
They read the daily box scores and recall the exciting days in the
States, but then they scan their bankbooks and relax.

"I liked it fine at Washington," says Roberto Ortiz, the big
outfielder, "but by the time I paid my living expenses and the
taxes, I got back to Cuba every winter broke. This is different
here."

The procession of American players keeps wending its way
south and the trail may grow deeper next year when the new
parks are built in Mexico.

"Then maybe you won't be surprised at seeing Ted Williams
down here," says Señor Pasquel proudly.

With Pasquel, nothing would surprise me. It is not true that
the Mexican government is backing him now, although he is a
friend of President Avilo Camacho, but if Miguel Aleman becomes the next president (and it seems a cinch for him now), the
league will definitely be a favored sport. Aleman and Pasquel
grew up together in Vera Cruz and are fast friends.

"Maybe even Bobby Feller next year, eh?" said Señor Pasquel
when we last saw him.

If that happens, the battle royal will really be on, and we will probably see contracts breaking in all directions. At least one American scout was lately run out of the Mexican ball park, just as we have been fighting off Mexican agents here. The happy gentry you will note on the sidelines will be the ball players, experiencing the millennium at last.

1947

ONE STRIKE IS OUT
By Stanley Woodward

FROM THE NEW YORK HERALD TRIBUNE
Copyright © 1947, New York Herald Tribune, Inc.

It is occasionally charged that sports writers feel that no other world exists outside of their own enclaves of gridirons and baseball diamonds, but these two pieces, a clean scoop, by the late Stanley Woodward, should have laid this canard to rest forever. They appeared in the New York Herald Tribune *on May 9 and 10, 1947. In them the indignation and wrath of the author at the intolerant and racist treatment of Jackie Robinson's debut into the major league is recounted with biting satire, and the author's deep humanity lays bare man's injustice to man.*

A National League players' strike, instigated by some of the St. Louis Cardinals, against the presence in the league of Jackie Robinson, Brooklyn's Negro first baseman, has been averted temporarily and perhaps permanently quashed. In recent days Ford Frick, president of the National League, and Sam Breadon, president of the St. Louis club, have been conferring with St. Louis players in the Hotel New Yorker. Mr. Breadon flew east when he heard of the projected strike. The story that he came to consult with Eddie Dyer, manager, about the lowly state of the St. Louis club was fictitious. He came on a much more serious errand.

The strike plan, formulated by certain St. Louis players, was instigated by a member of the Brooklyn Dodgers who has since recanted. The original plan was for a St. Louis club strike on the occasion of the first game in Brooklyn, May 6, in other words, last Tuesday. Subsequently the St. Louis players conceived the idea of a general strike within the National League on a certain date.

That is what Frick and Breadon have been combatting in the last few days.

It is understood that Frick addressed the players, in effect, as follows:

> *If you do this, you will be suspended from the league. You will find that the friends you think you have in the press box will not support you, that you will be outcasts. I do not care if half the league strikes. Those who do will encounter quick retribution. All will be suspended and I don't care if it wrecks the National League for five years. This is the United States of America and one citizen has as much right to play as another.*
>
> *The National League will go down the line with Robinson whatever the consequences. You will find if you go through with your intention that you have been guilty of complete madness.*

Several anticipatory protests against the transfer of Robinson to the Brooklyn club were forthcoming during spring training when he was still a member of the Montreal Royals, Brooklyn farm. Prejudice has been subsequently curbed except on one occasion, when Ben Chapman, manager of the Phillies, undertook to ride Robinson from the bench in a particularly vicious manner.

It is understood that Frick took this matter up with the Philadelphia management and that Chapman has been advised to keep his bench comments above the belt.

It is understood that the players involved—and the recalcitrants are not all Cardinals—will say, if they decide to carry out their strike, that their object is to gain the right to have a say on who shall be eligible to play in the major leagues. As far as is known the move so far is confined entirely to the National League. Ringleaders apparently have not solicited the cooperation of the American League players.

In view of this fact, it is understood that Frick will not call the matter to the attention of Happy Chandler, the commissioner. So far, it is believed, Frick has operated with the sole aid of Breadon. Other National League club owners apparently know nothing about it.

The *New York Herald Tribune* prints this story in part as a public service. It is factual and thoroughly substantiated. The St. Louis players involved unquestionably will deny it. We doubt, however, that Frick or Breadon will go that far. A return of "No comment" from either or both will serve as confirmation. On our own authority we can say that both of them were present at long

conferences with the ringleaders and that both probably now feel
that the overt act has been averted.

It is not generally known that other, less serious difficulties
have attended the elevation of Robinson to the major leagues.
Through it all, the Brooklyn first baseman, whose intelligence
and degree of education are far beyond that of the average ball
player, has behaved himself in an exemplary manner.

It is generally believed by baseball men that he has enough
ability to play on any club in the majors. This ability has asserted
itself in spite of the fact that he hasn't had anything resembling a
fair chance. He has been so burdened with letters and telegrams
from well-wishers and vilifiers and efforts to exploit him that he
has had no chance to concentrate.

It is almost impossible to elicit comments about Robinson's
presence in the National League from anyone connected with
baseball. Neither club owners nor players have anything to say
for publication. This leads to the conclusion that the caginess of
both parties, plus natural cupidity which warns against loss of
salaries or a date attraction, will keep the reactionary element
under cover.

When Robinson joined the Montreal club last year, there
was resentment among some Royal players. There was also a fear
on the part of league officials that trouble would be forthcoming
when the Royals played in Baltimore. Both the resentment and
the fear were dissipated in three months. Robinson behaved like
a gentleman and was cheered as wholeheartedly in Baltimore as
anywhere else. Incidentally, Baltimore had its biggest attendance
in 1946 and the incidence of Negroes in the crowd was not out of
proportion.

Since Robinson has played with Brooklyn many difficulties
have loomed, sometimes forbiddingly, but all have been circum-
vented. This was in part due to the sportsmanship of the fans
and in part to the intelligence and planning of the Brooklyn
management.

It is understood the St. Louis players recently have been
talking about staging the strike on the day that Brooklyn plays its
first game in St. Louis. Publicity probably will render the move
abortive.

The blast of publicity which followed the *New York Herald
Tribune*'s revelation that the St. Louis Cardinals were promoting
a players' strike against the presence of Jackie Robinson, Brooklyn's Negro first baseman, in the National League probably will

serve to quash further strolls down Tobacco Road. In other words, it can now be honestly doubted that the boys from the Hookworm Belt will have the nerve to foist their quaint sectional folklore on the rest of the country.

The *New York Herald Tribune's* story was essentially right and factual. The denial by Sam Breadon, St. Louis owner, that a strike was or is threatened is so spurious as to be beneath notice. The admission by Ford C. Frick, National League president, that the strike was contemplated was above and beyond the rabbitry generally adhered to by the tycoons of our national game. Such frankness, when compared with the furtiveness of other baseball barons, makes Frick the Mister Baseball of our time, whoever gets the $50,000.

From behind his iron curtain, Happy Chandler, through his front man, Walter Mulbry, denied any knowledge of the projected St. Louis players' strike. This is true. The commissioner was uninformed. Inasmuch as the projected strike did not transcend the boundaries of the National League, Abie was told nothing about it, or at any rate, that was the reason ascribed.

When this department was investigating the story, it was discovered that almost no one except the St. Louis personnel and the astute Branch Rickey, president, had knowledge of it, though numerous lesser Robinson impasses had badgered the Flatbush Mahatma earlier in the season. Rickey declined to talk about the case even though silence had not been imposed on him. The lack of such imposition was due to the fact that the commissioner, knowing nothing about it, had not got around to placing additional gags.

Frick also kept his peace, but due to a leak similar to the one seeping from Abie's office to *The Sporting News*, we were able to discover he had knowledge of it. Knowing him to be an honest man, we decided he would not deny the story. Therefore we went ahead and printed it. If Frick had denied it, its truth might still be unestablished. As it is, whatever Mr. Breadon may conjure up, people will laugh at him.

We made no pretense of quoting Frick verbatim in the ultimatum he delivered to St. Louis. We were wrong, apparently, in stating he personally delivered it to the players. It seems he delivered it to Breadon for relay to said operatives. In view of the fact that it is obviously the most noble statement ever made by a baseball man (by proxy or otherwise) we hereby reprint it, giving Ford full credit if he wants it:

If you do this [strike], you will be suspended from the league. You will find that the friends you think you have in the press box will not support you, that you will be outcasts. I do not care if half the league strikes. Those who do will encounter quick retribution. All will be suspended and I don't care if it wrecks the National League for five years. This is the United States of America and one citizen has as much right to play as another.

The National League will go down the line with Robinson whatever the consequences. You will find if you go through with your intention that you have been guilty of complete madness.

Enough of sweetness and light. Just to supplement our story, let us say Robinson's presence in organized baseball has been attacked by minorities ever since he joined Montreal last year. There was nothing but trouble throughout training this spring. Extravagant measures have been taken to see that untoward incidents do not occur. Most of the trouble has been caused by players from the Hookworm Belt, but at least one major-league owner has openly expressed his dim view of the situation. We hesitate to name him. He is fatherly and venerable.

It is also known that another tycoon, who has expressed no open disapproval, has filed with the commissioner a secret document in which he is supposed to have stated that the presence of a Negro in baseball jeopardizes the holdings of all the major-league owners.

Boy, are the clients going to run out to see Robinson when he tours the West!

1948

NOTES ON THE GAY SCIENCE
By Joe H. Palmer

FROM THE NEW YORK HERALD TRIBUNE
Copyright © 1948, New York Herald Tribune, Inc.

*The early demise of Joe H. Palmer deprived our country
of one of its wittiest track analysts. He paid much more attention to the two-footed bettors and touts than he did to
the four-footed main attractions inside the fences. The
present article is a case in point.*

Books on picking winners appear in the mails now and then. I
never read them, because the notion here is that the responsibilities of great wealth about balance its pleasures, and besides,
money got that way will never do you any good. But people
everywhere seem to enjoy bewildering themselves methodically. I
think this was originally said about theology, but it will do for
horse playing by system.

Conscience indicates, too, that this department has been
remiss about giving its constituents pointers on betting horses. So
a few notes are here set down, not exactly constituting a "system," but supplying materials on which a system may be built. As
you will see, everyone cannot operate it exactly the same way.

Shortly before the most recent war (not counting little wars)
several of the Midwestern tracks began to offer handicapping
prizes, usually of $1,000 a day, to people who could pick seven
straight winners. This was done because track managements like
to make people happy. Particularly stockholders in their race-
tracks. People who can pick seven straight races do not need
$1,000 prizes, but that is neither here nor there.

Well, at Arlington Park, if memory serves, a lady was paged
over the public-address system one afternoon and, when she
appeared, was informed that the ballot she had turned in before

the races had included the first seven winners, and that if she would sit down a moment, a $1,000 check would be forthcoming. Members of the expert racing press, most of them losers on the day, were present, and they discovered that not only had the lady made the proper selections but she had (1) played each of them on the nose, (2) had not played any other horses, and (3) had coupled the first two in the daily double. She then glanced at her watch and asked if she had time to nip out and bet on the eighth race. She had, she did, and her horse won galloping. Eight for eight, the double, and a $1,000 prize made the score for the day.

She was then asked if she based her selections on *Daily Racing Form*. She countered by asking what *Daily Racing Form* was. This avenue of inquiry was abandoned, and she was paid by a local publication to make selections for the following day. She picked eight horses, none of which was in the money, and afterward dropped from sight. This is the cornerstone.

Myself when young did eagerly frequent the old Kentucky Association track, and in about 1921 slapped a meeting around as I have never been able to slap one around since. It was strictly illegal, but I was tall for my age and the track needed the money. The method employed was to bet on horses carrying green and white silks, because those were the colors of the high school from which I was newly hatched. By a happy coincidence they were also the colors of E. R. Bradley, who was prepping a string there, and of George Collins, who had a barn full of horses all named Thistle Fern or something closely similar, and all hot as $2 pistols.

The method broke down because the subject subsequently went to one college and, after certain broad hints from the management, to another, and you cannot profitably play three horses in one race. The inference from this is that a man intending a career as a horse player should not pass high school and, I suspect, few of them do. Now you know why.

There are certain limitations to this. If you went to Michigan, you had better bet on football anyway, of course; the only horse you can bet on is a two-year-old named Jacopone, because he belongs to Larry MacPhail, who is the only owner I know whose silks are maize and blue. But the method isn't restricted to higher education. Graduates of P.S. 53 will, of course, couple five and three in the double, graduates of schools above 129 will have to scratch for themselves.

Then there was a visitor at one of the smaller Midwestern

tracks this fall who got $106.20 on a horse named Armed Man. Since the animal had run 37 times previously and still didn't know what a winner's circle was, she was asked to explain the chain of reasoning which led up to her selection. She said she'd been reading about the horse in the papers and she understood he was one of the best horses in the country. Hadn't he beaten Assault in a $100,000 race the fall before? Perfectly clear, said the questioner, beginning to cut out paper dolls.

For that matter, at our own Jamaica last Tuesday, a filly named Maid of Oz strolled in for the last race at $105.30. Friend of mine found a friend of his vociferously waving a winning ticket and asked what brand of tea leaves had brought about such a happy circumstance.

"Straight handicapping," said the ticket-holder indignantly, "He [sic] won here last November 3, didn't he?"

You will object that last Tuesday wasn't November 3, and that last November 3 wasn't Election Day. But you forget that this is leap year, and you have to allow one day. It's on such slender margins as this that winning systems are based.

There is no firm contention that these items can be woven into an infallible system. But it is confidently asserted that the methods outlined here are the only ones which can beat a 15 percent takeout. Thousands of bleached bones attest this.

1949

PIE IN THE SKY

By Tom O'Reilly

FROM TRUE

Copyright © 1949, Fawcett Publications

This debunking article tells what may have happened to the $2.50 you invested in the Irish Sweepstakes a short while ago. At present, many of our states are involved with their own gambling procedures, as evidenced by the manifold lotteries, legalized gambling, and "over the counter" attempts to raise revenue. This article holds more than a modicum of truth on the shenanigans of legal or quasi-legal wagering today, and it makes for interesting reading.

If you wish to make a tidy contribution to the Irish hospitals and take credit for it on your income-tax report, please do not let me stop you. The Irish hospitals are a worthy charity, of course. Although, with all the money they have acquired through the famous lottery on England's Grand National Steeplechase at Aintree, I wouldn't be surprised to hear that each biddy and bogtrotter in the old country has a private hospital bed.

If you wish perchance to dream and buy a sweepstakes ticket merely as an aid in constructing your castles in the air, I can't argue with you about that, either. Sweet dreams are hard to come by these days, and a sweeps ticket is certainly less damaging than an opium pipe or a bucket of Duggan's Dew.

If, however, you have any foolish idea that a sweepstakes ticket is going to bring you riches and can be taken as a serious gamble, wait for me before you make another move. I have a nice proposition in which you can get ten shares of Brooklyn Bridge at a nominal cost per share. I also have a neat line of gold bricks, underwater real estate, wildcat oil investments and Communist-stuffed pumpkins. Why gamble when you can have a sure thing?

I have seen the Grand National Steeplechase on which this lottery is based. I have seen (as who hasn't?) those wonderful newsreel and press pictures of an occasional lucky sucker with a family of 12 kids and no job, happily waving a winning ticket in the Irish Sweeps.

I have also seen newsreel and press pictures of persons who have found large sums of money in the subway, on city streets, and in old mattresses for more than 40 years. I will continue to look, but the moment someone wants to make an annual charge of $2.50 (the price of a ticket) for the privilege, I will stop. Even I, who still live in hope of getting a taxi the first time I whistle on a rainy night, know when the odds against me are too stiff.

Last winter in the snack bar of a train bound for Baltimore, two seamen flashed a book of Irish Sweeps tickets, and asked if anyone wished to buy one. Everyone looked at the tickets. Nobody bit. Two and a half dollars seemed like a large sum to hand over to a couple of chance acquaintances. Yet from the conversation that followed the departure of the seamen I gather that, they had been able to contact their prospects in private, they might have had greater success. It was mostly the fear of being ridiculed as suckers that stopped the folks from buying.

When the sweeps is coming up, of course, plenty of men and women enjoy flashing a ticket. They feel it is smart to be in on the big gamble. Often their friends express admiration at such a display of sporting audacity and ask where they can buy one, too. Usually the ticket-holder acts mysterious. He says, "I know a fellow who gets them straight from Dublin." There is a certain snob appeal in this daffy business. The ticket-holder appears to be in the know. If he admitted he bought it from a stranger on a train, they might laugh him off the premises.

The first big gamble anyone takes when he purchases a sweeps ticket is on the possibility of the counterfoil corresponding to that ticket being returned to Dublin and deposited in the great drums for the annual drawing.

You probably have seen newsreel shots of this drawing, which traditionally is started on the Thursday prior to the running of the race. The giant drums, made of glass and designed to spin on an axis, have contained as high as 10,000,000 counterfoils. Smaller drums contain the names of the 50 or more horses entered in the race. Before a galaxy of Irish hospital and government officials, a bevy of lovely colleens, attractively attired in photogenic cheesecake costumes, do the drawing.

Pipes skirl and bands play. There is much pouring of champagne and cheering. One of the spinning drums is stopped and a pretty colleen steps up to pull out a counterfoil. Then she reaches into one of the smaller drums and pulls out the name of a horse to go with the counterfoil.

When all 50 or more horses have been drawn out of one small drum, the process is repeated with another small drum. This is continued until 20 pools have been completed. Thus, there will be 20 winning ticket-holders and an equal number on the second and third horses. In addition, if, say, 50 horses start, each pool will contain 47 tickets worth $3,000 each, for that sum is awarded anyone lucky enough to draw a horse. Thus the number of prizewinners is about 1,000. The mechanics of the payoff on the winners is fairly simple. Obviously, if 10,000,000 tickets are sold, the entire pot is worth well over $20,000,000. Of this amount, approximately one half is returned in prize money. This prize money is divided into 20 pools, each of which is distributed in this manner:

$150,000 for a ticket on the winning horse
$ 75,000 for a ticket on the second horse
$ 50,000 for a ticket on the third horse
$ 3,000 for a ticket on each horse entered.

It should be repeated, however, that the first big gamble taken by the purchaser of a sweeps ticket is on the possibility of the counterfoil corresponding to his ticket being returned to Dublin for the drawing. Here you are not betting on a horse race or even entering a lottery. You are wagering on the natural cupidity of the human race. The best way to figure the odds on this proposition is to drop a $10 bill on the sidewalk and see if the fellow who picks it up returns it.

If anything goes wrong with your sweeps ticket, such as the counterfoil winding up in an ashcan, it will do you no good to complain to the National Steeplechase and Hunts Association of Great Britain, which stages the Grand National Steeplechase. The steeplechase people have nothing whatever to do with that Irish lottery. In fact, they disapprove. It is just as illegal to buy or sell a sweeps ticket in England as it is in the United States.

The Grand National Steeplechase has been running for well over a century on the same Aintree race course. It got along for 50-odd years without any help from the pixie gentlemen across the Irish Sea.

The sweepstakes was simply a grand idea thought up by

some sympathetic people who wanted to cure my Irish com-
patriots of runny noses by erecting a few nice hospitals. You will
never hear the operation more roundly condemned than in the
precincts of the Aintree stewards' stand, where officials take a
dim view of everything Irish anyway since Irish horses have a
disconcerting habit of winning this race with clocklike regularity.

Sweeps tickets generally come in books of 12 each. At $2.50
per ticket, the entire book is worth $30. To encourage distrib-
utors, however, the counterfoils for all 12 tickets will be accepted
in Dublin with a return of $25. In other words, the seller gets two
tickets free. He can either sell them and earn $5 or sign them and
get two free chances in the lottery.

One thing is certain: he can collect $30, which is his to keep
or send to Ireland. It is a fine testimonial to the hopefulness or
the stupidity of the human race that millions of stubs turn up
in those drums every year. And shortly after World War II, it
was estimated that 50 percent of the tickets sold came from
America.

Hundreds of thousands of Americans have Aunt Bridgets
and Uncle Pats in the old country who send them books of
sweeps tickets every year. The Irish are a dreamy race, and most
of these people are on the up-and-up. In fact, one year the sale of
tickets in this country was so good that a group of unscrupulous
scoundrels tried to flood the place with counterfeits. I can't
imagine which would be more distressing: to have my authentic
counterfoil wind up in a sewer or prove to be counterfeit.

It should amuse you to know that the Irish Sweeps officials
complained about this counterfeit problem to, of all people, the
United States postal authorities. It is against the postal laws, of
course, to send any lottery matter, counterfeit or authentic,
through the mails. In fact, post-office watchdogs are constantly
on the lookout for such matter. They call it using the mails to
defraud.

I dropped around to ask the chief postal inspector for the
state of New York, who, believe it or sue me, is named Rex
Napoleon Criss, how the tickets get into the country. Criss smiled
tolerantly. "It is our belief," he said, "that most of the sweeps
tickets are brought in either by seamen or visitors from abroad.
But the mails, of course, are inviolate. No man in the United
States has a right to open a letter unless it is addressed to him.
We respect those laws."

It was Criss, however, who made one of the greatest Irish
Sweeps lottery pinches in post-office history back in the thirties

when he confiscated some $179,000 worth of tickets held by a lady in upstate New York. Criss is reluctant to discuss how the catch was made. He only said, "She was a nice lady. She allowed a group of sharp operators to use her name for the sake of charity."

It seems that sharpers had convinced the lady she would be doing the hospitals in the old country a good turn if she let it be known that she had plenty of tickets. When word of this reached Criss, he moved in and pinched the whole crew, but the lady was excused since it was obvious that she did not figure to make a nickel on the deal.

The only way the postal authorities can intercept sweeps tickets is through complaints and with the cooperation of the public. Sometimes a letter will arrive in the New York post office stamped "Believed to contain lottery matter." In such instances, the inspectors telephone the person to whom the letter is addressed and invite him to the post office. They show him the letter and explain that they would like to see what is inside. Criss says, "Nine times out of ten people say, 'Go ahead. Open it up. If it has lottery tickets, you can have 'em.' The cooperation of the public is very encouraging."

So, let us suppose that you have purchased an Irish Sweeps ticket, either from a seaman, a visitor to these shores, or a broth of a lad with some relatives in the old country.

Let's even go further and assume that you are an unusually lucky party, that your counterfoil was not only returned to Dublin but actually was drawn from one of the great drums and matched up with a horse in the race. You are now far ahead of the game and are about to become involved in a big-money transaction.

When your ticket was drawn and matched up with a horse, you automatically won $3,000. Now, if your horse is not scratched, you have a chance of winning the top prize, which is $150,000, or the second prize, which is $75,000, or the third prize, which is $50,000. At least, those are the figures called for on your ticket, but don't let them go to your head. When Uncle Sam gets through cutting up those prizes, provided you win one, you'll probably begin to resent the time you wasted with those newsreel photographers.

Just to keep the records straight, we might take a quick peek at what the governments actually do to that kind of money with the tax laws that are in effect as this is written.

On a winning ticket, worth $150,000, the federal income tax

would be $111,820, leaving you $38,180. If you live in New York, moreover, the state income tax would take another $11,520, leaving you only $26,659. That is the most you could win, and the tax figures are based on the premise that you had no other income whatsoever during the year.

If your horse won second money of $75,000, Uncle Sam would take $46,170, while New York State would demand $5,746, leaving you $23,084. That, of course, is nothing to be sneezed at; it is only $3,575 less than first money and originally the idea was to reward the winner with twice as much.

If your horse finished third, winning $50,000 in the sweeps, the federal tax would be $26,820, while New York would take $3,821, leaving you $19,359.

Of course, if you have any other income at all, your sweeps winnings would push you even higher into the surtax bracket and your take-home winnings would be correspondingly smaller. For instance, the federal government wants 90 percent of everything you make over $150,000.

Now you know why authors who starve half their lives trying to write a hit show go completely nuts when they do score, only to find that Uncle Sam has stepped in to take the lion's share of the earnings.

All right, it is a bit rugged to find out that being an American citizen costs that much money, but this is still the best country in the world and fortune has smiled on you, so you won't grumble.

However, there is another important decision for you to make: should you sell your sweepstakes ticket or hang on to it? You will be amazed at the speed with which you will be offered a sizable sum for your ticket. There is a famous bookmaking syndicate in England which makes a business of buying up these tickets. It is the same firm that runs the lottery for the Irish hospitals. It knows where you live if you wrote your address on the ticket. It probably will write you a very interesting letter about that ticket, telling you where it can be sold.

This letter will come from Douglas Stuart, Ltd. That is the most famous bookmaking firm in the British Isles. It should be pointed out, incidentally, that bookmaking is not only legal but a highly respected profession in England. In order to get credit with Douglas Stuart, Ltd., a man must have the very best bank references. Racing is England's national sport, and British businessmen who have credit with Douglas Stuart, Ltd., telephone their bets to that firm after looking over the racing entries at breakfast each morning. In the afternoon the British businessman reads the results and marks them down carefully. At the end of the week he will get either a bill or a check from Douglas Stuart, Ltd., depending on his luck.

Douglas Stuart, Ltd., puts full-page advertisements in the big British magazines, many of them in color, depicting smart characters, obviously members of the peerage and attired in appropriate gray toppers, at Royal Ascot under the motto "Duggie Never Owes."

As the manager and operator of the Irish Sweepstakes, Douglas Stuart, Ltd., not only knows the address of every ticketholder in the United States but also the fluctuating odds on every horse in the race. The firm dispatches representatives to this country for the sole purpose of buying up sweeps tickets corresponding to horses in the race.

Douglas Stuart, Ltd., does not gamble, of course. It buys tickets on every horse in the race. The first three sweepstakes prizes—$150,000 and $75,000 and $50,000—add up to $275,000. Douglas Stuart, Ltd., by careful purchasing, never pays more than $150,000 for a complete set of tickets on each horse in the race. Therefore, it figures to win $125,000 on the deal.

The firm tries to get, and usually gets, four sets of tickets on each horse in the race. That means it buys up four pools, in each of which it is certain to get back $275,000 for an investment of $150,000. If you borrow your laundryman's abacus, you will find that this neat operation adds up to a $500,000 profit.

Being close to the race and knowing which horses are considered most likely to win, the firm naturally pays more for a red-hot favorite than for an outsider. In the Irish Hospitals Sweepstakes on the 1932 English Derby, which is a flat race and runs much closer to form than a steeplechase, Douglas Stuart, Ltd., paid $60,000 four times for tickets on a horse named Orwell. Orwell did not win. However, I will guarantee that Douglas Stuart, Ltd., didn't lose, either.

If your horse is just another 100-to-1 shot but you dislike Duggie's modest offer of $1,500 for your ticket (although that is over and above the $3,000 you have already won by drawing a horse in the race), perhaps you would like to gamble. In that case Duggie will buy one half of your ticket. The firm keeps its books in balance, of course. It buys another half on the same horse from someone else.

The manner in which these tickets are purchased in the United States is interesting. In the first place, there is no such person as Douglas Stuart. That is just a name with solid Scottish connotations that two gentlemen named Sidney Freeman and Martin Benson thought up when forming the firm. On the day of the sweepstakes drawing, their agents are in Glasgow, Liverpool, London, Capetown, Sydney, Montreal, New York, Boston, Chicago, and wherever enough tickets have been sold to make their appearance worthwhile. Originally, Freeman came to America with a staff, himself. In New York, Freeman's headquarters used to be the Ritz-Carlton Hotel. Incidentally, his name became so well known among Irish-Americans that whoever comes here now as the syndicate agent still retains the name "Mr. Freeman."

In case any American government official should be nasty enough to suggest that the sale of lottery tickets is illegal in this country, "Freeman" has an attorney with the proper answer. The Freeman legal eagle argues that when a man has drawn a horse in the Irish Sweeps, his ticket is no longer a mere receipt from the organizers of a lottery. It has been transformed into a security with a minimum value of $3,000. Therefore, Freeman is not buying lottery tickets. He is purchasing a $3,000 security for a possible rise in market value. The whole thing is quite legitimate.

Since Freeman pays cash in large, coarse banknotes, his room is carefully guarded. He gets the cash from a nearby bank. Usually the Irish Consulate has a lawyer on hand to witness the signatures on release forms and receipts.

If the ticket-holder wishes, he may bring a lawyer, too, although this generally means just handing the barrister 50 bucks after he sees that everything is on the square. Before a ticket-holder got to see Freeman there was a protocol to be followed. He had to come to an agreement on how much money he expected for his ticket with Freeman's agents in an anteroom. Freeman doesn't dicker. When the ticket-holder appears in the inner sanctum, he signs the proper papers, is handed his money, and is ushered out a different door from the one he entered.

Freeman's assistants are great hands at quoting odds and percentages. They have the latest line from the Aintree race course. They also have statistics to show that anybody who bets on the Grand National Steeplechase is crazy. The clinching argument comes, of course, when it is pointed out that Freeman is offering a neat prize from $1,500 to $15,000 over the $3,000 the ticket-holder already has won. Moreover, he will get it immediately with no strings attached. He is then asked if he would bet that kind of money on a horse race. If his answer is "Yes," they tell him about the Grand National Steeplechase. It is the craziest race on earth.

Fifty-seven horses started in last year's Grand National Steeplechase, which was won by J. J. McDowell's Caughoo, a 100-to-1 shot. Despite the seemingly large field, that might seem like a lot of money for the winner to pay. Actually, neither the size of the winner's payoff nor the starting field was unusual. In the last quarter century, the smallest field ever to start was 27 horses, in 1935, when Major Noel Furlong's Reynoldstown was the winner at 22-to-1. Moreover, no winner in the last quarter century has paid odds of less than 8-to-1.

Actually, 8-to-1 is usually the price quoted against a red-hot favorite. If the best horse in the field has only one chance in eight of winning (and I assure you English bookmakers do not make their odds with an eye toward philanthropy), you can well imagine why the English say, "See the National by all means. See it, like Naples, and die. But don't bet a jolly bean!"

Like all lovers of racing, of course, they do bet on the thing. But the average bet in England is two bob. That adds up to about 40 cents. In the Royal Paddock, bejeweled and befurred ladies may be seen calmly placing their 40-cent bets on each race. You may be sure that if any of these smart characters had a sweeps ticket for which someone was willing to pay $15,000, they would sell it without a moment's hesitation.

The Grand National is a spectacle that attracts between 300,000 and 500,000 persons. It has been called "England's annual spring festival." Business comes to a standstill throughout the British Isles on the afternoon the race is run. The race course is located at Aintree, a suburb of Liverpool, and is reached by race trains.

The race course is a tremendous thing, two and a quarter miles in circumference. The distance of the race is just short of four and a half miles, or twice around the oval track. This course is dotted with 15 decidedly tricky fences, each of which must be taken twice in the race. Because of the distance, the tremendous fields, and those fences, it is seldom that more than a dozen horses finish.

Every step of this horse race is packed with excitement. The start is like nothing ever seen in this country. The race is started at a point about a quarter of a mile from the first fence. When the starter turns the field of 40 or 50 horses loose, the race to that first fence resembles a cavalry charge. Many a prospective champion has met his Waterloo at that first fence, not because he wasn't fit and ready for the race of his life, but because he was knocked flat when 10 or 15 other horses tried to clear the same fence at the same time.

I saw Don Bradman (named after the Australian cricket star), one of the finest chasers ever to come out of Ireland, knocked flat at the first fence. He got up again, remounted, and finished sixth. Without that tumble, he surely would have won.

Three quarters of the field usually is eliminated on the first round of the great course. Horses tumble at Becher's Brook, a high hedge with a small brook on the landing side, so named because a Captain Becher nearly drowned in it when this race was first run over a century ago.

They go down at Valentine's Brook, a similar fence with a continuation of the same small stream on its landing side. They fall at the open ditches, the water, and the Canal Turn.

So, on the second time around, when a man's horse begins to feel the strain of this tremendous endurance test, the course is practically covered with loose horses, playfully zigzagging around, jumping fences on a slant, engaging in tag with the mounted racers, and otherwise turning the affair into a mad rodeo.

I saw H. Lloyd Thomas's Royal Mail win the Grand National in 1937, although there were two mares behind him who might easily have outdistanced the winner had it not been for a loose horse named Drim.

Drim lost his rider the first time around the course and then took a liking to the mares. He played tag for the rest of the race, while Royal Mail, just a few lengths in front, cantered to an easy victory.

The mare which finished second was Cooleen, owned by James V. Rank, brother of the motion-picture producer. Here is what Jockey Fawcus, rider of Cooleen, had to say after the race: "I was in the middle of the pack for the first circuit and nothing happened until one loose horse stuck on top of the first open ditch. My mare jumped the fence and missed him. As we approached the last fence, Drim came at Cooleen with his mouth open and tried to savage her. We were only two lengths behind Royal Mail, but that distracted the mare's attention and she tried to look at the loose horse and the fence at the same time. She hit the fence pretty low down and that took almost all she had out of her. Somehow she managed to keep on her legs. I think I would have beaten Royal Mail for speed in the run in. He was pretty well spent, and I felt I was on the fresher horse."

Pucka Belle, the third horse in the race, had E. W. W. Bailey, her owner, in the saddle. He said: "When Drim came for my mare, I tried to shake him off. Yet for something like two miles Drim and several other loose horses bothered her. I had to go way out in front, where I didn't want to be, to avoid them. Eventually she settled down, but her early exertions took too much out of her. Had I been able to escape interference and ride the race I wanted, we would have given the winner a busy time."

In 1928, out of a field of 42 starters, only two horses finished. The winner was H. S. Kenyon's Tipperary Tim, who paid 100-to-1. The second horse was Billy Barton, the greatest steeplechase ever bred in the state of Maryland. Billy Barton was leading Tipperary Tim by a quarter of a mile, coming into the last fence. He fell over the fence. Immediately he rose, however, and stood waiting for his jockey to remount. He had fallen in America's great timber race, the Maryland Cup, been remounted, and set a record. At Aintree, however, his jockey was knocked cold. He never got up until Tipperary Tim had passed them.

Books have been filled with similar heartbreaking incidents in this race. In 1936 a horse named Davey Jones had a comfortable lead. His owner, an amateur, was riding. Because the owner was a toff, his handlers put a fancy park bridle on the horse. Nobody expected Davey Jones to get much farther than the first fence. Coming into the last barrier, with the greatest steeplechase on earth in his pocket, that fancy bridle, built for the post parade, came apart. As it did, the horse swerved and ran outside the jump into oblivion.

And that is the race on which you hope to win $150,000 less taxes, or $26,659, provided the man from whom you purchased your ticket is honest, provided that the tickets given him were not counterfeit, provided your number is one of 1,000 in 10,000,000, and provided your horse is blessed with luck no steed should expect. Why not take a whack at an eight-horse parley some afternoon? The odds are about the same.

1950

MR. HENDERSON AND THE COOPERSTOWN MYTH

By John Lardner

FROM TRUE

Copyright © 1950, Fawcett Publications

*John Lardner, scion of the great Ring, here reveals that al-
though Abner Doubleday sighted the first gun fired back
from Fort Sumter in the Civil War, had the perception to
suggest the first cable car in San Francisco, and wrote
historical tomes about Chancellorsville and Gettysburg,
there was one thing he really didn't do: Invent baseball!
And from that point on in this delicious piece of American
trivia the risibilities of the reader are tickled as Lardner
gently erodes America's great baseball shrine in Cooperstown, New York.*

General Abner Doubleday deserves to live in American history.
He sighted the first gun fired from Fort Sumter in the Civil War,
which means, in a manner of speaking, that he kicked off for the
North. He wrote books about Chancellorsville and Gettysburg.
He suggested the first cable-streetcar railway in America, when
he was on Army duty in San Francisco. Any way you look at him,
he was a man of great resource and initiative.

There is practically only one thing he did not do. That was
invent baseball. In Cooperstown, New York, or anywhere else.

Today a state of sporadic warfare exists between the
Doubleday-Cooperstown faction on one hand and, on the other,
the only man in the world who knows and has proved the full
truth about baseball. Robert W. Henderson, Cooperstown's
staunch and singlehanded enemy, is a spare, gray, quiet fellow in
steel-rimmed glasses. He is chief of the main reading room of the

New York Public Library, and librarian of the Racquet and Tennis Club. He is not mad at General Doubleday. He gives the General credit for such honors as really belong to him. He thinks Cooperstown, New York, is a nice place. But, as a lifelong scholar and researcher, he believes there is no valid substitute for the truth. Baseball—meaning organized baseball, the powers and the glory, the leagues and their high commissioner—is using a substitute. As long as it does, it will have a fight on its hands.

I said it is war between Henderson and Cooperstown, but maybe "armed truce" is a better term for it just now. Baseball has recognized the Doubleday myth, officially, since 1908. That was the year when the late A. G. Spalding, the game's elder statesman of the period, showed his muscle and palmed off the myth on the public. In 1947, in a book called *Ball, Bat, and Bishop,* Henderson shot the story full of clean, round holes and published the facts about baseball's origin—namely, that it came to this country nearly intact from an English game that was first known as baseball (as far back as the seventeenth century) and later as rounders.

A brief, painful silence ensued. Then the Cooperstown people resumed firing their own, hand-tooled brand of history. However, a few months ago, a small number of officials of Cooperstown's National Hall of Fame and Museum sat down to lunch with Henderson. They told him that from now on they were going to be "neutral." Henderson went away from there quite pleased. "Neutral" seemed like a step in the right direction. What puzzles him is that since that time, they have gone right on worshiping the name of General Doubleday and dispensing the old, reliable propaganda.

"I guess their hearts are in the right place," says Mr. Henderson patiently. "It's a comfortable myth, and they hate to give it up. But you can't always be right and be comfortable at the same time. You just can't. I think General Doubleday would agree with me."

The fact is, the General could not have been more innocent of founding our national game if he had been born and raised in the Ural Mountains in the middle of the Paleolithic Age. He never said he did it, and I'm glad to be able to report that he went to his grave not knowing that he would be charged with it. It is a wrong rap. Just the same, it has been hung on him, so hard that it sticks, by a great many parties, including the *Encyclopedia Britannica,* the *Encyclopedia Americana,* and the *Dictionary of American Biography.*

Jim Farley brought the U.S. government into the deal by putting out a centennial stamp in 1939 to commemorate Doubleday's invention of the game in 1839. The Cooperstown taxpayers have built a shrine to the same purpose, and a memorial ball field, and a museum which houses baseball's most precious lore. The Doubleday story is perhaps the best example in modern times of mythology taking the place of history.

Cooperstown is a lovely village on the shores of Otsego Lake. Maybe this is not the time and place to point out that, by coincidence, it is consecrated to the memory of a powerful fabricator, James Fenimore Cooper. We will leave Mr. Cooper to Mark Twain, who once tore his books apart line by line. The Doubleday story is something else again. It is a pretty fable, preserved in a pretty setting. Baseball needs a shrine. It needs a museum. Cooperstown fills the bill. Where the people up there go wrong is to keep insisting, as they do, that the Doubleday story is not just a useful, tailor-made piece of malarkey, but the genuine scientific goods.

The myth habit is strong, though. In this case, it has strong backing, too, all the way from Commissioner Happy Chandler down (or up) the line in organized ball. After promising Mr. Henderson to be good, the Cooperstown people recently issued the latest of a series of brochures. It is a handsome job, put together by Jack and Alice Durant. Mr. Durant, who wrote the text, is an author and sports cataloger of high quality. But he is writing to Cooperstown orders, and once more the public is spoon-fed with a reassurance in behalf of General Doubleday. The sole authority for the Doubleday story, originally, was a very old gentleman named Abner Graves. Mr. Durant allows that he was very, very old. But he adds:

"In support of the Cooperstown belief are these sturdy links in the chain of evidence: the findings of the Commissioner which were officially sanctioned by organized baseball, and the discovery of the Abner Doubleday baseball."

Calling Mr. Henderson from his studious toil in the public library, I asked him what he made of the new catalog. Were the boys honoring the truce? Or were they off the reservation and selling snake oil again? It looked bad.

"It looks bad to me, too," said the scholar, "but there is one small point on which they have yielded. Maybe that's a sign of grace. That so-called Abner Doubleday baseball; up till now they've been claiming it was the very ball Doubleday used to invent the game. If you read on, you will find that they now admit it is just a ball—a lopsided old ball found in a trunk belonging to Abner Graves. I don't deny it was found in a trunk somewhere, or that it was once used to play baseball with. But, as the modern saying goes, so what?"

As for the other sturdy link, "the findings of the Commission," the reference there is to a commission hand-picked 44 years ago by Spalding to find out, "for all time," where in the world baseball did originate. We will inspect that link in its turn. What should be pointed out now is a curious fact about the war Henderson is fighting. It is a war against a dead man—not Doubleday, but A. G. Spalding. Henderson recognizes that fact. Visibly, his enemies are the Cooperstown people, the baseball industry, and Happy Chandler, all very much alive. But the tale they defend was chosen and set up in business by Spalding, for reasons of his own. Spalding is Henderson's true foe, and though 35 years dead, a tough one.

Spalding told baseball and the rest of the world to believe:

1. General Doubleday invented the game.

2. He invented the name of the game.

3. He did all this one day in 1839.

Henderson says, and has shown by documents:

1. The name of baseball appeared in print as early as 1700.

2. The game of baseball was known and played in America before and during the Revolutionary War.

3. The rules of baseball, as attributed to Doubleday in 1839, were identical with the rules of rounders as printed in England several years earlier. They were lifted intact from English rule books by American publishers, so that Doubleday could easily have read them.

4. Doubleday was not in Cooperstown in 1839, and never said he was.

Once Spalding was defeated in a run for U.S. Senate. Apart from that, as the Doubleday legend shows, he almost always had his way. He was a great pitcher as a boy, and a great player, manager, and organizer as a man. He started and developed the biggest sporting-goods business in the world. He launched the *Spalding Guide*, which was, while he lived, the official mouthpiece of baseball.

Spalding was a mighty man in the year 1905, but he was restless. One of the things that made him restless was to hear his old friend Henry Chadwick, who had been born in England, keep saying that baseball came from rounders. Chadwick, an oldtime sports writer, is known in some circles, including Brooklyn, where they have a monument to him, as the "Father of Baseball." He was certainly the father of baseball reporting and of the modern box score. He talked gently about his rounders theory, but he talked so long and so often that he drove Spalding slightly nuts. In the 1905 *Spalding Guide,* the boss announced that it was time to put a stop to this rounders twaddle of Chadwick's. He said that a commission must be appointed to study the facts and determine the true origin of baseball, about which nobody, at the moment, seemed to know anything definite whatever.

But the way Spalding put it, it was not just an origin that must be found—it was an American origin. Nothing foreign would do.

"I claim baseball owes its prestige as our National Game," he once declared, "to the fact that as no other form of sport it is the exponent of American courage, confidence, combativeness; American dash, discipline, determination; American energy, eagerness, enthusiasm; American pluck, persistency, performance; American spirit, sagacity, success; American vim, vigor, virility."

He also said, "It would be as impossible for a Briton, who had not breathed the air of this free land as a naturalized American citizen; for one who had not part or heritage in the hopes and achievements of our country, to play baseball, as it would for an American, free from the trammels of English traditions, customs, and conventionalities, to play the national game of Great Britain."

The members of the investigating commission were appointed by Spalding himself in 1906; and they could all take a hint. Their names were A. G. Mills, Morgan G. Bulkeley, Nick Young, Alfred J. Reach, and George Wright, with James E. Sullivan, president of the Amateur Athletic Union, serving as secretary. It was a stout collection of baseball names. Mills, an elderly lawyer and sportsman, had been very important to the game in the 1880s, when he created the famous "reserve clause" (Danny Gardella should tip his hat). Bulkeley, the first president of the National League, was U. S. Senator from Connecticut in 1906. Young, Reach, and Wright were former great ball players who had moved up to bigger jobs. They were very busy men indeed. There is nothing to indicate that any of them, except Mills, their chairman, ever read a line of the "extensive correspondence" and data collected by Sullivan in the next year and a half.

The tireless Henderson has bayed back on this trail like a bloodhound in spectacles; he found that a fire in 1911 later destroyed all of Sullivan's data and correspondence, so that we have no complete record today of what it amounted to. But Henderson learned something about it from a press release issued before the fire. It included several letters with descriptions of baseball as played in America in the 1820s and 1830s.

Evidence of that sort has been cropping up ever since. Henderson points to the autobiography of Thurlow Weed, a famous New York editor and political mastermind, who told of belonging to a baseball club in Rochester in 1825. Samuel Hopkins Adams, the author and expert on President Harding, has evidence of the same club in action in 1827. But there was only one letter in the Sullivan collection that suited the taste of A. G. Spalding. That was a letter from Abner Graves, an octogenarian mining engineer then living in Denver. The other letters did not burn till four years later, but for all the attention Spalding and the commission paid them, they might as well have been used to light cigars with on receipt.

Mr. Graves said he had seen baseball leap full-grown from the brain of Abner Doubleday, at Cooperstown, New York, one day in the spring "prior or following" the William H. Harrison hard-cider campaign for the presidency. That would mean 1839, 1840, or, possibly, 1841. If Graves had named General Harrison himself, Old Tippecanoe, as baseball's inventor, Spalding would probably have grabbed the idea in his arms and kissed it. However, he knew that Doubleday had been a general, too. Another thing he knew was that Doubleday had died in 1893, and was in no position to talk back. So, in 1907, the General became the posthumous father of baseball. In all his life, he had never mentioned this little peccadillo to a soul, even though baseball, by the time he died, was a national success and well worth boasting of. He may not have been the father then, but look at him now.

Spalding's fight talk to the commission is quite a document. I will quote from it, as a lesson to present-day salesmen.

"The tea episode in Boston Harbor," said the elder statesman, rolling up his sleeves, "had not been sufficiently forgotten in eighteen forty for anyone to be deluded into the idea that our national prejudices would permit us to look with favor, much less adopt any sport or game [he meant rounders] of an English flavor. . . ."

"I would call the special attention of the commission," he went on, now frankly waving the whip, "to the letter received from Mr. Abner Graves . . . who claims that the present game of baseball was designed and named by Abner Doubleday, of Cooperstown, New York, during the Presidential campaign of 1839. . . .

"In this connection it is of interest to know that this Abner Doubleday was a graduate of West Point in eighteen forty-two, and afterward became famous in the Civil War. . . . It certainly appeals to an American's pride to have had the great national game of baseball created and named by a major general in the United States Army."

In sum, Spalding said that Graves said that Doubleday, his schoolmate at Green's Select School in Cooperstown, outlined the first diamond with a stick in the dirt, invented the players' positions, drew a diagram of the field, made a memorandum of his rules, and coined the phrase "baseball," all on the same day in 1839. And see what the boys in the back room will have.

Mr. Henderson has read and copied the Graves letter. The cold fact is, he says mildly, that Spalding was reading Graves's mind. Graves did not really say all that Spalding said he said. He did not say that Doubleday made a diagram or a memorandum. He did not say that Doubleday was his schoolmate. He did say that Doubleday was a "boy pupil at Green's Select School," but in another letter, published in 1918, he wrote, "I was attending the 'Frog Hollow' school south of the Presbyterian Church, while he was at school somewhere on the hill." It's a minor conflict, but, major or minor, it all runs for Sweeney—because, as Henderson points out, Doubleday was not a "boy pupil" anywhere in Cooperstown in 1839. He was 20 years old, and a cadet at West Point. He had no leave in Cooperstown that year, or in any year after that.

The members of Spalding's Commission of Investigation took Spalding's word for the Graves letter—all except A. G. Mills, the chairman, who gave it a quick look. The story delighted this old gentleman. He ate it like honey from a spoon. As it happened, Doubleday had been his buddy. They belonged to the same G. A. R. post. Mills commanded the guard of honor at Doubleday's funeral when the innocent general lay in state in New York's City Hall, little suspecting the gaggeroo that would be played in his name 14 years later.

Some doubters, including Frank Menke, the sports encyclopedist, have charged Mills with the chief responsibility for slipping the Doubleday story across on the public. They wrong the old lawyer. The credit goes entirely to Spalding, with an assist from Graves. Mills was startled no little when he heard that his

dead chum had invented baseball, for the general had never
spoken of it to him. But he was willing to buy the angle—to
repeat, he loved it. He expressed his debt to Spalding, and closed
the case with these words:

"My deductions from the testimony submitted are:

"First: That 'baseball' had its origin in the United States.

"Second: That the first scheme for playing it . . . was devised by Abner Doubleday at Cooperstown, New York, in 1839.
Yours very truly."

He signed the paper, and the other commissioners lost no
time in signing it, too. As I said before, they were busy men. The
rest is history. Well no, not history. Just a substitute, with lacy
trimmings. We'll take up history, and Henderson, next.

"Sometimes I wish I could have talked to Mr. Spalding and
General Doubleday," says Mr. Henderson wistfully. "I think
they'd have liked to know the truth."

Henderson presents a printed reference to baseball in the
year 1700. A certain Reverend Thomas Wilson, a preacher of
stern principles operating out of Maidstone, England, looked
back on the 1600s and wrote:

"I have seen Morris-dancing, cudgel-playing, baseball and
crickets, and many other sports on the Lord's day."

So much for Doubleday's invention of the name.

At first, Henderson has shown, baseball was a simple, one-
base game like one-old-cat. Then it took on its diamond form,
with three outer bases and a home base. About that time, toward
the end of the eighteenth century, the name "rounders" came to
be used for it in England more commonly than "baseball." It was
still the same game as before, played by teams taking turns at
bat, with a pitcher in the center of the diamond, fielders scattered
about, and the batter at the home base. You scored a run when
you rounded the bases, and the team with the most runs won.

One of the last Britons to call it "baseball," instead of
"rounders," was a great lady, Jane Austen. On page 2 of *North-
anger Abbey*, if you go for Austen, you can read: "It was not very
wonderful that Catherine . . . should prefer cricket, baseball,
riding on horseback, and running about the country, at the age of
fourteen, to books."

When the printed rules of the game came over here, everything came with them, Henderson has proved, but the name
"rounders." We'd always called it "baseball" here, and we went
on calling it that. But we took the rest of it lock, stock, and blue-
prints. We did quite a bit of hijacking in those days, copyrights

being what they were, or rather, were not. A game book called *The Boy's Own Book* was published in London in 1829. It contained the rules of rounders and a diagram of the diamond. In the same year, it was pirated and published in Boston. The rules and diagram were kept intact, but the heading was changed from "Rounders" to "Base or Goal Ball." Other books hijacked from England were published all over the East in the next few years, the best of them, says Henderson, being a New Haven job, by S. Babcock, called the *Boy's Book of Sports*. Babcock, an honest fellow, admitted his debt to the English rules, but used the name "baseball" instead of "rounders." It was a simple switch, and a good one. He made one other change: he had his base-runners go counterclockwise, instead of clockwise, as was the English style. It's a clockwise country, England. Look at their horse racing. If someone wants an idea for a psychological essay, this one is on the house.

So much for Doubleday inventing the game.

Here, I should say, is what the Doubleday story comes to. It's possible that Doubleday played baseball some time in the 1830s. It's possible that he laid out a diamond diagram and recited the rules, for the rule books I have mentioned were tremendously popular in the 1830s everywhere east of the Great Lakes, and Doubleday could have read them.

Doubleday didn't name it. He didn't invent it. As Mr. Henderson says, he was nowhere near Cooperstown in 1839.

Your correspondent would like to point out, to appease the ghost of the late Mr. Spalding, that Henderson is not a mucker, in the pay of England (dollars are scarce enough there already). He was born in England years ago, but facts mean more to him than nationalities. He is an American ball fan today. As it happens, when Spalding said that baseball was foreign to the English character, he forgot or ignored the fact that two of the very first professional ball players in this country, Harry Wright and Al Reach, had been born in England. It's lucky for us that baseball is not unsuited to the characters of Irishmen, Germans, Central Europeans, and Italians—for those peoples, in successive waves of immigration, have supplied big-league baseball with some of its best material. However, Spalding was right when he insisted that the growth of baseball into a big-time game, a man's game, was peculiarly American. In England and France, during the seventeenth and eighteenth centuries, baseball was truly a kid's game. The kids there, when they grew up, took to football, cricket, or boxing.

So baseball's shrine and museum belong in America. Cooperstown is as good a place for them as any. What riles Mr. Henderson, in his quiet way, is that Cooperstown tries to make too good a thing of it, to reach for the factual chips as well as the mythological gravy.

In short, it ain't ethical. It ain't true. And, speaking of truth, I believe I *will* steal a little bit of Cooperiana from Mark Twain.

It seems that Cooperstown's first great hero, J. F. Cooper himself, was writing about how the Indians, those cunning fiends, operated in the old days. They were after scalps one time, and a paleface party was trying to float a house up a creek under their very noses. The house was about 90 feet long, the barge upon which it was floated was about 120 feet long. The Indians hung in ambush in a tree above the stream. A setup, you say? A sitting duck? Not the way Cooper tells it.

The Indian chief, with his knife in his teeth, dropped first, but he missed the target, the whole 120 feet of it, and fell a foot astern of the boat. The rest of the redskins dropped in turn, one at a time. The first one missed by 10 feet, the next by 20, and so on. The last of these cunning fiends could not have reached the barge by telegraph. That always struck Mr. Twain as quite a tale, the best that ever came out of Cooperstown. He didn't know about General Doubleday.

1951

FOOTBALL FAMILY
By Bill Rives

FROM THE DALLAS MORNING NEWS

Copyright © 1951, Dallas Morning News

This short article received warm appraisal from our judges. The author relates the unusual story of a Texas family with six sons, all at different colleges and all football players in spite of their parents' dislike of the game and its hazards. It is a heartwarming testimonial to family understanding and dedication.

The ill-advised sports reformers—those persons who cry that the imperfections of intercollegiate athletics make it necessary to destroy the entire program—should sit down for a half-hour, talk with Mr. and Mrs. W. A. Hawn of Athens, Texas. Most certainly it would cheer up their aggrieved spirits. In all probability it would make them understand that, although the body is feverish, there is no reason to demand its burial. Hawn is a lumber dealer in the East Texas town, a man who undoubtedly could retire to the placid life but who is horrified by such a suggestion. His wife—whose facial features and soft, dark eyes give evidence that in youth she was entrancingly beautiful—has borne him six sons.

Both of them are shy about revealing their age, but they admit being "over sixty." They traveled to Columbus to watch the SMU–Ohio State football game. Such weekend journeys during the autumn sports season are common to the Hawns. For more than 20 years they have followed SMU's football teams.

Hawn can recall only two trips which he and his wife have missed—the jaunt to the Rose Bowl after the 1935 season and a previous journey to California, in 1931.

He was traveling in Arkansas in his automobile at the time of the 1931 game with St. Mary's and he pulled off the highway and parked his automobile under a tree. He turned on his car radio just in time, he recalls with a smile, to hear a description of a pass play that carried from the Mustang quarterback to the arms of his son, Fritz Hawn, in the end zone. But Fritz dropped the ball and the Mustangs lost the game, 7 to 2. On every other occasion when the Mustangs played—in South Ben, Indiana; Atlanta, Georgia; Pittsburgh, Pennsylvania—the Hawns were in the stands.

Each of the Hawns' six sons played football, either in high school or college or both. Not all of them went to SMU. Charles and Joe Verne went to the University of Texas and Frank attended Schreiner Institute. The others—Fritz, Arthur, and Jimmy—went to Southern Methodist. Jimmy, the youngest, now is in his junior year and is an end on the football team.

The Hawns became attached to SMU when Fritz enrolled there in 1929. Ever since he started playing varsity ball the following year, they have been loyal fans. Theirs is the sort of loyalty a school needs, the sort that would end the coach-baiting and the player-pressuring that causes one of football's biggest headaches.

They view football in the proper light. They look on it and other sports as an important function in the development of youth.

There is no malice in their hearts when their son sits on the bench; they raise no shouts for the coach's scalp. They mutter no grumbles when the team loses.

It was not always thus with the Hawns, however. In the beginning they were opposed to football. When Charles, their firstborn, began playing football in grade school, they tried to dissuade him on the grounds it was a dangerous sport.

But, as with most boys, Charles wanted to play football more than he wanted to do anything.

Mrs. Hawn finally made the decision. "Either we have to tell him he cannot play, or we must encourage him all we can."

Neither of them had the heart to forbid the boy to play football. So they cheered him on, watching workouts and going to games.

In the beginning they knew little about the game—only that it was a violent form of sport in which the possibility of physical injury was ever present.

Doggedly they swallowed their fears and hid their anguish. Many times Mrs. Hawn felt the heart clutch that comes to a mother as she sees a son injured. The boys have suffered broken ribs, twisted knees, battered noses.

Anticipating injury, the boys sternly forbade their mother to go down to the field if they should be hurt. So Mrs. Hawn had to sit in the stands and pray silently as she fought back tears.

The sons did their best to hide these hurts. Once, when Charles received two cracked ribs in the final game of his college career, he trotted off the field, despite great pain, as though nothing had happened.

Why, through all these years, have the Hawn parents submerged their feelings and permitted their sons to participate in athletics?

Because they quickly learned that sports competition provided benefits that far outweighed the dangers.

"I think athletics is wonderful for a boy," Mrs. Hawn said simply. "Boys learn to take disappointments like men; they come under the influence of fine coaches. Sports teaches them to keep their habits clean. It also gives them a chance to form many fine and lasting friendships."

Each of their sons, except the youngest, who is still in school, has become a success. Charles and Arthur are partners in an automobile dealership; Frank is a dentist; Fritz is in the lumber business in Dallas; and Joe Verne is an executive with another lumber concern in the same city.

The broken ribs, the twisted knees, the battered noses have been repaired. Those damages were temporary, but, Mrs. Hawn feels, the lessons her boys learned in competition and the wholesome influences to which they were exposed are permanent.

Who has a better right to judge the value of collegiate athletics than this couple, who have watched six sons participate wholeheartedly over a span embracing more than 20 years?

The reformers might take a lesson from the manner in which the Hawns handled their problem when the oldest child first wanted to play football. Don't abolish the sport; encourage it in a wise and understanding manner.

1952

MAD MARATHON

By Jerry Nason

FROM THE BOSTON GLOBE

*If the Greek bards had need of any help in singing anti-
phonic praises for the Olympic games, Jerry Nason of the
Boston Globe would have been the perfect voice. He's
America's answer to the Greek lyricists, and his descriptions
over the years of the Boston Marathon have been warmly
received by both judges and readers.*

In an April fooler that was contested 18 days late, an impover-
ished cotton-mill worker from Guatemala named Doroteo Flores
brought his own weather with him yesterday and sped on
spidery legs to a formidable victory in the Boston Marathon.

Fluid-driving Flores, in whose veins flows the blood of Indian
forebears, was impervious to the scorching sun, which proved a
purgatory to the hopes of domestic favorites, and fled strongly to
the finish in 2 hours, 31 minutes, 53 seconds.

It was never a contest once he took command of the 26-mile,
385-foot race this side of Natick Square, after exchanging sprints
with his fellow countryman, Luis Velasquez, for approximately
10 miles.

When the 30-year-old Guatemalan reached the tape, his high-
boned cheeks flushed red through his brown skin, and his neat
mustachio shedding water like a damp toothbrush from his
improvised shower baths, he had forged a winning margin
without precedent in the past 15 years.

The second finisher, Victor Dyrgall, 31, an accountant from
Fort Lee, New Jersey, didn't arrive until 4 minutes and 47 seconds later, and confessed, "I never saw Flores from start to
finish!"

He was so right. Not since the gangling Montreal cop, Walter Young, flew away from Johnny Kelley to win the 1937 race by more than five and one-half minutes, has a marathon winner been so safe from pursuit as was the 130-pound, unpublicized Guatemalan yesterday afternoon.

Behind Flores' solo flight absolute chaos prevailed.

He was the seventh foreign runner in succession to win the Boston macadam classic, and on this particular day the domestic talent was really confident of restoring their rights to their own Olympic tryout.

But John Lafferty, the overwhelming Winter-book favorite, was overtrained, was seared by leg and stomach cramps before the hills of Newton had been reached, and came home, stilt-legged, in eleventh position.

The national champion, Jesse Van Zant, at no time a factor, put 24 weary miles under his tawny legs, then smoldering-eyed in his disappointment, yielded to the welcome temptation to desist.

And so, the roof fell in, and it was Flores, rated only second best of the three-man Guatemalan delegation, who, in finishing the first marathon race of his life, stirred up the storm.

Dyrgall was more or less expected to show inside the first half dozen. And it was no particular surprise that Velasquez, 32, the Guatemalan railroad timekeeper who had never before lost to Flores in such a long race, finished third. English-speaking Luis, stunned by Flores' footsy performance, then served as his countryman's interpreter.

Nobody really expected the Lincoln U. professor, Tom Jones, 35, to bowl over guys like Lafferty, Van Zant, and one or two others, but he did, and is in a very solid spot for the Olympic team.

A performance which incited approximately as much astonishment as Flores' was the output of a very tired, very game, and very small (5 feet 1 inch) Hawaiian named Norman Tamanaha, who finished fifth.

Norman was 45 years old on Good Friday, flew all the way from Honolulu last weekend to compete in the second marathon race of his life. In his first here, seven years ago, he finished forty-sixth.

The remainder of the first 10 was completed by Ted Corbitt, 32, Brooklyn physiotherapist and a newcomer to the marathon; the 5-foot, 40-year-old Turkish champion, Sevki Koru, now studying in New York; Ed Ramagnoli, a New York traffic cop who has been up high before; another wee fellow, Louis White, 37, who trained for only three weeks for the race, due to a heel infection; and Arnold Briggs, 36, a Syracuse mailman.

Thus the meteorology for the day (the thermometer reached into the lower 80s) favored the "old folks," for the youngest man in the top dozen was Flores, 30, and for the first time in history life in the marathon started at 40 for three of the Daily Dozen—Koru, who is 40; Johnny Kelley, who is 44 and punched himself out to get twelfth position; and the 45-year-old Hawaiian, Tamanaha.

The race unfolded in virtually the same manner and developed almost the identical pattern of the one the swift Svenske, Karl Gosta Leanderson, won in 1940. The Guatemalan emerged with the bit in his teeth just past the tenth mile, as Gosta had done.

There was a pronounced shift in sentiment to the Guatemalans, of whom the third starter was a little fellow entitled Guillermo Rojas, at the gathering point in the rural town of Hopkinton. The sun was hot and promised to be even more ardent by noon, when the field was to start.

Yet the fingers were pointed not at Flores, a man with black hair, and a blue running shirt, and a gold-capped tooth which gleamed when he smiled, but at Velasquez, their champion.

But Velasquez shrugged. He said, "No, no. I like it not so warm as this. Doroteo, he will like this warmth."

Doroteo, it developed, relished it as if it were gold from the blue above.

There was a temporary overcast when the 156 starters got away, without the mysterious Yugoslav, Ljubislav Draskovic of Sudbury, Ontario, who failed to check in.

It was significant perhaps that, while the sun was thus obscured, Velasquez was the more forceful of the two Guatemalans. He ran just a step ahead of Flores, and about 50 yards behind an early-blooming blossom from Philadelphia named Stanley Lindner.

When the first checking point, six miles, at Framingham railroad depot, was approached, Velasquez was at the wheel, with Flores 15 yards in arrears, in the fairly fast time of 32 minutes and 12 seconds.

They had a formidable lead, upwards of 500 yards, on anybody who counted, and a two-man race was a definite possibility then.

And so it remained down into Natick—Velasquez, a chubby sort of little fellow, with a bright face which always seems to be on the point of breaking into laughter, leading his hawk-visaged countryman by two or three steps.

It is just a trifle less than 10 miles to Natick. No more than the length of a football field beyond the square. Velasquez, as he had once before, paused to snatch a proferred container of water, taking a gulp, then sending the rest cascading over his wavy coiffure. The cool drops trickled down the backs of his chunky legs and gleamed in the hot sun.

Flores, however, paused for nothing. His eyes burning deep and dark under brows like raven's wings, he whirled right on past Velasquez and never again yesterday afternoon did an adversary see his face. It was just an incident, but an important one. It proved, indeed, that one Guatemalan feared the heat and the other was disdainful of it.

It was just a trifling lead at first, 10 yards, but it suddenly started to expand as Flores put fury into his running. His eyes were as black as the night, and he kept them riveted to the road just ahead of him as he started to dip into his store of stamina.

Three miles later, halfway home, at Wellesley Square, the man from the cotton mill was three minutes ahead of Velasquez and five minutes beyond the reach of any logical candidate for the role of destroying Doroteo's dream of glory this day.

He is not a picture-book runner, this Doroteo Flores. But he is neat. His stride is short, but it beat the pavement with the regularity of the second hand on the officials' stopwatches.

He looked almost fierce, like some bird of prey about to plummet upon a midday meal, as he now took complete mastery over the fifty-sixth Boston A.A. Marathon race and ruthlessly ran his opponents goofy from there to the finish.

There was a savageness to his performance that has been unequaled on the course since the Indian, Ellison Brown, dedicated his every ounce of heart and muscle to the task of smashing the record in 1930.

Flores wore a blue shirt, of deep hue, and white trunks, and his shock of jet hair, his deep brown face which was creased by a crayon stroke of mustache, and small muscle-sheathed legs, made a picturesque contrast to these garments.

But most impressive of all was the way his black eyes bored out of a sternly set face, seldom shifting from right to left—but most always fastened to the road six or eight feet ahead.

Like an indestructible little pony, he whirled down through Wellesley and Newton Falls, and into the hills at Auburndale, and not once, on the three topographical booby traps in Newton did he falter. On the longest and most cruel of them, Heartbreak Hill, Flores flogged steadily ahead.

It wasn't until he reached the crest of this terror, with no rival in sight, that the quick-gaited Guatemalan for the first time made an appreciative snatch for a water container.

He lifted it high to his lips, took one cool swallow, then poured the remainer on his black thatch.

From there to the finish Flores partook of a mobile shower bath. Water by the gallon sloshed over his head and down his body as he gratefully accepted offerings from spectators and officials, so that, when he pattered steadfastly into Kenmore Square, with the finish in sight, and the applause chattering like machine-gun practice all around him, his pretty running suit was a soggy satire and he shed drops of water like a Labrador retriever.

But moist he was, Doroteo Flores, unmarried man who works for hungry wages in a Guatemalan cotton mill, was not nearly so wet as the "experts" who selected everybody but Doroteo to win the marathon race.

1953

MICHIGAN STATE CONSTRUCTION JOB

By Tommy Devine

FROM SPORT

Copyright © 1953, Sport Magazine

Mr. Devine was at least 20 years ahead of his time when he cautioned that any athletically ambitious college team's rise to an eminent position in sports would be marked by bitter controversy that would backfire and demonstrate the virtual impossibility of athletic honesty and purity for victory-minded schools.

Want a prescription for big-time football success? Michigan State can furnish a guaranteed formula to any interested college, but along with it will come a note of warning: "USE WITH CAUTION—BEWARE OF OVERDOSE."

The Spartans' gridiron prescription is time-tested and effective. The advice relative to its use stems from experience which plainly demonstrates the lot of the winner isn't necessarily a happy one.

Michigan State is the defending national champion. The Spartans entered the 1953 season undefeated and untied over a stretch of 24 consecutive games. But State's rise to that eminent position has been marked by bitter controversy and sharpshooting which resulted in the Spartans drawing a year's probation from the powerful Western Conference, even before they had the opportunity to play their first football game as a league member, and a subsequent disciplinary slap by the National Collegiate Athletic Association.

The Michigan State story demonstrates the virtual impossibility of athletic purity for a school that is victory-minded and sharply etches the jealousies which develop and make the winner a consistent target.

The ingredients of Michigan State's rise from an also-ran in the football picture to a ranking power include an athletic-minded college president; an aggressive, free-spending, football-conscious alumni group; a head coach who is a sound fundamentalist; a staff of assistants who are talented and persuasive "salesmen"; a liberal academic admissions policy; one of the nation's finest athletic plants; and a superbly equipped campus that is a genuine lure for ambitious athletes.

Founded in 1855 as the Michigan Agricultural College, the East Lansing school was the first of its kind in the United States and furnished the cornerstone of the land-grant college movement which followed in the 1860s. The school's name formally was changed to Michigan State in 1925.

The college has been represented by a football team since 1896. Its gridiron history properly may be divided into five periods, as follows:

1. The Ancient Era (1896–1915)
2. The Age of Amateurs (1916–1928)
3. The Great Awakening (1929–1932)
4. The Struggles of an Independent (1933–1946)
5. The Glory Road (1947–1953)

For the first 32 years Michigan State was represented on the gridiron, football was merely a game and part of a well-rounded physical education program. Then there came to East Lansing as the Spartan's twelfth head coach an ambitious, energetic young man named James H. Crowley.

Crowley bore the nickname of "Sleepy Jim." It was strictly a misnomer. He had been one of Notre Dame's famed "Four Horsemen" under Knute Rockne and he knew what it took to achieve football success. He knew his coaching future depended on the development of a winner. His every effort was directed that way. Aware that the job couldn't be accomplished alone or through legitimate scholarship channels at the college, Crowley organized a "Downtown Coaches" organization to help him recruit and subsidize talented athletes.

From Crowley's standpoint the program was a success. In 10 years preceding "Sleepy Jim's" arrival, Michigan State had only one season in which it won more games than it lost. Under Crowley there was a winning edge every year and his composite record for the four seasons he remained on the campus was 22 victories, eight defeats, and three ties.

Dr. John A. Hannah, Michigan State's president who now is on a year's leave of absence serving as Assistant Secretary of Defense, has discussed freely and frankly what took place during Crowley's regime. "Jim had been at Michigan State only a short time before he organized a Downtown Coaches group that was large and active. Crowley was a fine mixer and had a persuasive way. The club raised a lot of money, spent a lot of money, and it wasn't long before good athletes began appearing on our campus."

The Spartans started winning, but all wasn't well with the athletic department.

"We had no control over the situation and conditions became quite impossible," Dr. Hannah said. "On occasions athletes would fall in arrears on their tuition, dormitory payments, or other obligations. When college authorities would question them, they'd say, 'When they brought me in, they promised they'd take care of everything.'"

Crowley left Michigan State after his short, successful, and eye-opening stay to go to Fordham, where he built the Rams into one of the great powers of the era. He was succeeded by another former Notre Dame star, Charley Bachman.

Bachman achieved the distinction of enduring longer than any other football coach in Michigan State's history—13 seasons. During his regime the Spartans made notable strides on the gridiron and in taking a commonsense approach to the troublesome twin problems of recruiting and subsidizing. College authorities didn't want a continuation of the sometimes reckless activities of the Crowley period. Yet they were realistic enough to realize some aid had to be extended if good athletes were to continue enrolling.

The method decided upon was due largely to the interest, foresight, and frankness of Dr. Hannah, who served first as Secretary of the State Agricultural Board, the governing force in Michigan State, and then was named the college's president in 1941. He was only 39 years old at the time of his elevation.

The plan was called "Jenison Scholarships," in honor of Frederick Cowles Jenison, a Lansing insurance executive who had been a rabid Michigan State fan. At his death in 1939 he left the college his entire estate, valued at $433,000, to be used "in any way whatsoever desired." Dr. Hannah was named the administrator of the estate.

"We decided to put the money to what we believed a legitimate and practical use by the establishment of athletic scholarships," Dr. Hannah explained. "We believe it desirable to be open and aboveboard in our aid to athletes rather than follow the methods we'd seen used in our own case during the Crowley era and which were in use elsewhere."

Under the Jenisons, an athlete was given tuition, books, room, and board. To hold the scholarship he had to maintain a classroom average of at least a C. If he lost the scholarship because of low grades, it could not be regained.

"I liked the idea of listing in the college catalog what was being done and how it was being done," Dr. Hannah said. "We had nothing to hide, nor anything of which we were ashamed."

Michigan State normally carried approximately 90 "Jenison scholars" on its rolls. These were divided among participants in all sports, but naturally football received the largest percentage. The Jenison plan worked well. It enabled the Spartans to come up with a steady flow of good athletic talent and to thrive on a balanced sports program.

There were two major sources of irritation to Michigan State officials during this period, however. First, the never-ending criticism on the part of some collegiate rivals of the Jenison program, and second, schedule difficulties, particularly in football, that were the lot of an "independent."

The criticism of Michigan State for the open use of athletic scholarships irked Dr. Hannah.

"There is frequent connivance on the part of many to point to the absence of athletic scholarships as a sign of purity," he said repeatedly. "Schools doing that are merely dealing from the bottom of the deck."

As the years passed and the criticism continued unabated, the Jenisons and what they stood for became a "crusade" for Dr. Hannah.

In a talk before the annual convention of the National Collegiate Athletic Association at St. Louis in 1946, Dr. Hannah said, "Few if any persons believe that the colleges and universities with great athletic traditions have their teams made up only of boys who naturally gravitate to their respective institutions without salesmanship, coercion, or aid in some form. Possibly, it is all within the scope of the rules, because most of the rules are worded very carefully to provide ample loopholes for individuals and agencies not officially connected with the college to do what the college agrees not to do.

"Why don't we be honest with each other and recognize it would be more effective to have athletic administrations adhere publicly and privately to some reasonable code of sportsmanship and ethics, rather than draw up a lot of rules and regulations that clever alumni and employees of the athletic department, or organizations set up for this purpose, can find a means of circumventing without violating the written word?"

Remember that last statement, for you'll soon see how appropriate it became to the situation that developed at Michigan State and which now casts a shadow that imperils the Spartans' continued athletic existence.

The Spartans' gridiron schedule problems were persistent. They had an annual scramble to fill the card and then often it was dotted with games that were meaningless and had little attraction at the gate.

In 1948, for example, Michigan State's 10-game schedule included five contests with teams west of the Rocky Mountains—Oregon State, Washington State, Santa Clara, Arizona, and Hawaii.

The chance to move from the "wrong side of the tracks" into an élite athletic neighborhood and put an end to the scheduling problems came when the University of Chicago finally decided to bury its "dead" athletic program and formally resigned its membership in the Western Conference on March 8, 1946.

Michigan State immediately applied for the membership, but the application was tabled. Dr. Hannah asked the application be made a "continuing one" for consideration whenever the Big Ten again would consider enlargement of the Conference. Then he enlisted the aid of another young and practical college president, Dr. J. Louis Morrill of the University of Minnesota. That was the first and most important step in a drive Michigan State carried on throughout the membership negotiations at the top administrative levels.

Big Ten athletic directors violently resented Michigan State "going over their heads," but the membership drive came to a successful culmination on December 12, 1948. The Spartans were in but not *all the way in,* for the jealous factions within the Conference had a trump card to play.

The Spartans still had to be "certified"; that is, a committee had to check again on Michigan State and express satisfaction that "rules and regulations and other requirements are completely in force." Because of this, Michigan State was barred from the football schedule meeting in December, at which time playing dates for 1951 and 1952 were arranged.

The Spartans received the certification, as everyone knew they would, on May 20, 1949. They began conference play in all sports, excepting football, with the school year of 1949–50.

To mix with Big Ten schools on a league basis, Michigan State has had to wait until this football season. Why? Conference rivals took the step to make doubly sure all the "impure" players who had enrolled under and benefited from the Jenison Scholarships had departed.

As a condition of Big Ten membership, Michigan State had to discard the Jenisons. It was a move Dr. Hannah made with great reluctance. "Obviously, I thought the advantages of Conference membership warranted the sacrifice of the plan," he said. "It remains my contention, however, that they were the decent method of dealing with the situation."

The junking of the Jenisons didn't end the well-regulated flow of young huskies to the East Lansing campus.

Remember Dr. Hannah's words to the NCAA that "few believe the colleges with great athletic traditions have teams made up only of boys who naturally gravitate there without salesmanship, coercion, or aid in some form"?

Dr. Hannah was realistic enough to recognize the athletic department would make "arrangements" to handle the situation. He didn't expect the Spartan coaches suddenly to change tactics.

"It is impractical to expect coaches and athletic directors to be interested in reform or strict regulatory measures on recruiting and subsidizing. The pressure is on them to win and their reputations depend on it," he said. "They are not going to take any steps which reduce their chances of victory."

Dr. Hannah has preached athletic realism and tight administrative control repeatedly. He was chairman of the "Presidents' Committee" of the American Council on Education in 1952 when a sweeping reform program was drafted which advocated, among other points, the elimination of all bowl games and spring practice. The recommendations never gained wide acceptance and Dr. Hannah's vigorous role in the movement was a source of embarrassment. Rivals who couldn't reconcile the Spartan's brilliant record with the aims of the Council said: "Why doesn't Dr. Hannah start practicing what he preaches?"

Michigan State's football reins had passed in 1947 from Bachman to Clarence L. (Biggie) Munn. The former University

of Minnesota All-American had prepared himself well for the
"big chance" by 16 years of coaching as an assistant under Bernie
Bierman, Ossie Solem, and Fritz Crisler at Minnesota, Syracuse,
and Michigan, and as head coach at Albright and Syracuse.

Munn's debut with the Spartans was a stunning 55–0 defeat
at the hands of Michigan's smooth-working combination, which
went on to win the Big Ten title and then bury Southern California, 49–0, in the Rose Bowl game.

Munn never forgave his former associates at Michigan for
that one-sided walloping. Yet it helped bring him closer to his
players and to put across the gridiron program. The Wolverines
have paid dearly for that victory. Munn and his Spartans have
beaten Michigan the last three years in a row.

In the locker room after the walloping, Munn told his
players: "Forget it. Let's start a new season."

The Spartans lost only one other game that season, a 7–6
setback to Kentucky. They won seven.

In 1948 Munn and Michigan State had a record of six victories, two defeats, and two ties, and in 1949 the record was six
triumphs as against three losses. The Spartans won their first two
games in 1950—from Oregon State and Michigan—then dropped
a 34–7 decision to Maryland.

Note that defeat, for it was the last time in a three-season
stretch the Spartans were to lose. They swept through their last
six games of 1950, won nine in a row in 1951 for the college's first
perfect record since 1913, and then grabbed nine more consecutive victories in 1952.

The sweep last season resulted in the Spartans' being voted
the nation's No. 1 team and winning the Reverend J. Hugh
O'Donnell Memorial Trophy, which is presented annually by the
Notre Dame Monogram Club to college football's top 11.

Munn's background as a builder of stout lines, particularly
for Bierman and Crisler, and his emphasis on fundamentals led
to a belief he lacked an "offensive imagination." It was an opinion
that grew after Michigan State installed a varied and effective
attack that included phases of the single wing, the straight T
formation, the split T, the short punt, and the double wing.

Credit for the intricate Spartan offense generally went to
assistants such as Forrest Evashevski, now head coach at the
University of Iowa; Kip Taylor, now head man at Oregon State;
and Lowell (Red) Dawson, now coaching Pittsburgh.

Munn resents the charges that his team's system of attack is the product of the imagination of others. After Michigan State edged Maryland 14–7 in 1949, a Detroit newspaper carried a story which said in preparation for the contest Munn sought advice by telephone from Bud Wilkinson at Oklahoma on suggested defensive measures to stop Maryland's split-T offense. Munn sizzled when he read the story. He demanded and received a retraction.

In one of the tightest squeezes of the long winning streak, Michigan State kept its record intact with a late 24–20 victory over Ohio State in 1951. The winning touchdown came on a long pass play known as the "Transcontinental."

A post-game story claimed that Red Dawson, who was working the press-box-to-bench phones, dictated the successful call. Munn pointedly said: "The call of the play was a staff decision and not that of any individual."

Week after week last season as the Spartan powerhouse rolled on and on, one rival coach after another said: "Michigan State unquestionably has the best squad in the country. Maybe somewhere there's a team that can match them player for player on the first 11 or 22 men, but nobody will touch them on an overall basis."

After the Spartans beat Texas A&M 48–6, the Aggie's coach, Ray George, said: "It isn't so much what the first or second teams do, but the third, fourth, and fifth teams murder you."

There was great individual talent and depth on the Spartan squad of 1952 and Munn molded them for maximum efficiency. Joe Williams, sports columnist of the *New York World-Telegram and Sun*, stressed this point at the time of the "Coach of the Year" award to Munn when he said: "Manpower is one thing, what the coach does with it is the criterion. And nobody would know more about this than the coaches themselves. There is probably no group in sports more informed as to what a coach has and what he gets out of it than his brother coaches. Munn did not get to the top on riches alone; it was the skill, ingenuity, and sagacity with which he spent his wealth that commanded the respect of his rivals."

This fall, when Munn led his troops into Big Ten combat for the first time, the enthusiasm of the college and its alumni was somewhat tempered by a formal reprimand from the NCAA and an accompanying threat of landing on the organization's black list. The troubles stem from the activities of a group known as the Spartan Foundation and its ally, the Century Club. These are extravagant names for a downtown coaches' association. Over a period of four years they collected $55,000 to be used for worthy causes—a needy halfback here, a destitute tackle there.

The Spartan Foundation was a corporation which had been issued a charter by the Secretary of State. The Century Club—so named because its members contributed $100 each—had 136 members when the Big Ten investigation broke.

A letter signed by Jack Breslin, then Alumni Field Secretary for Michigan State, in behalf of the Spartan Foundation and the Century Club, touched off the lengthy Big Ten investigation. In the letter, which eventually fell into the hands of Commissioner Kenneth L. (Tug) Wilson, Breslin said:

> *Dear Century Club Member:*
>
> *Through the compliments of Biggie Munn we would like to present you with this secret practice pass. This pass will admit you to all Spartan football sessions during the fall, with the exception of Saturday afternoon, September 15th. This practice will be closed to all.*
>
> *Biggie also has asked me to extend to you his thanks for your interest in the Foundation.*
>
> *Just a word from the writer—we need 100 more Century Club men. If you will get just one more yourself, we will get the additional 100 easily, for at this writing we have 136 Century Club men. Give it a try.*

The letter was written in 1951. Once in Wilson's possession, it became a thorn in Michigan State's athletic side. There followed 18 months of investigations and hearings with the climax coming last February when the Big Ten announced Michigan State's probation.

Of the $55,000 the Spartan Foundation collected, it turned over $33,500 to the college when dissolved at Dr. Hannah's request. It satisfactorily accounted for the legitimate expenditure of another $4,000. That left $17,500 for which Wilson wanted an accounting.

Between the time of the Big Ten probation and the August crackdown by the NCAA, Michigan State had whittled the "unaccountable fund" to $5,400. Now both the Big Ten and the NCAA have made a full accounting of that sum a condition for the Spartan's return to good standing. Michigan State officials insist they are powerless to furnish more information.

Dean Edgar Harden, Michigan State's faculty representative to the Western Conference, sums up the situation in this fashion:

"It is completely out of our hands. We have tried to get the report, but there's been no luck. I merely hope that NCAA and Big Ten authorities will recognize our problems."

Claud Erickson, Lansing engineer who was president of the Spartan Foundation, bluntly refuses to furnish investigators additional information relative to the money. "This money was disposed of over seven terms prior to the time Wilson assumed investigative powers for the Big Ten. I don't think it is anybody's business," he says.

Thus the matter stands and the consensus of outside observers is that Michigan State is damned regardless of which way it turns. An accounting of the missing $5,400 would bring additional punishment and the failure to supply it likewise would result in censure.

One Michigan State official put it this way: "We're being asked to supply the evidence to convict ourselves."

As might be expected, the Spartans' run-in with the NCAA and the Conference has left them wide open for dozens of other charges, many of them groundless. Every time a well-known schoolboy athlete shows up on the campus at East Lansing, members of rival athletic departments raise their eyebrows. It is unthinkable, in some quarters, that a young football star should go to Michigan State of his own volition.

Two cases in point are those of Gerald Musetti, a 185-pound sophomore from Detroit, and Earl Morrall, a 180-pound quarterback from Muskegon.

Musetti originally indicated an intention to attend Michigan. He spent several days on the Wolverine campus. Then, suddenly, he had a change of heart and enrolled at Michigan State. Tongues wagged freely. There were charges and countercharges. They reached such proportions that Commissioner Wilson ordered a full-scale investigation of the case. The Spartans were absolved of any wrongdoing.

Morrall was Michigan's top high school player in 1951 and was sought eagerly by college scouts. He finally narrowed his choice to Michigan, Michigan State, and Notre Dame. The Spartans eventually got the nod. Again, there was much talk of what Michigan State alumni had "given" to get him. Morrall finally took it upon himself to answer, through a letter to a Detroit paper. He said in part:

During my senior year in high school I felt sincerely I would like to go to college at Notre Dame, Michigan State, or Michigan.

I was told my marks were high enough to enter any of them. During the winter of my senior year I never felt I was pressured by Michigan State. . . .
*   I have a scholarship at Michigan State. . . . It is administered directly by the school and I must keep a high average to retain it. I am taking an engineering course. If I was asked the main reason why I chose Michigan State, I would say the friendly and helpful attitude of the coaches, players, and students was the most important factor in my decision. I felt I would receive a good education.*

The Musetti case was one of 15 charges against Michigan State which have been officially investigated since the Spartans were admitted to league membership. There unquestionably will be more, because jealous rivals are enjoying "spanking" the Big Ten's baby member in the legislative and judicial councils when they can't do it on the playing field.

The Spartans went into their first Big Ten season as co-favorites with Ohio State for the championship. Michigan State would have been a stronger favorite if the two-platoon plan had not been abandoned by the Rules Committee.

While bitter over the change at first, Munn finally philosophized: "We won't be hurt any more because of it than any other team."

A Big Ten crowd in the first season of gridiron competition and a New Year's Day Rose Bowl berth at Pasadena would be balm for many a Spartan wound. If the Spartans don't get the twin prizes, rest assured they'll be carried out on their collective shields while making the attempt.

1954

BROCKTON'S BOY

By W. C. Heinz

FROM COSMOPOLITAN
Copyright © 1954, by W. C. Heinz

Rocky Marciano (né Rocco Marchegiano) and his home town, Brockton, Massachusetts, became one entity as the fighter went through the mundane daily routine of his preparation for the heavyweight championship fight with Jersey Joe Walcott (né Cream). The adoration felt for this folk hero by the ordinary citizens of the town is both touching and inspiring.

On September 23, 1927, in Brockton, Massachusetts, Mr. Fred Denly, of 18 Everett Street, succeeded in bringing to bloom a two-headed dahlia. Twenty-five years later, to the very day, Mr. Rocco Marchegiano, of 168 Dover Street, same city, distinguished himself in still another field. In Philadelphia he hit Mr. Arnold Cream, of 1020 Cooper Street, Camden, New Jersey, on the chin and won the heavyweight championship of the world.

Whatever the implications of Mr. Denly's botanical accomplishment held for Brockton, they have been lost in the years. It is safe to say, however, that as long as there is boxing and a Brockton 20 miles due south of Boston, the impact of the punch with which Rocky Marciano (né Marchegiano) knocked out Jersey Joe Walcott (né Cream) will be felt.

In Brockton today, for example, there is a young man named Nicholas Rando, who lives at 69 Bartlett Street—the street, incidentally, where Rocky delivered the *Brockton Enterprise-Times* as a boy—who will forever be lacking the first joint of two fingers of his right hand. When Marciano, with his own right hand, flattened Walcott, the excitement that raged through Brockton's Ward Two Memorial Club reached such a pitch that Rando, then fourteen years old, fed his hand into a ventilating fan.

In the state of Virginia lives Mrs. Dorothy Brown Therrien, widowed nine days after the victory over Walcott. Her husband, 54-year-old Frederick J. Therrien, manager of the Brockton office, State Division of Employment Security, and former drum major of Brockton Post 35, American Legion, had been warned by doctors not to overexert himself. When it was announced there would be a parade to welcome home the new champion, however, he couldn't resist and dropped dead in front of the YMHA on Legion Parkway, Brockton, while marching as a marshal's aide.

At St. Colman's imposing fieldstone Roman Catholic Church, Wendell Avenue at Lyman Street, Brockton, the Very Reverend LeRoy V. Cooney, who married Marciano and Barbara May Cousins there on December 30, 1950, will not forget Marciano, either. Just before the second Marciano-Walcott fight, televised from Chicago on May fifteenth of that year, he was directing the un-crating of a 30-inch television set, a gift to the church by the fighter and friend, when he stumbled off the stage in the recreation hall and fractured his right leg.

Despite such occurrences, however, the effect on Brockton of Marciano's rise to the most coveted, most romanticized throne in the world of sport is hardly a tragic one. A manufacturing city of 62,862 residents, many of whom, or their progenitors, came from Italy, Ireland, Lithuania, Poland, Sweden, and French Canada to work in its shoeshops, Brockton has benefited by what has happened to Marciano in ways that can hardly be measured.

Last year Brockton exported 12,384,378 pairs of shoes as well as unrecorded tonnages of carpet ticks, storage batteries, sausages, and burial vaults. It is the unchallenged opinion of the manufacturers that no matter what the product, sales were helped immeasurably by the fame that has accrued to the city through the fistic prowess of the 30-year-old son of Pierino Marchegiano, ex-shoe worker.

"Why, Rocky Marciano has done more to make this city famous than all the shoes ever made here," says Perley Flint, president of Field and Flint, shoe manufacturers. "Now they've heard of Brockton in places they don't even wear shoes."

"Anybody who travels out of Brockton and only carries one line," says J. W. Mahoney, assistant sales manager of the same firm, "also carries Rocky. In Chicago, at the National Shoe Fair last year, they expected anybody from Brockton to be able to predict not only Rocky's next opponent but who would win."

Brockton's delegates to the 1952 political conventions in Chicago found themselves faced with the same questions and so did the 37 Boy Scouts from the Brockton area who attended the National Jamboree near Santa Ana, California, last July. And the *Brockton Enterprise-Times* reported that Brocktonians visiting New York TV studios found themselves plucked for audience-participation shows as soon as they revealed their home town.

"I've talked to customers on the West Coast," says George Stone, head of the Independent Nail and Packing Company, "and they say, 'Oh, yeah? That's Marciano's home town.' There's one machine-tool manufacturer in Milan, Italy, who exports to this country, and do you know what he wanted? An autographed photo of Rocky."

"In Birmingham, Alabama, last year," says Dick Stevens, a salesman for Field and Flint, "I wasn't having much luck getting into one of the stores. There were some hard feelings, so I just dropped in and didn't talk business at all. We just talked Rocky. I never said a word about shoes, but now the orders are coming in."

As a matter of fact, the Brockton boy is also an instrument of shoe research. Each year the Doyle Shoe Company presents Marciano with ten pairs of black Vici kid road shoes, size 10½-EE. Even when he isn't in training for a fight, the champion does daily road work, and recently he returned one pair that, worn through on both soles, had carried him 700 miles.

Marciano's ring shoes, size 10-E, are made, two pairs for each fight, by the Howard and Foster Shoe Company, of black yellow-back kangaroo uppers applied to a lightweight sole manufactured by the Pitvin Shoe Company, also of Brockton. They are probably the lightest boxing shoes ever made.

Last year Charles R. Armey, vice-president of Howard and Foster, decided to put a lightweight street shoe on the market. The first lot went to a fashionable men's store on South Michigan Avenue in Chicago. Some time later the factory received a letter from the retailer stating that the first pair had been bought by Ezzard Charles, former heavyweight champion of the world, who is now challenging Marciano.

"It's a small world," says Armey, "but the important thing is that our employees feel as though they're helping Rocky in the ring. Just last week the women in the stitching room came out and asked if they could sign their names in Rocky's shoes. We decided they could sign one pair."

The economic influence of Marciano on Brockton industry is confused, of course, by many other factors governing business profit and loss. A clearer index is afforded by the effect of his success—45 wins, 40 knockouts, and no losses—on the finances of various individuals.

"A lot of working people in this town are a lot better off because of Marciano," says one Brocktonian. "There are families that have suddenly moved into brand-new homes. The man is a factory worker and everybody knows what he makes. They say, 'Where does he get the money to buy a house like that?' It's obvious. He's been bétting on Rocky.

"And these guys who have pyramided their cars. They started out with old rattletraps when Rocky started fighting in Providence in 1948. They borrowed what they could on the cars. They won and bought betters cars and borrowed again. Today they're driving high-priced automobiles that are paid for."

Before Marciano fought Rex Layne in Madison Square Garden on July 12, 1951, one old Italian woman pulled out of a kitchen coffee tin $500 she had saved in her lifetime without her husband's knowledge. Through a relative, she placed it with a local bookmaker, and when Marciano knocked out Layne in the sixth round, she got back her $500 plus another $1,000.

"When Rocky was getting ready to fight Louis," says Ed Lalli, a Brockton auto dealer, "a guy I never saw before comes in here. He says he wants to sell his car to bet on Rocky. I say to him, 'Look, friend, don't do it. We all think Rocky is gonna win, but suppose something goes wrong? Be smart. Go to a finance company and borrow $200 on your car and 12 months to pay off the loan.'

"So he did it, and after the fight he comes back. You know what he says? He says, 'You make me lose a lot of money. Look at all the money I could have today if I don't listen to you.'"

It was two weeks before the Louis fight, the most important in Marciano's career up to that point and the second Marciano fight to be televised, that the avalanche struck Brockton's 27 television dealers and 12 TV-service firms. By the day of the fight, it was impossible to buy a new receiver in Brockton or to get immediate repair service.

"People who never had trouble with their sets before," says Joe Nesti, of Corola, Inc.," wanted us to go and check them. They wanted us to guarantee they wouldn't have trouble during the fight. Who can guarantee a thing like that?"

A Marciano fight also exerts a marked influence on Brockton's social life. On such an occasion, it is *de rigeur* on the well-to-do West Side for Brockton's matrons to hold cocktail and supper parties in the stately white Colonials and imposing fieldstone mansions where live the city's industrial magnates and more successful doctors and lawyers. Elsewhere in town, bars are crowded and so are Brockton's 15 fraternal and social clubs that own television receivers.

In factories that employ night shifts, power is shut down between 9:45 and 11:00 P.M. and employees gather before TV screens. Brockton's three motion-picture theaters are almost empty.

On the evening of May fifteenth of last year, for example, when Marciano fought Walcott the return bout that was televised from the Chicago Stadium, the Center Theater, with 1,034-seat capacity, had 16 adults and 10 children in the house. At the other two theaters, the Brockton and the Colonial, business was equally bad.

"When Rocky fights on TV," says Bob Riordan, city editor of the *Brockton Enterprise-Times*, "the streets are deserted. You can look the length of Main Street and not see a soul. Then between rounds, you see a couple of people hurrying across the street. They're changing bars, looking for better reception or a better look at the screen. The moment the fight ends, everything busts right open."

Cars, their occupants and their horns sounding, tour Brockton streets until 2:00 A.M. Most of these finally descend upon Ward Two, where Marciano was born and grew up and where the Ward Two Memorial Club, of which Marciano is a charter member, is the nerve center of the celebration. The club, which started 19 years ago in a garage on Winthrop Street, now owns, a hundred yards from Marciano's parental home, a single-story, brown-shingled clubhouse on which a $4,000 mortgage has been lifted, thanks to Marciano's fighting ability.

When Marciano's fights are neither telecast nor broadcast, crowds gather before the red-brick front of the *Brockton Enterprise-Times* at 60 Main Street, where two loud speakers are hung from windowsills of the third-floor editorial rooms. For the first Walcott fight, anxious residents began collecting an hour and a half before fight time, and when the first succinct announcement was made—even round-end blow-by-blow reconstructions of the fight were banned by the International Boxing Club—there were 10,000 waiting before the windows.

"The first round was a bad one for Rocky," came the announcement, edited from the copy received by direct wire from ringside in Philadelphia. "He was down."

Considering that this was the first time Marciano had ever

been knocked off his feet in a ring, it can be imagined with what trepidation the almost silent crowd received at three-minute intervals, the cryptic comments, which varied from that extreme to the occasional opinion that Marciano seemed to be doing a little better but still had a hard fight on his hands. Suddenly, at 11:34 P.M. there came the word.

"The new heavyweight champion of the world," said the voice of staff man Ken Wheeler, "is Rocky Marciano!"

That started it. Four Marines were arrested for street fighting. Three additional police cruiser cars were dispatched to Ward Two, where young Rando was to lose part of his right hand and a man named Francis C. Reed of 55 Indian Head Street, Hanson, was to lose his wallet and $260.

At police headquarters the members of the night shift assigned to house duty sat back satisfied. They had managed to pick up, on the shortwave radio, a blow-by-blow description from a Canadian station. When it had started to come over in French, they had moved the radio back to the cell block where a Bridgewater prisoner of French extraction had provided them with a translation. The next day in court, the bilingual benefactor was fined five dollars for drunkenness.

Marciano has, naturally, complicated the ordinary routine of the Brockton Police Department. Following his knockout of Louis, the department, the *Brockton Enterprise-Times,* and Rocky's mother, Mrs. Pasqualina Marchegiano, all got postcards threatening Marciano's life. The cards were traced to two teenagers.

On the night of the first Walcott fight, all police leaves were canceled and 20 men were assigned posts on the block on Main Street from Green Street to Legion Parkway, which includes the newspaper's offices. When Marciano returned home after that fight to be paraded before a crowd of 50,000, all leaves were again canceled and 60 policemen were requisitioned from the nearby towns of Randolph, Abington, Whitman, Avon, Easton, and the three Bridgewaters. These, plus the hundred men on the Brockton force, were supplemented by a hundred civil-defense volunteers and six motorcycle men of the Massachusetts State Police.

Marciano, of course, could exert tremendous political influence on his city. So great was his appeal after he knocked out Louis on October 26, 1951, that he was exiled from his home town for three weeks during the close battle being waged for the mayoralty by the Republican incumbent, Melvin B. Clifford, and the present mayor, Democrat C. Gerald Lucey, who ultimately won by a margin of 343 votes out of 29,094.

"I was advised right after the Louis fight," says Marciano, "that if I wanted to stay clear of politics, I'd better wait until after the election before I went home. So Barbara and I went to all the shows on Broadway and lounged around for three weeks."

In 1952, during the presidential campaign, Mayor Lucey discovered the heavyweight champion had more than local political significance. He received a request from Washington to arrange for Marciano to ride on the Adlai Stevenson campaign train between Providence and Boston. Although past heavyweight champions had received thousands of dollars for backing presidential candidates, Rocky turned down the request in order to maintain outward political neutrality.

"Then last year," he says, "Paul Keith, who was running against Lucey, came to my house. He said, 'I just want to meet you because people ask me if I know Rocky Marciano and I want to tell the truth.' So we shook hands and then he left."

Brockton Republican leaders claim, of course, it was Mayor Lucey's many public appearances with Marciano that helped swing the last election for the Democrats. The latter, as naturally, assert it was the usual issues—streets, sewers, and schools.

Brockton has 272.36 miles of streets and roads, 123.78 miles of sewers, and 27 schools. Where Marciano, as a manual laborer for the Brockton Gas Company and the Brockton Department of Public Works, once made a pick-and-shovel imprint on the first two, he now exerts another influence on the last.

Before Marciano's first fight with Walcott, the pupils of the first three grades of the Belmont Elementary School sent him a scroll they had signed. In Brockton High School, where Marciano played one year of varsity football before leaving school to work, the champion is a constant subject of class discussion and a constant inspiration to the athletic teams.

Every coach in the school, according to Charley Holden, athletic director, has used the example of Marciano's climb at some time before or during an important game. Between halves of the Brockton-Quincy football game in 1952, with Brockton trailing 14 to 0, Marciano himself strode into the dressing room. He spoke to the team about Brockton's fine football tradition, about its fine coach, Frank Saba, and about the responsibility that rested with the players. Brockton won 19 to 14.

Of all Brocktonians, however, those who have been the most deeply affected by the Marciano ascension are, besides the man himself, the members of his family, his childhood friends, and others who, in one way or another, played a part in his life. One of these is Dr. Josephat Phaneuf, who is now 66 years old and head of the red-brick 94-bed Phaneuf Hospital, at 688 North Main Street. At 1:00 A.M. on September 1, 1923, however, he was still a young, hardworking general practitioner who was to go on to deliver, in all, 7,235 babies in and around Brockton.

"I remember a delivery at that time at 80 Brook Street," he says. "I recall it was fairly difficult because of the size of the baby."

The previous year Pasqualina Marchegiano had lost, in birth, a 13-pound boy. When Rocco, the first of six living children—three sons and three daughters—arrived, he weighed 12½ pounds.

"I say to the doctor," says Mrs. Marchegiano, "I ask him, 'How much this cost?' He say, 'Forty dollar.' I say, 'Well, Doctor, I give you cash.' He say, 'Well, thirty-five dollar.' "

"Strangely," Dr. Phaneuf says, "I have never seen him fight. A great many of my patients talk about him, though, and when they do I say, 'I was the first one ever to hit him.' "

In Brockton now, Red Gormley is a letter carrier. Less than 10 years ago, however, he, like Marciano, was a good amateur baseball player, and they shared their dreams of making the big leagues together, Gormley as a shortstop and Marciano as a catcher. In the spring of 1947 they reported together in an old car to the Fayetteville, North Carolina, farm club of the Chicago Cubs.

"In April," Gormley says, "they released us. We went to Goldsboro, and they didn't want us, either. Our arms were gone. We couldn't throw. We were broke, and I guess we looked like a couple of bums, so we decided to come home."

Gormley's territory is in Ward Two. Standing in front of 168 Dover Street, his mail sack over his shoulder, he looks across at the five-and-a-half-acre James Edgar Playground, where he and Marciano, day after day, year after year, played ball.

"We were driving back in the old car," he says. "Finally Rocky said, 'The heck with it. I'm through with baseball. I'm gonna get some fights, and you're gonna handle me.' There I was, sitting right next to half the money in the world, and I didn't even know it."

He hitches his sack higher on his shoulder and starts up the steps to 168. It is the two-family, green-shingled house where Marciano lived from the time he was 11 years old until last year and where the Marchegianos still live. To this address it has now become part of Gormley's job to deliver some of the mail that comes to the heavyweight champion from all over the world.

"So what's the sense of talking about it?" he says, turning back. "I've got a wife and three kids now."

The bulk of Marciano's mail is a burden on the backs of Norman Fenn and Bill Riley, who deliver it to the cottage at 54 Woodland Avenue, where live Mr. and Mrs. Arthur Bellao. Bellao, a short, intense, brown-eyed young man who sells cars for a living, is an old friend of the Marchegianos and owns a typewriter. When the mail begins to submerge 168 Dover Street, he volunteers to answer it.

"It picks up just before and after a fight," he says. "When Rocky became champ, there were a hundred letters a day, some of them from Saudi Arabia and the British West Indies, asking for autographs or pictures or pieces of equipment to be used for raffles. My wife and I were working from 6:00 A.M. until 8:30 A.M., and then from 8:00 P.M. until 1:30 A.M. to handle it."

It is in the five immaculate rooms on the first floor of 168 Dover Street, of course, that Rocky's impact is strongest. For more than 30 years Pierino Marchegiano, born 60 years ago in Abruzzi, Italy, and gassed and wounded fighting with the Second Marines on the Marne and in the Argonne, left at seven every workday morning with his lunchbox under his arm to work as a No. 7 bedlaster in the shoe factories. The machine he ran forms toes and heels of shoes, and shoe workers say it takes more out of a man than any other machine in the shop. Two years ago he retired.

"Now I go back," he says, "and I see my old friends and everybody says, 'What a difference, Pete. Years ago you couldn't talk with the super, and now he take you around the shop.'"

Pasqualina Marchegiano, now 52, was born near Benevento, Italy. She, too, worked in the shoeshops before the children came—Rocco, now 30 years old; Alice, 28; Connie, 26; Elizabeth, 22; Louis, 20; and Peter, 13.

"I lose my first baby," she says. "The doctor say, 'You gonna have no more baby' I cry. After a while I say, 'If God want me to have baby, and if God give me children, I gonna do the best I can.'

"All I want is to keep my house clean. I keep my children clean, I make my supper. Always at breakfast I tell my children, 'Now try your best in the school.' I tell them the same like when they go to church.

"Now it's just sit in my heart. It's hard to say the beautiful thing that happen with Rocky. You feel happy, and you feel like crying when you think."

Pierino and Pasqualina do not move as freely in Brockton now as they once did. They are quiet people, and unexpected attention embarrasses them.

"I don't go downtown," Pierino says. "Too much talk."

"I don't go but one day a week," says his wife. "Last week I went to post office and there is a big line and I wait and a man I don't know says to me, 'How is our boy?' I say, 'Fine.' He say, 'You know, we're very proud of him down at the Cape.' Then he introduce his wife and his sister. Who is this man?

"I walk on the street and a woman come up to me. She say, 'God bless you, Mrs. Marchegiano. My son and my son-in-law, they make a fortune on your boy. I tell no one, but I tell you because I want to thank you.' Who is this woman?

"I go in a store. In the store the man say, 'If you need credit, Mrs. Marchegiano, you get credit. Your son make me a lot of money for us.' I go to Rocky's house and I see a letter there from someone who wants his picture. I bring it home and I look at the letter and I say that God been so good to my son to give this beautiful luck, why can't I give to people who like my son? So I sent these poor people the picture. Sometimes I cry."

In Goddard Junior High School, where the Marchegianos' youngest child, Peter, is a pupil, he, too, finds he is different. On the day of the second Walcott fight, John Zoino, the science teacher, announced a test.

"Then he asked me," says Peter, "if I thought I could take it. I said, 'I'm afraid I can't today.' Then he let me take it the next day."

When it was revealed in the *Brockton Enterprise-Times* last year that Marciano and his wife had bought a new home at 46 Harlan Drive, a neighbor counted 500 cars that stopped there on the following weekend so the occupants could examine from the outside the as yet unfurnished $35,000, nine-room, brick-field-stone-and-clapboard ranch house. Marciano, most of whose time is spent in training camps, on personal-appearance tours, or relaxing with his wife and their 18-month-old daughter, Mary Anne, at Grossinger's in the Catskill Mountains of New York State, has been home only a total of two months since he won the title, and then he found little privacy.

"When Rocky got home from that tour of the Pacific last December," says Al Columbo, his closest friend since childhood and the man who has helped train Marciano for all his fights, "he got into town late and nobody knew he was here. I went around to his house the next morning to walk with him before breakfast. While we were walking he said, 'You know, it was great to come back to my own home and to wake up and find my wife and the baby there and to have nobody else around.' We walked about five or six miles, and when we got back, there they were—five cars in front of the house."

Vic Dubois, *Brockton Enterprise-Times* sports editor, has appealed to his readers to allow Marciano some privacy. The champion and his wife, however, are reconciled to the inevitable attention focused on the heavyweight champion of the world. What disturbs them more is the change that has come over their old Brockton friends.

"They don't drop in like they used to." Marciano says. "When they do come around, they act different. They even talk different. I know what's bothering them. They think they're bothering me and they're not and I can't convince them."

"It's the same with my old girlfriends," his wife says. "When I'm home alone it's fine, but the minute they come in and see Rocky, something comes over them. It's a shame."

As Brockton generally, however, basks in reflected glory, there is but one dark cloud on the horizon. That is the possibility of a Marciano defeat. Neither Brocktonians nor boxing experts envision that in the near future, but the hope is everywhere in Brockton that when their hero starts to slip, he will retire before succumbing to an opponent.

"God help this town if he ever gets licked," says one taxi driver. "There's one old Italian couple here I pick up before every fight and take up to a loan office. The last time they borrowed $3,000 on their house. Can you imagine what it will be like if he ever gets beat?"

ROOMMATE: BOB COUSY

By Al Hirshberg

FROM SPORT

Copyright © 1955, Sport Magazine

This intimate study of Bob Cousy, the player who first put the Boston Celtics on the basketball map and who was instrumental in keeping them the leaders in the NBA for over a decade, is about the man as well as the athlete. The author roomed with Cousy on a five-day trip and regales the reader with the stellar player's penchant for cards, movies, dreams, reactions during and after the games, and with his total dedication to basketball.

For the swing around the western half of the league, the Boston Celtics had chartered a Northeast Airlines DC-3 which, complete with crew and flight agent, would carry us on the whole trip, from Boston to Rochester to Minneapolis to Milwaukee to St. Louis to Fort Wayne and back to Boston. I arrived at Logan Airport in East Boston with a few minutes to spare and hurried aboard the plane. There was a single row of seats on the right and a double row on the left, and everyone seemed pretty well settled when I arrived. Bob Cousy was in the front single seat, busily shuffing a deck of cards. Bill Sharman was directly across the aisle from him, and Johnny Most, who broadcasts the Celtics' games on the radio, was on the window seat next to Sharman. Fred Scolari sat right behind Cousy, with Ed Crowley, the radio engineer, and sportswriter Larry Claflin of the *Boston American* opposite him. The six of them were deep in a card game before the engines had begun warming up.

I was curious to know what they were playing but I couldn't see; another card game was blocking my view. This one numbered Ed Macauley, Red Auerbach, the coach, Bob Brannum, and Dwight (Red) Morrison. Sitting on aisle seats opposite each other, they had constructed a card table out of a blanket spread across the aisle and hooked on the arm rests of each of the four seats. They were playing bridge.

Further back in the plane, I sat down next to Jack Barry of the *Boston Globe* and said conversationally, "I'd like to sit and talk to Cousy for a while."

"You might as well forget about talking to him until we get to Rochester," he said.

"Why?"

"Because he won't get up off that seat and neither will those guys playing bridge."

"What's Cousy playing?"

"Oh, hell," Barry said.

"What's the matter?" I asked him.

"Not a thing," he said cheerfully. "Why?"

"Why'd you say, 'Oh, hell'?"

"Because that's the name of the game."

"Oh," I said, relieved. "How do you play it?"

"Hanged if I know," Barry said. "You'll have to ask Cousy."

We took off at 10:45 and Cousy lit a cigar the moment the "No Smoking" sign went off. I passed the time talking to Barry and to the non-cardplaying Celtics, Togo Palazzi, Frank Ramsey, Don Barksdale, and Jack Nichols. Joan Barrett, the pretty blue-eyed stewardess, came by from time to time with cookies and coffee. Once in a while she handed cartons of milk to Cousy and Sharman, who would surely drink up all the profits if they were dairy farmers. The trip to Rochester took about two hours and 15 minutes and they must have guzzled a quart and a half apiece.

It was bitter cold at the Rochester airport, but the boys in the "Oh, hell" game were in no hurry to get into the terminal. Instead, they crowded around Cousy as he stood beside the plane, working with a pencil over a complicated chart of figures on a sheet of paper. Finally, Cousy announced the results. With nothing at stake, I was already retiring to the warmth of the airport building.

"How did you come out?" I asked Cousy, as he came in.

"Lost half a buck."

"Anybody lose more?"

"Not much. Nobody ever loses more than a buck or so at this game."

"And you guys stood around and froze to settle 50-cent accounts?"

Cousy shrugged. "I'd rather die from freezing than from worrying," he said.

Since we weren't staying overnight in Rochester, those of us who were supernumeraries left our luggage on the plane. Only the players carried their grips into town. In the lobby of the Hotel Seneca, Auerbach said, "Mind if your career as Cousy's roommate doesn't start until we get to Minneapolis? The boys will only be here for the afternoon."

Cousy's regular roommate is Sharman. The two were standing in the lobby, staring at a 1955 model automobile on display.

"Reminds me of a Christmas tree," Cousy said.

"I'll bite," I said. "Why does an automobile remind you of a Christmas tree?"

"Because I can't figure out how they got the car in here and how they'll get it out again."

"What's that got to do with a Christmas tree?"

"Because I can't figure out how they'd get a Christmas tree in and out of here either," he said.

"What are you going to do this afternoon?"

"I'm undecided whether to sack out or go to the movies. I might even eat."

He ended up eating—about a side of beef, two glasses of milk, and a huge plate of ice cream. By the time he got through, it was after three o'clock. Then with Sharman and Palazzi, he went to the movies. After that, he had a quick sandwich and some more milk, then headed for the arena.

The Rochester Arena is a big barnlike building, with tiers of seats rising from the floor on both sides of the basketball court. There is a reverberating echo in the place, and the name that bounced around it most was Cousy. Everyone was either cheering or jeering him, but, apparently impervious to the crowd reactions, he played a solid, steady game. The Royals won 107–101. Cousy, with five field goals and 14 successful foul conversions, had 24 points, a good night's total.

"Those noises bother you?" I asked him later.

"I'd be out of business if they did," he said.

"Some of the riding was pretty rough."

"They paid their money. They had a right to say anything they felt like."

"Some guys resent it," I remarked.

"Any professional athlete who resents anything a paying customer says ought to have his head examined," Cousy said.

We ate at a diner near the airport, with Cousy packing away two sandwiches, a huge piece of pie, and two glasses of milk. As we walked to the plane for a midnight takeoff, he asked, "You going to play 'Oh, hell'?"

"Don't know how," I told him.

"Want to learn?"

"Sure," I said.

We got back into the plane, and I took the front window seat. Cousy was beside me and Sharman sat in the single seat across the aisle. Crowley sat in one of the seats behind us, with Houbregs, who had met us at the airport, in the other. When the game began, I figured we'd play for an hour or so and then call it a night, but I was living in a fool's paradise. Hour after hour the boys kept dealing, and by 3:00 A.M. I was ready to throw in the towel.

"Look," I asked, "how long are you guys going to play?"

"Until we get to Minneapolis," Cousy said blandly.

"Until *when*?"

"No sense breaking up the game right in the middle, as long as we've got players."

"Don't you intend to get any sleep?"

"You one of these guys who sleeps his life away?" he needled me. "Come on, now, don't be a spoilsport."

So I played "Oh, hell" all night.

Well, not exactly all night. We stopped in Milwaukee at 4:30 in the morning to fuel up, and had sandwiches and coffee (milk for Cousy and Sharman) while we were waiting. On the way back to the plane, we bought chocolate-covered ice cream sticks out of a slot machine and ate them as we walked toward our DC-3. When we got aboard, we found Crowley and Houbregs asleep, and the game had to be rearranged. Scolari sat in the seat behind Sharman, and he played for an hour or so. When he wilted, Brannum moved in. By the time we reached Minneapolis at 6:00 A.M., Cousy, Sharman, Brannum, and I were staggering through the last hand. I lost $2.70.

"I thought you said nobody ever loses more than a buck at this game," I remarked.

"Never in my entire career," Cousy said earnestly, "have I run into as lousy an 'Oh, hell' player as you."

"I'll learn."

"You'd better. There are only eight people in the whole world who know how to play it and they're all on this trip."

"Oh, hell" is not a difficult game to learn, as I found out later when, refreshed from a whole three hours of sleep, I could think fairly straight. Depending upon the number of players in the game, eight or ten cards are dealt on the first hand, and a card is turned up as trump. Each player announces how many tricks he expects to take, and the cards are then played out as in bridge. Players who take exactly as many tricks as they predicted get a 15-point bonus; otherwise, only as many points as they take tricks. In each succeeding hand, one less card is dealt, and the game ends on the one-card deal.

I played the game practically every single minute we were airborne and I never did learn how to keep score. Furthermore, Cousy, Sharman, and Scolari weren't too sure of themselves. Even Cousy and Sharman, who, for all I know, might have invented "Oh, hell," were halfway into the next game before they had figured out the results of the last one.

Minneapolis was cold, colder than Rochester. Between a long delay waiting for luggage and a long ride in from the airport, we couldn't check into the Hotel Nicollet until about 7:30—an hour and a half after we landed. Just before we got into the elevator to go to our room, Auerbach said, "Leave a call in time to meet at 12:30." Cousy just looked at him and nodded. I shuddered.

We rode up without a word, then headed for our room. The only sound that came from either of us was Cousy's grunted "Long halls—I hate 'em" as we struggled with grips which suddenly had become as heavy as lead. Once in the room, Cousy left a call for noon. The two of us took off our clothes and flopped into bed without even opening our suitcases. It was nearly eight o'clock.

The next thing I knew, Cousy was wheezing, from the depths of his blankets, "What time is it?"

I looked at my watch and wheezed back, "11:30."

He got up, jumped out of bed, took his toilet kit from his suitcase, rushed into the bathroom, and started shaving. Ten minutes later he poked his head out and barked, "What time did you say it was?"

"11:30."

"What did you wake me up for?"

"I didn't wake you up. You woke me up," I said.

"The hell I did! I messed myself out of half an hour's sleep. Well, I'll get it now." And he flopped back into bed again.

Fifteen minutes later, the operator rang with our noon call, which we had both forgotten. With murder in my heart but sugar on my tongue, I thanked her, then got up. At 12:15, I woke Cousy, and a quarter of an hour later, we were on our way downstairs to meet the rest for the ride to the game.

"Do you do this sort of thing often?" I asked him.

"This," he said, "is practically routine."

"How do you feel?"

"Terrible."

"Then how can you play?"

By this time we were getting off the elevator in the lobby.

Cousy turned to me and said, "I can play all right. What worries me is how I can eat. It's too soon before the game to have a big meal."

"But the game doesn't worry you?"

"Oh, I'll have trouble trying to score. I always do in this town."

"Why?" I asked him.

"On account of Slater Martin. That little guy is the greatest guard in the league. He sticks to me like court plaster. Whenever I play him, I'm glad to settle for ten points."

"And the way you feel now?"

"I'll settle for five," Cousy said.

He had a light breakfast—orange juice, toast, and milk—we headed for the Armory at about 1:15 for a 2:30 game. Everyone looked tired, although some of the boys had slept fairly well on the plane. Neither Cousy nor Sharman, who had sat up all night, appeared to be ready to play a basketball game, and, with the Lakers in their own home town, this one figured to be a slaughter.

But Minneapolis was lucky to win. Once the game got under way, they put up a real battle before losing 115–108. The Lakers didn't clinch the issue until the last two minutes of play. It was the second time in a row that the Celtics had scored over 100 points in a losing cause.

Cousy, a hard loser, was grim and silent for an hour or so after the game. He had hit for 21 points, with five baskets from the floor and 11 foul shots, in spite of the fact that he had neither eaten nor slept well. Yet he was very unhappy.

Later I said to him, "You didn't really expect to win, did you?"

"Well, I never go into a game expecting to lose."

"I know, but look what you guys had been through. And you certainly scored more than five points off Martin."

He smiled, then said, "Y'know something? That's the best day I've ever had against him."

We had dinner a couple of hours later, and Cousy demolished a tremendous slab of roast beef. Sharman and Palazzi, who were rooming together, joined us, along with Ed Crowley. At about 6:30 we went to the movies. When we came out, it was nine o'clock.

I yawned and said, "Well, guess it's time to go to bed."

"Bed—at nine o'clock? You crazy?" Cousy said.

"Have you got any better ideas?"

"Sure. There's another movie across the street."

That was too much. I watched the boys buy their tickets and go into the show, then I picked up some newspapers and went back to the hotel. Playing cards all night on an airplane was all right. So was going to one movie. But two movies in one night was more than I could take.

"You must be daffy about the movies," I said to Bob when we got up Monday morning.

"Once in a while, you see a real good one. Mostly, I just go to pass away the time."

"Do you ever see the same show twice?"

"That I won't do," Cousy said. "But I can always find a show somewhere I haven't seen before."

"What time did you get in?"

"About 1:30. We had something to eat after the show."

"Aren't you tired?"

"Sort of," he said. "But there's no sense in my going to bed early. I just toss around half the night and then get up exhausted."

The phone rang, and Cousy, after talking for a few minutes, hung up and said, "That was one of my campers. He apologized for not coming to the game."

Bob is part owner of Camp Graylag in Pittsfield, New Hampshire. He has 100 boys, some from as far away as the West Coast.

"Basketball is the greatest game in the world," he said, "and I'll do anything I can to sell the game. Now, take our league. We've still got a few kinks to iron out, but we're getting there. I'd like to see teams in cities like Chicago and Detroit and I think we'll have them some day. The new rules have worked great. They're made for a faster, better, more exciting game than ever."

He was referring to the 24-second rule, which makes it necessary for a team to take a shot at the basket within 24 seconds after getting possession of the ball, and the six-foul rule, which gives an extra penalty shot for every foul over six in a given period.

"Before the new rules, the last quarter could be deadly in a pressure game," he said. "The team in front would hold the ball indefinitely, and the only way you could get it was by fouling somebody. In the meantime, nobody dared take a shot and the whole game was slowed up. Of course, the new game is tougher on the ball players, and I'm trying to work something out to protect them."

Cousy has spent considerable time in the last two years forming a players' association, similar to the group operating among professional baseball players.

"The players have as much at stake as the owners," he said. "If the league weakens or folds, it will cost a lot of guys their living. I think we should have more to say about how the league is run."

"What would you want done?" I asked.

"Well, we've kidded around a lot about this trip, for example, but it's really a killer. Just imagine—playing in Rochester one night and in Minneapolis the next afternoon! Today's our only day off this trip—Milwaukee tomorrow night, St. Louis Wednesday night, Fort Wayne Thursday night! And we're not the only ones. That sort of thing happens to everyone in the league. We've got to work out something that makes more sense.

"And there should be some kind of minimum salary, and better incentives. We don't even have a Most Valuable Player award, or an award for the highest scorer or anything like that. The boys should be given more to shoot for than just those postseason bonuses.

"I'd like to see a good minor league developed," he said. "The way it is now, there's no place for a boy to go if he's dropped from an NBA squad. There are only a few independent teams and no farm league. Some of the younger fellows need nothing more than experience, but where can they get it? Instead of taking a chance on struggling back into the NBA some day, most of the promising kids quit the game altogether if they don't make the big league on their first try.

"I don't know what the solutions are, but I want to do something to help find them. There's no reason why we can't be consulted for ideas. That's one of the big reasons why we're forming this association."

On the way to the airport—we were scheduled for a 1:30 P.M.

takeoff for Milwaukee—I said, "How come you didn't drop dead during the game yesterday afternoon?"

"It really wasn't so bad."

"But didn't you *ever* feel so tired you thought you'd have to call it a day?"

"Well," he said, "there are always times when I feel that way. I can run up and down the floor twice at constant top speed without getting tired, but when I have to do it a third time, it really gets me."

"That's right," said Sharman, who was in the taxi with us. "You run the ball down, lose it at the other end, and then run back, all without stopping, and you're all right. But if you steal it at your end and have to move back down again without breaking your stride, it's murder. As a matter of fact, it's easier on the Cooz than on any of us."

Cousy is not a robust-looking athlete. On the contrary, with his long, thin face and his sloping shoulders, he looks actually frail. And at 6 feet 2 inches, he is a great deal shorter then the average professional basketball player.

"Where does all the stamina come from?" I asked.

"My legs," Cousy answered. "They're my strongest asset. The bulk of my weight is below my waist. I look about 160, but I weigh around 185. Nobody ever believes that until they see me standing on the scales."

"This guy can run forever," Sharman said.

"I grew up playing basketball on concrete outdoor courts on Long Island," Cousy pointed out. "I never played indoors as a kid. I built up my legs on those hard courts, and when it came time to play on wooden floors, it was that much easier for me."

We took off from Minneapolis at 1:45 P.M. and landed in Milwaukee an hour and three-quarters later. During that brief time, Cousy, Sharman, Scolari, and Houbregs officiated while I dropped six dollars at "Oh, hell."

"If I hadn't seen it with my own eyes, I wouldn't have believed it possible," said Scolari.

"Don't let him get away, boys," Cousy added. "This is his only trip."

At the desk of the Hotel Wisconsin, Auerbach said, "You've got two roommates instead of one this time. Sharman's going in with you."

As soon as we had checked in, Cousy and Sharman went to the Milwaukee Auditorium, where the Hawks were working out, to visit Chuck Cooper, who had roomed with Cousy when he was with the Celtics. The two are close friends. Cousy had once refused to stay in a Raleigh, North Carolina, hotel because it wouldn't accept Cooper, a Negro.

I didn't see Cousy until four or five hours later when he and Sharman walked into a movie palace around the corner from the hotel. The theater was advertising a triple bill, so I knew it would be a long evening. It was. The boys got out at one o'clock in the morning, and by the time they had eaten and gone to bed, it was after two.

When we got up the next morning, Tuesday, I asked them why, on the one day off, they didn't take advantage of the chance to get to bed early.

"Because it throws our schedule all out of kilter," Cousy said. "We play most of our games at night, so we gear our lives accordingly. We eat a big meal at around three in the afternoon, then take in a movie or loaf around the room and go to the arena an hour or so before the game. Then we eat again after it's over and get to bed at 1:30 or 2:00 in the morning. On our days off, we do the same thing, because we don't have enough days off to shift to a more normal routine."

"You know how baseball players hate to go from day games to night games and back again," Sharman pointed out. "Well, we're the same way, except we play more nights than ball players do. The worst thing for us is a day game, because that messes everything up."

Sharman is an authority on the subject of baseball players. He is still an outfielder in the Brooklyn Dodgers' chain. He didn't play in 1954, but he's toying with the idea of returning to baseball this year.

The boys had a big breakfast at about 10:30 Tuesday morning, and then went to the movies. They ate again in the middle of the afternoon, then rested for an hour or so. That ended their longest free period of the trip.

The game Tuesday night was played in the Milwaukee Auditorium and it marked the Hawks' debut of Frank Selvy, who, like Houbregs, was a refugee from the Baltimore Bullets. The rookie star from Furman got a big buildup locally, and a good crowd showed up for a well-publicized Cousy-Selvy duel.

The fans were on Cousy all night, but, as usual, he showed no sign of being annoyed. One leather-lunged observer kept yelling, "Cousy, you're a bum! Cousy, you're a bum!"

But Cousy was no bum that night. On the contrary, both he and Selvy built up impressive point totals. When Cousy scored his thirty-fourth point late in the game to set a new Milwaukee record, his heckler yelled, "Don't that bum ever miss?" A minute later Selvy, who had 33 points himself, racked up two more, and Cousy's tormentor was back in business. As the game ended, the walls were jumping again with the raucous "Cousy, you're a bum!" But Cousy was all smiles as he ran off the floor. The Celtics, hitting the hundred mark for the third straight game, won a 118–99 victory.

Cousy was bubbling and grinning and swapping wisecracks when I walked into the locker room 10 minutes later.

"Now everything's fine," he said. "We finally won one."

"Did you hear that guy yelling at you?" I asked.

"You mean the foghorn? There's one like that in every town. Long as they pay their way in, they don't bother me any."

Later about 10 of us sat down for a "snack." Cousy's consisted of a full-course dinner, complete from soup to nuts and featuring a thick, juicy steak. It was exactly midnight when he started cutting into it.

"Hey, Red, what time do we meet tomorrow morning?" he asked.

"Nine o'clock, in the lobby." Auerbach replied. "It's two and a half hours to St. Louis and I don't want to get there too late."

Cousy turned to me. "How about a card game back in the room?"

"You mean tonight?" I said.

"Sure."

"But we won't get started until about half-past one."

"That'll be all right."

"How long do you want to play?"

"Well," Cousy said, "we have to be out of here by nine. We can't play any longer than that."

So we played cards—but not until nine in the morning. That would have been all right with Cousy and Sharman, but the rest of the boys broke it up at four. Grateful for small mercies, I was happy to settle for four hours' sleep in the pungent atmosphere of drying uniforms. Both Cousy's and Sharman's were draped along the radiators.

"How come I never noticed this fragrance before?" I asked, as I struggled out of bed Wednesday morning.

"Very simple," Cousy explained. "I didn't have time to hang my suit up after the Rochester game and by the time we got into the room Sunday night at Minneapolis, it was all dry. We had an afternoon game there—remember?"

"I wish they were all afternoon games," I muttered.

It was snowing hard when we took off from Milwaukee, and we found out later that we ran away from a blizzard. We got off the ground at about 10:30 A.M., and landed in St. Louis two and a half hours later. On this trip, Johnny Most, the radio announcer, helped Cousy, Sharman, Scolari, and Houbregs relieve me of $3.75.

"A game of pennies, and the guy loses in dollars," said Most. "Where have I been? You been keeping him to yourself?"

"Don't worry," Cousy told him. "We've got time for a couple more sessions. Don't worry, you'll get your share."

Scolari, the elder statesman of the ball club, rode with Cousy, Sharman, and me into St. Louis from the airport.

"How old are you really, Freddie?" Cousy asked him.

"I'm 32. I'll be 33 in March."

"You've been 32 for years. You were playing in this league before I was in high school."

"This is my ninth year. I started when I was 23," said Scolari haughtily.

"That's your story. Hey, Willie," Cousy said, turning to Sharman, "how many ages have you got?"

"Three," said Sharman. "One for baseball, one for basketball, and one for when I first got into Southern California."

"Which is the right one?" Cousy asked him.

"I don't remember which is which. Anyhow, I'm 26."

"Twenty-six?" roared Scolari, "Why, you've got a daughter in high school!"

"That's my kid sister," said Sharman.

"And I'm Childe Harold. Why don't you guys be like me and tell the truth?"

The game at the spacious new St. Louis Arena was scheduled for 9:30 Wednesday night. Sharman roomed with us again, and after we checked into the Hotel Melbourne, he and Cousy had their big dinner and then went off to the inevitable movie.

The Hawks, who came in from Milwaukee by train, arrived early in the evening. A fair-sized but hardly neutral crowd was on hand for what turned out to be an easy game for the Celts. St. Louis is Ed Macauley's home town, and as far as the Celtics were concerned, the game might just as well have been played in Boston.

Cousy had another great night. Besides piling up 31 points to lead both clubs, he put on a bewildering show of dribbling behind his back, scoring from odd angles, and looking in one direction while passing the ball in another. He banged in 12 baskets from the floor and, as usual, played practically the whole game.

The Celtics won their second in a row, and for the fourth straight time scored over 100 points. The score was 101–90, thanks not only to Cousy's hit streak but also to Macauley's 28 points and a magnificent job of defending against Selvy on the part of Sharman. The Hawks' rookie, who had finished up with 44 points the night before in Milwaukee, was held to 15 points.

It was Cousy's game all the way, but he was particularly brilliant in the last period. The Celtics had a seven-point lead going into it, and Cousy made some unbelievable shots as he racked up five field goals. When the lead had increased to 16, he dug into his bag of tricks, and delighted the crowd with his passing, shooting, and dribbling.

"The guy's the greatest," said Auerbach after the game. "There isn't anyone in the business who can come close to him. He's had 65 points in two nights. And when he gets a chance to put on a show the way he did tonight, he's in a class by himself."

"Why don't you do that sort of thing more often?" I asked Cousy later.

"The only time I can do it is when we've got a safe lead," he said, "and in this league, that doesn't happen very often. I can't fiddle around out there just for the sake of fiddling around. My job is to help win ball games. When a stunt will help me out of a jam, I'll use one. Otherwise, I have to play it straight.

"The behind-the-back dribble which seems to attract a lot of attention was originally a desperation measure. I picked that one up while I was at Holy Cross. We played Loyola one night and the only way I could get around a guy was by shifting the ball from one hand to the other. He had me so well guarded that I couldn't do it in front, so I did it behind my back.

"As a matter of fact," Cousy added, "I'm not the only guy who can do that. I've seen others work it, and I imagine everyone on a club like the Harlem Globetrotters can do it as a gag. I guess maybe I'm the only one who does it consistently, and as a strategic measure during a regular game."

"Do you mind being called a basketball magician?"

"Hell, no. It suits me fine. If people want to think of me as a magician, that's wonderful, just so long as they don't think of me *only* as a magician. I'm a professional basketball player, and I have to be a lot more than a so-called magician in order to be a successful one."

Cousy, as a matter of fact, is almost as proud of his defensive ability as of his passing, shooting, and legerdemain. When he first joined the Celtics five years ago, he had some defensive weaknesses. They since have been ironed out, and he is now a comparatively stingy opponent. "Of course, I'm not the best in the business," he said. "Nobody on our club is a defensive genius. If we were as good on defense as on offense, we'd be unbeatable. We're the highest-scoring team in the NBA, but we lose a lot of ball games because opponents score heavily on us. But the game we play is wide open, and I'm sure the customers like it better that way."

The usual midnight "bite" was another steak. At about 12:30 I went back to the room for what I hoped would be a night's sleep. We had to meet in the lobby at nine o'clock the next morning for the flight to Fort Wayne, where the Celtics were winding up the trip Thursday night. I left a call for 8:30, read the papers for a while, and put out the light at one o'clock.

It didn't stay out long. Just as I was dropping off to sleep, the door burst open and in trooped Cousy, Sharman, Houbregs, and Ramsey.

"Come on, come on, get up!" yelled Cousy. "This is no time to be sleeping."

"Ga-a-a-," I grunted.

"Half-past one and you're in bed? Where do you think you are—in a hospital?"

"I will be by the time you guys get through with me."

I struggled up to a sitting position, while the boys dragged a table and some chairs over by my bed. Cousy took a deck of cards out of his pocket and started shuffling. Before he began dealing, he said, "We're going to play buck-up."

"Buck-up?"

"You know the game?" asked Cousy.

"Never heard of it."

"Well, Ramsey never heard of 'Oh, hell,' and he's too young to teach."

Buck-up is a fast, three-card game which we played for a fast two hours. At 3:30, when Ramsey and Houbregs finally left the room, I collapsed.

"Look at that crumb, Willie," I heard Cousy say. "He died on us."

"Better it should happen to you," I snarled from under the pillow.

"You going to bed, Willie?" he asked Sharman.

"I guess so," was the reply. "There doesn't seem to be anything else to do."

"Well, I'm not tired," said Cousy. "I'm going to read a while."

Cousy and I were the last ones out of the hotel the next morning. Sharman was up and dressed before either of us had set our feet on the floor.

"What time did you get to sleep?" I asked.

"About 4:30, I guess," Cousy yawned.

"Did you read all that time?"

"Sure."

"What did you do that for?"

"Good book," he said.

Palazzi was waiting for us on the sidewalk. The youngster started to get into the back seat, but Cousy said, "Why don't you sit in front, Togo? It's more comfortable."

Cousy and I climbed in back, and, when the taxi started rolling toward the airport, Cousy said casually, "Say, Togo, did you notice that sign on the dashboard?"

When Palazzi shook his head, Cousy told him to read it aloud.

" 'The right front is the most dangerous seat in the car,' " Palazzi read slowly. " 'Please do not sit here unless all other seats are taken.' "

Cousy killed himself laughing. He was still chuckling when we arrived at the airport. Palazzi climbed out of the cab looking like a man who had just sat in an electric chair with the power off.

It was exactly 10:30 when we took off from St. Louis, and, with a one-hour change back to Eastern Standard Time, we got into Fort Wayne at 1:45 P.M. During the two and a quarter hours I lost only $1.25.

"You're getting there," said Cousy.

"In another week you'll be playing us even," Sharman added.

I lost my roommates at the Van Orman Hotel. Since we were leaving right after the game to fly back to Boston, there was no purpose in my checking in. Besides, I couldn't be with Cousy anyhow, since several of his campers live in Fort Wayne and he would be busy until it was time to go to the Coliseum, which, incidentally, is the most beautiful arena on the NBA circuit. We arrived there during the early stages of a game between Milwaukee and Minneapolis, since the Celtics-Pistons contest was the windup of a doubleheader.

With no Sharman to guard him, Selvy had a field day against the Lakers. He scored 42 points, setting a new Coliseum record, and the first to congratulate him after he left the floor was Cousy.

"That boy's great," Cousy said later. "He'll be good for a long time, too. He's only a kid, fresh out of college."

The game at Fort Wayne started as if it would be a cinch for the Celtics. At the end of the first quarter they had a 28–21 lead, but they slipped in the second and held only a one-point advantage at half time. It was 71–71 at the three-quarter mark and then the roof fell in on the Celtics. The Pistons scored 45 points in the last session and piled up a 116–98 decision. It was the only game on the whole trip in which the Celtics failed to score 100 points.

After the first period, when he scored four times from the floor, Cousy was held to one basket. He was glum and uncommunicative when the game ended, but hamburgers and milk at the airport helped bring back his normal good humor. He didn't even get mad when I asked, "What makes a bad night?"

"Maybe you—maybe the other team—it all depends," he answered.

"Well—like tonight."

"I guess it was a combination of the two. We were hot at first, and then we cooled off. And the Pistons are in a terrific streak. A good club going well is the hardest combination in the world to beat."

"You started out as if you were going to have another big night."

"It looked that way, didn't it?" he nodded. "But I went cold. Those shots that rolled in when we played at Milwaukee and St. Louis just dropped out here."

"Do you keep track of your baskets during a game?"

He shook his head. "I don't even try," he said. "If I only get a few, I don't want to know the total, and if I get a lot, I can't add them up."

We were sitting at the airport, waiting for the writers, who were still filing their stories from the Coliseum. Someone griped about the delay, and Cousy quickly turned on him.

"Never squawk when writers are working," he said. "If you're lucky, they might be writing about you."

"They might be beating my brains out, too," the other man remarked.

"I'd rather have them beat my brains out than not mention me at all," Cousy said.

"There are athletes who don't have much use for writers," I commented.

"I feel sorry for them. They don't realize how much help writers can give them. I don't know where we'd be without the writers. Basketball is over 50 years old, but the game never really caught on until the writers began telling the world about it."

He leaned forward. "Y'know," he said slowly, "there are some people who think they're more important than anyone else just because they have some God-given talent—maybe they're athletes, maybe artists, maybe stage or screen people, maybe even writers. But I'll tell you this, no matter how big a person is, there's never an excuse for his having a big head."

We got off the ground at 1:15 in the morning, with two stops before Boston ahead of us. We were hitting Washington to refuel and landing in Worcester to drop Cousy off.

"They always do that for you?" I asked him as we sat down for the last "Oh, hell" game.

"What do you want 'em to do—drop me off by parachute?"

"That wouldn't be so bad," Scolari commented.

"Deal the cards, Gramps," Cousy said, "and try not to look at them while you're doing it."

The game lasted all night. At about 3:30 A.M. the plane began pitching and tossing. Joanie, the stewardess, walked by and Cousy asked, "Is this Washington or bad weather?"

"Washington," she told him.

We were there nearly an hour. Back in the plane, we picked up the game again, and kept going until we started coming down in Worcester. Just as the wheels touched, Sharman, who was keeping score, was ready with the results.

"How did I do this time?" I asked.

"You won a quarter," he said.

We were on the field now, rolling toward the main building. Cousy stood up, bowed deeply, and said, "Congratulations. I never thought you'd do it."

He walked up the aisle toward the door. When he got there, he turned and yelled something that sounded like, "Don't think it hasn't been swell, buddy, because it hasn't!" I can't be sure. I was practically asleep.

I slept all the way to Boston—the whole 30 minutes. It's lucky Cousy wasn't there to see me. He'd have thought I was an awful sissy.

1956

BROOKLYN'S BRAINIEST BUM

By Stanley Frank

FROM TRUE

Copyright © 1956, True

One of our judges, John Hutchens, remarked of this piece by Stanley Frank that it was one of the best backstage baseball pieces he ever remembered reading. He particularly liked the fine organization of the story, in which data and anecdotes are combined with remarkable skill.

On Thursday, July 14, 1955, an emergency meeting was held in the office of Brooklyn Dodger President Walter O'Malley. Despite the fact that Brooklyn was 11½ games ahead, the five men who attended that meeting looked like candidates for a game of Russian roulette. The team was in terrible shape and, with 70 games left to play, the panic was on. Yet, on that seemingly dismal day, the Dodgers wrapped up the National League pennant.

"I'm in a bad jam and I need help fast," Manager Walter Alston was saying, "I've got nobody to pitch. Six guys have sore arms—Newcombe, Erskine, Loes, Podres, Spooner, and Koufax. Meyer is in the hospital with his neck in a brace. That leaves me Labine, Roebuck, and Hughes. I need Labine in the bullpen. Roebuck has shot his bolt with all the relief work he's done. Hughes is over the hill."

Alston snuffed out his cigarette and abstractedly lit another. "The trainer tells me the guys with sore arms will be all right in a week or 10 days, but in the meantime we've got three doubleheaders coming up. In the last week three full games have been shaved off our lead and, at that, we're lucky. If it hadn't been for the All-Star break, we'd be in a worse fix. We've got to get some pitchers right away, or we may blow the pennant."

The four other men in the room recoiled visibly at the mention of the ominous phrase "we may blow the pennant." They had good reason to be gun-shy. It brought back vivid memories of the two most catastrophic collapses in baseball history. In 1951, the Dodgers were out in front by 13½ games in mid-August and lost the pennant to the Giants on Bobby Thomson's sudden-death homer in the play-offs. In 1942, Brooklyn finished second after holding a 10½-game lead the first week in August. Now, with nearly half the season to go, the Dodgers had one foot on the toboggan again and a slight push could send them on a sickening slide.

Nothing was said for a long half-minute. Alston, O'Malley, Vice-President Buzzie Bavasi, and Al Campanis, a scout, looked expectantly at Fresco Thompson, chief of the Dodgers' farm system. "Are there any pitchers on the farm clubs who can help us?" O'Malley asked.

Thompson nodded, turning to Alston. "Which would you rather have, a right hander or a southpaw?"

"Hell, I don't care how the guy throws as long as he can get somebody out!" Alston snapped.

"The best bets at St. Paul are Pendleton, a right hander, and Bessent, a southpaw," Thompson said thoughtfully. "I like Bessent."

"What's his record this year?" O'Malley asked.

"He's won eight and lost five."

"That doesn't sound so hot to me," O'Malley said doubtfully.

"He's ready for the big leagues," Thompson answered. "He can win up here."

"Who've we got at Montreal?" Bavasi asked.

"Craig has won 10 out of 12," Thompson said without reference to notes. "He's coming along fast."

"Craig?" Alston said. "Jeez, he was in the Piedmont League last year. Going from Class B to the majors in a couple of months is an awfully big jump for a kid."

"He's got good stuff. He can cut the cake for you," Thompson said. "The best way to settle this is to get the opinion of each manager." He looked at his watch. It was shortly before noon. "We can't reach them by phone because they're on the way to the ball park. A wire will be faster." He called in a stenographer and dictated identical telegrams to Max Macon at St. Paul and Greg Mulleavy at Montreal: "Please advise which pitcher on your club can help Dodgers immediately. Urgent."

Within two hours the answers were delivered to Thompson. Macon recommended Bessent. Mulleavy picked Craig. Both rookies were ordered to take planes to New York the following day. They arrived on Friday and were given a day to learn the team's signals and get themselves squared away.

On Sunday the two kids drew the starting pitching assignments in a doubleheader with the Reds. Craig won the opener 6–2, with a three-hitter, and Bessent captured the nightcap 8–5. During the next week the Dodgers won six games and the pair of rookies brought up by Thompson accounted for five of them.

Brooklyn's sore-arm brigade, given a good rest while the two new men were doing the brunt of the work, came to life. The Dodgers went on to clinch the earliest pennant ever won in the National League, and then scored a more notable first by knocking off the Yankees in the World Series.

"We wound up the champions of the whole wide world, but nobody knew how close we were to falling flat on our kissers," Thompson confides. "The fact that our pitching staff was shot last July was not nearly as disturbing as the team's morale. Everybody associated with the Dodgers gets a bad case of buck fever when a big lead starts to go down the drain. All of us are haunted, I suppose, by nightmares of '51 and '42. You never really recover from a shock like that.

"The big problem when a team hits the skids is the panic that spreads through the players like an epidemic. They begin to think they can't do anything right and the harder they press, the deeper they go into the slump. The psychological lift Craig and Bessent gave the team was worth a lot more than the actual games they won."

Most baseball executives spend their time sitting on their fat rumps and operating their teams as hobbies rather than business enterprises. No matter what the courts say, baseball is a business and it's the businessmen who win the pennants. The general managers and their staffs who put in eight full hours of work a day, five days a week, 52 weeks a year, can be counted on the fingers of one hand. The rest couldn't last a month in other jobs paying comparable cushy salaries.

Lafayette Fresco Thompson is a shining example of a brass hat who knows his job and ranks as just about the top front-office manager in baseball today. Since 1949, when Fresco was put in charge of the ivory-hunting department, Brooklyn has won four pennants and barely missed two others on the final day of the

season. The Dodgers unquestionably are the class of the National
League, and rookies now ripening on the vine in the minors will
make them the team to beat well into the 1960s.

But it's not necessary to peer into the misty future to get a
tip-off on Thompson's ability. More than any one man, Fresco is
responsible for bringing to Brooklyn the greatest collection of
bargain-basement players ever assembled on one team. The
talent that flattened all comers last year was acquired for a total
cash outlay of $118,388 in purchases, drafts, and bonuses. And
$42,500 of that figure was paid for one man, Pee Wee Reese.

Eleven members of this championship squad were purchased for a total of $37,333—a fraction of the sums lavished on
two conspicuous busts of recent years. Billy Joe Davidson,
handed a bonus of $125,000 to sign with Cleveland a couple of
seasons ago, could have been picked up, in the last minor-league
draft, for $10,000. Paul Pettit, a young pitcher who cost the
Pirates a hundred grand, has given up the mound and is currently trying to fight his way out of the minors as an infielder.
They were both up for grabs in the last draft, with no takers.

Only two big-league teams, the Senators and the Cardinals, spent less than Brooklyn for the players in the field last
season, and both needed radar to keep within sight of the contenders. Before sandlotters began demanding—and getting—fancy
bonuses, the Cardinals won pennants with squads that cost less
than the 1955 Dodgers, but those days are gone forever. It's
extremely unlikely that a club will hit the jackpot again with an
ante as small as the Dodgers' unless, of course, it has an ace in
the hole like Thompson.

It is no exaggeration to say that Thompson is the key man in
the Brooklyn setup. He had a hand in scouting, signing, or
coaching every player on the Dodger roster last year except
Reese and three second-stringers—Walker, Meyer and Kellert,
who were acquired in trades. All the other Dodgers were strictly
home-grown farm products.

Buying established major-leaguers or outbidding the opposition for hot-shot bonus kids is no great achievement. Anyone
with an unlimited bankroll can do it. The trick is to beat the
bushes for inexpensive diamonds in the rough, make an accurate
appraisal of their potential ability, and come up with such as
Podres, Craig, and Labine. On a total investment of $10,500,
these three accounted for all the pitching victories in the last
World Series. The majority of the Dodgers were fantastic bar-

gains, as the following list of purchases and bonus payments indicates:

Pee Wee Reese	$ 42,500
Billy Loes	21,000
Sandy Koufax	12,000
Carl Erskine	8,000
Johnny Podres	6,000
Don Bessent	6,000
Roger Craig	4,000
Junior Gilliam	3,333
Jackie Robinson	3,000
Ed Roebuck	3,000
Don Zimmer	2,000
Roy Campanella	1,700
Don Newcombe	1,500
Gil Hodges	1,300
Sandy Amoros	1,000
Duke Snider	800
Karl Spooner	500
Clem Labine	500
George Shuba	150
Carl Furillo	105
Don Hoak	0
	$118,388

A couple of odd items on the list, such as the $3,333 tag on Junior Gilliam, require explanation. That is purely an arbitrary price, because Gilliam was one of three players in a $10,000 transaction. Actually, he cost next to nothing. In 1951 Brooklyn dickered with the Baltimore Élite Giants, a Negro team, for Pitch Leroy Farrell, but Thompson thought the asking price of $10,000 was a little too steep for a rookie who was still in the Army. To clinch the deal, Thompson casually suggested that the Élite Giants throw in two unknowns. One was Gilliam. The other was Joe Black, who wrapped up the 1952 pennant for the Dodgers with his relief pitching. Farrell? He came out of the Army hog fat and never was worth a quarter.

Another strange entry is $105 for Carl Furillo, and a stranger story goes with it. We'll let Thompson, who was in on the ground floor, give the details.

"Back in the fall of 1940 a guy named Eddington, who

owned the Reading Club in the Inter-State League, got fed up
and offered to sell out to Larry MacPhail for $5,000. That was
dirt cheap for a franchise—20 players and two full sets of uniforms—but the thing that intrigued MacPhail was the new bus
which the team used on road trips. This was a year before Pearl
Harbor and most automobile production was earmarked for the
armed forces.

"MacPhail figured the bus was worth $2,500 and 40 uniforms
cost at least ten bucks apiece, making another $400 worth of
equipment. That meant Brooklyn was getting 20 players for
$2,100, or $105 apiece. Conditionally, MacPhail had another
angle. His son Lee had been graduated from Swarthmore a few
months before and he thought Reading would be a good spot for
breaking in the boy as an executive. I'd just been hired by Mac-
Phail and he sent me to Reading to manage the team and help
Lee learn the ropes. It was one of those screwball deals MacPhail
loved and he came out of it looking like a genius. Brooklyn
eventually realized double the purchase price by selling Walt
Nothey, a pitcher, and Bill Heltzel, a shortstop. Incidentally, we're
still using the bus at Vero Beach."

And thanks to Thompson, Brooklyn is still getting a lot of
mileage out of Furillo, one of the 20 accessories who went with
the bus. Listed on the Reading roster as a pitcher, Furillo had
such a powerful arm that he could throw the ball through a brick
wall—provided the wall was 20 feet long and two stories high. In
his first mound assignment, Furillo faced five batters and conked
three with pitched balls. Thompson hustled the youth out of
there before he was arrested for manslaughter, and converted
him into an outfielder. A dozen years later Furillo won the
National League batting title and was recognized as the best
right fielder in the trade.

"That's the thing that makes scouting a fascinating and a
frustrating job," Thompson remarks. "You're gambling with in-
tangibles all the time. A scatter-arm pitcher may be another
Furillo and you worry whether you've wasted $1,300 on a muscle-
bound shortstop and he turns out to be Gil Hodges, the best first
baseman in circulation.

"This is the only business in the world in which you pay a kid
money, sometimes a fortune, before he proves his ability. No
matter how good a sandlotter looks, you have no guarantee he'll
reach the big leagues. If you sign every promising prospect who
comes along, you're going to go broke because the odds against
any amateur making the grade as a pro are at least 50 to 1. But,

on the other hand, if you pass up too many kids you'll land in the cellar."

We asked Thompson what he looks for in casing a prospect.

"Something you can't see," he answered, tapping his heart. "More than half the kids who disappoint you haven't got it here. It's not only a matter of courage. They may be confirmed bushers because they haven't the ambition to learn their trade. And you never know how they'll react to the hooray and adulation of the big leagues. A kid who sings in the choir and tips his hat to nice old ladies may turn into a boozer or a dame chaser. You're guessing all the time."

What are the most important physical assets in rating a rookie?

"Good actions, fluid movement. Speed is a must because it's the only attribute used on both offense and defense. A good arm is the next thing I check because there are only two spots, first base and left field, where a poor thrower can get by.

"Potential ability rather than actual performance is the big thing. If a prospect swings well and has nice wrist action, he has a chance to be a good hitter. Power is a secondary consideration. That may come as he develops physically. If a kid is afraid of a pitched ball, though, he'll never overcome it. A small pitcher must have more stuff to get by, perhaps, but otherwise size is not as important as a lot of people think. Hustle compensates for lack of muscle. I'd rather have little guys like Reese, Rizzuto, and Ford than a ton of big oafs. I won't mention any names, I may want to sell a couple."

Cultivating fresh talent for the Brooklyn varsity is only one facet of Thompson's job. He also must produce a surplus of players who can be sold to other teams to cut down the annual deficit of $600,000 piled up by the farm system. This is a particularly urgent problem for the Dodgers, who have the biggest payroll and next to the smallest ball park in the National League (only Cincinnati's Crosley Field has fewer seats). It's no secret that Brooklyn would have wound up in the red in recent seasons if not for World Series windfalls—and about $750,000 realized from the sale of superfluous farmhands.

The news that Thompson is a high-powered executive will come as a great surprise to friends and fans who remember him as a low-pressure ball player who seemed to be more interested in pulling gags than winning games. Fresco, a better than fair second baseman, bounced around the National League from 1925 to 1934 and compiled a respectable lifetime batting average of

.298. In 1929 he climbed to the giddy eminence of .324 with the Phillies, but when baseball people gather in bars and hotel lobbies to cut up old touches, they talk of Fresco's quips rather than his hits.

There was the time the Phillies played an exhibition game at Brooklyn's training camp in Clearwater, Florida. The club house was so crowded that the visitors had to share lockers with the home team. Fresco was assigned to the locker used by Babe Herman, a redoubtable slugger who was also noted for fielding fly balls off his skull. Herman threw a fit when he saw Fresco sitting in front of his cubicle.

"It's a hell of a note having to dress with a .250 hitter," Babe Herman grumbled.

"How do you think I feel dressing with a .250 fielder?" Fresco snapped.

During the war, when Fresco went to New Orlens to manage the Pelicans, he received enthusiastic advance reports on a French-Canadian outfielder named Paul Merrinow. It developed that Merrinow could run like a deer and throw like an angel, but he was somewhat deficient with the bat. It was said that he couldn't hit a pitcher walking past the plate with the ball in his hand, and somebody asked Fresco what Merrinow's trouble was.

"He's thinking in French and they're pitching to him in English," he answered gravely.

On the same club there was another youth who had flawless batting form and enough power to make new exits in fences with line drives, but his rhythmic swipes at the ball agitated only the atmosphere. "I don't know what's wrong, Skipper," the kid told Thompson. "I just miss the ball by this much." He held up two fingers about a half-inch apart.

"Tell you what to do," Fresco said. "Get yourself a pair of inner soles, put them in your shoes and you'll be just the right height."

Abusive fans who attempted to ride Fresco were sitting ducks for his squelches. For some unknown reason, a surgeon in Williamsport, Pennsylvania, got on Fresco while he was managing the local entry in the Eastern League. One day late in a game, Fresco went to the mound to relieve a pitcher who weakened suddenly after going eight good innings. As Fresco went back to the dugout, the surgeon yelled, "Another mistake, Thompson?"

"Yeah, but my mistake will work tomorrow," Fresco retorted.

Nothing more was heard from the surgeon for the remainder of the season.

Toward the end of his four-year sentence with the Phillies, who finished out of the cellar only once, Fresco was appointed captain of the team. It was not the distinction it appeared to be. "I was tapped for the job because everybody else was conserving his strength for hitting and didn't want to waste it taking the lineup to the umpires before games," he explains.

Before a contest with the Pirates, Fresco delivered the Phillies' lineup to Umpire Bill Klem, who glanced at the card and then turned 18 shades of purple. In the ninth position for the pitcher, Fresco had carefully written, "Willoughby and others."

"Young man," Klem roared, "you are making a travesty of the game."

"It's a travesty all right," Fresco agreed amiably, "but don't blame me. Wait till you get a load of our pitchers."

The Phillies used six hurlers in the game, which was par for the course. In that four-game series, both sides scored in double figures in every game.

Nothing was sacred to Thompson in his pursuit of laughs, and he still enjoys one as much as the next fellow. But responsibility has sobered his approach to baseball. His office is the nerve center of a network that covers all of North America and the Caribbean and extends to South America. This past spring, at the central clearing house for rookies in Vero Beach, Florida, there were candidates from 38 states, five Canadian provinces, Cuba, Mexico, Puerto Rico, Venezuela, and Costa Rica.

Thompson's office is a huge room, 40 feet square. Two walls are covered from floor to ceiling with blackboards listing all the teams and players in the farm system. Once the season gets under way, the blackboard is smudged with erasure marks as players are shifted and juggled to spots that will accelerate their development. The two other walls are lined with ordinary filing cabinets.

"If you want to put in a touch of the cloak-and-dagger bit, there's our secret weapon," Thompson said recently, waving to the cabinets. He pulled out drawers at random. Each one was crammed with odd pieces of typewritten and scrawled papers.

"In these cabinets we have a rundown on every professional ball player in America," he explained. "All the managers in our chain are required to submit written reviews after each game, including appraisals of their own and opposing players. If they note that a hitter is weak on a low-breaking ball, let's say, or a pitcher tends to come down the middle on a 3-and-2 count, we know the faults that must be corrected. If the players get to the majors with another team, we may be able to win games by exploiting his weakness.

"Since we no longer have farm teams in every minor league, our scouts case all the players in every circuit at least twice a year and give us the poop on all the personnel in it. We also keep a record on all the free agents we look at, including those we reject. These reports are especially valuable during the winter, when minor-league waiver and draft lists are drawn up. We can move in and take advantage of a slip-up in office routine or grab a player who's impressed us more than his own organization. For example, the Yankees didn't think much of Bessent when they had him at Binghamton, but our reports were favorable, so we drafted him for $6,000.

"Don't get the idea I'm trying to embarrass the Yankees or build us up as masterminds. Every team makes mistakes. Just for openers, we once turned loose a kid who became the best third baseman in the business. A guy named George Kell."

Ball games are won on the field, but the individual skills that achieve the end result are fed into the hopper by Thompson and his staff of 24 full-time and 16 part-time scouts. In the final analysis, the Dodgers are only as good as Thompson's judgment and there is no better testimonial to it than the world championship flying over Ebbets Field.

A modest fellow, Thompson is the first to point out that the present Dodgers are the product of three regimes. He is the link, though, that has given some sort of continuity to the radical switches in the team's talent-procurement programs. Fresco lasted through the regimes of both Larry MacPhail and Branch Rickey, learning a little here and discarding a little there, refining the technique down to his present approach.

Thompson's indoctrination in the Brooklyn organization under MacPhail was, in a sense, the worst possible training for his present job. MacPhail, who spent money like a drunken sweepstakes winner, was obsessed with the idea of getting the pennant at any cost. He poured out $888,100 for 47 players in four years, a spending spree topped only by Tom Yawkey a few years before. There was one vital difference between MacPhail and Yawkey, however. Yawkey did not win a pennant until 1946, long after his original high-priced stars had passed out of the picture. MacPhail put together a team that climbed from seventh to first place in three years.

As MacPhail's liaison man in the field, Thompson was in the thick of the spending orgy. But the chief MacPhail talent that impressed him was not his uncanny ability to distribute funds but his immense capacity for work.

After MacPhail left to go into the Army in 1942, the Dodgers were taken over by a man with a positive horror for spending money. Branch Rickey would never buy an established star, operating on the theory that he would catch enough big fish if he threw a net over every unattached sandlotter in sight. At one time Brooklyn had nearly a thousand players under contract, on a total of 32 farm teams. To his credit, however, it must be mentioned that it was Rickey who developed the nucleus of the current team—Campenella, Robinson, Snider, Hodges, Erskine, Newcombe, and Loes.

Rickey replaced most of MacPhail's assistants with his own men, but he promoted Thompson to the top managerial job in the chain, at Montreal. That could have been Thompson's springboard to the Dodger managership. It's a matter of record that he was Walter O'Malley's first choice for the job in 1953 when Charley Dressen was released in a hassle over a long-term contract. Thompson was itching to accept, but he turned down the offer for the same reason that impelled him to ask Rickey for a transfer to the front office a few years after taking the Montreal job.

"When I went to the winter meetings I'd see 60 managers who'd just been fired hanging around looking for jobs," Thompson confides. "There were only two or three unemployed front-office men. The odds looked good."

As Rickey's field supervisor in the farm system, Thompson was instrumental in picking Jackie Robinson as the right man to break the baseball color line, and his confidential reports were largely responsible for the signing of Don Newcombe and Roy Campanella.

Thompson became Rickey's troubleshooter during the turbulent postwar era, and on at least one occasion found that troubleshooting meant just that. He went down to Venezuela in 1948 to scout Chico Carrasquel and Jim Pendleton. The morning after he arrived in Caracas, Fresco descended to the lobby of his hotel and found guns waving all over the joint. It turned out that there had been a revolution during the night and the new government had declared a state of martial law which prohibited, among other things, public assemblies for such events as counterrevolutions and baseball games.

Fresco gave Carrasquel's and Pendleton's managers a hurried sales talk and persuaded them to stage a private workout behind locked gates. After a fast, apprehensive look, he signed both players. Carrasquel was sold to the White Sox a year later for $50,000 and Pendleton was trade bait in the swap for Russ Meyer. This can safely be called the best baseball deal ever made during a revolution.

Meanwhile, back in Brooklyn, stockholders were revolting against the heavy deficits piled up by Rickey's octopus-like farm system, claiming it was unnecessary to support 32 farms to insure the trickle of young players needed by the Dodgers.

Rickey was succeeded by Walter O'Malley, who wasted no time in putting through a drastic change in policy. He made Thompson a vice-president and ordered him to cut the farm system down to 13 teams, and to instruct his scouts to be more selective in recommending prospects. He made it plain that Thompson was expected to maintain a steady flow of fresh talent without resorting to either MacPhail's undiscriminating spending or Rickey's wholesale signing.

As an indication of how well Thompson has done on the tight budget which allows him to corral only 125 new prospects a year, he has already contributed Podres, Gilliam, Amoros, Labine, Spooner, Zimmer, Roebuck, Koufax, and, of course, Bessent and Craig.

To further complicate his problems, Thompson was also told to step up the output of surplus players who could be sold to other teams. And he had to be damn sure that he wasn't selling off a Willie Mays or Ronin Roberts who might come back to haunt him. As a result of this policy, there are now 40 former Dodger farmhands on every major league team except the Cardinals, and the majority of those brought the fanciest prices were unloaded by Thompson. Rickey got his biggest bundle, $50,000, for Chico Carrasquel. Thompson sold Billy Hunter to the St. Louis Browns, of all people, for $125,000. He peddled Irv Noren and Danny O'Connell for $65,000 apiece. The 75 grand the Dodgers got from the Braves for Andy Pafko should also be credited to Thompson's account, for he had uncovered the rookie outfielders that made the sale feasible.

Among these 40 players, only eight could conceivably help the Dodgers now, and those chiefly in reserve roles. They are Noren, Carrasquel, Hunter, Dee Fondy, Paul Minner, Johnny Klipstein, Eddie Morgan, and George Kell. The one real prize in that group who got away was Kell.

"He and I are sort of baseball kinfolk because we got into the Brooklyn organization the same year, 1940," Thompson says. "He was sent to the deepest bush in the Northeastern Arkansas League and didn't look much of a hitter. Nobody could. Most of the games were played at night and your cellar was lighted better than those ball parks. He always had a back misery or something, so we let him go. Well, as we used to say on the Phillies when we were losing a hundred games a year, you can't win 'em all.

"I shouldn't be telling you this because it can hurt us when we try to sell players, but if we're convinced a kid is a potential star, we'll keep him, regardless of the price he'll bring. All our scouting effort is beamed to the Dodgers.

"We're getting into a critical period now because we'll need replacements soon for a number of key men who are getting up there in age—Robinson, Furillo, Campanella, Hodges, and Reese. Give Reese a raincheck. It seems to me I've spent half my life hunting for Pee Wee's successor at shortstop and it's beginning to look as though he'll be here forever."

During the season Thompson divides his time between scouting and supervising minor-league affiliates. That's standard operating procedure for all farm directors, but it is in the off-season that Thompson gets the drop on the opposition. While competitors are telling amiable lies about ringtailed wonders they've shaken out of trees, Thompson is doing intensive home-work on the Dodgers' secret weapon. He's digesting those voluminous reports for leads that turn up men like Gilliam, Podres, Labine, Amoros, and Zimmer, making mental notes of the Craigs and the Bessents who can be pulled out of the hat in an emergency.

1957

THE MAN BEHIND THE MUSCLES

By Murray Olderman

FROM TRUE

Copyright © 1957, Murray Olderman

This article is a profile or close-up of Doc Anderson, the chiropractor-trainer of the Cincinnati Reds from 1951 or 1952 to 1959. It tells how deeply the players felt about their trainer and the tender and solicitous care they received from him. The piece is chock-full of instances and examples of why some Cincinnati players called Anderson the most important man on the team.

The ball rocketed off the bat of the Milwaukee lead-off man and shot toward the mound, faster than Joe Nuxhall's eye could follow it. Before the big Cincinnati pitcher could throw down his gloved hand to intercept the white streak, it smashed against his right knee. Nuxhall fell to the ground in a lump.

Manager Birdie Tebbetts leaped from the dugout and trotted anxiously toward the crumpled figure on the hill, a frown cutting between his eyes as he contemplated, smack in the middle of the pennant race, the loss of the only reliable left hander on his staff. This was August, 1956, and the Reds, Braves, and Dodgers were running neck and neck for the National League championship.

Behind Tebbetts followed a chunky white-trousered man. He was Wayne (Doc) Anderson, trainer of the Redlegs, and what he did in the next half hour would determine whether or not the southpaw ace of the Cincinnati staff would be available to his hard-pressed team in the next crucial month.

"Can you get up, Joe?" asked Tebbetts.

Nuxhall winced and shook his head.

116

"Let's get him to the dressing room," snapped Anderson. A quick wave to the dugout brought three bench-warmers on the run. Two grabbed him under the shoulders, another by the legs, they carted him off the field. Tebbets, watching Nuxhall's knee swell, was writing him off for two weeks at least. And it was the kind of injury that could easily keep a man on the shelf for a month.

In his trainer's quarters, Anderson probed gently above the knee. "You've got a ruptured blood vessel between the muscle and bone, Joe," he announced. "I'm gonna throw an ice pack on it and keep it there for 12 hours. That way it won't puff up overnight. Tomorrow we'll start in with whirlpool baths and diathermy. Then we'll see."

The date was August 19. Three days later, on August 22, Nuxhall faced the Pittsburgh Pirates and, without a trace of a limp, easily subdued them 6–3. The big southpaw went on to contribute five important triumphs as the Redlegs made a run for the pennant down to the next to the last day of the season and finished only a pair of games behind the winning Dodgers.

A $3,000,000 investment in pennant-contending baseball talent was at stake when Anderson made his quick diagnosis of Nuxhall. The insurance on that investment is a trainer like Anderson. If you want to know how the players feel about their walking insurance policy, just ask them:

"Doc alone keeps me in the lineup," says Roy McMillan, a spindly, sure-handed shortstop whose chronic bad back would prevent him from even knotting his shoelaces if it weren't for the strong-fingered Redleg trainer.

"Nothing is too big for Doc to tackle," grins Ted Kluszewski, a first baseman of monumental proportions whose maze of muscles would defy the probing of a Congressional investigator. (When big Klu was sidelined last season with an injury to a "small muscle," a reporter cracked, "I didn't know he *had* any small muscles.")

Doc's reputation has spread far beyond his own team, and he has been consulted by such stars as Stan Musial, Roy Campanella, and Robin Roberts (who flew out to Cincinnati last winter so that Anderson could look at his valuable pitching arm).

"If I ever manage a big-league club," Pee Wee Reese once confided to Anderson, "I want you as my trainer."

Eventually General Manager Gabe Paul of the Reds was forced to insert a specific clause into Doc's contract forbidding him to treat players on other clubs, because the traffic into the

Cincinnati dressing room was getting so heavy that Doc didn't have enough time for his own players.

An intense, chattering refugee from Los Angeles, the light-haired, open-faced Anderson looks young enough (he's 36) to be one of the players he massages. His office is an airy room tucked among the girders of Crosley Field in Cincinnati. There he's boss. Players drift away from their nearby lockers and cluster on the boxes and trunks strewn around the room. Robinson is autographing a baseball. Big Hersh Freeman, the relief pitcher, thoughtfully draws on a cigarette. Center fielder Gus Bell leafs through a magazine. On the rubbing table a muscular mass is stretched out contentedly. Anderson pats his rump and growls hoarsely:

"All right, this ain't no whorehouse. If you want to get rubbed, there's a Turkish bath down the street. Next!"

McMillan, torso bared, climbs onto the table, flat on his stomach. Doc reaches over to a shelf and pulls down a yellow-tinted bottle. "Hot oil," he says. "He's got a stiff back. See there."

He points to a slender scar in the small of Roy's back.

"He had a spinal fusion before he ever come up to the majors. I have to rub hot stuff on it every day. It don't take very long. He's not very big—no more than one of Klu's legs."

Kluszewski, hearing his name, grins amiably. He's due on next. Anderson takes an elastic garter and slips it over the big man's thighs. "Cut these down from ladies' girdles," winks Anderson. "Hell, he practically got muscles on the hair of his legs, so I got to keep watching to make sure he doesn't get tied up."

For three hours Doc probes muscles, tapes legs, prescribes aspirins, and talks in a steady drone as Cincinnati players move in and out of the trainer's quarters. Suddenly it's vacant. The Redlegs are out on the field chasing fly balls, hopping in and out of the batting cage, getting ready to play a ball game.

In Anderson's room, only the starting pitcher remains, left alone to work up a competitive edge for the nine innings ahead. He stomps out a cigarette, paces nervously.

"Let's give it a stretch," Doc suggests. He grabs the arm, yanks it deftly up and over as if to pull it out of the socket. "I'm stretching the muscles to get the oiling mechanism in order," he explains. "You never get a pitcher ready by rubbing his arm. That was the way the old trainers did it—throwing on some alcohol and slapping at 'em. And that's why all smart pitchers used to keep away from their trainers."

The ritual over, the pitcher goes out to throw some warm-up tosses, leaving Doc alone.

"I figure," he says, "I'm doing my job best when I'm sitting around on my butt doing nothing. Three-quarters of my salary is for the accidents that don't happen. I got a thousand different kinds of remedies in my office"—he waves at the cluttered shelves—"but half the ball players' problems is in their noodles.

"A trainer is like a priest to ball players. They tell you their troubles. They don't ask your advice. You can't afford to be a stooge, like they make you on a couple of teams in this league. You're done if they stick a fork in you. I'm part medicine man, part con man. Treating guys like Ewell Blackwell brought out the con in me."

When licensed chiropractor Anderson joined the Cincinnati club in 1951, after a lengthy minor-league apprenticeship, the big star was Ewell Blackwell, as great a pitcher as modern baseball ever featured—when he felt like it.

"One morning," recalls Doc, "Blackie phones my room at the hotel. 'Doc,' he says, 'I feel lousy. Howinhell can I pitch today? I got a cold and my arm aches something awful. It's killin' me.'

" 'Meet me in my office in half an hour,' I tell him.

"Blackie comes in looking green. I show him a batch of coated pills. I tell him, 'Every time you feel an ache coming on, I'll see you get one of these codeine tablets.'

"Before Blackie goes to warm up, I slip him a pill. He lets loose a pitch, holding up his arm and throws me a wink. Game time I slip him another pill, slyly, so he thinks no one is looking.

"Out on the mound, he's throwing and winking. The codeine is killing the pain. The Braves got just one hit off Blackwell in the best-pitched game I ever saw. Blackie doesn't know to this day the pills I slipped him were nothing but coated aspirins."

Facing the St. Louis Cardinals one afternoon, Blackwell stopped dead in the middle of his stretch, threw the ball and glove on the ground and walked off the mound. He motioned to Anderson in the dugout.

"Doc," he moaned, "I can't go on. I can't lift my arm at all, no kiddin'."

Anderson looked it over and stretched it once or twice with a cracking sound effect. Blackwell's lean face brightened.

"Now it feels great," he said, and went right back to his pitching.

"All I did," shrugs Anderson, "was pop my knuckles to make

the cracking sound. It worked. I didn't do a damn thing to his arm."

The Cincinnati trainer dabbled in the same kind of psychology last year with Hersh Freeman, their vital relief ace. But unlike Blackwell, Hersh really did have a bad arm. In seven years of pitching in the Boston Red Sox organization, the 6-foot-2, 228-pound right hander from Gadsden, Alabama, had won only two major-league games. The Reds picked him up on waivers in the spring of 1955 and he responded with seven victories and four defeats as a reliable relief pitcher. Last year he was a heroic and vital figure in the spurt which moved the Redlegs from 1955 fifth place finish into the first division and thrust them within a deuce of the National League flag. He made 64 pitching appearances and won 14 games against five losses.

"His arm," admits Doc, "was tighter than the top of a table. He was working it like a sonofagun day after day, but we needed him because every game counts when you're going for the flag. I had instructions to tell him how loose his arm is.

"How in the hell, if it's hurting him, can I keep telling Hersh every day how good his arm feels? Pretty soon he's gonna wake up and say, 'This Anderson is for the birds.'

"So on a day I figure Freeman won't be used because we got a strong starter and there's some fresh men in the bullpen, I whisper, 'Today I'm gonna tell Birdie your arm is tight.'

"Now I got him feeling I'm with him. I'm sympathetic to his problems. The next day he comes into my office and says, 'Yep, sure was tight yesterday. That one day rest was all I needed.' I give his muscles a quick stretch, and he's ready to go again."

Naturally, Anderson's preoccupation with the neuroses of a ball player doesn't go unnoticed by Birdie Tebbetts, the sharp, glib philosophy major who clucks over the Redleg brood as manager and guiding genius.

"You know he's with you all the time," affirms Birdie. "He's a fine asset to the club because, besides his regular swell job for us, he can do things that a regular doctor wouldn't be able to handle."

For example, when Tebbetts suspects the opposition is on to his signals, he doesn't hesitate to use Anderson as a decoy to relay signs from the bench to the field. More to the point, as the caste division of manager and player prevents a close personal relationship, Birdie has often taken advantage of Doc's peculiar position as a confidant of ball players. If a rookie's performance is suffering because he's worried about money problems, and he's embarrassed about taking his case to the front office, Anderson is likely to find out and bring it to the attention of management. Sometimes, at Tebbetts' behest, he'll do a selling job to imbue a player with confidence.

An example is Johnny Klipstein, one of Cincinnati's starting pitchers, who is known in the trade as an "Edison." He likes to experiment with a variety of deliveries to the detriment of his stock in trade, a live fast ball which ranks with any in the majors.

On September 11, 1955, sticking to the fast ball, he pitched a one-hitter against the Brooklyn Dodgers, the lone safety coming with one out in the ninth. The entire game Klipstein threw but three breaking pitches.

In his next start, five days later, he turned cute again with half-speed pitches and was blasted from the box. "I know that Birdie wants him to stick with the fast one," recalls Anderson. "Before his next start, against Milwaukee, as I'm loosening up his arm in the clubhouse, I keep telling him, 'I hope you have that fast one working again today, John. Like you did against the Brooks.'"

Klipstein went out and, using fast balls, handcuffed the Braves for seven innings and won breezing. That was his last 1955 start. The season was over before he had another chance to assimilate the prodding. Last season Klipstein achieved his major-league high of 12 victories and finished over the .500 mark for the first time.

Coddling pitchers, though, is only part of Anderson's work in ministering to the physical and mental peculiarities of 25 different ball players. His biggest and most important project is Ted Kluszewski, who doesn't require any con job.

"Physically," says Anderson, "Ted demands more time than any ball player I ever handled because of his peculiar muscle structure that leads easily to pulls. I'm in the clubhouse an average of three or more hours before a game, and Klu's on the rubbing table at least one-third of the time."

There was a time in 1946 that Anderson despaired over getting the big slugger in shape. Kluszewski had let his weight climb over 250, and early in spring training he pulled a deep muscle in his leg that wouldn't respond to medical treatment. So Anderson put his strong, sensitive fingers to work and muscle-rubbed him back into the lineup. The big guy never did get his poundage down to normal last season, but did spiral his batting average up to a respectable .302 and contributed 35 homers.

During the winter, Anderson, who lives in Cincinnati and

works for the ball club on a 12-month basis, outlined a stringent weight-trimming program, and big Ted was down to a playable 240 before he reported to spring camp. It was back trouble, not weight, which kept him out of the lineup during the early part of the season.

In addition to the brawn brigade, the Reds are blessed with finesse ball players who provide speed and fielding balance. With them you have to pay particular attention to the legs. Typical of this is second baseman Johnny Temple, who, with Roy McMillan, forms the best double play combination in the game.

Anderson's ingenuity salvaged Temple's career, imperiled by a leg that was badly burned around the shinbone when he was a kid and covered with grafted skin. When bruised or scraped, grafted skin doesn't heal, and the traffic's pretty in injuries around second base.

To protect the shin, Johnny first tried abbreviated catcher's guards, but they were too bulky and got in his way. Then Anderson devised a fiber-glass guard, molded to the contour of Temple's leg, that fits snugly inside his stocking and offers maximum protection.

To effect cures and miracles, Anderson has at his disposal the most modern medical aids. His training room under the stands is white-tiled and air-conditioned. In it are two diathermy machines ($600 each), a whirlpool bath, ray lamp, shortwave machines (for blood clots and deeper injuries), an electric relaxi-cizor to soothe tired muscles, an ice tub, and a refrigerator for penicillin.

On the shelves are 103 different kinds of medicines, salves, drugs, ointments, oils, and vitamins, and Anderson's bag contains several sets of surgical tools, a sewing kit for buttons, scalpel blades, hay-fever remedy, laxatives, electric and safety razors, shaving cream, and face and hair lotions. The door on the right leads to a laundry and modern heat room where uniforms are freshened daily.

He can remember as a clubhouse kid hanging around Wrigley Field in Los Angeles in 1931, when players paid for their own sweat socks and wore them till they got so dirty they stood on end.

"All a trainer carried around with him was an alcohol bottle, scissors and tape, olive oil and Sloan's liniment. He was either an ex-pug or an old catcher with bent fingers. The bellhop in one hotel where the team stayed became the trainer the next day because he talked fast."

The trainer of today is a licensed chiropractor, like Anderson, or an osteopath, like Dr. Harold Wendler of Brooklyn, or schooled in physiotherapy by the Army, like Al Scheuneman of the Cubs.

"I became a trainer," says Anderson, "because Eddie Leishman, a second baseman for Oakland, told me, 'Kid, as an infielder, you'd never make a pimple on a ball player's butt.' "

Leishman, now a minor-league owner at Salt Lake City, took a paternalistic interest in the kid and sent him to the University of Washington, where he was graduated from the American School of Chiropractics.

His first job after World War II (he was in the submarine service) was assistant trainer for Casey Stengel, then managing Oakland. Casey finished his schooling by sending him to Boyes Springs, California, where Detroit trainer Denny Carroll, famed healer of sore arms, "taught me to feel with the tips of my fingers." A couple of years later, advanced to the head job with Sacramento in the Coast League, he dug up Bill Bevens and made the reputation which landed him in the majors.

The Bevens case was a baseball tragedy. A strong-armed Yankee right hander, he had a no-hitter going against Brooklyn in the fourth game of the 1947 World Series until two were out in the ninth. Pinch-hitter Cookie Lavagetto then made history by driving a double to right which cost Bevens the game and the first Series no-hitter. Worse, Bill's arm went dead.

By 1949 he was down to pitching softball in Salem, Oregon. He tried needles, drugs, everything he could think of to relieve the shoulder pain. Nothing helped, until Anderson got him on a rubbing table.

"I'm stretching his arm," Doc relates, "when I feel a lump under his shoulder as big as a golf ball. Whenever he moved his arm over in a normal pitching motion, his shoulder blade pressed against the calcified deposit and caused pain. I reduced the lump by heat treatment and constant rubbing with my fingers to dissolve the calcium."

Tears streamed down the big right hander's face after he returned to organized baseball with a strong effort against the San Francisco Seals. He went from the mound to Anderson and planted a kiss on Doc's forehead. Bevens made it as far back as a 1952 spring trial with the Reds, but by that time it wasn't a bad arm that licked him. He was too old, and bad legs kept him from getting in shape to throw.

"Actually," says Doc, "the best job I did in baseball was on

Al Benton after the Detroit Tigers gave up on him and shipped
him to Sacramento. Al came to us with a sore arm. He couldn't
raise it to throw natural because of extra weight around his
shoulder socket. He was just plain fat. So I simply wrapped 10
yards of flannel around his chest and sweated the fat off him and
put him back in the big leagues as a fine relief pitcher in less than
a season. He pitched in the majors for three more years."

The impressed Reds brought Anderson up in 1951. Brach
Doc, youngest trainer in the majors at 30, promptly became the
first medic ever thrown out of a spring exhibition. It happened
after he told Gabe Paul, "A trainer has no business getting on a
ball player or an umpire from the dugout."

"You're human," Gabe answered. "You gotta say something."

"Nope, I don't say nothing."

In a game at Lynchburg, Virginia, Anderson sat on the
bench between manager Luke Sewell and pitcher Herman
Wehmeir, his first pal on the Reds.

"Open your eyes, rockhead!" Wehmeier yelled at the plate
umpire, who whirled and glared at the Cincinnati bench: "I'll run
the sonofabitch who said that."

"You haven't got the guts to run anyone," Wehmeier shouted.

"You, ANDERSON, OUT!" The umpire pointed to the
trainer.

"Who, me? I didn't say anything." Doc turned to Sewell.
"Luke, tell the man. You know I kept my mouth shut."

Sewell shrugged.

Then Anderson got sore. Passing home plate on the way to
the dressing room, he stopped and barked, "You ARE a rockhead!"

Two days later, sweating out a $250 fine and a wire from the
commissioner's office, he discovered it was all a hoax, plotted by
Paul and the other Redlegs. The next season Anderson was
kicked out of a game legitimately for pouncing on a Pittsburgh
outfielder named George Metkovich. During a field riot involving
the Reds and the Pirates, Metkovich collared Manager Sewell
with a stranglehold, so Doc, 50 pounds lighter at 140, whacked
him across the kidneys and rolled him in the dirt. And the league
henceforth banned trainers from the field unless summoned.

Anderson had no such predisposition to protect his next
Cincinnati manager, gruff Roger Hornsby, who took over in
August, 1952. The Rajah, like a lot of old-time managers, had no
use for trainers. He belonged to the tobacco-spit school of medical
treatment. If that didn't work, rub on some iodine. To him,

Anderson's chief function was running errands and relaying instructions to the coaches, to whom Hornsby never condescended to speak.

At Hornsby's first spring-training camp he split the squad into A and B groups for practicing games in other cities. Anderson had his first-aid bag packed, expecting to accompany the A squad. Hornsby casually nodded to a clubhouse boy to tag along instead. Doc decided he was to go with the B boys and walked to the team bus. Hornsby was there.

"We won't need you with this group, Anderson," he snapped.

"Where *do* you want me to go?" puzzled Doc.

"Go see a movie."

Luckily the spring passed without incident. And Hornsby's disdain of trainers is a minority attitude in baseball. The first aid administered immediately after a player is struck down can affect the career, even the life, of the injured man. When Ted Williams caromed off the left-field wall at Comiskey Park in the first inning of the 1950 All-Star game, he stayed in the game until the ninth—and was lost to the Boston Red Sox for the rest of the season when X rays revealed a fractured elbow.

"I read they massaged the elbow and gave it heat," says Anderson. "It was the worst thing they could have done, to stimulate circulation around any kind of break."

Because a trainer knew his business, the life of Hall of Famer Mickey Cochrane was saved in 1937 after a wild pitch crashed against the temple of the Detroit catcher-manager in a Yankee Stadium game. The Yankee trainer of that era was Earl V. Painter.

"I was the first one out of the dugout," Doc Painter remembers, "and I could see he was bad off. That day Mickey was in luck. Of all the 16 teams in the major leagues, the Yankees alone had a stretcher as part of their equipment.

"I was careful not to move Cochrane, and I didn't let anybody touch him, only made the umpire stand in front of him to shield his face from the sun. I gently raised his head, then his body to put the stretcher under him. The doctors who successfully operated on his fractured skull later told me he only had one chance in a thousand to live anyhow, and he got that chance because somebody knew how to put him on a stretcher."

While appreciating a trainer's capabilities in a crisis, a manager like Tebbetts, who took over the Reds in 1954, is more interested in the prosaic matter of keeping the Reds in shape to play ball every day. On this Doc has firm ideas.

"A player's living," he insists, "is in his legs. I run, run, run 'em. It's the key to condition. Each of us has a built-in temperature gauge. The idea is to get your heat mechanism in order so that in the summertime you can play ball and get overheated quickly and not lose your stuff. That's the mark of a man in shape.

"Times have changed, but one thing hasn't—they still come to play ball. Funny, but nobody shows up hurt on a big day.

"Johnny Temple slides hard into second and I can tell by the way he gets up he's injured. He'll come back to the dugout and scoff. 'Naw, there's nothing wrong with me.' He's all keyed up and don't feel it."

Anderson will probe the spot.

"Ouch," says Temple, "that hurts."

He doesn't leave the game. Doc massages the bump quickly between innings to lessen the tension and keep him loose. After the game he applies a cold press. That way it doesn't stiffen up overnight and cause the player to lose a couple days' action in the heat of a pennant race.

"Pitchers have their earned-run averages to tell them how they're doing," Anderson says. "The hitters have their fielding and batting averages. A trainer has a b. a., too.

"Every time a player misses a turn from the lineup, I'm batting .ooo."

1958

20 SECONDS + A FEW INCHES FROM HOME

By Jack Mann

FROM NEWSDAY

Copyright © 1958, Newsday

For most football enthusiasts, Jack Mann's story of the first sudden-death overtime game in pro football depicted an enthralling championship event. All three judges were impressed with the story of a Cinderella-like Giant team contending with a lavishly talented Baltimore Colt club. All three judges gave it their vote in the coverage. John Chamberlin noted, "A tingler, preserving all the values of the game itself," while John Hutchens noted how Mann kept the sequence of highlights entirely lucid.

The Giants' Cinderella run for the National Football League championship finally ended yesterday. Their coach will tell you where: "Twenty seconds and a few inches from home."

The lavishly talented Baltimore Colts won the NFL playoff game 23–17. They are clearly a superior team to Jim Lee Howell's tattered New Yorkers, but it took them eight minutes and 15 seconds in the league's first sudden-death overtime to make the Giants believe it.

If they believe it yet. Two minutes from the end of the normal 60-minute game, the Giants were perpetrating another "miracle." They had boot-strapped from 11 points behind—largely on the clutch pitching of old Charley Conerly—to lead the favored Colts 17–14, and they had the football.

It was third-and-four on the New York 39 and a first down would lock the title for a team whose coach "didn't think they'd win four games." Frank Gifford, who had fumbled twice to arrange the Colts' 14–3 lead at the half, was given the job. He cut back over tackle and hard-nosed into a cordon of Colt tacklers.

It was the toughest kind of pro football collision. It shattered the right ankle of Baltimore's star end, Gino Marchetti, and they had to wait until he was stretchered away before they could measure for the first down. The Giants hadn't made it; referee Ronald Gibbs held his hands up to the crowd to show the six or seven inches they lacked. And there they were: a few inches from home.

But what was to worry about? "We have the league's best punter, or at least the second-best," Howell observed later, and Don Chandler booted 60 yards in the air, leaving Baltimore safety Carl Taseff no choice but a fair catch on the Colts' 14.

Johnny Unitas missed with his first two passes. Now all Baltimore had to do was cover 86 yards in the remaining minute and 16 seconds. With Unitas throwing and end Ray Berry catching ("With that Lenny Moore keeping us busy," Howell pointed out), such projects are not implausible. Berry took a button-hook pass and ran through a number of Giants for a first down at the 50. Unitas hit Berry for 15 more yards, then found him again as he cut away from Carl Katilivacz. Berry scooted to a first down at the Giant 13. Now the Giants were 20 seconds from home.

It doesn't take that long to kick a field goal. Steve Myrha, who had kicked one into Sam Huff's ribs in the first quarter, didn't miss this time and the score was 17–17, with 10 seconds to kill.

They tossed the coin at mid-field and the Giants won. A roar went up from the 64,185 customers when the ref patted co-captain Kyle Rote on the helmet. That meant the Giants would receive, and in pro football possession was supposed to be tantamount to victory in a sudden-death overtime. Pro football has now learned something about sudden-death overtime games.

Daring Don Maynard swooped in for the kickoff and muffed it. He picked it up and reached the 20. Gifford went off tackle for four yards. Conerly made a convincing fake to Mel Triplett but missed Bob Schnelker with a pass over the middle. Then Conerly rolled out to his right and couldn't find a receiver. Old (37) Charley had to go it alone, and he made five yards. There were the Giants again, this time 24 inches from home.

Pro football's second-best punter chased Taseff back to the Colts' 16, and the Giants' downfield crew decked him at the 20.

This time Unitas and company had to cover only 80 yards, with almost no time limit. They could have played all night. L. G. Dupre bolted off tackle for a first down at the 30. Lenny Moore scooted down the sideline and Unitas unleashed a 65-yard heave. It was the play that embarrassed Lindon Crow in the earlier game with Baltimore, costing a touchdown, and the same one Moore plucked off Crow's shoulder for a 60-yard gainer in the first quarter yesterday.

But by now Crow was used to the play, and he broke it up. Dupre went for three yards and a swing pass to Allan Ameche gave the Colts another first. Dick Modzelewski barged in to nail Unitas for an eight-yard loss. Unitas took note of Modzelewski's down on their 41, after Dupre gained three more, barging.

Unitas hit Berry for another first down on the Giant 43, and on the next play Modzelewski barged again. It was a trap play, and Unitas sprung Ameche through the hole for a 23-yard ramble. Karilivacz and Jim Patton made the last-ditch tackle, but the Colts had still another first down at the Giant 20.

Sam Huff smashed Dupre for no gain, but Berry got loose again, Unitas hit him with a spot pass, and Berry ran and dived to the nine. Ameche gained two, and another quarterback would have kept the ball on the ground, holding the lock-cinch field goal as the last trump. Another coach would have fainted when Unitas pitched a bullet to the right flat, where Jim Mutscheller caught it and crashed out of bounds on the one. Baltimore coach Weeb Ewbank is used to Unitas, and Howell wouldn't knock it: "Great call," he said. "You have to do things like that in this game."

The drunks were careening onto the field and the several thousand Colt fans were planning their demolition of the goal posts (new pro record: 18 seconds flat) before Ameche formalized the victory by plunging the remaining yard.

The Giants weathered their customary adversity from the game's beginning. Don Heinrich was at quarterback for his usual exploratory work during their first three sets of downs, but they survived by the grace of a Unitas fumble, Karilivacz's interception and Huff's block of Myrha's field goal. Gifford's 38-yard run set up Pat Summerall's 36-yard field goal for a 3–0 lead at 12:58.

Gifford's fumble at the Giant 20 was recovered by Gene (Big Daddy) Lipscomb early in the second quarter and Ameche plowed over for a 7–3 edge. Gifford later fumbled on the Colt's 14 and Unitas conducted a 14-play march that culminated in a 15-

yard pass to Berry, who slipped between Patton and Emlen Tunnell to score unmolested. So at the half it was 14–3 and the Giants exited stumbling.

The Colts were poised for the KO punch in the third period when Unitas' pinpoint passes to Berry and Moore made a first down at the Giant three. Then the defensive team showed why the Giants beat teams that are better than they are. Two thrusts by Ameche and a sneak by Unitas couldn't get the ball inside the one. On fourth down Cliff Livingston belted Ameche for a five-yard loss.

That goal-line stand, followed by a spectacular play, revived the Giants. Operating from his own 10, Conerly faked to everybody, then lofted a soft pass to Rote, who made a circus catch at the Colts' 40. At the 30 Andy Nelson nailed him from behind and the ball bounced loose. From nowhere, like the U.S. Cavalry, appeared Alex Webster. He scooped the ball up and galloped to the one. It was an 86-yard play and Mel Triplett capped it with a dive for the touchdown. Summerall's conversion made it 14–10.

Conerly passes to Schnelker, good for 17 and 46 yards, brought the Giants to the Baltimore 15 in the first minute of the last (it was supposed to be the last) period. Conerly then pitched a swing pass to Gifford, who encountered a Colt at the 5 and bowled him over en route to the TD. Summerall converted and the Giants were ahead 17–14.

The defensive platoon, thus inspired, contained Unitas and company almost to the end. Twenty seconds and a few inches from the end.

1959

"CHING, CHING, CHINAMAN"

By Al Laney

FROM THE NEW YORK HERALD TRIBUNE

Copyright © 1959, *New York Herald Tribune, Inc.*

> *Our judge John Hutchens, in commenting on the stories of the year 1959, wrote of this piece by Al Laney on Ching Johnson, Ranger hockey star: " 'Ching' is a beauty of its kind, full of heart and unsentimental nostalgia. It is one of the relatively few stories I have read that gives one a real idea of why and how a great athlete can be not only admired but held in true affection."*

The big, rugged man with the bald head came in out of the cold and stood inside the door of the Union Station in Washington. He looked around and, having located the information booth, came barging across the rotunda. Suddenly, nearly there, he smiled, and no one who ever attended a Ranger hockey game in Madison Square Garden between 1926 and 1936 would have needed an introduction.

Ching Johnson, gone from our town these 20-odd years, looks just about the same. His weight is exactly the same at 210 pounds and his belly is flat. And he still has the look of a mischievous but wholly captivating small boy when he turns on the old smile the hockey addicts knew so well.

Back in the now almost prehistoric days before loudspeakers were in use there used to be a fellow sitting in the mezzanine at hockey games who didn't need one. With an unusual sense of timing he would cup his hands around his mouth at intervals during Ranger games and give off with a piercing "Ching, Ching, Chinaman."

This cry would soar above the other crowd noises and, as

though he had been waiting for the signal, the battle-scarred old ice cruiser with the shining dome and the flashing smile would take the puck, circle behind the net, and start straight down the middle on a one-man rush toward the enemy goal.

By the time he had got well under way the whole crowd was on its feet. When he crossed mid-ice the noise had reached a deafening crescendo, finally to burst with explosive voltage as irresistible force met seldom immovable defensive objects.

They have been playing hockey in the Garden for going on 35 years now. All the greatest players of the game have appeared there and still are appearing. Some of the National Hockey League's most exciting dramas have been enacted on this strip of ice and one at least of the goriest of Stanley Cup brawls occurred there.

But never in our town, either in hockey or any other sport, has there been anything quite to equal those delicious moments when the old Bald Eagle made his lone sorties into enemy territory. Knocking to the ice violently all who got in his road, bearing down on the goalie like a runaway tank, he finally would skate away wearing the grin that removed all the venom from his violent actions.

Ching Johnson captured the hockey crowds as no other ever did. He became a gallery favorite overnight at his first appearance here and he will remain a permanent New York legend so long as hockey is played in the old Eighth Avenue barn.

Ching came in with hockey when it began in New York or anyhow just after the start. It was in 1925 that the Garden decided to experiment with any sport that might bring people into the new arena on those nights, six each week, when there was no boxing, the sport that paid the freight in the early Tex Rickard days.

So the New York Americans were brought in and a few dates allotted to them. Before the first season was done it was clear that the stepchild would become a breadwinner and so in 1926 came the Rangers. They came from Western Canada and the old Northern League to join the NHL and with them came Ching. With them also came others who were to write hockey history— Bill and Bun Cook, Frank Boucher, Taffy Abel, Murray Murdock. Abel was Ching's partner on the back line and it may be that hockey never has had such a pair as these two.

But this story is about Ching, who already was pushing 30 when he arrived in town with this remarkable group. He was to have 11 wonderful years in the Garden and other NHL rinks and he did more to popularize the game in New York than any of them. For he had that rare ability to establish immediate communion with the crowd. In our time and in our town only Babe Ruth has had it to the same extent as Ching.

Year after year he went about the league, his body seamed with cuts, welts, and scars, knocking people down, bringing roars from the galleries everywhere, and smiling his wonderful smile. And how he could throw a body check! He operated in a day of vicious defensemen—Eddie Shore and Red Horner, for inatance —but none hit harder than he. And there never was another such of whom friend and foe alike agreed that in all the years he played and in all the hundreds of bruising checks he handed out he never once resorted to the dirty tactics so common in this fast and furious game.

Ching was no speed demon and no fancy Dan on skates, but he was a clever one indeed at poke-checking, and at body-checking he hit with a force that bounced them off the ice and sometimes left them in shock. And there were two things about him that apply to no other of comparable ability. His stick, a lethal weapon in other hands, invariably was out of the way when he hit and always there was that sheepish, almost pixielike grin as he sent his man sprawling. To Ranger fans this smile was angelic. To fans in other cities it was diabolic.

But we have left Ching standing too long at the information booth. It would be good to learn what and how he has been doing in the years since he left us after one final part-time whirl with the Americans when he was 40 or so.

"The wife and daughter have gone shopping," he says. "There's a nice place down the street a way where we can sit and visit while we eat."

Ching did not wind up his hockey-playing days in New York. He is credited with rejuvenating hockey in Minneapolis in two years as a playing coach and then he went to Washington in the same capacity. That lasted only one season and then Ching, believing himself done with the game, went to California to dispose of some property he had there. That finally did lead to the last fling.

"They saw me skating on a Hollywood rink," he explained, "and asked me if I wanted to play with the local team in the Pacific Coast League. We won the title that year, 1944."

So that made it an even quarter century of hockey for the Chinaman, who carried the name hung on him as a small boy in Winnipeg through all his playing career. His name really is Ivan, but now he has adopted Ching and that's all you will find in the Washington telephone directory.

Ching entered hockey late. He had scarcely played at all when he returned in 1919 from four years with a trench mortar outfit in World War I, then broke in with the Winnipeg Monarchs while attending the University of Manitoba. "Trench mortar" is now a term more antiquated than "hansom cab," but it can emphasize the long span over which Ching was a brilliant performer in perhaps the roughest game of all.

Having cleaned up his business and finished his hockey in Los Angeles, Ching came back to Washington and for many years now he has been with Perrin and Martin, a heating, plumbing, and air-conditioning firm with offices and plant in Arlington, Virginia. Ching installs these things and has a big crew working under him. They just hand him a blueprint and he takes his bunch and goes to work in a building new or old. He is doing all right.

He and Mrs. Johnson live in an apartment just over the district line in Maryland. Their kids are grown up now, and Jimmie, who finished at the University of Maryland and took his graduate degree at Illinois, is in South America for his company at the moment.

Since Ching is a legend, even the newer addicts know about him, but just in case there should be some skeptics, young or old, among them, let us return for a moment to one of the most remarkable scenes in any sport. This was in Detroit's Olympia Stadium and the time, the evening of April 1, 1937.

The Rangers had just lost the Stanley Cup to the Red Wings, beaten in the final game of the final round. It was the last game Ching would play as a Ranger. There was nothing official but it was generally understood that he was through.

Now, for 11 years Ching had been going into Detroit, banging the Wings about, hurting them, beating them. Nowhere in the league had the boos for him been louder. The Olympia crowds had reviled him, shouted insults at him, thrown things at his bald head. Now he had played his last game among them and gone.

It was a long time after the game was over before Ching was packed and ready to start back to Winnipeg. At last the door of the visitors' dressing room opened and the familiar bald head, hanging low now, poked out. But hundreds of Detroit fans had waited outside for this and when they saw him, they lifted the rafters with their cheers.

They rushed him and mobbed him. They wanted to touch him, slap him on the back, and have his autograph. They spoke to him, called his name affectionately. No longer was he a villain. Now he was a departing great one to whom they would pay tribute.

They milled about him and would not let him leave. Finally three cops pushed through and rescued him. And the last thing that he heard as he left the building was the old familiar chant, "Ching, Ching, Chinaman." Although Ching Johnson played on for a while next season, this really was the end. And what a moment for him! And how well deserved.

1960

THE METHUSELAH
OF BOWLING
By Bob Cole

FROM THE WINSTON-SALEM (N.C.) JOURNAL
Copyright © 1960, Piedmont Publishing Co.

It's not very often that we get bowling stories that engender enough interest to be included in Best Sports Stories, *but Mr. Cole's account of an old-time kegler received two enthusiastic votes from our judges—an "aye" from Mr. Chamberlain, who maintained it was a beautiful character sketch, and one from John Hutchens, who wrote: "Speaking of entertainment unfamiliar to this observer, bowling is even further removed than track. But there is an irresistible quality about this genuine character study of a man so absolutely dedicated to a sport. If the writer had been a novelist, he might well have had a first-class novel of this life."*

Much of the time he sits hunched forward in a straight-back chair, silent except for spasmodic wheezing . . . chain-smoking . . . staring through round, gold-rimmed glasses . . . his large-veined hand stroking the gray combed-back hair and the gray stubble that frame his eroded face. . . .

This is Sarge Easter, the Methuselah of bowling, looking down the alley at a 7–10 split of hourglasses.

And he doesn't have many trick shots left at 69. Or 72, or 79, whatever his age.

He has trouble walking through the modest four-room house at Walkertown, or driving 10 miles to Walnut Cove for drugs to kill the pain and help clear the lungs.

Emphysema has cost him his optimism, ability to exhale easily, 40 pounds of weight, and his consuming love-vocation.

It's been almost a year since he last bowled. He's lost most of his contact with the game, although the other day he got an hour-long phone call—at the rate of $1.10 for three minutes—from a touring team that stopped in Greenville, South Carolina.

Then he got a letter from a promoter asking him to bowl in a proposed national bowling league. But Sarge has a tough time putting on his bowling shirt every morning, much less rolling a 16-pound ball 60 feet with the accuracy he once achieved.

So he just sits and thinks . . . back. The memory is not clear. Too many times the years have been shuffled to please the Army, the sports writers.

Too many strikes, too many miles . . . sometimes it's a blur of khaki, of black ball exploding white pins, of currency green passing over his palm.

The beginning of his odyssey is clear, violent, A moonshiner's shotgun blast killed his father, Dunkard minister Joseph Anderson Easter, and sent his family from its home near Cana, Carroll County, Virginia, to a small tobacco farm near Walnut Cove.

It was 1904. Sarge was 12 years old, one of seven children his widowed mother somehow raised to comfort.

His four brothers and two sisters called him "Ed," from the initials of his given name, Ebber Darnell. His was almost the only non-Biblical name among a Simon, Peter, Jonah, Keziah, etc.

At 14, nose pressed to a grimy glass front on Liberty Street, Ed saw his first bowling alley. Love at first sight wasn't cynical in 1906.

He went home, successfully pleaded for a small patch of tobacco, and cultivated bowling money. At 10 cents a line (it's 50 cents now) Ed was in heaven from noon until six o'clock.

Five years and a falsehood passed before he bowled again. Tired of farm life, 18-year-old Ed connived with a Roanoke, Virginia, Army recruiter to circumvent the parental consent requirement.

"You're husky enough," the recruiter told the 5-foot-8, 180-pound stump of a youth. The Army agreed, and made Ed a physical-training instructor.

When the United States entered World War I, Ed was sent to Canada to learn bayonet tactics, then to California to relay the lethal lessons to Europe-bound infantrymen.

During those first 10 years of service, Ed bowled nearly every night he wasn't on guard duty. He also discovered his other athletic abilities.

Trading his khaki for wool flannel on a three-month furlough in 1920, he pitched for Spokane of the Class A Pacific International League.

He was also a fair trackman, in the quarter mile and broad and high jumps. Later, he became a left-handed golfer—because he used left-handed clubs the first time he played, although he is right-handed.

After his third enlistment period ended, in 1921, he pitched and switch-hit his summers away for two years in the minor leagues, several more in semipro baseball.

He won a game in Winston-Salem for Raleigh in 1922, but lost it when the local team protested that he was one of too many veterans on Raleigh's roster.

He pitched against Satchel Paige in spring training for Spokane, little dreaming he would join the Negro star in sports antiquity.

After pitching the 10-inning, 1–0 losses in a doubleheader, he turned down a shot with the Philadelphia Athletics in 1921.

Maybe he later regretted the decision. He drifted around the country in the twenties, shucking corn and catching rivets and bowling for industrial teams in the Midwest, mining coal in West Virginia, living everywhere by wit and daring—as a bachelor can.

Broke in West Virginia, he rented a theater and in one day promoted a "fiddler's convention" that cleared over $1,000.

A pool shark who'd bite for a fin, he would stroll into an emporium, enter a game with no financial backing, run the table.

"But what if you ever lost, Ed?" he was asked.

"I'd get a cue stick cracked over my head," he said with a shrug. "But I couldn't lose. There was money on the line."

The bowling world later would learn this, but Sarge foresaw no such dream-come-true. With a penchant for a pension and Army security, he looked for a recruiter who would overlook the fact he was 38 and even older by Army records.

He found one, and was "in" again in 1930, on his way to fame and self-fulfillment. The route was indirect, to Hawaii and back to Chicago.

The return trip was to his first American Bowling Congress tournament in 1938, and it temporarily cost him his staff sergeant's rank.

His enlistment period had nearly ended when the tournament came up, and he could keep his sergeant's rating if he reenlisted immediately. When Ed asked for a furlough to bowl, his commanding officer told him, "Take a leave or a promotion."

The CO knew Ed's dependence upon the Army, but not his love of bowling. Ed was at least 46, with no skills, no money. He went bowling.

Twenty-six days later, he was back in khaki, a buck private. He was sent to the University of Wisconsin (at Madison) as an ROTC rifle instructor.

Taking an apartment next to Schwoegler's ("sh-waig-ler's") Lanes, he hung around the alleys like a hand towel on a ball rack. When not on the firing line—where he says he hit 80 straight bull's-eyes from 50 feet—he was on the foul line.

The Schwoeglers "took a liking to the old (at least 47) gent," put him on one of their league teams, and . . .

"When he came here in '39, all he had was a straight ball," Mel Schwoegler recalled. "No science. Worse, he had a pronounced backup [his delivery faded from left to right instead of right to left as a hook does].

"So Dad [the late Tony] taught him a hook, and Connie [Mel's brother, one-time ABC Bowler of the Year] worked a lot with him.

"He and Connie experimented with different grips, after studying slow-motion movies of ball-and-pin action.

"Sarge developed his 'Easter grip,' and it was popular while he was.

"Funny thing about Sarge. He was always coughing. We would draw straws to see who would room with him on trips."

This was emphysema ("em-fuh-seem-uh") in its early stages. As the disease progresses, it turns the lung muscles to flab, making exhalation difficult and causing the lungs to remain nearly full of stale air—air from which the body has assimilated most of the oxygen.

But Sarge had no time for sickness. He had 33 years of duffer bowling to make up. On weekend passes he sped around the Midwest tournament circuit and back to Madison for a nap before reporting to the university at 8:00 A.M. Monday.

He won a few tournaments and usually finished in the money, but most amazing was his match game success—especially at Schwoegler's. Driven by a hungry ego and betting money, and fortified by tremendous stamina, he could bowl challenge matches all night.

As a gray-haired prodigy, he quickly gained a national

reputation. After his Army manipulations, his age was as much a mystery as Jack Benny's.

The ABC Who's Who lists his birthday as November 20, 1882, cites him as its oldest champion (for his membership on its 1950 champion team). But another ABC record says he was 69 in 1953, which would make his year of birth 1884.

Sarge says his birthday is March 8, 1889. The family Bible kept by his sister, Mrs. R. W. Sands of Walnut Cove, says he was born March 8, 1892.

However inconsistent his age, these things are certain: He was at least 50 before he won a major tournament, at least 65 when he left the pro circuit. Popular stories make that age span 60 to 75.

In 1946, Sarge was retired from the Army as a staff sergeant after 26 years of service. The next 11 years he spent bowling in the Midwest and California, or driving cross country.

His most memorable trip was a two-day tear from Long Beach, California, to Detroit. Scheduled to bowl with the midnight shift in a Long Beach tournament, Sarge had planned to skip a tournament beginning two days later in Detroit.

But the Detroit sponsor called that night: "Sarge, the mayor and governor are going to be here. It's opening night for my alley. You got to come!"

Sarge came. leaving Long Beach at 2:30 A.M. Wednesday after winning that tournament, arriving in Detroit at 8:00 P.M. Thursday—just in time for opening ceremonies.

The governor presented him the check he won in Long Beach. "Sarge, you made it in 40 hours! You must have averaged 70 miles an hour," the proprietor said, beaming.

Well, not quite, but even 70 would have been slow for Sarge. His record was somewhere over 120 mph—or so the Tennessee state police told him when they finally caught him at their road block. That little spin cost him only $16.50; he was as smooth a talker as a bowler.

"Want to get even?" Sarge asked, counting his money.

"Yeah."

"Then bet on me from now on, not against me."

Less than a year later, the wiser but flatter Detroiter was in a bar watching television. Sarge and his Detroit Pepsi-Cola team were in the finals of the 1950 ABC team championships.

Sarge was anchor man. If he bowled strikes in the last two frames and one in the extra frame, his team would win the title by one pin.

"Hundred says he can do it," the Detroiter said to the man on the next stool.

"You're crazy, but I'll take you."

The Detroiter wasn't crazy.

Sarge took a bet like a dare, especially when the odds were against him, as when:

—He lost his regular partner on the last day of a 1953 national doubles tournament in St. Louis. So he teamed with a so-so shooter, and they shot a three-game score of 1,483, best of the year. He struck out on the last frame and the team won the tournament by a pin.

—Although just recovering from a siege of influenza and ptomaine poisoning at the 1953 St. Louis All-Star tournament, he agreed to bowl with his team until a substitute arrived.

The sub didn't arrive until the sixth frame. Sarge had six strikes and said, "I'll bowl until I miss a strike." He stopped after a perfect game—which, according to ABC records that list him as 69 in 1953, made him one of the two oldest men ever to bowl a 300 game in sanctioned league play. He was at least 61.

Sarge was through as a pro bowler in 1957. He had spent three seasons in Detroit, one in St. Louis, most of the rest in Burbank, California.

A Burbank proprietor gave Sarge a special chair near the door of his alley, away from the hum and splatter of the bowling area. When not sitting, he was betting at Santa Anita race track. His favorite wager: a three-horse round-robin parlay.

Last January Sarge left his bachelor brother and the Burbank motel room they shared, and moved here to live with his widower brother, Simon, at Walkertown.

He took his bowling equipment to a local alley, told the proprietor he hoped to "get in a few more games before I go."

He did, dropping by occasionally for trick-bowling exhibitions, such as bowling two balls simultaneously, so that they cross midway down the alley and roll on to knock over the No. 7 and No. 10 pins—which are set in the far corners of the alley.

But the emphysema worsened. And after a life of freedom and good health, Sarge became depressed when the disease became manifest. For the first time in his life he entered a hospital—with reluctance—for two weeks.

Doctors told him he would have to be confined; no one could care for his internal hemorrhaging at home. At first, he seemed to take confinement as an admission of defeat, but adjusted so well he had to be persuaded to leave.

Soon after he was out, brother Simon's son graduated from high school, and it appeared the boy might not be around home too long. Simon told Sarge:

"Us two old men can't stay here and try to care for each other. We're both weak. You're under sedative at night. We're going to have to move."

So last week Sarge staggered out to his car with his topcoat and winter suit.

"Don't know whether he's going to take 'em to the cleaners or try to drive to Denver [Colorado]," Simon said. "Says he wants to enter the veterans' hospital out here.

"He ain't got no business trying to drive to Denver, but I won't try to stop him. We're a hardheaded family, and he won't listen to nobody."

The money from his winnings was big ("I've had as many as 18 checks for him when he'd come home," Simon recalled), but his traveling expenses were high. There apparently is not much left.

But Sarge still has his bowling ball, shoes, and bag, and one more goal: to make the ABC Hall of Fame, which he barely missed last winter.

"I should make it next year," he said. "But the way I feel now I don't know if I'll be around to celebrate."

1961

THE MONGOOSE

By Jack Murphy

FROM THE NEW YORKER

Copyright © 1961, The New Yorker Magazine, Inc.

At the age of 44, when most boxers have faded into the past, Archie Moore emerged as the most elderly of all boxing champions. All of our three judges were so enthralled that they gave author Murphy at least one vote. To quote part of judge John Chamberlain's review: "The close-up of Moore is a beautiful job of extensive coverage—Archie has had a long life which he has adorned with the expenditure of much wit and grace and Jack Murphy has done a superior job in delineating this human being."

Archibald Lee Moore, the lightweight boxing champion of the world, is 44 years of age by his own account and 47 by his mother's. She says that he was born on December 13, 1913, in Benoit, Mississippi, but he insists that the year was 1916 and, on occasion, that the place was somewhere in Missouri, or perhaps Illinois. "My mother should know, she was there," he has conceded. "But so was I. I have given this a lot of thought, and have decided that I must have been three when I was born." Whoever is right, Moore is the most elderly champion in the history of boxing. By all the rules of the game, he should have faded into retirement long ago, like his contemporaries Joe Louis, Joe Walcott, Ezzard Charles, and Rocky Marciano, all of whom have settled into a sedentary life appropriate to their gray hairs and accumulating paunches. Moore's hair is gray and he is often grievously overweight, but he just doesn't seem to age. "I don't worry about growing old, because worrying is a disease," he says. Not long ago, he was chatting with a friend in a Los Angeles gymnasium after a workout when he chanced to overhear a couple of young fighters discussing him. "That old man should quit," said one of the apprentices, nodding toward Moore. "He should get out and let us take over. Look at him, with his old gray head!" Moore walked lightly over to where the two fighters were standing, and said, smiling, "It isn't this old gray head that worries you young fellows, it's this old gray fist."

Moore has been a professional boxer for 26 years, starting as a middleweight, winning his championship as a light-heavyweight in 1952, by beating Joey Maxim in 15 rounds, and on two occasions fighting for the heavyweight title—first, in 1955, against Rocky Marciano, and then, in 1956, against Floyd Patterson, both of whom knocked him out. He has had 214 fights to date, and has won 183, 131 of them by knockout—a record unmatched in pugilism. However, because his build is undistinguished and his countenance unscarred, there is nothing about his appearance that hints at the violent nature of his trade, and he affects a wispy bebop goatee that gives more the look of a jazz musician than of a fighter. His taste in wearing apparel is something less than severe—he usually goes into the ring draped in a gold or silver silk dressing gown festooned with sequins, and he has been photographed at Epsom Downs in England wearing a gray topper, striped pants, and a cutaway, and on Fifth Avenue strolling along, cane in hand, in a white dinner jacket and Bermuda shorts—but his natural poise and his almost regal bearing enable him to carry off such trappings with dignity. Moore calls himself "the Mongoose," but although he is sharp-sighted and agile and fearless, like a mongoose, he has practically none of the irritable nature of that ferocious little animal. Moore's warm personality and rough-and-ready wit make friends for him everywhere. People come up to him on the street to shake his hand, and motorists wave to him. He can go unannounced into a nightclub in Harlem or its Los Angeles counterpart and soon the management will have him on the bandstand, entertaining the customers with his light patter. Children respond to him enthusiastically. "Wouldn't it be awful if a man had to go through a day—even one day—without a little music and laughter?" he once said when somebody complimented him on his happy disposition.

Moore is probably the most widely traveled boxer of all time—largely because there was a period of some years when it was impossible for him to get fights in this country with anyone near his class—and he is proud of the attention he has received from Toronto to Tasmania. "I have passed the time of day with President Eisenhower and, if you will pardon me, several dictators," he remarked some time ago. "I was once criticized for some newspaper pictures showing Juan Peron with his arms around me. I can only reply that when the head of a government invites me to meet him, I think it is judicious to do so. I have been in Germany, too. I posed with all the West German politicians, policemen, generals, and fighters. When I ran out of dignitaries. I went to the parks and posed with the statues. I really dig that historic stuff, you know. However, I am not a political person. I am an ambassador of good will."

In actuality, Moore isn't quite the political innocent he often pretends to be. He is a registered Democrat and, as a San Diego resident of some 20 years' standing, has worked in behalf of several California office seekers. Moreover, in 1960 he ran for a lame-duck term as assemblyman in California's Seventy-ninth Assembly District, but he was beaten, probably because he didn't bother to train—a tendency that he had carried over from his professional life. (Instead of campaigning for the office, Moore went off to Rome and rounded up a suitable challenger for his championship—an Italian fighter named Giulio Rinaldi, who outpointed him in a nontitle bout.) When Moore took out his nominating papers, he listed Mississippi as his birthplace on one affidavit and Missouri on another. Advised that he'd have to make a choice, he protested, on the ground that both states deserved this honor. Eventually he decided in favor of Mississippi. (In Nat Fleischer's *The Ring*, though, he is quoted as having said he was born in Collinsville, Illinois.) He also listed his occupation as "the light-heavyweight champion of the world," but a deputy registrar pointed out that California law permits only a three-word description on the ballot, so he reluctantly settled for "light-heavyweight champion."

If the deputy registrar had chosen to make a point of it, he might have questioned that capsule description as well, for although Moore is the recognized champion where it counts—in New York, Massachusetts, and California, and abroad—the National Boxing Association, which presides over the small-time, or remaining 47 states, decided late last year that he was not defending his championship often enough and declared the title vacant. Moore, who has had a running feud with the National Boxing Association for years, appealed to the United Nations. It hadn't previously occurred to anybody that the United Nations had jurisdiction over boxing, but when Moore's camp sent a telegram to Ambassador Henry Cabot Lodge asking him to help a "great internationalist," the NBA backed up and granted Moore an additional period of grace in which to contract for a championship fight. Moore paid no heed. "When I wanted the NBA to recognize me as a challenger, they let me wither for five solid years," he said. "I think I've made a definite contribution to boxing; if everybody is going to forget that, why, I'll get a job or go into the movies or something." When the deadline was up, the NBA defrocked Moore a second time and arranged for a fight between the two leading contenders—Jesse Bowdry, a 23-year-old St. Louis fighter, and Harold Johnson, whom Moore had fought five times and defeated four times, the last fight being a championship bout at Madison Square Garden in 1954, when Moore knocked him out in 14 rounds. Johnson knocked out Bowdry in nine rounds, and the NBA said he was champion. The fact remains that Moore is in the big money and Johnson is not.

Johnson currently declares that he is no longer interested in fighting Moore. "Archie is an old man, and they can put you in jail for beating up old men," he said not long ago. "Why, Johnson is my protégé," Moore countered. "I have always looked after Harold and said nice things about him. The trouble with Harold is that he is under the impression the clock of time has stopped. As soon as the young man"—Johnson is 33—"makes a reputation for himself, I'll be glad to give him another shot at my title." At various times, Moore has announced that he intends to keep his championship for 16 years, or until 1968 ("That would help me get even for the 16 years I waited until they finally let me fight Maxim"), and that he will continue to defend his title until he can pass it along to his son, Hardy Lee. Hardy Lee recently observed his first birthday.

Moore loves to talk. "I am a great sidewalk talker," he once said. "I can talk Mexican-fashion, squatting on my heels, or big-city style, with my spine up against a lamppost or a building, or even garment-center technique, with my backside at the edge of a curb." He is a frequent after-dinner speaker, and he plans his post-fight speeches, which are usually addressed to a nationwide radio and television audience, with loving care. "When I am invited to speak at a prison, I usually accept, because nobody walks out in the middle of my speech, and there is no heckling," he says. Moore sometimes talks while he is fighting, too. In 1957, when he knocked out Tony Anthony in the seventh round of a championship fight in Los Angeles, Anthony's manager, Ernie Braca, complained that his man had been befuddled by Moore's line of chatter. "Archie is a smart old guy," he said. "He talked his way to victory." "Please remind Mr. Braca that I mixed a few punches into the conversation," Moore responded.

Moore acknowledges certain defects in his conversation. "I'd rather use six little words than one big one," he says. "I tend to draw a pitch out. I say this to say that. Eventually, however, my meaning comes clear. Like the night I was fighting Bobo Olson. I hit him in the belly with a left hook and followed with a right to the head. The right was slightly high, but Bobo got the message. Still, there is, I fear, that one chink in my armor. I am inclined to waste words. In fact, I throw them away. It is my only excess." The last statement is not entirely accurate. Moore has such a tremendous fondness for food that he regularly eats himself out of shape—so far out that every time he has defended his championship he has been obliged to take off from 25 to 40 pounds in order to reach 175 pounds, the weight limit of his class. The sports columnist Jimmy Cannon once accused him of gluttony, to which he replied, with all possible solemnity, "No, Jimmy, I am not a glutton—I am an explorer of food." According to his associates, the difficulty is that he chooses the wrong terrain to explore, and Moore himself admits that "the things I like to eat are not becoming to a fighter." He is particularly attracted to starches and to fried foods, and between meals he finds an icebox irresistible. Some months ago, when he was in New York with his lawyer on business, the two men shared a hotel room, and one night, a couple of hours after they had retired, following a seven-course dinner, the lawyer, awakened by a stealthy noise in the room, turned on the light just in time to see Moore walking in his sleep through the door. Leaping out of bed, the attorney grabbed him by an arm and steered him back into the room. "Archie! What are you doing?" he demanded. Moore mumbled sleepily, "Where is the icebox in this house?" He then awakened, ate a bagel he had bought that evening from a street vendor, and slept quietly until it was time for breakfast.

Although Moore contends that "fat is just a three-letter word that was invented to confuse people," his battles with the scales have often provided more excitement and suspense than the ring battles they prefaced. He always waits until the last possible minute to start reducing. "In order to lose weight, I must get myself into the proper frame of mind," he once said when he was facing such an ordeal. "I'm circling the problem now, looking it over carefully. I may pounce at any time." When Moore pounces, the mongoose in him comes out. He believes in trimming down the hard way, by means of a low-calorie diet and savage exercise—a combination that would almost certainly hospitalize a lesser man—and the regime makes him a bit snappish. In the summer of 1955, while Moore was training for his championship fight with Bobo Olson at the Polo Grounds, he took off 23 pounds, the last few at Ehsan's Training Camp, a dreary, unpainted sweat pit in Summit, New Jersey. His trainers closed the doors and windows of the gymnasium early every afternoon, quickly transforming it into a steam cabinet, and in this suffocating atmosphere Moore, swaddled in a skin-tight rubber costume, went through his ritual of shadowboxing, sparring, bag-punching, and rope-skipping, giving off sprays of water like a revolving lawn sprinkler. The close air was almost unbearable, but he drove himself furiously, and during the last 24 hours before the weigh-in had nothing to eat or drink except half a lemon. The method seemed extreme, particularly for a middle-aged athlete, but it was effective. Moore made the weight by two pounds, and knocked out Olson in three rounds.

Last May, when Moore started training for his most recent title defense—on June 10th, at Madison Square Garden, against Rinaldi, the man who had outpointed him in a nontitle match in Rome the year before—he weighed 198 pounds. For the Rome fight, Moore had agreed to weigh in at a maximum of 185 pounds or forfeit a thousand dollars. He started taking off surplus weight, mostly in steam cabinets, only six days before the match, and the best he could do was a hundred and ninety, so he lost the thousand. Furthermore, Rinaldi took the decision. For the New York match with Rinaldi, when the title was at stake, Moore diminished himself with such a desperate crash diet ("You can eat as much as you like, as long as you don't swallow it," he was fond of saying at the time) that the fight crowd began speculating on whether he would have enough strength left to mount the steps into the ring. Rocky Marciano, who visited Moore's training camp, called Kutsher's in the Catskills, was appalled by his training methods. "I don't believe Rinaldi can lose the fight," he said. "The weight-making will beat Archie—that's the big thing." The promoters of the bout, alarmed by the possibility that the star would either collapse from exhaustion or be disqualified by excess poundage, invited the *alter* champion, Harold Johnson, to serve as a standby. "Hasn't Harold always stood by?" Moore asked when he was told about it. Moore made the weight by half a pound, and Dr. Alexander Schiff, who examined him for the New York State Athletic Commission, marveled at his condition. "I don't know his age, but he has the body and reflexes of a man

of 30 or 32," the doctor said. A great sigh of relief was heard from
Harry Markson, general manager of boxing for Madison Square
Garden. "I feel as though I had lost that weight myself," he said,
beaming. Johnson was not surprised. "I knew he'd make it," he
said. "Archie wasn't going to let me have all that money." Moore
won an overwhelming 15-round decision, and seemed as fresh at
the finish as he had at the start. Fascinated by this time with the
whole subject of weight removal, he issued an invitation to
newspapermen: "Come to my home town a year from now and
you won't find a fat man in San Diego. I'm going to open a chain
of health studios." He hasn't got around to it yet, but at last
report he was still thinking about it.

A self-styled expert on nutrition, Moore frequently speaks of
a "secret diet" that he says he obtained from an Australian
aborigine in the course of his travels. ("Did you ever see a fat
aborigine?" he asks.) He declares that he got the diet in exchange
for a red turtleneck sweater, and he regarded it as a professional
secret up until last year, when he included it in his autobiography. *The Archie Moore Story*, written in collaboration with Bob
Condon and Dave Gregg, and published by McGraw-Hill. The
diet proved to be about like most other diets, except that it
placed uncommon emphasis on the drinking of hot sauerkraut
juice for breakfast—an idea that the aborigine had somehow
overlooked. Unfortunately, the appearance of the diet coincided
with the embarrassing disclosure that Moore was asking post-
ponement of a fight with Erich Schoeppner, a German light-
heavyweight, because he was unable to make the weight.

Moore's alternating periods of feast and famine subject his
physique to such drastic restyling that he finds it convenient to
buy clothes in three sizes. There's one rack of suits for the
heavyweight Moore, at around 215 pounds; another for the junior-
heavyweight Moore, at 190; and still another for the championship weight. Moore tends to regard his smallest self as something
of a stranger. Studying his profile in a mirror before one of his
title fights, he said critically, "I look sort of funny when I get
down to 175. I'm not skinny, exactly, but I don't look like me."

Once a fight is over, it doesn't take long for Moore to become
recognizable to himself again. When he is in residence in San
Diego, he likes to entertain his friends with cookouts at which the
staple item is barbecued spareribs, and when he is fooling
around at his rural fight camp, a small ranch situated on a ridge
of rocky but oak-shaded hills 30 miles northeast of San Diego,
and known as the Salt Mine, he often takes a skillet in hand and

fries up a tasty batch of chicken, which is one of his favorite dishes. "Fried chicken has a personality of its own," he says. "You can eat it hot or cold, with a fork or free-hand style." As a matter of fact, Moore's home, a two-story brick house on the edge of downtown San Diego, was built on the site of a restaurant that he owned and operated for a number of years and that was called the Chicken Shack. Under his personal supervision, the house has been remodeled and expanded, at a reported cost of $150,000, until it has become one of the showplaces of the city. The creature comforts include a swimming pool in the shape of a boxing glove; a poolside cabana that is equipped, fittingly, with both a barbecue pit and a steam room; a soundproof music studio, where he plays a piano or a bass fiddle in occasional jam sessions, or listens to an extensive collection of jazz records; and three rumpus rooms—one for himself, one for his wife, and one for his children. In his rumpus room, Moore has a regulation-size pool table, imported from England. "I play piano, but will shoot pool with tone-deaf guests," he says. "After all, a man can't spend his whole life just fightin' 'n' fiddlin'."

He is also an expert pistol shot (he practices frequently on targets at the Salt Mine), a skilled angler, a student of boxing history, and a handyman who is equally at ease with an electric drill or behind the steering levers of a bulldozer. "The main secret of true relaxism is diversion," he says. "A person who has no hobby has no life." He is devoted to the current Mrs. Moore— the former Joan Hardy—a tall, attractive, light-complexioned woman, who has borne him two daughters and two sons in six years of marriage. Because she is a sister-in-law of the actor Sidney Poitier, she is not much awed by her husband's celebrity, and she cheerfully makes allowances for artistic temperament. She didn't complain, for example, when Moore insisted that she shorten the heels on her shoes by a full inch. He is 5 feet 11 inches tall, and she is only an inch less. The champion didn't want his wife towering over him, and he refused to wear elevator shoes. Since he wouldn't go up, she agreed to come down. (When Moore first sprouted his goatee, along with a light mustache, a reporter asked him if his wife didn't object to the new growth when he kissed her. Moore smiled indulgently and replied, "A girl doesn't mind going through a little bush to get to a picnic.") Mrs. Moore—she is his fifth wife—has been a stabilizing influence on her husband. Not only has she given him domestic happiness, but her quiet efficiency has brought a measure of order to his once disorganized social and business affairs. Until she assigned herself the duties of secretary, bookkeeper, and business manager, Moore was surrounded by clutter and chaos. Well-meaning but irresponsible, he would accept half a dozen speaking engagements for the same date and ignore them all. Now his appointments are cleared through his wife, and he usually shows up on schedule.

Mrs. Moore is also secretary of Archie Moore Enterprises, Inc., a firm that was established two years ago for the purpose of supervising the champion's investments and maintaining amicable relations with the Director of Internal Revenue. Moore is the president of the corporation; the vice-president is Bill Yale, a young San Diego attorney; and the treasurer is Clarence Newby, a San Bernardino CPA who serves as Moore's accountant and tax expert. The president's income from boxing and related activities goes to the corporation, which pays him a salary. Moore doesn't like to talk about his financial affairs. "I am wealthy in terms of happiness, because I have a wonderful wife and fine children," he says, "but I still must scratch for a living."

Moore's professional entourage, whose members wear uniform blue coveralls as they go about their various duties at the Salt Mine, includes an odd assortment of friends. There is, for instance, Redd Foxx, a sort of court jester, whose admiration for Moore is so extravagant that he once had his hair barbered to form the letter "M." There is a wizened little man in his late seventies, known as Poppa Dee (his real name is Harry Johnson), whom Moore calls "the medicine man of boxing." "I like to have Poppa in my camp because he makes me feel good," Moore says. Then, there is a sparring partner called Greatest Crawford, who has made a substantial reputation in the ring on his own hook, and a masseur called Big Bopper (his real name is Richard Fullylove), who stands 6-foot-2 and weighs 298, and who used to play football for a small Negro college in Texas. At one time, Moore planned to farm him out between fights to the San Diego Chargers, of the American Football League, but the Big Bopper was unable to pass the Charger physical examination. He had high blood pressure. Moore has had three trainers in recent years—Cheerful Norman, Hiawatha Grey, and the incumbent, Dick Saddler. Cheerful Norman left the Moore entourage five years ago, and Hiawatha has quit several times after minor disputes with Moore, but the two men remain firm friends. Hiawatha, like Archie's other trainers, and like Archie himself, is a Negro. "He is a very wise old owl," Moore has commented. "It would be wise to be married to him 14 years before you call him

Hiawatha, because he doesn't like the name. Most people just call him Hi. He goes his own way." Saddler has been the most enduring of Moore's trainers, and his staying power can probably be attributed as much to a happy nature and a talent for playing the piano as to his technical qualifications. Moore's authority is unquestioned when he's in training, but Saddler's clowning relaxes him, and when he's relaxed, he willingly takes orders. (Nevertheless, Moore insists on taping his own hands before a workout or a fight—he is the only pugilist of stature to do so— and won't wear protective headgear while sparring in the gymnasium, lest he come to depend on it.) When Moore is skipping rope, a routine that invariably attracts a crowd at training headquarters, Saddler accompanies him on the piano, usually pounding out a boogie-woogie beat. "My only trouble with Dick is that he is a ham," says Moore. "He tries to upstage me. I put the piano behind a curtain, but he insists on being seen." Saddler is satisfied with the relationship. "I guess Archie hired me because I can play piano," he says, "but he admits I know a little about fighting, too." Another long-time friend and camp follower is Norman Henry, a drowsy sort of man who is always welcome at the Salt Mine, even though he is a fight manager and fight managers, collectively, are anathema to Moore. Moore simply enjoys his company. One afternoon when Henry was catnapping in a chair, Moore nodded toward him and remarked to a visitor, "At the dawn of civilization there were three men. One, watching lightning strike, saw the possibilities of fire. Another invented the wheel. Norman? Well, Norman was asleep. He had already invented the bed."

Last winter, Moore's Salt Mine sparring partners included a handsome young boxer out of Dallas named Buddy Turman, who a short time later turned up as Moore's opponent in a 10-round nontitle bout in Manila. (Fighting one's sparring partners, it should be explained, is an old and cherished custom in the fight game. Rocky Marciano fought a series of harmless exhibitions with one of his relatives a few years ago, and Young Stribling, a fighter of an earlier era, was—until Moore deposed him—the all-time knockout champion, thanks in no small measure to his custom of flattening his chauffeur in one small town after another.) Moore usually has two or three rookie fighters on tap at his training camp, and for a brief period the cast included a distinguished young man named Cassius Marcellus Clay, who, having made a reputation by winning the Olympic light-heavyweight championship in Rome the summer before last, had decided to learn what he could at the feet of the Master. Accompanied by a woman lawyer, Clay flew to San Diego last fall and announced that, since he planned to turn professional, he was going to spend at least a month studying under Archie Moore at the Salt Mine. Clay said he admired the Mongoose more than any other fighter in the world and would gladly do anything asked of him—that no sacrifice would be too great, no chore too mean or small. He devoutly hoped that Moore would become his manager. It sounded like an ideal arrangement, but within two weeks Clay had turned in his blue coveralls and left, saying, "I wanted Archie to teach me to fight, but the only thing I learned was how to wash dishes. Who ever heard of a fighter with dishpan hands?" Clay is now fighting under other management and remains unbeaten after eight bouts. He is considered a long-range threat to Patterson.

It was at the age of 15 that Moore determined to become a fighter. His color was chiefly responsible for this decision, because boxing was the only way he could see for a Negro to rise above the kind of poverty he grew up in. He was born Archie Lee Wright, but his parents were separated shortly after his birth, and he and his sister, Rachel, and his half-brothers, Louis and Jackie, were all brought up in a St. Louis slum by his Uncle Cleveland and his Aunt Willie Moore, whose surname he adopted as a convenience. His uncle died when Archie was 14, leaving only a small insurance policy, and it was up to Aunt Willie to support the family. "We had a tie of affection in our home—oh, it was so beautiful," Moore recalls fondly. "As they say, we were too poor to paint and too proud to whitewash, so we kept everything spotless. We had bare wood floors, and on Saturdays we scrubbed them with lye soap. We kept our house so clean it was like a hospital. My auntie taught us that we might not have the best furniture or wear the best clothing, but we sure could keep them clean." Despite the best Aunt Willie could do to bring them up properly, however, both Archie and Louis had brushes with the law in their teens (as Moore recalled in his autobiography, "Louis was light-fingered by nature, and somehow a man's watch got tangled up in his hand, and the man sent the police to ask Louis what time it was"), and Archie spent a 22 month term in the Missouri reformatory at Booneville for hooking coins from a streetcar motorman. Of the reformatory experience, he says, "I don't say I enjoyed it, but I'm grateful for what it did for me. It was a glorious thing in my life, because it forced me to get eight to ten hours of sleep every night; it gave me an opportunity to have three hot meals a day; it gave me a lesson in discipline I would never have got at home. They used to pay me a little something for the work I did, but it should have been the other way around. I should have paid them for what they did for me."

Shortly after Archie returned home from Booneville, he and his aunt had a conference about his future. "I had thought about what I could do, and I told my auntie I wanted to fight. For a Negro starting a career, that was the only way. It was the last road. I considered the other possibilities. I could get an education and become a postman or a teacher; I could become a policeman or fireman; I could play baseball. There weren't many opportunities then, even for an educated Negro. As a teacher, the most I could become was a school principal. As a policeman, I couldn't advance beyond the rank of lieutenant or captain. I couldn't be a police chief or a fire chief; my color made that impossible. Professional baseball didn't offer much, because at that time all the colored ball players were in Negro leagues, and Satchel Paige was the only one of them who was making big money. He had a reputation and his big drawing power, so he took a percentage of the gate. The other colored ball players were lucky to earn $300 a month. Remember, this was right in the middle of the depression. I began to read in the newspapers about the boxers. Kid Chocolate was my first hero. I suppose I liked him because his name sounded so sweet. His skin was ebony; he was like patent leather. Most of all, the money intrigued me. I read that Kid Chocolate was fighting for a gate of $10,000, and that seemed like all the money in the world. I knew Kid Chocolate got 25 percent of the purse. According to my figures, that was around $2,500, and he was a rich man. *Twenty-five hundred dollars!* Do you know what kind of money that was then? Do you know how much it was to a family that depended on the government for a basket of food each week—for a family that waited for a government check each month to pay the rent? It was fabulous. It was my way out."

It is unlikely that any fighter has ever put more thought and effort into learning the boxing trade than Moore. He was skinny as a boy, but he developed unusual strength with exercises of his own invention. One of his stunts was walking on his hands. He'd go up and down stairs on his hands, and sometimes around the block, or around several blocks. The boy also developed his arms and shoulders by exercising phenomenally on a chinning bar.

While still in his teens, he once chinned himself 255 times, and he used to shadowbox hour after hour in front of a mirror. "The idea was to take myself out of Archie and put me into my image," he says. "I tried to visualize what I would do to Archie if I were the fellow in the mirror. I wanted to anticipate the reaction to my moves. I learned boxing from beginning to end and from end to beginning." To develop his jab, he got the idea of practicing before a mirror with a five-pound weight in each hand. He would wrap his fists around a pair of his Aunt Willie's flatirons and spar for six minutes without a rest. Then he'd pause for breath and repeat the procedure. "I knew I'd be wearing six-ounce gloves in the ring," he explains. "If I could spar with five-pound weights, the six-ounce gloves would feel as light as feathers. I'd never have to worry about becoming arm-weary." He credits his stinging jab to the flatirons. "I had the best jab in the business, Joe Louis notwithstanding," he says proudly.

In the course of events, Moore went to work in one of the Civilian Conservation Corps camps, at Poplar Bluff, Missouri, and there had a chance to take part in the Golden Gloves competitions, which gave him excellent training. After a while, he was fighting and winning what are known in the trade as "bootleg fights," in which technically amateur fighters make a little side money fighting anybody they can get a match with. One of the earliest such bouts he remembers was with Bill Simms, at Poplar Bluff, in 1935. Moore knocked him out in two rounds. This sort of campaigning—in Missouri, Arkansas, Oklahoma, and Illinois—kept him on the go, and he was learning fast. "When I was fighting as an amateur, I used to ride the freight trains, and once I had an experience I'll never forget," Moore recalls. "I was on a freight returning to St. Louis when a brakeman got after me. I had been standing there on the side of a tank car—it had molasses in it, I think—and I was daydreaming, without a care in the world, when a sixth sense told me I was in danger. I pulled back just as the brakeman swung at me with a club. He missed, and the club splintered on the handrail of the car. It would have killed me sure if he had hit me. I was scared and excited, but I got away from him. I ran. I was as sure-footed as a goat. I've always wondered why that fellow wanted to kill me. I was just a harmless hobo. I wasn't bothering anybody. I suppose that brakeman will never know the grief he caused me. When he swung that club, I dropped the little bag I was carrying. I lost all my fighting equipment. I had a pair of nice white trunks, a pair of freshly shined shoes, and my socks all neatly rolled. Those things meant a lot to me, and I was heartbroken over losing them."

Moore's first professional fight, to the best of his recollection, was against Murray Allen, in 1946, at Quincy, Illinois, and he won a decision, breaking his right hand in the process. His share of the gate was three dollars, which was two dollars less than the sum required for a boxing license. ("The commission was very generous," says Moore. "When they told me that I'd have to take out the license, they agreed to waive the other two dollars. I didn't fight in that state again until 1951. By then, I guess the license had expired.") The newspapers and the record books had not yet deigned to take notice of young Archie Moore, but before the year was out he had begun to establish himself. According to the latest edition of *The Ring*, Moore won 13 fights in a row that year, all by knockouts, and then lost the next three, by decisions, and won the seventeenth, by a decision. The first of the recorded knockouts was over Kneibert Davidson. The following year, 1937, he fought a dozen times and won the middleweight champion-ships of Kansas, Oklahoma, and Missouri, all 12 bouts by knockout.

Early in 1938, Moore headed for California, where he hoped to establish himself by fighting the prominent middleweights of the day—Bandit Romero, Eddie Booker, Swede Berglund, and others. He was riding in an automobile driven by a St. Louis mechanic named Felix Thurman, who was his manager at the time, when, near Bartlesville, Oklahoma, a car in the opposite lane suddenly bore down upon them. Thurman had a split-second choice—meet the other car head on or pile into an irriga-tion ditch. He chose the ditch. The car flipped over and landed on its roof, knocking Thurman unconscious. Moore, unharmed but frightened, tried to pry open a door, but it wouldn't budge. Then he heard the sound of dripping liquid. It was water drib-bling from the upturned wheels, but Moore thought it was gasoline, and was afraid the car would catch fire. In a panic, he smashed a window with his right fist, and then crawled out through the jagged glass, cutting an artery in his right wrist. Unaware that the cut was bleeding badly, he made a desperate effort to lift his unconscious companion from the wreckage, but he couldn't, so he stood beside the road, helpless and bewildered, until a car came along—carrying, as luck would have it, two interns. They quickly administered first aid to Moore and re-vived Thurman, who was not seriously injured. "Do you know

how long you would have lived with the blood spurting like that?"
one of the interns asked Moore. "About 14 minutes!" Moore still
speaks with awe about the kindness of the two men who saved
his life. "It was almost too much for me to understand," he said
some years later. "I figured that anybody in Oklahoma seeing two
Negroes overturned in a ditch would drive on. Yet the first car
stopped and came to my aid. I don't know whether God is a
white man or a black man, but I knew then He truly made us
all."

Fortunately, the automobile, once it had been turned right
side up and towed to a filling station, proved to be still navigable.
Thurman straightened the dented top with a mallet he had
brought along in his tool chest, and the two resumed their
journey. The tow job had cost them $12, leaving them with a
capital of $23, and this was reduced by $5 the next day, when
Thurman developed a toothache and was obliged to go to a
dentist and have a tooth pulled. When they ran out of money
completely, Thurman began trading his expensive mechanic's
tools for gasoline, yielding his treasures piece by piece. A spray
gun got them their last tank of gasoline, and they arrived in La
Jolla, where Thurman's wife had preceded them, at three o'clock
in the morning, weary and hungry, having driven several hundred miles and eaten only a sack of peanuts and two oranges in
the past 24 hours. Moore, always an early riser, awoke at 6:30
and went for a pre-breakfast sprint along the beach, in the course
of which he noticed a great column of smoke arising from the
direction of nearby San Diego. He wondered idly where the fire
was, and later that morning, when he and Thurman called on a
San Diego boxing promotor named Linn Platner, he learned that
it was at the Coliseum. The aspiring young fighter had arrived in
San Diego on the day the boxing arena burned down.

For the next several years, Moore moved around a great deal
but moved upward in the boxing world only a little. He toured
Australia and Tasmania and came off very well, winning four of
his seven fights there by knockout and the others by decision, but
when he returned to this country, there still seemed to be no
place for him in the big time. Not long ago, Moore was asked
whether he thought racial bias had kept him out, and he said, "I
would rather believe it didn't. In fact, I would be making excuses
for myself if I blamed my troubles on color. Joe Louis, Henry
Armstrong, and John Henry Lewis were Negroes, and they all
won championships during that period. Racial prejudice couldn't
have been the main reason. My problem was that the people who

handled me didn't have good enough connections. Looking back, though, I'm glad that's the way it was. The people who handled me did not deliver me to the element that controlled boxing. I don't want to talk about that element. I'm just happy I never came under the control of those people. I'm not saying, mind you, that I have any affection for fight managers. If it weren't for managers, a lot of fighters would have been millionaires. I have emancipated myself from the pit of boxing, and I am no longer tied down by managers." Moore was particularly aggrieved, it seems, because the last manager to hold his contract—Charlie Johnston, with whom he parted company in July of 1958—insisted on doing some of the talking for the firm. "Charlie was the sort who always wanted to speak for his tiger," Moore says. "But he didn't bother to call when our contract ended; he knew better. I have finally earned the right to meet the press and public the way a fighter should." Not long ago, Moore outlined a plan for turning his ranch into a haven for aged and indigent managers. "Every day, I would come in with a blacksnake whip and get them up. Then I'd have them do five miles of roadwork around the ranch. That would be good for their health and also give them a chance to understand their fighters a little better. But I wouldn't be altogether harsh. I'd furnish them with cheap cigars, and give them plenty of time to lie and boast to each other. Of course, I'd have a small problem remembering all their names, because most fight managers look alike to me. But I'd overcome that. I'd have a common name for them—Bum. That's what they spend their lives calling the kids they live off."

Moore's current manager, Jack (Doc) Kearns, has the official title of "boxing representative," because the champion can't stand the word "manager." A veteran of the boxing world, Kearns gives his age as 69, though 80 is probably closer to the mark. He has been part of Moore's life since Moore won the championship from Maxim, in 1952. Maxim was then managed by Kearns, and Moore had to guarantee Maxim $100,000 for the fight. This gave Moore a clear idea of the value of the championship and of the value of Kearns, and when the title changed hands, Kearns came along with the franchise. Moore, who received only $800 for winning the championship, not only adopted Kearns but adopted his policy of demanding $100,000 guarantee for putting his title at stake. The only contract between him and Kearns is a handshake. "I cut my purses with Doc because I like him," says Moore. "Doc is for his fighter. He made my big matches with Olson, Marciano, and Patterson. We've had a fine relationship. Doc is a promoter, a talker, a guy who knows how to maneuver. You could give Doc 200 pounds of steel wool and he'd knit you a stove."

In 1941, Moore was industriously beating his way through thickets of contenders on his way to the middleweight title, and had achieved the eminence of fifth rank in that division, when, in March, he collapsed on the sidewalk in San Diego and was taken unconscious to a hospital. His illness was diagnosed as a perforated ulcer, and an emergency operation was necessary to save his life. The newspapers reported that if Moore survived, which seemed doubtful, he would never fight again. He was in the hospital 38 days, and spent an even longer period convalescing, and then came down with appendicitis, which necessitated another operation. Then, late in the summer, gaunt and wasted, he appeared in the office of Milt Kraft, who at the time was overseer of a government housing project that was about to get under way in San Diego, and asked for work as an unskilled laborer. "When Archie came to see me, he was so weak he could barely stand," says Kraft, who now owns a wholesale sporting-goods business in San Diego. "Three different kids who were working for me put in a word for him, separately. They all said he was sickly but a good worker. 'Don't worry about this guy—we'll see that his work gets done,' they said, but I didn't want it that way. If I hired a man, he had to be able to do a job, to pull his own load. Archie obviously wasn't in shape for heavy work, but I decided to find something for him. You don't turn away a man when three people speak up for him. When that happens, the fellow is pretty sure to be something special. I had an opening for a nightwatchman, and I offered the job to Archie. We had a big trailer camp where the workers were going to live, and about 550 empty trailers to look after. I gave Archie a key to one of the trailers, and told him to lie down and rest. I asked only one thing—he'd have to get out every hour during the night and check the trailer area. 'I'll do anything,' he said. 'I'm desperate.' " Moore had been on the job about a week when Kraft began receiving reports of strange activity in the trailer camp. People in the neighborhood complained of a phantom runner in the night, and, investigating, Kraft found Moore jogging along among the trailers as he made his rounds. "My association with Archie was the most inspiring experience of my life," Kraft says. "I've never seen a man with such determination. Here was Archie, down on his luck, a physical wreck, the doctors telling him he would never fight again—yet he was positive in his own mind that he'd become a champion."

Kraft and Moore soon became firm friends, and the fighter

got into the habit of reporting early for work each evening. "Archie came early because he wanted to talk," says Kraft. "He told me about himself and he wanted to know about me. Somebody told him I had won the national bait-and-fly-casting championship in 1939, and he began examining me like a trial lawyer. He had to know everything about me. He asked me if I had been confident before the tournament, if I had been sure I was going to win. He wanted to know at what point I became sure of myself, whether I had been afraid or excited. I told him I had been very confident, and positive that I would finish high among the leaders. That made his eyes shine. He told me, 'Mr. Kraft, I feel exactly the same way. I'm absolutely certain I'll be champion of the world someday.' "

Many years later, after Moore had indeed become champion of the world, the two men went fishing on the Colorado River, in California. It was the first time Moore had ever held a casting rod. Kraft showed him how to grip it and where to throw the plug. "When he reeled it in, he had *two* bass, weighing two pounds apiece," Kraft says, smiling happily at the memory. "Imagine catching two bass with one cast the first time you wet a hook! A man who can do that can do anything."

Moore, disqualified for military service because of his two operations, returned to the ring early in 1942, and won his first five fights by knockout, but it was not until 11 years and 54 knockouts later that he got a chance at a world's title, and by this time he was officially a light-heavyweight and was occasionally taking on heavyweights. He met Maxim, the light-heavyweight champion, in St. Louis on December 7, 1952, won a decisive victory on points, pocketed his $800, and shook hands with Doc Kearns. Prosperity was just around the corner. During the next 19 months, he won 13 fights, including two more with Maxim, and he was just beginning to get his share of the big money when, in the course of a routine physical examination for the California Athletic Commission before a scheduled bout with Frankie Daniels, in San Diego, in April, it was discovered that something was wrong with Moore's heart. The boxing world was stunned. The Daniel's fight, which was called off, was to have been a warmup for a bout at Las Vegas between Moore and Nino Valdes, who was then the No. 2 ranking heavyweight. Moore was ordered to bed in a San Diego hospital, and the diagnosis was confirmed by a heart specialist. The doctors held out little hope. Moore's heart ailment was organic; he would never fight again, and he would have to forfeit his championship.

Friends who visited him in the hospital at the time found him close to despair. "This is so cruel," he said, clenching his fists in anguish. "I've been fighting all these years and I've never made any real money. Now I've got a chance to cash in, and this happens." He turned away, rolling on his side to face the wall. For the first time that anybody could remember, he seemed utterly defeated.

Doc Kearns was the only person who didn't lose courage. With nothing to go on but faith in his fighter (the title "Doc" was conferred on him by Jack Dempsey, and not by a medical school), he convinced himself that Moore's heart condition was correctable. At any rate, he was certainly not going to accept the judgment of two local doctors as final. He obtained Moore's release from the San Diego hospital and flew with him to San Francisco to consult another specialist. The verdict there was the same: Moore had a heart murmur, and fighting was out of the question. Then Kearns, Moore, and a friend named Bob Reese— an automobile dealer from Toledo, Ohio—took off for Chicago, where they went to Arch Ward, sports editor of the *Chicago Tribune,* for advice. Ward himself, as they knew, was receiving treatment for a heart ailment, and he recommended that they see the Chicago specialist who was treating him. Once more the news was bad: Moore dare not fight; no commission would license him. Ward, who later died of a heart attack, wrote a column urging Archie to retire. Then Moore and Kearns decided to go to the Ford Hospital, in Detroit, for an examination by Dr. John Keyes, of the cardiology department. "Detroit was our last hope," Kearns recalls. "I'd been told that they had the greatest heart doctors in the world at the Ford Hospital. If they couldn't help Archie, I knew he was finished." Dr. Keyes' findings brought the sun up again for Moore and Kearns. The heart condition wasn't organic, after all; Moore had a fibrillation—an irregular heart rhythm that was correctable with medication. "They put me to bed, and I began receiving medication every two hours," Moore says. "This continued for four days. On the fifth day, I had another electrocardiogram, and the heartbeat was regular again. The doctor gave me a clean bill of health, and I got my walking papers."

A month and a half later, on May 2, 1955, Moore fought Valdes as scheduled, in the Las Vegas ball park. Many of Moore's friends thought that he was foolish to fight so soon after recovering from a heart ailment, and some sports columnists were ghoulishly speculating that he might die in the ring; they warned the Nevada State Athletic Commission against assuming responsibility for the bout. Sports writers arriving in Las Vegas a couple of days before the fight found Moore exercising before a paying audience in a ballroom above the Silver Slipper gambling casino. He looked terrible. Free to enter the ring at whatever his weight happened to be on the day of the fight, he had allowed himself to balloon to 200 pounds, and he was in such poor shape that he had difficulty lasting three minutes with a sparring partner. He spat out his mouthpiece after 30 seconds in the ring, because he could barely get his breath. The fight itself was scheduled for 15 rounds. When it began, Valdes was as trim as a panther, and Moore looked like the winner of a pie-eating contest. Silhouetted against the evening sky, he shuffled about the ring, his long trunks flopping in the breeze. He landed a few blows and was clearly exerting himself as little as possible. The crowd began to jeer him, and Valdes steadily piled up a lead on points. Then, starting in the eighth round, the old man suddenly became the aggressor. He began scoring with his left hook, he jolted the Cuban with right-hand leads, and now and then he banged Valdes with stinging combinations. It became obvious that Moore was using the bout as a training fight—that this was merely the first step in his preparations for bigger bouts later in the year, with Olson and Marciano. As the contest progressed, Moore became stronger and Valdes faded. There were scattered boos when the referee, Jim Braddock, who was the only official, awarded the decision to Moore, but most of the working press at ringside agreed with Braddock.

Seven weeks later and 25 pounds lighter, Moore defended his light-heavyweight championship against Olson at the Polo Grounds, and knocked him out in three rounds. In September, back up to 188 pounds, Moore attempted to take the heavyweight title away from Rocky Marciano, at the Yankee Stadium, and succeeded in flooring him with a short right uppercut in the second round, but Marciano got up and pounded Moore down and out in the ninth. (A year or so later, the two were reminiscing about the fight, and Marciano said, "When you had me down in the second round there, Archie, it was too close." Moore replied graciously, "Rocky, it's like I've always said—it was a pleasure to fight you.") Marciano never fought again. The next spring—in April, 1956—he announced his retirement from the ring, and on November 30th of the same year Moore and Floyd Patterson, who had been adjudged the ranking contenders, met in the Chicago Stadium for the vacant title. Moore's best fighting weight is between 182 and 185 pounds, but he came into the ring at 196 pounds, looking like a Buddha in boxing gloves. He was 39 (or 42) years old. Patterson, at a trim 182¼ and 21 years old, knocked him out in the fifth round with a looping left hook that Moore, normally an extremely clever defensive fighter, should have avoided easily. It was probably the worst performance of Moore's career, but when the writers trooped into his dressing room after the fight, he received them with his customary aplomb. Instead of sulking, he stood on a bench and courteously answered questions during a long interview, but his lame explanation that he was overtrained obviously failed to satisfy the critics. Nevertheless, when the inquisition finally ended, he thanked the writers for their time and their company. "God bless you, Archie, you're wonderful!" shouted the late Caswell Adams, then boxing writer for the *New York Journal-American.* Boxing writers are a cynical breed and seldom applaud anybody, but this time they cheered.

For all Moore's popularity with the sports writers and with other students of boxing, who were aware of his artistry from his early days, the public regarded him as just another good colored fighter, though one with a flair for publicity, up until three years ago. He was suspected of being something of a fraud—a glib con man who, incidentally, could punch. Then after 22 years of struggling for recognition, he suddenly became a celebrity. The transformation came on the night of December 10, 1958, in Montreal, when Moore was pitted against a brawling 29-year-old Canadian fisherman named Yvon Durelle. For the official weigh-ing-in ceremonies at the Montreal Forum, Moore showed up wearing a homburg and a midnight-blue shawl-collared tuxedo, and carrying a silver-headed cane. The fight mob was transfixed. "I'm only trying to give boxing a touch of class," Moore explained. "Why, Durelle, there, is dressed like a farmer!" Moore got his deserts a short time later, when Durelle nearly slaughtered him in the first round. He knocked Moore down three times then, and once more in the fifth, but Moore somehow weathered the merciless beating, outlasted his younger opponent, and, in the eleventh round, battered him unconscious. It was as wild and savage a spectacle as anything that has been seen in the television era of boxing, and it did more for the Mongoose than any other victory or combination of victories in his long, improbable career. For the first time, he had earned the respect, affection, and sympathy of the public. Instead of a personification of bravado and bluster, the public saw a resourceful and cunning fighter of surpassing grace and skill, a man of fierce pride, a man with a special kind of valor. There was a certain majesty about him, and when the end finally came, and Moore's hand was raised in tribute to the hundred and twenty-seventh knockout of his career, the emotion of the crowd was so powerful as to be almost overwhelming.

When Moore crashed to the canvas for the third time in the first round, no one would have blamed him if he had called it a night. Instead, he recalls, he regarded himself with cool detachment ("I asked myself, 'Can this be me? Is this really happening to me?' ") and set about redeeming himself. He got through the first round largely on instinct, and from then on he fought with all the guile and mastery he had acquired through the years. At the end of the fifth round, when he had been knocked sprawling a fourth time, Doc Kearns wouldn't let him sit down but told him to stand there in his corner and wave to his wife in the audience. Moore couldn't see her, but he waved anyway, and Durelle, across the ring, thought Moore was waving at *him*, disdainfully. It took the heart out of Durelle, and from then on Moore was in charge. Durelle wilted completely in the eleventh round, and as referee Jach Sharkey stood over him, completing the count of 10, Moore, according to Doc Kearns, was calling to the prostrate challenger, "Please get up, Yvon! I got up for you!"

All in all, it was probably the most violent and taxing night of Moore's life, but when they put a microphone before him and trained in the television cameras, he sounded as though he had been taking tea with the Governor-General. "I enjoyed the fight very much," he said. "I am happy everybody was satisfied with it." Later in the evening, when the furor in the dressing room had quieted, Archie behaved like an actor on opening night, waiting impatiently for the early editions. "Was it a good action show?" he asked a friend who had dropped in. Assured that it had been the hit of the season, he said, "I'm glad I gave them a good show. At my age and at this stage of the game, I just *had* to win!"

In 1959, largely as a result of his astonishing rally against Durelle, Moore was voted the boxing world's equivalent of the Pulitzer prize—the Edward J. Neil Memorial Trophy as the fighter of the year—and on the occasion of its presentation he was given the full treatment as a newly arrived celebrity. The ceremony, which took place in the course of a banquet at the Waldorf-Astoria, was, of course, one of the grander moments of his life. When Moore got up to accept his award, instead of going directly into his speech, he looked out into the banquet audience and requested permission to make an introduction. Then he asked Durelle to rise. "It takes two to make a fight," he said. Until then, few of the guests had realized that Durelle was in the room. From this time on, Moore was in great demand at public functions, and as the banquet season progressed, his account of the Montreal fight became increasingly entertaining. He would describe in rich and dramatic detail for his various audiences the thoughts that passed through his mind while Sharkey was counting over him. As he elaborated on this fascinating theme, it often seemed that he must have been on the floor for hours instead of seconds. One version began, "I was lying there and I said to myself, 'This is no place to be resting. I'd better get up and get with it.' Every time I looked up, I looked into Sharkey's face. I got tired of looking at that man." Another version featured his eldest daughter, Rena, then just over a year old. "When Durelle knocked me down the first time," Archie related, "I had a peculiar idea. I remembered that I had left my baby, Rena, on the bed at the hotel. She was wearing red pajamas. I was dazed by the punch, and I got the idea that if I didn't get up somebody was going to take those red pajamas away from her. I loved to see Rena in those red pajamas, and I didn't want anybody taking them away. So I got up."

The American Broadcasting Company sent Moore an unedited film of the famous evening, complete with commercials and curtain speech, and one evening Moore, in a darkened room at the Salt Mine, watched it for the first time, with immense enjoyment. As he saw himself on the canvas after the first knockdown, a pathetic figure groping in a shadowy world as he desperately tried to regain his balance, Moore jeered, "Look at the poor guy. He can't even find the floor." When Durelle dropped him for the third time, Moore seemed faintly amused. He watched himself clutching at the ropes and trying to get up before Sharkey's count reached 10. "Now he's so dazed he can't even find the ropes," said Moore, with a soft chuckle. When the lights went up, however, he seemed thoughtful. "That guy belted me so hard he knocked out my bridge," he said. "And my elbow was sore where I fell on it. Being hit like that isn't much fun. It won't happen again—not if I can help it."

The two fighters met again in August of 1959, and Moore knocked Durelle out in three rounds. The champion is a great one for putting away an opponent as soon as the opportunity

presents itself. "In this game, you have to be a finisher," he says.
"I call it 'finishing,' and you don't learn it in Miss Hewitt's school
for young ladies."

Moore is acutely aware of his special position as a champion—and, more particularly, as a Negro champion. "A Negro
champion feels he stands for more than just a title," he says
gravely. "He is a symbol of achievement and dignity, and it is
tough to be a loser and let down a whole race." In 1959, not long
after the Durelle fight, Sam Goldwyn, Jr., invited Moore to try
out for the role of Jim, the runaway slave, in a movie version of
The Adventures of Huckleberry Finn. Both Moore and his wife
were leery of what they called "handkerchief-head parts," and a
Negro publication cautioned him against taking an "Uncle Tom"
role, but he proceeded with the screen test, was offered the part,
and signed a contract with Goldwyn. Moore is unconscionably
proud of the fact that he won the role in competition with professional actors as well as amateurs. (Among the latter was Sugar
Ray Robinson, who was then the middleweight boxing champion.
"Ray lost the part because he was too sleek," said Archie. "They
didn't have sleek slaves in those days.") Moore has boasted about
how, although he was training for a title fight at the time, he
memorized a 16-page script for his screen test and went before
the cameras after only one rehearsal. The way he tells it, his
performance in the test alone entitled him to an Oscar. At the
end of the scene, as he recalls it, the professionals on the set—
electricians, stagehands, and the like—broke into spontaneous
applause. "Tears came from the directors eyes," says Archie.
"Goldwyn was dabbing his eyes and shaking his head in wonder.
An electrician told me it was only the second time in 30 years
that he had seen such emotion during a test." However accurate
these recollections may be, the director of the movie, Michael
Curtiz, appears to agree with Moore's own estimate of his talent.
"Archie has instinctive acting ability," said Curtiz. "He seems to
know just the right inflection to give a line, and his facial expressions are marvelous."

When Moore first saw the script of the movie, he noted that
the offensive word "nigger" appeared in it now and again, but he
said nothing about this until the part was his and the contract
signed. Then he began maneuvering. "I'm not a clever man, but I
know how to get things done," he said later. "The script used the
word 'nigger' at least nine times. I went through it with a pencil
and struck out the word everywhere I found it. Then I took it up
with Mr. Goldwyn. I told him I couldn't play the part unless he

would agree to the deletions. I told him, 'You are a young man, Mr. Goldwyn, and times are changing. How could I play this part when it would cause my people to drop their heads in shame in a theater?' Goldwyn thought about it and he agreed with me. He ordered the deletions. The man who wrote the script was furious; his anger meant nothing to me. I had saved my people from embarrassment." (Actually, the word was used only once in the movie, and then when Moore was off camera.)

During the filming of the picture, Moore's career was the subject of a program in the television series *This Is Your Life,* broadcast from a studio in Burbank. Since surprising the honored biographee is the cream of this show's jest, Moore was not told what was in store for him but was whisked away from the *Huckleberry Finn* set with the explanation that he was needed at Burbank for some publicity shots. He had grown a stubble beard for the part, and, being vain about his appearance, he was momentarily thrown off stride when he realized that he was being seen on television screens all over the country in this woefully unbarbered condition. By the time some of his cronies got a chance to tease him about it, though, he had recovered his aplomb, and retorted, "Us slaves can't afford razor blades."

Moore the character actor became quite a lion at Hollywood cocktail parties during the period, and on one occasion a determined actress shouldered her way through a swarm of publicity men, actors' representatives, and newspaper people surrounding him and demanded his attention. "Archie, there's something I must know, and I must have an honest answer," she declared in a compelling voice. "What was your greatest thrill—getting a starring role in *Huck Finn* or winning the championship?"

Moor seemed surprised. "Why, it was winning the championship, of course."

The woman persisted, "But you're an *actor* now, remember that."

"I am a fighter," he said softly. "A fighter first, last, and always."

After the whole Hollywood episode was over, an old friend asked him why—aside from the monetary reward, which was far from negligible—he had got so wound up in the part of Jim. "I wanted to prove that I could act without losing any dignity," he said. "I don't agree with those who said the role belittled the Negro. Slavery was a fact at the time; there's no escaping that. Jim had something to say that was important even for today. He was a man searching for freedom. This man Jim is really every man who is trying to be free. Jim is spiritually free, but he yearns to be free physically, so he can buy his wife and his two children out of slavery. Every man wants to be free in a different way. Jim is just one in the long history of man's struggles to be free."

For all his eloquence about Jim, Moore has seldom made an issue of his color, and, unlike baseball's Jackie Robinson, say, has not been known as a supporter of the National Association for the Advancement of Colored People and allied causes. For this reason, many of his admirers were surprised when, seizing the microphone after his Madison Square Garden victory over Rinaldi, he used the prize ring as a platform for endorsing both the NAACP and the Freedom Riders. He announced, with some 19,000,000 people listening, that he was donating $1,000 of his purse to the Freedom Riders, another $1,000 to the United Fund in San Diego, and a $500 lifetime membership to B'nai B'rith, and was also purchasing a $500 lifetime membership in the NAACP. Certain fight fans, particularly in the South, wondered where he had got the idea, and whether he has been coached. A man who has known Moore for a long time asked him later on whether the incident had simply been an impulse of the moment. "I wouldn't be telling the truth if I said it was an impulse," Moore replied. "I'd thought about it. This has been brewing inside me for a long time. I knew what I wanted to do. Of course, I always rough out my speech before a fight, because I always anticipate victory." He smiled. Then he was asked whether the idea had been his own. "Nobody puts words in my mouth!" he said sharply. With less heat, he added, "Let me tell you how I feel about this. As a colored champion, I have a responsibility to my race. I have a minor voice. So long as I have popularity, I can make my voice heard, though that isn't always enough. Joe Louis had great popularity, but he wasn't articulate. Some of my white friends were surprised when I spoke out, because they know I am not a militant man—they know I am not militant outside the ring. But they know the depth of my feelings. I read something not long ago that expresses what I believe. The writer said, 'He who would deny one person freedom does not himself deserve freedom.' I believe that. I knew I would vex certain people, but it didn't matter. In my own way, I will do whatever I can that is right, because right will always stand."

Some years ago, Moore and one of his numerous newspaper friends were returning to San Diego together after watching an afternoon boxing card in the bull ring at nearby Tijuana, Mexico. They had gone to the fights separately, and met there by chance, whereupon Moore had insisted on driving his friend back to San Diego in his Cadillac. The newspaperman soon noticed that Moore was strangely moody and subdued. They drove for several miles in silence, and then Moore remarked, "A fellow called me a nigger today." Startled, his companion kept quiet and waited for Moore to continue. "I heard there was some property for sale near the Salt Mine, and a friend drove me over to take a look," he said. "We were driving around the property, looking for the owner, when we saw a watchman coming toward us. We waited. The watchman wanted to know what we were doing on private property. Trying to break the ice, my friend said to the watchman, 'Archie Moore lives around here; do you know him?' The watchman said, 'Oh, yeah, I know him; he's just another nigger to me.' My friend was shocked. I've had my place, the Salt Mine, in that area for quite a while, and he figured everybody knew me. I think he was afraid I might jump out of the car and shake that fellow, or something. Then he said to the watchman, 'I've got a man here I want you to meet—this is Archie Moore.' The fellow gulped. I mean I could *see* him gulp. I sat there and looked at him. Here was a man who looked like he was past 60; he had lived all his life with no respect for a Negro. I wondered how a man could be so ignorant. The watchman recognized me, and then he was trembling. He said, 'If you wanted to, I guess you could get out of that car and knock me down.' I didn't want to hit him. I felt compassion for him. I told him, 'No, I don't want to hurt you; I wouldn't waste my time. I just feel sorry for you, Mister. I offer you my sympathy.'"

The long left hook that knocked out Archie Moore for the sixth time in his career and made Floyd Patterson the heavyweight champion of the world was photographed by movie and television and newspaper cameras from almost every conceivable angle. Patterson had clearly put the last ounce of his enormous punching power into the blow, and it stretched Moore out flat on the canvas. It seemed impossible to the crowd that he could get up before the count of 10, but he did—at nine—only to go down again under a flurry of punches. He struggled to his feet a second time, but referee Frank Sikora, convinced that Moore was through, stopped the fight. As the days went on, gossip began to arise in the boxing world to the effect that Moore had taken a dive. Not long ago, a visitor to Moore's home in San Diego asked him about it. They were sitting over a pot of coffee in his rumpus room, where Moore had been writing letters—mostly to newspapermen, with whom he carries on a steady correspondence.

(He takes particular pleasure in composing letters to Red Smith, the *Herald Tribune* sports columnist, but for reasons known only to himself he always addresses them "Mr. Red Smith, care of Mr. Al Buck, *New York Post,*" Al Buck being another sports columnist.) Stationery and envelopes were scattered about the floor, the mouth organ music of Jimmy Smith was emerging softly from Moore's hi-fi set, and the Big Bopper, the resident sparring partner of the moment, was dozing in a chair at the far end of the room. Moore poured a cup of coffee for his guest before replying. "It was one of the worst beatings of my life, but it was on the level," he said. "I didn't dump the fight. I strongly resent all this whispering, too. It's been said I took a dive because I had bet on Floyd. Well, it takes at least two to make a bet. If the man I bet with will come forward, I will be glad to meet him for the first time. If I had beaten Patterson, I would have been both the heavyweight and the light-heavyweight champion. Don't you suppose I could make more money with the title than by selling out in one fight? Forget my pride for a moment and look at this objectively. The odds weren't right for a gambling coup. I was a 6-to-5 favorite. The odds didn't change. If you rule out money, what other reason would there be for me to take a dive? I lost that fight because I was being harassed by a Cleveland woman at the time and I was upset. I lost because I got ready too soon. If the fight had been held three days earlier, I would have been the champion. The worst mistake a fighter can make is to come along too fast."

The talk turned to the Valdes fight, and Moore was asked how long he thought he could get away with, in effect, using men as dangerous as that for sparring partners. Moore reflected a moment, and then replied obliquely. "They wonder how an old fighter like me can keep going," he said. "The secret, my friend, is experience. I learned many things in my youth, and these are the things I have going for me now. Naturally, I fought Valdes with a plan. I've always had an uncanny sense of pace. In all my years as a fighter, I've been forced out of my pace only twice. The first time was in 1940, when I was fighting Shorty Hogue in San Diego. I had banged him up pretty fierce, and a kind referee would have stopped it. I thought he was hurt real bad and I got careless; I abandoned my plan of action and tried to finish him. He caught me with a sucker punch, then he rallied in the last two rounds, and they gave him the decision. Marciano was the other fighter who forced me out of my pace. He was so strong, so difficult to hurt. I hit him with punches that would have knocked out any other fighter, but he kept on coming. I wanted to box, but I had to slug it out to keep him from killing me. They asked me if Marciano was the greatest fighter I ever met, and I don't know how to reply. I don't want to seem ungenerous—but it is well to remember that I was 38 when I boxed Marciano."

Moore went on to say that, pound for pound, Henry Armstrong, the former welterweight champion, was the best fighter he had ever seen in the flesh, but that the boxer he most admired was the late Jack Johnson, who held the heavyweight championship from 1908 until 1915. Moore had recently seen a film of the 1909 fight between Johnson and Stanley Ketchel, which ended in a twelfth-round knockout by his hero. "Johnson knocked out Ketchel as easily as I would toss a ball out a window," he said. "Believe me, he would be something in these days and times. Johnson loved to punish a man; he got a great pleasure from it. He was a counterpuncher, and he got the most out of a minimum of effort. He was a master of the art of self-defense, and there have been very few masters."

In due course, the conversation got around to the current crop of fighters, and it developed that Moore has his own way of estimating their worth. According to him, there are old-old fighters, old-young fighters, and old fighters who stay young forever. It isn't hard to imagine where Moore fits himself into this scheme. He described Ingemar Johansson, the Swedish heavyweight, as a 10-year fighter. (This was after Johansson had won the heavyweight title from Patterson and then lost it in a rematch.) "The Swede is a 10-year fighter, but that takes in his entire career, including his amateur fights," said Moore. He was reminded that Johansson had already been fighting 10 years. "Yes, I know," Moore said. Since there has been talk of a fight between Moore and Johansson, possibly in Goteborg, Sweden, and possibly in Philadelphia, Moore's guest said he'd been wondering if Johansson could make much trouble for him. "No, I'm afraid not," said Moore. "The Mongoose knows too much."

His guest asked Moore how he expects to be remembered by boxing historians, and the thought seemed to excite the champion. He said he wanted to make a statement, and wanted it taken down verbatim. This is what he dictated: "After 26 years, it is more and more apparent there never has been a perfect fighter and there never will be. It might be said in years to come that there was the Will-o'-the-Wisp—meaning Willie Pep. There was the Saccharinated—meaning Ray Robinson. There was the magnificent Benny Leonard and Joe Gans, before our time. The

Wisp, the Sweet One, they both have the marks and have
suffered the wounds of the club fighter. More especially, Sweet
Raymond has undergone several facial liftings and eyebrow
archings. But there are still some of the writers who want to be
identified with this era who swear by the beard of the false
prophet that these were the only two gladiators. Meanwhile the
Merry Mongoose, after more than 213 battles, fighting men in
their time who were rated and qualified practitioners of the art of
boxing, have suffered no more hurts than wounded feelings and
only a quarter-inch scar between the eyebrows by being anxious
to see what damage, if any, he had done to Floyd Patterson, by
looking up suddenly and then incurring a butt—this is the only
mark Moore has garnered in 26 years of boxing. Will-o'-the-Wisp,
Sugary One—ring immortals? Poppycock—you can have them!"
Moore got up and paced the floor for a few moments, and the
Big Bopper stirred in his slumber. Then the Mongoose's mood
changed, and he was off on a lecture about "breathology" and
"escapeology." "Very few fighters know how to breathe properly
nowadays," he said earnestly. "Breathology is an art I mastered
many years ago, and it still serves me well. It served me very well
in my second fight with Willi Besmanoff. I didn't get him until
the tenth, but I got him. The punch that did it was something
quite special. You may have thought it was just an overhand
right, but that punch was delivered at a 90-degree angle and
it had 500 pounds of pressure per square inch. It traveled eight
inches and had enough pressure to drop a Missouri mule. I bent
his horn and got his undivided attention! Now, against Rinaldi I
used the technique of Applied Muscular Tension. By feinting and
moving according to a predetermined plan, I exhausted the
Italian from muscular tension. I myself was unaffected by muscular tension, because my moves were calculatedly relaxed—
oily and easy. It's all in knowing the art of escapeology. Some of
the boxing writers were critical of Rinaldi because he was as
awkward as an amateur, punching wildly and without any plan.
All that could be part of the cleverness of Moore. Please keep in
mind that even the great Marciano missed me 39 consecutive
times, though he finally caught up with me, aided and abetted by
the law of averages."

The hour was late, and Moore's guest stood up to leave, but
Moore detained him long enough to say, "One of these days, the
law of averages, or maybe the law of gravity, will catch up with
me. I can't last forever. I've been thinking about how I want to
go. I want to be respected. When I'm finished, I want people to

say only one thing of me. I want them to say, 'There goes a man.'" At the door, he added, "When I retire, I'm going to write a book in my own hand, and the last chapter will be entitled 'The Prolonged Sunset.' I've been looking at the sun for a long time, but it still hangs there on the horizon. When it goes down, it will go all of a sudden."

1962

TEN TERRIBLE DAYS

By Elwyn (Bud) Myers

FROM OUTDOOR LIFE

Copyright © 1962, Popular Science Publishing Co.

For the past 30 years the hunting story has been a popular segment of Best Sports Stories. *Elwyn Myers, the author, and his guide managed to get themselves lost in western Ontario after beaching their boat to hunt for moose. A severe snow storm, the loss of their clothing, tent, matches, and compass combined to make this an intriguing adventure which instituted one of the biggest air and land hunts that Canada had ever launched.*

I want to say something right at the beginning that has been said 1,000 times before, but I want to say it louder: don't ever leave camp or walk off a trail in wild country without a map, compass, and matches in a waterproof container.

My ordeal started out as a moose hunt that promised to be about as dangerous as a game of Ping-Pong. It turned into a life-and-death affair, and death almost won.

I got out of high school at Pentwater, Michigan, in 1953, out of the Marines in 1957, and out of Central Michigan University in June of 1961. I had a job waiting in the fall with the Fish and Wildlife Service, and I also had plans to get married in about a year.

I had hunted since I was a kid—foxes, deer, partridges, and ducks—I loved it. All along, however, I wanted to go to Canada for a moose. With the job and the girl in the offing, I concluded the fall of 1961 might be my last chance for quite a spell.

I picked the area northeast of Lake of the Woods, in western Ontario, left Pentwater on Wednesday, October 25, drove 28 hours, and reached the town of Vermilion Bay, 50 miles east of Kenora, before noon the next day.

I had reservations at a hunting camp, but I learned that an early freeze had forced it to close three days before. So here I was, 1,000 miles from home, all set for my first moose hunt, with no place to go. On the advice of a restaurant counterman, I got in touch with Archie Webb, who operates a bush-flying service, does some outfitting, and maintains tent camps on a few remote lakes. We made arrangements in a hurry. Webb would fly me to Portal Lake, 35 or 40 miles to the north, for a four-day hunt. He'd supply a guide, tent, boat, sleeping bags, and the rest of the gear. We wrapped it all up and in two hours were airborne.

Archie landed at McIntosh, on the Canadian National Railroad, to pick up guide Tom Strong, a local Indian, 31 years old, who had lived all his life in the area and knew it well. Quiet, he looked and acted capable, and I liked him from the start.

From McIntosh we flew to a small lake where Webb had a tent camp, and he left us there for the night. Next day he moved us and the camp to Portal Lake, setting us down shortly after noon. We got the gear ashore and Archie gunned his plane off the water, leaving the guide and me with a good outfit, plenty of provisions, and a big chunk of roadless bush. Webb would fly over every day or so, check to make sure things were okay, and fly my moose out if I was lucky.

The sun was up when Tom nudged me awake next morning, Saturday. "Look out the flap," he said. A big cow moose was standing at the edge of the lake about 40 yards away. I could have killed her without leaving my sack, but I hadn't come to Canada to get a moose that way; besides, I wanted a good head for mounting.

I had a hard case of moose fever by the time she wandered back into the woods, and we didn't wait for breakfast. We paddled the 12-foot aluminum boat down the lake, spotting two more cows but no moose with horns. Finally we went back to camp for breakfast.

The morning was so still that Tom was sure if there were bull moose knocking their antlers against trees we'd hear them. "All cows here," he said.

When we finished eating he proposed a hike to a small bog lake he knew about. It was only two miles away, and we'd be back in time for lunch. "Lots of bulls back in there," he said.

We paddled across the lake, pulled the boat up on shore, and left it there. That probably saved our lives.

The idea of making any special preparations never entered my mind. We'd be gone only a few hours, the guide had been to the place before, and it was a fine, warm October day. There was no reason to think about survival gear.

We were both lucky in our clothing. I was wearing light underwear, a sweatshirt, cotton shirt, wool vest, insulated hunting pants, an army field jacket, fur cap, two pairs of sweat socks, and thermal rubber boots. Strong had on long underwear, two shirts, two pairs of pants, a wool jacket and cap, and low rubber pacs over two pairs of wool socks. By sheer accident I had a pair of wool mittens in my pocket. Tom was less fortunate on that score. Paddling, he used only one glove, and that was all he had with him.

I carried my .30/06 converted Springfield and eight shells. I also had a hunting knife and binoculars. Strong had a few kitchen matches and I was carrying some paper matches. We had maybe a dozen between us, enough for a cigarette now and then.

We reached the bog lake in less than an hour and found fresh tracks. The place looked good, so we waited. The clear, warm day was changing now. The sky turned overcast and a raw wind came up. When we started to get cold the guide suggested we head for camp. We'd go back another way, he said, to keep out of muskeg and swamp. We crossed a ridge and struck into the bush. The sky was getting darker, the wind was blowing harder, and soon it began to snow, a blinding squall of big wet flakes that whitened the ground fast. We walked an hour, and I expected to see Portal Lake any minute. Then we came over the top of a ridge and looked down on the bog lake we had just left.

I had heard about men walking in circles, but I found it hard to believe we had done it. There was no doubt about it, however, so we turned back and trudged away once more. We walked two hours that time, broke out of a dense swamp, and stared in disbelief at the bog lake.

"I walk circles," Tom grunted. "You try."

So I took the lead, lining up one tree with another. In about an hour we came out on a smaller lake we had not seen before.

"I here last fall," the guide assured me. "Camp that way," and he drew a crude map in the snow with a stick. But after two more hours of hard hiking we came back to the same spot and found our own tracks. When we tried again, the same thing happened.

Once more I took the lead, and we did not see that lake

TERPSICHORE IN TRIPLICATE by Joe DeNarie, *San Francisco Examiner*. Joe DeNarie made this shot 30 years ago for his paper, from which he retired some years ago. He now is in the real-estate business in San Rafael, California. (Copyright © 1944, *San Francisco Examiner*)

THE OLD SCHOOL TRY by Jack Frank, *New York Herald Tribune*. Home-plate play in New York City Public Schools' Athletic League championship game between Grover Cleveland High School and Samuel Tilden High. Cleveland won and Frank received first prize with the shot in the Press Photographers' Association exhibit. (Copyright © 1945, *New York Herald Tribune*)

DEATH TAKES A WINNER by Carl E. Franks, *Cedar Rapids* (Iowa) *Gazette*. In this split-second photo, death has already struck the driver whose car is end up. The race took place at Cedar Rapids and the victim, who won this race, has just hit a car he had lapped, thus causing the accident. (Copyright © 1946, Carl E. Franks)

THE CATCH by Harry Harris, *The Associated Press*. Bill Swiacki, Columbia's All-America end, making the catch in the Baker Field game that marked the end of the Army's winning streak of 32 games. He caught the ball five yards from the end zone, near the end of the game. Army was leading 20-14 at the time and Columbia went on to win 21-20. (Copyright © 1947, Associated Press)

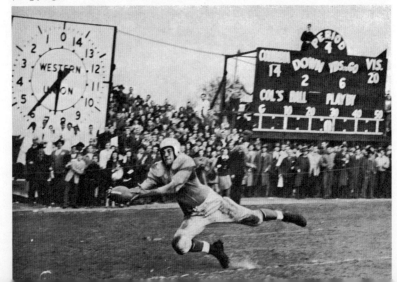

No. 3 by Nat Fein, *New York Herald Tribune*. This poignant and dramatic shot shows Babe Ruth's last appearance as a player in Yankee Stadium. It was a ceremonial day given to the "Bambino" in which many of his old teammates participated. (Copyright © 1948, *New York Herald Tribune*)

SOCK TREATMENT by Charles Hoff, *New York Daily News*. A tremendous punch thrown by Sugar Ray Robinson that paralyzes Kid Gavilan is depicted here as Sugar Ray held on to his welterweight title. (Copyright © 1949, *New York Daily News*)

DIRT EATER by Paul Siegel, *Minneapolis Star and Tribune.* The photographer has caught this unhappy player giving his all to Mother Earth in his attempt to steal a base. (Copyright © 1950, *Minneapolis Star and Tribune*)

AFTER THE BALL WAS OVER by Barney Stein, *New York Post*. After Ralph Branca, Dodger pitcher, had dealt out a "gopher ball" to Bobby Thompson to blow the pennant in the crucial play-off game, this scene was enacted in the Dodger dressing room. Lying on the steps overcome with grief is Branca, and sitting next to him, sharing his dejection, is coach Cookie Lavagetto. (Copyright © 1951, New York Post Corporation)

GLASSES FOR THE UMPIRE by Bob Campbell, *San Francisco Chronicle*. The unknown "Hilda" and her satiric thrust, the thumb of the umpire, and the bewilderment of the catcher all tend to make this picture irresistibly humorous and placed it a co-winner in the 1953 book. (Copyright © 1952, *San Francisco Chronicle*)

BEGINNING OF THE END by Harry Leder, *United Press International*. Rocky Marciano sends challenger Roland La Starza through the ropes in the eleventh round. One moment later he was acclaimed the victor by Ruby Goldstein, the third man in the ring. (Copyright © 1953, United Press International, Inc.)

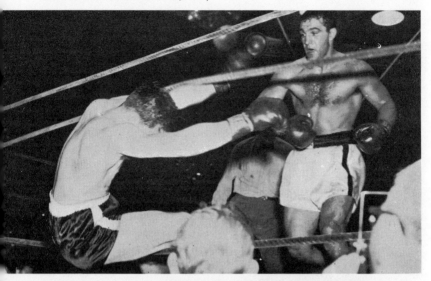

HEADS UP by Ernest Anheuser, *Milwaukee Sentinel*. This striking pose was created when Bobby Morgan of the Phils popped high into the air. The hopeful catcher, mask flying, is Del Crandall of the Braves, and the umpire is Frank Secory. (Copyright © 1954, *Milwaukee Sentinel*)

THE BITTER END by Andrew Lopez, *United Press International*. The light-heavyweight champ, Archie Moore, lies against the ropes, a helpless, beaten fighter. Rocky Marciano, the heavyweight titleholder, floored Moore four times during this bout and retained his title. (Copyright © 1955, United Press International, Inc.)

THE LAUREL FITS by Paul Maguire, *Boston Globe*. The Mayor of Boston in this unusal tribute keeps pace with the winner of the yearly Boston marathon and bestows a laurel upon his brow. (Courtesy of the *Boston Globe*. Copyright © 1956, *Boston Globe*)

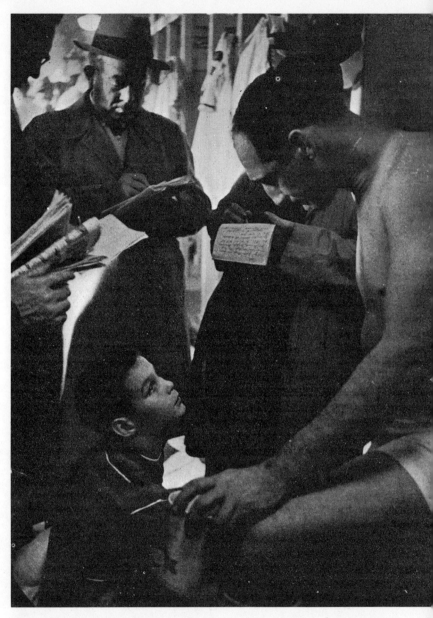

THAT'S MY POP by Art Rickerby, *United Press International*. Hero worship by son for father is expressed by 8-year-old Gregory Spahn after his father, Milwaukee s Warren, won the fourth game of the World Series between the Braves and the Yankees. The photographer has caught his subjects at the perfect instant of rapport. (Copyright © 1957, United Press International, Inc.)

PRO-AMATEUR MISS by Joe Kordick, *Chicago Sun-Times*. Earl Torgeson goes all out after a foul ball, while Nellie White, also of the White Sox, takes in the proceedings. (Copyright © 1958, *Chicago Sun-Times*)

FOOTBALL BALLET by Howard Swift, *Des Moines Register and Tribune*. Pat Fischer, lightweight Nebraska halfback, hauls down Iowa State's Gale Gibson after he intercepted a pass. Nebraska won 7-6. (Copyright © 1959, *Des Moines Register and Tribune*)

FLYING HIGH by Ken Ross, *Memphis Press-Scimitar*. This extra jump availed little as Harry Smith, a PBA bowler, failed to get his strike and ran out of the top money. The photographer got the strike. (Copyright © 1960, *Memphis Press-Scimitar*)

OUT BY A FOOT by Frank Hurley, *New York Daily News*. This winning action shot graphically illustrates how Jimmy Piersall, Cleveland outfielder, put an end to the harassment of one of two tormentors who ran onto the field to express their antagonism. The wild scene took place at Yankee Stadium. (Copyright © 1961, *New York Daily News*)

AMERICAN BEAUTY by Ted Kell, *New York Herald Tribune*. The sun, waves, wind, and Mr. Kell all conspired to be at the right place and the right time to catch this honey of a picture. It depicts the American yacht *Weatherly* in action against the Australian boat *Gretel*. (Copyright © 1962, New York Herald Tribune, Inc.)

HEAD HUNTER by Niels Lauritzen, *Milwaukee Journal*. Night Train Lane, Detroit Lion back, brings Jim Taylor of the Green Bay Packers to earth with this turn-of-the-head tackle. The Lions held the Packers to a tie and helped Chicago capture the Western title of the National Football League. (Copyright © 1963, *Milwaukee Journal*)

I'M HAVING A BALL by Bob Doty, *Dayton Journal Herald*. This feature-winner picture was taken during a Cincinnati baseball game. Mr. Doty captured three first prizes in this anthology with his shots, which usually were in the feature class. (Copyright © 1964, *Dayton Journal Herald*)

A Stick-to-it-iveness by James R. Kilpatrick, *Detroit News*. Bobby Hull of the Chicago Black Hawks thrusts his stick out for a shot while taking a tumble. The ensuing tumble of Detroit's Doug Barkley and the power and dexterity of the great Hull demonstrate the speed and excitement of this sport. (Copyright © 1965, *Detroit News*)

When the Cheering Stopped by Bob Ray, *Nashville Banner*. There is nothing to cheer about for Cameron, West Virginia, which has just seen its basketball team beaten in the last few seconds of a state regional tournament. (Copyright © 1966, *Nashville Banner*)

DOUBLE DUTY by Paul J. Connell, *Boston Globe*. This amusing shot of Arthur Hill performing as a linesman and as a helping husband occurred during the National Women's Indoor Tennis Tournament in Winchester, Massachussetts. (Courtesy of the *Boston Globe*. Copyright © 1967, Globe Newspaper Company)

CATCH AS CATCH CAN by Charles L. Pugh, *Atlanta Journal-Constitution*. This shot shows a miraculous backhand catch of a pass. The receiver, No. 20, is Robby North of Tucker Hill High School in Atlanta. The unbelieving defender, No. 22 of Therrell High, tries mightily, but in vain as his school lost. (Copyright © 1968, *Atlanta Journal-Constitution*)

THE BATTERY IS FULLY CHARGED by Paul DeMaria, *New York Daily News*. Pictured here is the extreme elation of Jerry Koosman, the winning Met pitcher, who has jumped on his Met team catcher, Jerry Grote, after he beat Baltimore in the 1969 World Series. (Copyright © 1969, New York News Syndicate Company, Inc.)

A Lunge to Victory by Larry C. Graff, *Chicago Sun-Times*. Billie Jean King, world's No. 1 women's tennis player, stretches to return a volley in match with Australian Kerry Harris in tournament at Lake Bluff, Illinois. (Copyright © 1971, Newspaper Division, Field Enterprises, Inc.)

Expos' Last Stand by Jerry Rife, *San Diego Evening Tribune*. This eye-filling photo, winner in the action division, shows what baseball players sometimes have to go through to get away from a close pitch. His team, the San Diego Padres, lost a close one to the Montreal Expos in spite of Jim Gosger's histrionics at the plate. (Copyright © 1970, *San Diego Evening Tribune)*

CONFRONTATION OF THE GIANTS by John E. Biever, *Milwaukee Journal*. This winning action shot expresses perfectly what professional basketball is all about — size! Pictured here is Milwaukee's center, Kareem Abdul-Jabbar, jousting in midair with Wilt Chamberlain of the Lakers, both over seven feet in height. The action occurred in 1972 during an NBA Western Division play-off, won by the Lakers. (Copyright © 1972, John E. Biever. Reprinted by permission)

INNOCENT BYSTANDER by Bill Serne, *Tampa Tribune*. This is the winning action photo in *Best Sports Stories—1974*. It shows a misdirected punch thrown by Willie Cheney that connected with referee Lee Sala instead of opponent John Pinney. Sala was not hurt and Pinney went on to earn a split decision in the fight at Curtis Hixon Hall, Tampa, Florida. (Copyright © 1973, Tampa Tribune Company)

again. By late afternoon we were mixed up in a chain of lakes and ponds connected with channels winding through bogs.

An hour before dark we came to a large lake that Strong was sure he recognized. "Camp over there," he said, "beyond big swamp." We found the swamps and fought our way through, but by then it was getting dusk and we decided to camp for the night.

The snow had turned to rain and sleet, and everything was dripping. We had six matches left, some of them wet. We stripped bark off a birch tree, gathered half-dry wood from windfall, and Tom tried to get a fire going. He did—with our last match.

We built up a roaring blaze, dried our wet clothing, and gathered wood and green boughs for a bed. We slept fitfully, getting up often to replenish the fire. The storm let up before daybreak, but the morning was gray and cheerless with a cold wind. We had no food but found a few wintergreen berries, which we munched while debating the next move.

We faced a grave decision. With our matches gone, this would be our last fire. Should we stay beside the fire and wait for rescue or try to get back to camp? I hated to leave, but Tom insisted he knew how to get to Portal Lake, and in the end I gave in.

We had been without food for more than 24 hours, and when we spotted a grouse in a tree I concluded raw meat would be better than nothing. I tried to blow the bird's head off with the .30/06 but only cut a feather or two from its topknot. Shortly after that I did better on a snowshoe hare. We picked up the headless rabbit and took it along.

We walked the rest of that day without finding anything the guide recognized. An hour before dark we came to a chain of small lakes. "You know these?" I asked.

"Never see before," he admitted.

"Then we're really lost." He nodded gravely.

It was a tough thing to face. I'd heard and read about it but had never thought it would happen to me, and knowing we'd let ourselves in for it by our own mistakes didn't help any. Right then I'd have given a year of my life for a map and compass. We were trapped in country as wild and rough as any in western Ontario, all hills and swamps, lakes and streams, muskeg, beaver ponds, and windfalls. Twenty-odd miles south was the CNR, running east from Winnipeg to Sioux Lookout and through

Tom's home town of McIntosh. About the same distance east was
Highway 105, leading north from Vermilion Bay to Goldpines.
Tom and I both thought the road lay southeast of us rather than
east, however—a mistake that came close to finishing us.

We built a crude lean-to by propping logs against a ledge,
covering it with green boughs, and gathered more for a bed.
Then we tried to start a fire by shooting into a handful of birch-
bark shavings and a piece of crumpled paper from my wallet, but
we had no way to extract the bullet. The blast charred the paper
but blew away the shavings. Nothing ignited, and we realized we
could not make fire that way.

Next we tried to eat some of the raw rabbit, but it tasted too
strong and wild. Maybe we were not yet hungry enough. We
each managed two or three bites of fat but couldn't choke down
the unsalted lean and finally threw the whole thing away.

Snow began to fall at dark, and the night was bitterly cold.
We slept in snatches, getting up often to walk warmth into ourselves. We were undecided next morning whether to wait for
rescue or try to find our way out. I had flown enough to know
how slim our chances would be of being spotted from the air
without a fire, so in the end we walked away. But before we left
we laid four logs together to form a rectangle in an open place on
the rocks, with an arrow to point our direction. We were not able,
after that, to write signals in the snow because we could find no
open areas big enough that were free of brush and grass.

An hour after we left we found a blazed trail. Bark had been
chipped off trees and the scar marked with an S in red paint. We
figured the S meant south, so we followed the blazes in what we
thought was that direction.

That morning Archie Webb flew over our camp and noticed our boat on the shore across the lake from the tent. He
had seen it there the day before and went down to investigate.
He found the camp unused, our clothing still packed, no sign of
recent fire, and only the rifle missing. He taxied across the lake to
the boat, discovered old footprints leading into the bush, and
realized he had a pair of lost men on his hands. The boat, left
there on the shore, had touched off a prompt alarm. Webb flew
back to McIntosh, picked up an experienced Indian guide, Tom
Payash, and returned to Portal Lake to launch a search that was
to grow into one of the biggest and most intensive manhunts ever
carried out in that part of Canada.

Strong and I followed the blazes all day. Late in the afternoon we saw that they crossed a river rimmed with new ice. The

barrier was formidable, but we could see the blazes on the far side so we hunted along the bank until we found a log to cross on. It was under almost a foot of water and so slippery it seemed doubtful for footing, but we had no choice. We pulled off our boots and socks, for the first time in four days, and when I saw my feet I was scared. They were white and puckered and Tom's weren't much better. Unless we could get our feet out of the boots at night we were in for trouble.

We got poles for balancing, and I tied my boots around my neck, slung my rifle on one shoulder, and inched out on the log. It was like grease, but I kept going. When I was safe on the other side Tom followed. A mile farther on, the blazed trail petered out at the edge of a big marsh. That was as bad a letdown as I'd ever had.

We built a lean-to against an upturned stump and cut marsh grass for our bed. It was dry and warm, and our camp that night was one of the best we had. But now I had another reason to worry. Cutting boughs in the dusk, I'd sliced a finger to the bone. I tore off a strip of shirt for bandage, but it worked loose in the night and the cut was dirty and swollen next morning. It looked as if I might have an infected finger added to my other troubles.

We decided to follow the blaze line back. Maybe hunters had blazed it out from a fly-in cabin on a lake. That would mean shelter and fire. Starting at first light, we recrossed the river on the sunken log, and went on.

We had seen deer frequently, and I decided to kill the next one. We needed meat if we were to keep going, and more important maybe we could wrap our feet in the skin at night and get our socks partially dry. Late in the afternoon we saw a doe 60 yards away and shot her.

We stopped for the night and tried to eat some of the warm venison. Tom couldn't get the lean down but ate a few bites of the fat. I didn't like the unsalted stuff but ate a slice half as big as my hand and felt better.

That night we took our boots off for the first time and put our socks inside our shirts to dry, wrapping our bare feet in the deerskin, hairy side in. It was even warmer than we'd expected.

Our pants had been ripped from brush and windfalls, and wads of insulation were hanging out of mine. Next morning we sewed them up with strips of deer hide, but they soon tore again. When we left the lean-to, in a hard snowstorm, I carried a hindquarter of the doe and Tom was wearing the green skin around his shoulders.

In the early afternoon the blazed trail ended on the shore of a lake. The last blaze was a crude picture of a cabin, and for a little while we were sure we'd find the cabin nearby, but we searched in vain. I'd still like to know who blazed that apparently meaningless trail, and why they did it.

About an hour after we left the lake, a rifle shot rapped out in the distance. We listened, hardly daring to believe our ears. In the next few minutes two or three more shots followed. They seemed to come from all around us. Then, sounding from less than a mile away, two were fired in quick succession. Certain they were a signal, I touched off two quick ones in answer, and almost instantly we heard a single shot reply.

This was the first proof we'd had that a search was under way. We had heard distant aircraft a few times but never close enough to raise our hopes. Now, however, we felt sure that rescue was near.

Of the eight shells with which I had left camp, I had but two left and dared not risk them except as a last resort. We waited for another signal, but none came. We decided to go and met the searchers.

I was sure of the location of the last shots, but when Strong jerked a thumb and said, "Come from over there," he pointed in the opposite direction. For a second I lost my temper. "What's the matter with you? They came from that way."

Tom shook his head. "Over there," he said.

It was the only argument we had, and I knew better than to let it grow into a quarrel. If we separated I was certain at least one of us would wander until he died. "Okay," I said at last, "we'll try it your way." We'll never know which was right.

That morning Webb had enlisted the help of two more pilots, Ron Booi of North Star Camp on Clay Lake and Emile Mayling of Vermilion Bay. He had also flown a party of 12 ground searchers to Portal Lake, established a camp there, and put Walter Booi, owner of the North Star Camp, Ron's father and a veteran bush man, in charge. Then Webb, Ron, and Mayling began an air search that would eventually cover more than 1,000 square miles.

Ground searchers had fired the shots. At that moment we were hardly more than a mile from help, but we missed contact completely, and those were the last shots we heard. The next day the searchers gave up their firearms. Those in charge knew that shooting in an area where men are lost is likely to confuse them or even excite them to panic.

Strong and I walked three hours, stopping now and then to yell and wait hopefully for an answer, before we gave up. I'd never been more discouraged than I was right then, but there was greater disappointment to come.

We found a place to camp at the edge of a muskeg and were gathering dry grass when we heard the drone of a plane. The sound grew louder, and the plane came into sight just over the trees bordering thé marsh, flying low and less than 500 yards away.

We ran for the open muskeg, stripping off our coats, waving and screaming like madmen, but the aircraft kept its course. It was a small bush plane and we could see the pilot, but he did not see us. We watched until he went out of sight above the timber. I guess that was the worst disappointment I ever faced.

Before dark, a second aircraft came over, flying a little higher. Again we raced for the marsh, but again the plane flew on, passing directly over our heads. I said grimly to Tom, "That settles it. If we're going to get out at all we'll have to walk out on our own." I didn't admit even to myself that I wasn't sure we'd make it.

That night our feet were in better shape. Our socks, tucked inside our shirts, never really dried but were drier in the morning than when we lay down, and the deerskin was warm on our bare feet. I debated shooting a second deer so we'd each have a skin, but with only two shells left decided to wait.

The final days of our ordeal blurred into a nightmare of torment, wandering while daylight lasted and huddling under open shelters at night, shaking with cold. I kept my watch wound and tried to keep track of time, but I must have lost count because we were lost two days longer than I thought.

We were turning into gaunt scarecrows. When we broke ice for a drink, I studied my reflection in the black water and hardly knew myself. We grew weaker each day. I was eating a little raw venison. It was almost like cold cuts out of a refrigerator. I realized I was risking dysentery by eating raw meat, but that possibility was better than eating nothing. Tom had given up on it, however, and was in worse shape than I. Once, when we were crossing a big muskeg, he dropped so far behind he was barely in shouting distance. After that I was careful to watch and wait for him.

The quarter of doe meat froze so hard at last that we threw it away. Neither of us seemed hungry, and we told ourselves that if we needed more we could kill another deer. We didn't suffer much actual discomfort from lack of food, but I dreamed constantly of hot chicken dinners.

The cold and wet were far harder to bear. There were about five inches of snow on the ground, and the bogs and sluggish creeks, often flooded by beaver dams, were frozen over but not hard enough to hold us. In many places we broke through, occasionally sinking above our knees. Our boot laces were broken and knotted, our tattered and ice-caked pants flapped around our legs, and at night our wet clothing froze stiff. At first I had slept with my mittens on, but when they became soaked I drew my arms out of my sleeves and folded them inside. I had lost my fur cap the first day (I also lost my binoculars, but I don't know when) and at night I tied a red handkerchief around my head, pulled the jacket up over it, and buttoned it tight. Tom and I crowded close for warmth, each pressing his bare feet against the other inside the deerskin. But in spite of all we did the cold kept us awake, and the nights were long. As we grew weaker we slept more soundly, however, and toward the end the cold no longer bothered us much.

We didn't know it then, of course, but I have learned since from official Canadian weather records that the daytime temperature in the Kenora area never climbed much above 40 degrees the 10 days we were lost, that it was below freezing most of the time, and that the nights got down as low as 15 above.

My cut finger was swollen to bursting, but I had too much on my mind to worry about it. I wondered a lot about my family and my girl. I knew they'd be praying, waiting hopefully for the phone to ring, lying awake at night.

The tantalizing thought of our well-supplied tent was seldom out of my mind. I'm sure we were never more than 10 miles from it, most of the time much less. It was hard to realize we might die of cold and starvation so close to it. In fact, I never really admitted that possibility; I told myself over and over we'd get out somehow. I don't know what Tom thought, for he said little. His wife had been ready to go to the hospital to have a baby the day we left McIntosh, however, and he worried openly about her.

There were days when we walked in circles, coming back repeatedly to our own tracks. Each night we built our lean-to at the edge of an open marsh where we'd have a chance of being seen by aircraft. We saw or heard planes every day, but after the first sighting when the two flew overhead none came close.

The plight of lost men begets a peculiar kind of universal

pity. Certainly that was true in our case. We were headline news in cities 1,000 miles away, and the Canadians pressed the search for us in every way they knew.

More bush planes volunteered, and the Search and Rescue Wing of the RCAF at Winnipeg came in until there were 11 aircraft flying and two helicopters standing by. The country for 20 miles around Portal Lake was laid out in a grid pattern and all of it covered. All the lakes big enough to land on were combed by small planes that taxied around the shore as their pilots looked for tracks, a dead fire, any sign of us.

High winds and snow hampered the searchers, and there were days when the planes could go up for only an hour or so. Archie Webb and Ron Booi flew under almost impossible conditions, when trim tabs and pontoon rudders froze and they had to land to break the ice off, even cracking shell ice with their pontoons to taxi ashore. My dad flew up from Pentwater to the search camp and went out on flights or waited helplessly for word of us.

On Saturday, November 4—a week from the day we had wandered into the bush—the Kenora Bush Search and Rescue Unit, a volunteer outfit made up of experienced bush men and timber cruisers, was called in. Constable George Orosy of the Ontario Provincial Police, area commander of the unit, flew to the camp and took charge. By that time he had 20 men.

The searchers began to feel they were looking for dead men. From what had been found in our tent they knew we were without food, and because no smoke had been sighted, they were sure we had no fire. There was a limit to the time we could survive, and many believed we had reached it. Hope was almost gone, but there was no thought yet of abandoning the search.

Orosy was more optimistic. We were both young and in good condition. Strong was used to roughing it, and he thought I would last as long as the guide. "It will take more than a week to finish them," he told Dad confidently.

The ground search was widened to cover more territory. Four members of the Kenora group walked 20 miles east to Highway 105 in three days but found no sign of us. Next, Orosy had three-man teams flown to lakes from five to 10 miles north, south, east, and west of Portal with instructions to walk a compass course back to the search camp. If they found us they'd light two fires as a signal, and bush planes were assigned to support these teams.

Everything that seasoned rescue workers could think of was

being done. Every man in the quest knew that unless we were found soon there would be no further use to look for us.

The morning the widened ground search got under way, Tom and I awoke to see the sky clearing and the sun breaking through for the first time since we had walked away from the bog lake on October 28. Now at last we could get our bearings. That first sight of the sun seemed to put new life in us. We'd walk out now. Just a few more days and we'd be back safe and sound.

Which way to go? It was no use to look for Portal Lake since we had no idea of its location or ours. We agreed our best chance was to try for Highway 105, which we believed lay to the southeast. We struck out in that direction, walking as fast as we could.

Actually, we were headed toward the railroad and Quibell, 30-odd miles away, and I know now we could never have made it. The Wabigoon River and a chain of big lakes was in our way, and we would not have been able to get across. Our strength was about gone, and our wanderings would have ended somewhere along the Wabigoon. Orosy told me later that we walked in a more southerly direction than southeast, I suppose partly because our way was barred time after time by streams and flooded bogs.

We tried to hurry all that day, setting our course by the sun. When we stopped for the night we thought we'd covered 12 to 15 miles. It was more likely five or less.

Now, at last, the search was closing in. While we stumbled weakly on that Sunday afternoon, one of Orosy's search teams— Louis Ashopenace, Tom Payash, and Charlie Fobister—cut our tracks going south two miles west of Portal Lake. They were old, but the three Indians followed them until shortly before dark and camped on a lake. Just after they got their fire built, an RCAF plane flew over, misread their signals, and reported we had been found.

Tom and I spent that night, our ninth in the bush, as we had spent the others, shivering under a lean-to. But we were only a few miles ahead of the search party. The sun was still out the next morning, and we started off to the southeast once more.

Orosy doubted that we had been found, and at daylight he and Archie Webb flew out to investigate. They went back to the base camp and airlifted three more Indians out to help the search team. About noon they came on the camp where we had spent the night and found blood on the snow from Tom's frost-bitten legs. They made four miles through a dense swamp in the next hour.

My recollections of that day are hazy. Once when we

stopped to rest in the thickets of a big swamp, Tom looked at me dully and said, "I don't think I make it."

That was the first admission of defeat from either of us, and I knew I couldn't be of much help. We even talked of throwing the deerskin away but decided against it. Tom was still carrying it around his shoulders with his bare hands wrapped in it, and I staggered along with the rifle.

About three o'clock we came to a low ridge, the first dry land we'd seen for hours. There was a big windfall with plenty of dead poles, so we stopped for the night. Before the lean-to was finished, Tom crawled into it and wrapped the deerskin around his feet without taking his boots off. He had not done that before, and I realized he was at the end of his rope.

I was helping him tuck the half-frozen hide around his legs when I saw a man walk out of the swamp, following our tracks. He saw us in the same instant, whistled sharply, and broke into a run, and then five more came in sight in single file behind him. We were found!

It took the idea a few minutes to soak in, then we shook hands all around. One of the Indians told us, "You're tough guys. We think you both dead." Then they went to work.

They had axes, food, coffee, tea, and dry socks. In minutes a big fire was crackling. They pulled a log up in front of it, and Tom and I soaked up the most wonderful heat I had ever felt, while our clothes started to steam dry. We drank tea and half a cup of hot soup apiece, and when that stayed down we tried a few bites of bread and cheese. About that time Ron Booi flew over.

He counted eight men and knew the long search was ended. He came down low enough to shout for us to wait where we were, then flew off to make his report. Our rescuers started to clear a place for a helicopter to land, but Booi was back in a little while, circling low again, pointing south and shouting, "Lake. Go that way."

We walked less than a mile before we came to the lake and found Archie Webb's plane waiting at the shore. We learned later that two 'copters standing by at Winnipeg and Kenora were grounded by 55-mile winds. Waves were hammering against the pontoons of Webb's plane, the sun was gone, and it was a dark, dreary November day. Tom and I climbed weakly up into the cabin. "You're late," Archie greeted us with a dry grin.

"About a week," I acknowledged.

Minutes later we were looking down into the snowy bush

where we had spent those 10 terrible days. Suddenly the whole thing seemed like a hideous dream.

Webb landed us at McIntosh, and my dad and Orosy met us there. Orosy said later that he did not think Strong could have survived another night in the open. "And I'd have given you just one more day after he went," he added. I hadn't realized either of us was that far along, but maybe he was right. We were both in pretty rough shape.

Webb's wife, who had kept the search camp supplied with hot soup and food, drove us to the General Hospital at Dryden, 40 miles southeast of McIntosh. We were there shortly after dark, but by that time it was snowing hard.

My weight had dropped 22 pounds, and Tom, thin to begin with, had lost about as much, but neither of us suffered any lasting damage. My finger healed quickly, Tom's frostbite was not severe, and by some miracle—and thanks to the deerskin—we escaped frozen feet. I spent three days in the hospital, eating about every two hours, and Tom was there a little longer. His wife had a baby boy before he got home and they named it Bud, for me. I couldn't have had a nicer compliment.

I still want a moose, and one of these days I'll go back and get one. But when I do you can be sure that every minute I'm in the bush I'll know exactly where I am.

1963

THE SAD END OF BIG DADDY
By Edward Linn

FROM THE SATURDAY EVENING POST

Copyright © 1963, Edward A. Linn

It was Quentin Reynolds, one of our judges, who termed this story a "small classic." The reader can only wonder why Big Daddy Liscomb at the summit of his career died by his own hand from acute heroin poisoning. Tragic, and yet the author, through a sensitive blending of poetry and reasoning, makes the event seem almost inevitable.

*John Henry told the Captain,
"A man ain't nothin' but a man
And if I don't beat your steam drill down,
I'll die with a hammer in my hand.
Lawd, Lawd,
I'll die with a hammer in my hand."*

John Henry, as any folk singer worthy of his union card can tell you, was a legendary Negro giant who hammered himself into the grave, gloriously, because he was unwilling to live in a world where the machine took the place of nature's muscle and sweat.

Eugene (Big Daddy) Lipscomb was a fun-loving Negro giant who really lived. He was so great and so colorful a football player that he had become almost legendary himself before he died, ingloriously, on May 10, 1963, at the age of 32. According to official records he died of acute heroin poisoning, accidentally, but by his own hand. Daddy lived grandly, but he died bad. Which proves again that, one way or another. the world has its ways for grinding down the man of muscle and sweat.

*I tell you something true as life,
And, Big Daddy, you better be believin';*

187

You lay that needle down right now,
Or your friends will all be grievin';
You lay that needle down, boy,
Or your women will be grievin'.

What the official report omits is that none of Big Daddy's
friends, none of the thousands who mobbed his funeral, is willing
to believe that he could have stuck a needle into his vein of his
own free will, even though the alternative is, if not unthinkable,
certainly improbable and unprovable. "Whiskey and women,
yes," they say to a man, "but drugs, never."

"I'm a B and B man," Daddy liked to boast. "Booze and
broads." And his capacity to handle both was one of the wonders
of the civilized world.

Big Daddy worked hard on a football field, and when the
game was done, it was time to get around some and have a little
fun. "Let's go out and get me a jug," he'd say. "Let's have a
taste." A jug to Gene Lipscomb was a fifth of whiskey and he
could throw down the fifth the way you or I would throw down
a beer.

To no small extent, Gene made himself up. He got his nickname during his early years with the Los Angeles Rams when he
was better known for rough, dirty playing than for ability. He
took to calling everybody "Little Daddy," which—since he stood
6-feet-6 and weighed 285—was a sly way of inviting them to call
him "Big Daddy" in return.

It wasn't until Baltimore bought him in 1956 for $100 on
waivers that Eugene Lipscomb became "Big Daddy" for real. On
the field he wore his uniform sloppily, his pants drooping, his
shirttail flapping. He had tremendous speed for a man his size.
He was so fast that he could beat almost any halfback in a 50-
yard dash. Generally two or three rival linemen were given the
assignment of keeping Big Daddy off the passer. The Cleveland
Browns usually set four men to harass him. In Baltimore Big
Daddy led the Colts to two successive championships.

One of Lipscomb's favorite tricks was to let a blocker make
contact with him so that the ball carrier would be encouraged to
skirt him. Then he'd flip the blocker away and run down the ball
carrier. "Where you going, little man?" he'd say, as he clubbed
his arms around him. "This is Big Daddy, and once Big D puts
the clamps on you, you're dead."

His real delight, though, was to burst in, his shirttail flying,
and flatten a passer.

Little passer, you better be nimble,
Little passer, you better pray,
'Cause if you get in Big Daddy's way,
Tomorrow will be yo' burying day,
Lawd, Lawd,
Tomorrow will be yo' burying day.

In case he hadn't made his presence known to everybody in the park, he'd linger for another moment to pick up the passer and carefully brush him off. And the smaller the passer, the longer Daddy would linger. With that sure instinct for the dramatic, he was the first professional lineman to take the play away from the backs and become a personality himself.

Off the field he dressed for effect, except here he was dressed not to maim but to kill. Well, when Big Daddy came swinging into a bar with that easy, dancing step of his, you could hardly keep from noticing him, what with a diamond ring on his little finger, a white silk shirt like a rock 'n' roll singer, a tie so red that it threw off heat, and alligator shoes that crawled right on his feet. And didn't Big D always look pretty grand in that small-brimmed hat with a feather in the band?

And Daddy would twist to that driving beat
Till he danced those chicks right off their feet.

"Gene didn't need to take drugs for kicks," his cousin Walt Chattman, himself a pro football player with the Philadelphia Eagles, says. "Being Big Daddy was all the kicks he ever needed."

His appetites were gargantuan and insatiable. A typical breakfast consisted of a dozen eggs and a pound of bacon, washed down by a pint of booze. Having learned to cook in the Marine Corps, he would make huge meals, run to the bathroom and throw up halfway through, then come back and finish off the food.

His fondness for variety in women cost him three marriages, as he freely admitted. His favorite story was about the time he passed underneath the room of one of his teammates, just before they were to play an exhibition game in Texas, and caught the echo of a soft and sibilant sigh. Daddy shot up the stairs with a mighty roar, while his teammate, showing quick reflexes, slammed shut the door and tossed the girl into the closet.

Well, now, Daddy went poking around, sniffing at the air until his eyes reached the keyhole and stopped right there. As he always said, and he didn't lie, "All I seen looking back at me was one big eye."

Big Daddy stepped back and Big Daddy was smiling. "Big Daddy is here," Big Daddy cried.

Well, Daddy had a lot of women chasing after him, a lot of the time, and he was never known to run the other way.

Drugs take away a man's appetite for liquor and women both, and that's one reason, his friends tell you, the official story of his death just can't be true.

What makes it even more ridiculous, they tell you, is that Gene had escaped from the streets of Detroit, at the age of 16, by joining the Marines. He never knew his father, who died in a CCC camp. When Gene was 11, a plainclothesman came to the house, put his arm around his shoulder, and told him his mother had been stabbed 47 times by a boy friend while she was waiting on a street corner for a bus. Gene was reared in Detroit by his maternal grandfather, who tried to keep him from running wild. Gene rarely talked about those early days, but he would occasionally tell how his grandfather had once tied him to a bedpost and whipped him as punishment for stealing the old man's whiskey. Even here, though, he would tell the story with affection, as if he were trying to show that someone had cared enough about him to go to all that trouble.

Signed out of the Marines by the Los Angeles Rams, he was one of the few pro football players without a college education, a condition that always bothered him. Still, he had a quick, if profane, wit, and after he became so famous and popular, under his magic "Big Daddy" cloak, he would grin and say, "When we're on a football field, man, I got a degree, too."

He knew what he had escaped from, and he had a peculiar, all-encompassing phrase for it: "the scum." The phrase, for him, covered the whole condition of the ghettoized Negro: the slum itself with its dirt and its crime, plus all of its human oozings— the junkies, the hustlers, the pimps, and the bums. He would walk through the worst sections of the cities with his closer friends and he would say, "Doesn't it make you feel great to be able to walk through here like a king, with your head held high?"

Buddy Young, the old Illinois All-American, who became Gene's tutor and conscience, says: "If somebody told me Lipscomb died in an automobile accident or in a fight over a woman, I'd believe it. If it had happened when he first came to Baltimore, a hoodlum and a thug, I'd have believed it. But Gene had grown out of hiding and had come face to face with reality. A man doesn't take away from himself the one thing he has to offer, his ability to play football. Football was his past, present, and future, and nobody knew that more than Gene. He knew what his image was, because he himself had made it himself. He wouldn't destroy that with drugs."

Gene was so jealous of that image that he quit the wrestling circuit when he was asked to become a villain. "That ain't Big Daddy," he said.

It has fallen to Buddy Young to protect that image and to protect it, curiously enough, against a man he has never seen, a man as different from himself as any other man could possibly be.

Young, who is now a Baltimore radio executive, exudes good will and sincerity and, if the word isn't too embarrassing, goodness. He has the solidity and conservatism of the self-made man. He can use words and expressions which would sound unbearably pretentious coming from someone else. ("I was often reminding him of his responsibility as a professional football player to be conscious of his actions, of refraining from expressing himself with vituperativeness.")

Buddy Young made himself a sort of den father for a group of Baltimore players, including Daddy, tackle Jim Parker, wingback Lenny Moore, and defensive back Sherman Plunkett. Daddy lived with Plunkett in the tree-shaded, middle-class Hanlon Park section of Ashburton, not far from Buddy Young's own home, although Daddy had been traded to Pittsburgh and Plunkett to San Diego of the American Football League.

But still, the Baltimore writers who were closest to Daddy knew that he would grow uneasy around the businessmen Young tried to surround him with, and that, from time to time, he would feel the need to cut out to the "back of town" district where he felt more at home. It was at the Uptown Bar in the "back of town" that he first ran into Timothy Black, the man who saw Big Daddy die.

Timmy Black, 27, is a slim, sparrowy man who came to Baltimore from the South 17 years ago, his left leg withered from a boyhood attack of polio. Even more than Lipscomb and Young, he is a man of his time and his place. His place is in the slums Daddy escaped from. His time stretches back a hundred years.

He is, admittedly, a man who would do his best to get you liquor, women, or drugs according to your taste—the functions, he says, he served for Big Daddy. He has, he admits, been in jail, although he balks at revealing the charges. At first glance he seems to be a shy, mumbling, naïve man, soft of voice, quick with deference, apologies, and respect. He has a delicacy of language that leads him to refer to the women he has dealings with as "young ladies" and "lady friends."

"Daddy and I weren't friends," he says, correcting you quietly, as if he is a man who has accepted his curious uses in life. But people close to Timmy Black called him "Hap," and every now and then you see the features shift a little under the slight tilt of his summer straw hat, and you catch a fleeting glimpse of another man underneath, the man who has committed himself to whatever he has to be to survive in his jungle. He is, too, a man with a sick and pregnant wife. Four months ago he got himself a job on the assembly line of a bottling company, a job he still holds.

When Black tells the story of Big Daddy's death, he leaves the impression that it was Daddy who wouldn't let him alone. According to Black, Lipscomb first asked him to get him a "deck" of heroin about six months ago, right after the end of the football season. "No," Black says, not volunteering the information but only answering the question, "he didn't act like it was the first time."

From then on, says Black, Daddy was taking heroin on the average of three times a week, the last time only two or three days before his death. Once, Black says, Daddy even "shot" himself in his car. "All it takes is a whiskey cap to put the stuff in, and a match to boil it up."

Impossible, say Daddy's friends. "He would come to the house never less than three times a week," Young says. "Walk through the door—I can see him now bending his head to get through—and he'd always call out to my wife, 'Hello, Sweetiecakes. Here's the Daddy.' He couldn't have walked in here and faced me, because I would have known it. He couldn't have lived with Plunkett, day in and day out, and not have him know."

Big Daddy's third wife, Cecilia, who lived only a block away from him, is equally incredulous. "He could never have put a needle in himself," she says. "He was terrified of pain. He got a splinter in the bottom of his foot one time, and the way he carried on you'd have thought he'd lost the leg. He wouldn't even let the dentist pull a tooth without my sitting in his lap. I saw him three or four times a week, and he never could hide too much from me. I could read him like a book."

Young last saw Lipscomb on Wednesday, May 8, a burning-hot morning two days before Daddy died. Daddy had come to see him at station WEBB and waited outside until Young got off the air. "He was in brown khaki pants and blue *sleeveless* sport shirt. It was one in which he had torn the sleeves off. His shirttail was out, and he was wearing a pair of—what would you call them?—shower shoes."

Daddy wanted to tell Young he was going to drive to Pittsburgh on Friday morning to sign his contract. Daddy had never made more than $14,000 a year, and he intended to ask for a two-year contract at $15,000 a year, the figure he had always looked upon as the ultimate goal. He had called Buddy Parker, the Steelers' coach, to ask if he'd have trouble getting the raise. He also asked Dan Rooney, a Steelers publicity man, to send him $500 "to meet an insurance payment on my car," the first time he had ever asked the Steelers for an advance.

On Thursday morning he cashed the $500 check at the Union Trust Bank. "Besides the money from Pittsburgh," Buddy Young says, "he had $400 that I know of. He put $200 in his checking account and paid two small bills that came to $40. That means he went out on Thursday with more than $600 in his pocket. Find what happened to that and you'll know why Daddy is dead."

If there was one thing Gene liked as much as football it was pitching softball. He played in a doubleheader that evening, and, after the games were over, took a couple of the boys from his team to have some drinks. "When Daddy had a lot of money on him, he'd take his wallet and lock it in the trunk of his car. I talked to the players he was with that night, and before he went into the bar, he locked the wallet in the trunk."

Daddy had another odd habit. Before he was to go on a motor trip, he would always stay up all night. When they were leaving the bar, around 11 o'clock, he asked one of the softball players to double-date with him, but the man already had a date. "If only that guy had been free," Young says, "Daddy would be alive today."

Timmy Black, the sparrow, worked late that night at the bottling plant and didn't get home until eight. After dinner, as was his custom, he went to the Uptown Bar. "I was outside on the corner of Monroe and Edmondson most of the time," Black says. "A guy came by who lived on the next street to me, and I asked if he could drive me home. But he wasn't going home; he was going the other way. If I'd only went home like I asked to, I wouldn't be in the trouble I'm in today."

Around midnight, Black says, Daddy came by in his big yellow Cadillac convertible—there was another fellow with him

—and called him over. "I had an idea he wanted heroin, figuring I might know where to get it, but he didn't say anything about it then, because he didn't want everybody to know."

As soon as Daddy dropped his passenger, presumably one of the softball players, he and Black headed out in search of heroin. Instead, Black says, they ran into two young ladies. Then they bought a six-pack of Country Club, a malt beverage, and took the girls to Black's apartment. At 3:00 A.M. the young ladies asked to be taken home. At some time after three o'clock, then, Daddy, according to Black, asked, "You still think you can get down?"

Black could try. "Daddy drove to Pennsylvania Avenue on 'The Block' [Baltimore's large strip-joint center]. We parked near the corner where we could be seen. There was a fellow right up the street in front of a restaurant, just a few yards away. Daddy gave me the money to get down for him and I bought a $12 bag." A "$12 bag" contains enough heroin for two or three users.

And now Daddy drove back to Black's apartment, at 434 North Brice Street, and from this point on all his movements take on that heavy finality that comes when you know in advance that all of the thoughtless, everyday actions are the last he will ever make.

North Brice Street is small and narrow, little wider than an alley, really, and less than 100 yards long. On either side of the street there is one low, flat continuous row of connected apartment houses, constructed of light brown brick. It is a neighborhood with a reputation second to none for teen-age addicts.

Black's apartment was on the second floor. Daddy walked up a single flight of stairs, so narrow that he must have filled it completely, like a big ship squeezed into a small berth. When he reached the top of the staircase, he was also in the apartment, the bathroom a step ahead, the kitchen ahead to the right.

It was a small kitchen, painted yellow, dominated by a large table against the near wall. Across from the table were a refrigerator and a small stove. At the head of the room, alongside the door leading to the back porch, was an old-fashioned radiator. Overhead hung a bare bulb. A man Daddy's size would have difficulty moving through the open space without bumping something.

It was in such an apartment that Gene Lipscomb lived out his early days in Detroit. It was as if, at the end, the "scum" had reached out to bring Daddy home.

The heroin was cooked up in a wine cap and sucked into a homemade syringe, with a piece of paper providing the neck where the needle and the syringe joined. Daddy, says Black, "shot" himself first and then handed the needle over to him so he could "shoot" himself, too.

Heroin is not a stimulant but a depressant. After the first shock it sends the user into a "nod," a sort of semiconscious daydream in which the user sees himself living out the life he would like to be leading. Black's first warning that something had gone wrong, he says came when Daddy's lips began to vibrate rapidly. Little rivers of foam formed at the sides of his mouth. Black, roused by fear, went to the refrigerator for some ice to press on the top of Daddy's head and underneath his testicles.

At this point, says Black, a third man, Robert Waters, came into the apartment, put a solution of salt water into the syringe, and shot it into Daddy's arm, an old-wives' antidote which possibly has some value, though not very much.

When Daddy still failed to come around, Black says, he told Waters to go out and phone for an ambulance. The call was made at about 7:15 A.M.

After Waters left, Black tried to revive Daddy by slapping him across the face. That only served to bring about the final indignity, as Daddy toppled off the chair and fell to the floor, face down upon the worn linoleum.

The police arrived first, followed shortly by an ambulance. Black handed the police Daddy's car keys and $73. "I knew the ambulance would take him away," Black explains, "and, you know, I took it out of his wallet to protect it."

Big Daddy Lipscomb was still breathing when he was carried out to the ambulance to be rushed to Lutheran Hospital. He was DOA—dead on arrival.

"We split the bag in half," Black insists. "I took the same half he did and it didn't kill me. But he was drinking in the bedroom with the young lady and I didn't know it. If I had known . . ."

It is true that alcohol "potentiates" the effect of drugs. But Daddy had not been drinking that much. The autopsy showed the alcoholic content of his blood to be .09 percent. Daddy's drinking through the years did have its effect, though. The autopsy also showed that his liver was somewhat damaged. Since detoxification takes place in the liver, the heroin remained in his system longer than normal.

The autopsy was performed by the assistant medical examiner of Baltimore, Dr. Rudiger Breitnecker. As he explains, it is not the heroin itself that does the damage, because heroin breaks down immediately upon injection. One of the main degradation products is morphine, and morphine is the killer. Daddy had about 10 milligrams of morphine per 100 cubic centimeters of bile, which would correspond to 11.3 milligrams of heroin.

When morphine is used therapeutically, it would be rare for more than a two-milligram dosage to be prescribed. In other words, Daddy's body contained *more than five times* what might normally be considered a safe dosage. "Any dose would have a serious effect on a beginner," Dr. Breitnecker says, "but, speaking generally, 10 percent is a lethal amount. It would take a hardened addict to survive 10 percent."

The question that arises, of course, is whether there is any medical evidence that Daddy had ever taken drugs before. There isn't. A needle mark, as anyone who has ever taken a simple blood test knows, heals completely within a couple of days.

Doctor Breitnecker did find "at least" four needle marks that were only two to four hours old. ("If that's true," Black says, "then three of them would have to be the salt-water injections. He only took one shot of heroin.")

In the course of the autopsy, Dr. Breitnecker also took one very small, very thick slice of skin from the inside of the elbow and, by the use of dyes and high magnification, came across an old needle mark, which was still identifiable only because a small fiber, which seemed to be cotton, was lodged in the puncture. Most addicts filter the cooked solution through cotton or bread as they suck it up into the syrings. Still, one needle mark is just like any other, and no man would be foolish enough to state that a piece of fiber couldn't have become lodged in any hypodermic needle, used for any kind of shot.

And so, while nothing Black says is inconsistent with the findings of the autopsy, it is also true that nothing Daddy's friends say is inconsistent, either. "There is hardly evidence to call him an addict," Dr. Breitnecker says. "We cannot, as a matter of fact, say positively that he ever took more than one shot of heroin in his life." The diagnosis, for the record, is that he died of acute heroin poisoning.

The key question, in the fight to save Daddy's reputation, is whether he could have been knocked out before the heroin was put into his system. To this, at least, Dr. Breitnecker can give a flat reply. "My answer to these attempts by a loyal public to explain away the fact that Big Daddy did take heroin, at this time, of his own free will, is that our tests showed he was not under any sedative, that he was not intoxicated, and that there was not a scratch on him of any kind."

But Daddy's defenders still make out their case. Robby Waters is hardly the passing stranger Black tried, at first, to make him out to be. In their statement to the police, the two young ladies had Waters getting into Lipscomb's car, taking the wheel to drive them to the apartment, and then returning from time to time while they were still there.

What gripes Daddy's friends is that there is only Black's story of the last hours. "Who is this man Black?" Buddy Young asks. "None of Daddy's friends ever saw him or heard of him."

Black was held, at first, on a charge of involuntary homicide, but it was quickly changed to mere possession of narcotics paraphernalia. The original bail of $10,000 was reduced to $3,000.

Black is not an addict. He has not used any narcotics, he insists, since the night of Daddy's death. He is a married man and he has a job. There seems little doubt that when his case comes to court he will be placed on probation.

Black faces the unasked question in his own indirect way. "I was the one who told Robby Waters to call the ambulance," he says. "I didn't want to take Daddy out and throw him in an alley. Right today you pick up the paper and find they die on steps or in an alley. I was frightened. Seeing that happen to Daddy was the worst thing that ever happened to me. I liked Big Daddy."

To which Buddy Young replies, "Nobody knows what happened in that room before the police were called. Nobody knows who was in the room or how long it took to call the police.

"Gene Lipscomb had a soul, he had a faith, and I'd walk with him all the rest of my life without believing that he was an addict. I know you can never tell what a person will do, but Daddy wasn't Marilyn Monroe out to commit suicide. He was at the summit of his career, he had come to the place he wanted to be. He knew how big he was."

And then, Buddy Young smiled, and the legend of Big Daddy had taken over again. "He'd have liked to have seen the crowd he drew at his funeral. I could hear him saying, 'See, Young. See, Little Man. You never knew how big Big Daddy really was, did you?' "

Don't weep for me, Little Daddy,
Don't bother with no prayer;
I don't want to go to heaven
Unless they swing up there.
Don't take me up to heaven, please, Lawd,
'Less there's kicks and chicks up there.

1964

A BAD DAY FOR CONSERVATIVES

By Bill Conlin

FROM THE PHILADELPHIA BULLETIN

Copyright © 1964, Bulletin Co., Philadelphia

"It was a bad week for Conservatives in Ohio, once a stronghold of the Right Wing in politics and football.

"Barry Goldwater lost.

"Robert Taft, Jr., lost.

"And today, Wayne Woodrow Hayes lost.

"Penn State completed the Conservatives' bleak week by blasting Ohio State, 27–0, in one of the most startling upsets of this or any football season."

One judge who voted for this piece noted that these lead sentences caught the eyes of the reader and wouldn't let them go. The other two judges had the same idea and the author won first-place money in the feature division of this sports anthology.

It was a bad week for Conservatives in Ohio, once a stronghold of the Right Wing in politics and football.

Barry Goldwater lost.

Robert Taft, Jr., lost.

And today, Wayne Woodrow Hayes lost.

Penn State completed the Conservatives' bleak week by blasting Ohio State, 27–0, in one of the most startling upsets of this or any football season.

It was the third time that Coach Rip Engle has brought a Penn State team here to upset the mighty Buckeyes, and it was the Buckeyes' first shutout in 45 games.

It was also "Dad's Day," but the only thing Dad saw Ohio State win was the opening toss.

The Buckeyes were unbeaten (6–0) and ranked No. 2 in the

polls when they trooped into sun-swept Ohio Stadium to the cheers of a capacity mob of 84,279.

When they limped to their dressing room, they were perhaps the most thoroughly whipped team in Ohio State's illustrious football history.

Listen to these statistics:

—Penn State rolled up a 201–33 plurality in rushing, supposedly the hub of Hayes's grass-roots approach to football.

—Penn State outpassed the Buckeyes 148–30. Thus the Lions led 349–63 in total offense.

—Penn State controlled the ball for 79 plays to only 37 for Ohio State and rolled to 22 first downs against 5. The Buckeyes were shut out completely in the first half—no first downs and minus-14-yards total offense.

—Penn State played errorless ball. Ohio State lost the ball four times, twice on fumbles, twice on interceptions.

After the rout, Hayes was a stunned football coach. "That's the soundest trouncing we've ever had," Woody said. "We could not establish anything. They made only one mistake and they fell on that for a touchdown."

Hayes was referring to a freak bounce of the ball on the last play of a tremendous 65-yard first-period march by the Lions.

Bullish Tom Urbanik, who was a fullback cast in the Ohio State mold, smashed the middle from a yard out. Tom was rocked loose from the ball, and it dribbled into the end zone. Right halfback Dirk Nye, who was completing his block, landed right on the ball. Sophomore kicker Gerry Sanker added the first of three extra points and the rout was on.

The rest of the game was completely the property of Penn State. Either the Buckeyes had been masquerading as a top-flight football team for five weeks, or Penn State is the most underrated 4-4 team in the country.

Hayes leans toward the latter theory.

"I'll tell you one thing," he said, "they haven't been playing that kind of football—or they wouldn't have lost four games. They have a well-balanced attack and they sure used it."

Woody is right. Penn State wouldn't have lost four games if it had played the kind of football it played here today.

After that first touchdown, State played savage, alert, and errorless ball. On a man-for-man basis, it won every battle in the line. Linebackers Bob Kane and John Runnells outplayed Tom Bugel and Ike Kelly, by reputation the best set of linebackers in the country.

Ohio State's offense was so intimidated by the fierce Penn State charge that once the Buckeyes punted on second down and twice punted on third.

It did little good. After State drove 69 yards only to miss a field goal, Joe Vargo fielded the second down punt and went 12 yards to the Buckeye 35.

Five plays later, quarterback Gary Wydman rolled out to his left and followed a sliver of daylight into the end zone.

Ohio State lost none of its inertia in the second half and the Lions lost none of their momentum. As the physics text say, bodies at rest tend to remain at rest, bodies in motion tend to remain in motion unelss acted upon by some outside force.

There was no outside force to save the Buckeyes. Ohio State finally broke up the perfect no-hitter midway through the third period.

The initial first down for the Scarlet and Gray was a dribbling little infield hit, a 15-yard penalty against the Lions for grabbing a face mask, and when the sticks were advanced, the near-record crowd let out a mighty sarcastic roar.

While the crowd was worrying about first downs State was either scoring or threatening.

Don Kunit, the halfback who isn't happy unless he gets five yards on every carry, swept over from the three for the first of his two touchdowns. Kunit's run—Don got 33 yards on seven carries—capped a seven-play drive from the Buckeye 36. Dick Gingrich's interception of a Don Unverferth pass set up the drive.

When Kunit scored again from the three midway through the fourth period, he was running with the third midway through the fourth period, he was running with the third team. That's how undignified the proceedings got for Ohio State.

With the scrubs digging in on the Ohio State 40, Ohio State made a last bid to cross mid-field. For the first 55 minutes they were unable to pass beyond its 41.

"That's the first time I ever saw a goal-line stand on the 50-yard line," quipped someone in the press box.

The Bucks passed the 50. They even got down to the nine. But defensive back Tom Bedick intercepted Unverferth's pass on the one and quarterback Jack White ran out the clock.

"Even if Penn State is from the East," said a wide-eyed partisan filing toward the exit, "I think we oughta' send 'em to the Rose Bowl."

1965

MICKEY MANTLE: OKLAHOMA TO OLYMPUS

By Gerald Astor

FROM LOOK

The bones of his knees were gone. The ligaments in both legs were old and elastic. He couldn't stop abruptly or throw any longer. Yet this authentic American hero captured the hearts of baseball buffs with his heart and guts. Once the greatest figure in the game, he complained little as deterioration set in before his time. He still loved the game and left it too early, without a whimper.

Henry V, a great field manager from another time, another place, exhorted his players, "In peace there's nothing so becomes a man/As modest stillness and humility./But when the blast of war blows in our ears,/Then imitate the action of the tiger./Stiffen the sinews, summon up the blood,/Disguise fair nature with hard favor'd rage./ . . . lend the eye a terrible aspect. . . ./Now set thé teeth and stretch the nostril wide,/Hold hard the breath and bend up every spirit/To his full height."

If Shakespeare's Harry had added a few words about aiming for the seats, he would have given a nifty description of baseball's most explosive warrior, Mickey Charles Mantle of the New York Yankees.

He came out of Oklahoma 14 years ago wearing a straw hat, lugging a $4 cardboard suitcase. He was that unique specimen, the instant star. He hit the long ball longer. He hit it more often, and he hit it from either side of the plate with equal violence. Any other strong boy's maximum effort inevitably came to be compared with several hit by Mantle in the same yard.

Before he began to tear his body apart with his own strength and zeal, he became an expert center fielder. Until his legs began to break down, the measure of a man's speed was how close he could come to Mickey in the critical 90-foot dash from home to first.

Mickey Mantle, Mickey Mantle: say the name fast, say it slow; it has a lilt to it. A trick of poetry, that trochaic, alliterative name, but man and name draw the people. Only the grace of Willie Mays rivals the fury of Mantle in crowd appeal (and salary). As a reigning demigod, he is hunted by squadrons of autograph and status seekers. In quest of signatures or the laying on of hands, they have banged on his hotel door at 3:00 A.M., knocked a steak off his plate and, in one terrifying encounter, punched him in the face. Some inevitably go away mad when refused an autograph. To survive, Mickey must avoid open ground where crowds can form. Near his home in Dallas is an amusement park. "My boys, they love it, you know?" said Mickey once. "Merlyn, my wife, has to take them there alone. Just once, I'd like to be able to go and watch them on those rides."

He is a shy man, a phlegmatic one, and some of this ultimately goes back to Commerce, Oklahoma, population 25,000. You hear some of Commerce when Mickey talks. There's a soft Southwest burr; consonants drop off the ends of words. He says "younder," and "that there," and "mah" is his first-person possessive. But he is not a hayseed. One New York writer irks Mickey by carefully printing his slightest fracture of grammar. The writer compounds the jibe with a feeble witticism at the athlete's expense. "He makes me sound hicky," says Mickey. "Hell, I know what a double negative is." He also hears the nuances of other people's speech. After listening to a traveler to Dallas recently, Mickey turned to the visiting Billy Martin, his old Yankee teammate, and said, "He talks just like Whitey [Ford]. Notice how he says 'water.'"

Oklahoma means far more than diction. It is Elven (Mutt) Mantle, aboveground straw boss of the Blue Goose Zinc Mine near Commerce at a top salary of $75 a week and a perennial sandlot baseball player. "If my dad had gotten a chance, I believe he could have played big-league ball," says Mickey.

Ten years before Casey Stengel popularized two-platoon baseball, Elven Mantle told his son that the complete hitter of the future was the switcher. The boy practiced for hours batting left-handed against his right-handed-throwing father, then crossed the plate to swing against Grandpa Mantle, a lefty.

Elven Mantle did more than coach his son in the art of baseball. He burned into him the hunger to excel. "I just wanted to please him more than anything else. I had so much respect for him. I could never take a drink or smoke in front of my dad."

When 19-year-old Mickey slumped in his first season with the Yankees and was shipped to the minors, his father visited him. The kid expected sympathy, but Elven Mantle, already tormented with a fatal disease, told him it would take "guts, not moaning, to make it." Otherwise, Mickey could come home to Commerce to "grub" for a living like his father. Mickey's slump ended.

Elven Mantle's faith was baseball, but he was a heretic around Commerce, for this is football country, and Mickey flung himself into that sport. Kicked in the leg during a high-school game, he developed osteomyelitis, a sometimes progressive bone-marrow disease. But penicillin halted the infection.

"I was a helluva football player," recalls Mickey, who weighed only 140 to 160 pounds in high school. As a halfback for Commerce High, he ran, passed, and kicked with the same ferocity that marks him in baseball. "I had a friend, a real close friend named Bill Mosely, and he gave me that feeling of always playing all out. In football, if somebody hit me real hard, I wanted to try him again." From football comes the distinctive Mantle style of running, chest high, knees piston-pumping high to discourage would-be tacklers. "Runs like a man whose feet hurt," said one student of the running Mantle.

"I still love football," says Mickey, "and I watch it anytime I can." The particular objects of his affection are the Dallas Cowboys, and he sits in the box of Bedford Wynne part owner and Mickey's lawyer, at every home game.

The osteomyelitis eliminated football as a career, but Tom Greenwade, a Yankee scout, spotted Mickey's quality as a baseball player. While other teams spent hundreds of thousands for bonus boys, the Yankees signed Mickey for $1,000. After one season in the minors, Mickey came to watch Commerce High play Picher, a neighboring mining town. Merlyn Louis Johnson, a redheaded majorette from Picher, caught his eye between halves, and they began dating. "My dad said to me, 'You marry Merlyn and have a redheaded, freckle-faced kid.' We did get married, and little Mickey is redheaded and freckle-faced."

Elven Mantle did not live long enough to see this first grandson. He died of Hodgkin's disease, a lymphatic cancer, at 41. In a book, *The Quality of Courage*, ghosted for Mickey by Robert

Creamer, the epitaph for Mutt Mantle is: "He didn't die scared and he didn't live scared," and the dedication to "the memory of my father and to my sons" reads: "I hope that each of them will grow to be as brave a man as he was."

The slow, painful death of the father he idolized still hangs over Mickey, and other family losses add to the melancholy. When conversation drags around to the prospects of the long-term future, Mickey may remind a companion, "You know, my two uncles died of cancer before they were 40." Mantle's sense of death need not set one to charting the Freudian swamps in Mickey's mind. All of us fear death. Approaching an age at which a father and two uncles died is apt to set anyone to brooding. In Mickey's case, the continued breakdowns of his own body, while outside the context of fatal disease, cast a steady shadow.

But when Mickey reported to the Yankee camp at Phoenix in 1951, the only shadow was that of the aging Yankee giant, Joe DiMaggio. Fake reports persist that DiMaggio snubbed the kid who began to gather press notices at Phoenix. Always somewhat aloof, DiMaggio comported himself with a magisterial dignity. "He was like a senator," says Mickey. "He would come into the locker room, take off his pants, and call for a can of beer. Sometimes he would say to me, 'Hi, kid,' and talk a bit. Sometimes he didn't say anything." Spavined in the legs, shoulder sore, DiMaggio in his final season still rates with Mantle as "the best all-around ball player I ever saw."

At Phoenix, Casey Stengel happily watched the *Wunderkind* drive baseballs into the seats and over the stands. He also watched Mickey play his position. "Casey called me over one day and said, 'Kid, you ever think of playin' the outfield?' I'd set a record at Joplin with 77 errors at shortstop [the record book credits Mickey with only a horrible 55], so I went to the outfield."

Tommy Henrich, another aging Yankee hero, taught Mickey to play right field. "I was a terrible outfielder then," says Mickey. "But he had that speed," says Billy Martin, himself a half year out of the minor leagues at the time, "and he could make up for misjudging a fly ball."

Martin, the dead-end brat from California, who now coaches for the Twins, became Mantle's close friend, and they roomed together until Martin left the team. Martin and Mantle, with Whitey Ford, thoroughly explored the pleasure principle—partying, practical jokes, and general good times. In the early 1950s, ball teams made their road trips by train. Martin and Mantle

amused themselves and their teammates by stripping to their
shorts for wrestling matches in the Pullman aisles. Contest rules
gave Martin choice of the initial hold, but inevitably he finished
on his back. "I fixed him once, though," says Martin. "I put my
fingers inside his mouth, got him by the gums. He threw me, but
he couldn't eat for two days." The gnarly old master of the
Yankees viewed such scenes with nervousness. "You're going to
hurt that boy," Stengel cautioned Mantle.

Another Pullman sport was a game called "nose poker." The
winner in a head-to-head hand of poker selected a card from the
deck. If it were a 10, he would take 10 swats at the loser's nose
with the card. In the hands of a skilled practitioner, a celluloid
card smarted enough to bring tears and a cherry-colored nose.
"Once, the train gave a lurch. Whitey caught me right on the chin
with his left fist," says Mickey. "That bled me."

In Martin, Casey undoubtedly saw something of himself, the
spirit who soared above his native skills. In Mickey, he saw the
greatest pure talent he had ever managed. Mantle and Martin
simultaneously delighted and tormented Casey.

When the Yankees clinched one pennant, Martin and Mantle
partied long after official club celebrations ended. In fact, they
went straight to the ball park from one party. At that, they
missed batting practice, but since regulars ordinarily were excused following a pennant clinching, the two did not hurry their
dressing. Suddenly, Martin swept up his uniform, shoes, and
glove and scurried to the toilet. "I couldn't figure out where Billy
went," says Mickey now. "I looked up and there was Casey, so
mad he could barely talk. He pointed a finger at me and said,
'You're playin'.' He left me in most of the game. I messed up a fly
ball, and I couldn't hit at all."

When the Yankees toured Japan in 1955, Martin and Mantle
partied so vigorously they could barely play. "The Japanese
expected another Babe Ruth," says Mickey. "All I did was strike
out."

The Martin-Mantle-Ford combination broke up in 1957,
when they and several other players with their wives became
involved in a clouded brawl at a New York nightclub. A group at
another table kept shouting unpleasantries about Sammy Davis,
Jr., the evening's entertainer. Some Yankees objected to the
language. When the uproar subsided, one of the members of the
whooping group lay unconscious on the floor.

A grand jury could not determine who did what to whom,
but the Yankee front office, fearful that Martin would lead

Mickey too far down the primrose path, traded him off. The chagrined Martin felt that Casey had let him down, and for seven years did not speak to his old mentor. Casey was not always easy on Mantle, but Mickey says, "I like Casey; he did a lot for me. When I signed a contract with the Yankees in 1951, Casey got me $2,500 more than the minimum."

Just before the baseball meetings in Houston this winter, Martin visited Mickey in Dallas. Mantle kept after Billy to forget about the past. "What you ought to do is just walk up to him and say, 'Hi, Case.' " A newspaper story from Houston later that week reported, "A seven-year feud ended when Bill Martin walked up to Casey Stengel and said, 'Hi, Case,' to the old man's obvious delight."

Martin and Ford remain Mickey's closest friends in baseball. "What I like about Mickey is he's such an earthy man," says Martin. "There's just nothing phony about him. Over the years, he's been a good friend to me. I just hope someday I can do something for him."

For his part, Mickey naturally admires in Martin and Ford their toughness on the field and their total commitment to the game. In Martin and Ford, Mantle sees future managers. Himself? No. "I could never be a manager. All I have is natural ability." In his own eyes, he lacks the ability to lead. Peculiarly enough, one of the many assets he brings to the Yankees is a form of leadership, the inspiration he gives to other players by his presence in the lineup even though he is in pain. He is in effect a platoon leader, a man who leads by deed. He cannot be a general because he cannot tell subordinates what to do.

Mantle remains immensely popular with ball players. Rough Hank Bauer, a former teammate and now manager of the Baltimore Orioles, says, "Nothing you say about Mickey would be too good or too nice."

Part of his charm is a certain diffidence. To be sure, in a city like Dallas, where private clubs abound, he will walk up to a maître d' and softly say, "I'm Mickey Mantle. Can we come in for a spell?" Or he may leave his Cadillac in a bus zone at an airport and reassure an anxious companion, "Don't worry, I'm very big in this town." A small-boy grin erases any touch of the overbearing.

In contrast, not long ago a hotel bureaucrat failed to give proper service to Billy Martin. The sinner received a prompt ear-rapping. Mickey admitted: "I could never do that. I couldn't chew a guy out to his face. If I owned a business, I'd sure appreciate being told that my manager was no good, though." When a writer prints something Mantle finds offensive, he does not strike back with the humiliating ear-rap before players and the writer's peers. He just stops talking to that writer.

His retiring nature does not suggest one can step on Mantle without some sort of retribution. A few years ago, Mickey, Ford, and Ken Hunt, a nonhitting, piano-playing outfielder, visited the apartment of a friend. Also present was a local loudmouth who kept claiming he had been a magnificent footballer. Mickey finally said, "I played a little football in high school. Let's see you run over me." Mantle got down between several chairs, and his opponent charged. Mickey threw him over a chair. The bragger picked himself up and then admitted his real forte was defense. Mickey allowed as how he'd been a halfback and now would carry the ball. The man got down; Mickey trampled him, leaving him in ruins. The losing team seated himself next to Mickey, and after several brooding minutes said, "I owe you something for that." Whereupon, in a suicidal impulse, he rapped Mantle across the mouth with the back of his hand. The host recalls, "Mickey's punch traveled maybe six inches. 'Play loud,' I shouted to Ken Hunt at the piano, and Ford called, 'Let's all have a drink.'" A three-time loser now, the noisome one lay stone cold on the floor.

Mantle smiles much more readily than he punches. His small-boy grin covers some minor transgression at home or accompanies the Oklahoma-honed wit: "Waitress, could I have some hearts of palm? My mom always used to put 'em in my lunch bucket when I worked in the mine."

Springing from rural Oklahoma, Mickey has the Westerner's appreciation of a man for what he is. Not long ago, he said: "I haven't had a roommate on the road since Billy left. But if I had to take my choice of any man on the club, I'd want Elston Howard. I really love that man"—Mickey's supreme accolade for any human. Mantle refuses to knock anyone in baseball, and adds: "I like Yogi Berra and Casey Stengel, but I really love Ralph Houk. If he were to tell me to run through that brick wall there, I'd start banging my head against it. And I know he'd be right there alongside me."

Most of all, Mickey appreciates his family. After bearing four boys, Merlyn Mantle can still put on a pair of slacks and slow traffic. She wears her once-red hair platinum blonde, and "her fried chicken and gravy is the greatest." "She's the best thing that ever happened to me," says her husband, "and I wouldn't give her up for anything."

The two older boys, Mickey, 11 and David, 9, already show unmistakable signs of the Mantle physique—narrow waists and shoulders that look as if someone forgot to remove the coat hangers from the shirts. Little Mickey follows baseball, but his athletic passion is football. When his father effortlessly throws sidearm passes of 35 yards, the boy returns with punts. This winter, a photographer tried to get a shot of Mickey, Jr., waving good-bye to his father after being driven to school. The boy flapped a very feeble imitation of a wave and trotted away. "He doesn't like a fuss in front of other kids," said his father.

"The boys idolize their father," says Merlyn. "If I say, 'Sit there,' to one, they all sit," proudly says Mickey. "We don't ever have to hit 'em." Like most American males, the head of the family does not verbalize his affection. At breakfast, he beams at the kids spooning up cereal. "That's right, boy, hog it up," he says to seven-year-old Billy, named for Martin. But more often, the father communicates his affection by touch. He constantly stops to pat a son upon the head, squeeze the knee of the one beside him on the couch, put his foot against that of one sprawled on the floor before the television set or wrap an arm about little Danny, four. The same holds true for his wife. He gives her a light hug while she makes breakfast or suddenly nuzzles her as they sit at dinner in a restaurant.

In the off season, after the boys leave for school, Mickey heads for the golf course. Once again, fair nature becomes disguised with a hard-favored rage as he rips into the ball. Using only a three wood, he hits some 300 yards from the tee, and it is a rare hole on which he requires a second wood or a low iron to reach the green. Unfortunately, an occasional drive will sail far over a highway into a neighboring pasture or out of bounds. Then, as in his vocation, Mantle casts his eyes down to the ground and marches off, black with anger at himself. He is considered the world's record holder for booting a batting helmet, and spectators often boo the gesture. Other players do not consider such action bush on Mickey's part. "Hell, he's just mad at himself for not doing better. How can you boo a guy for wanting to hit so bad?" says one. Mickey remains his most vinegary critic. Talk of the 1964 World Series, and he says little of his three home runs. "I gave them four runs," he says in disgust at his fielding.

When not at the golf course, Mickey may drop in to visit his Dallas lawyer, Bedford Wynne. Over the years, Mickey has made a number of investments with indecisive results. His motel in Joplin, Missouri, he sold at a decent profit, but his Dallas bowling alley he escaped from only with a loss. Currently he is an investor in the Miss Teen-Age America Pageant, is part of a group sponsoring the Mickey Mantle Billiard Parlors, recently bought a piece of an insurance firm, has a few small oil investments, and owns some registered Aberdeen Angus cattle roaming about Colorado. While he is by no means a project for the War on Poverty, Mickey's financial future is less than assured. The Dallas home is in the $100,000 neighborhood, and the taxes are fierce. Summers, he rents a place for Merlyn and the boys in New Jersey, and for years he has contributed to the support of various relatives. His clothes are on the sharp side, but there is an attractive, neat look to him. Although he occasionally indulges himself with handsomely styled alligator shoes at $155 (they will last a lifetime), Mantle does not throw his money around. He still remembers working in the mines after high school at $35 a week. Nor is he tight-fisted; he will always pick up his share or even the entire check. The difficulty is that Mantle is an Internal Revenue man's delight. "If you're incorporated," says Mickey with the expertise of the accountant," and more than half of your income comes from your personal services, like mine, then they say your corporation is just a personal holding company, and it's taxed like ordinary income."

The hero is now 33, an age at which many ball players are in their prime. Infirmities, not time, have dimmed the flourish of his youth, however, and never again will he be the outfielder he once was. "I can't stop fast and throw, so I have to wait for the ball to get to me," says Mickey. "There's nothing wrong with my arm. I can still throw, but I give away a step to the runner by having to wait for the ball." Mantle cannot stop abruptly because the cartilage or cushion between the bones of his knees is gone. "My ligaments in both knees are like old elastic," which makes lateral movement at the knee a precarious business as well. To build up his weakened groin and hamstrung muscles, he works out during the winter at the Cowboys' field, chasing a football with a friend, George Owens, does isometric exercises, and takes physical therapy from the Cowboys' trainer.

Still relishing the contest when at bat, Mickey says, "I'd like to play another five years. If there was just me and that pitcher there, I'd still want to hit him. There's just nothing like that feeling when you hit a home run, especially like that one in the ninth inning of the World Series."

But if he finds he can no longer summon the blood, Mickey offers no complaint. "I figure I got all the breaks in spite of my legs. Otherwise, I'd have been in the mines." And the Blue Goose is a long, long way from Olympus.

1966

THE SILENT SEASON OF A HERO

By Gay Talese

FROM ESQUIRE

Copyright © 1966, Gay Talese

DiMaggio! It was our judge Robert Harron, a former New York sports writer, who said that this story provided a notable picture of the man so many had known and so many millions had admired and yet so few understood. This piece will help the reader to know this great outfielder better and will even increase the esteem in which he is held. One of our other judges felt that he had never read a better overall story about the Yankee Clipper and was held enthralled by his personal grief and dignity under the pressure of intrusion by dopes, opportunists, and even well-meaning admirers.

"I would like to take the great DiMaggio fishing," the old man said.

"They say his father was a fisherman. Maybe he was as poor as we are and would understand."

—ERNEST HEMINGWAY, *The Old Man and the Sea*

It was not quite spring, the silent season before the search for salmon, and the old fishermen of San Francisco were either painting their boats or repairing their nets along the pier or sitting in the sun talking quietly among themselves, watching the tourists come and go, and smiling, now, as a pretty girl paused to take their picture. She was about 25, healthy and blue-eyed and wearing a turtleneck sweater, and she had long, flowing blonde hair that she brushed back a few times before clicking her camera. The fishermen, looking at her, made admiring comments, but she did not understand because they spoke a Sicilian dialect; nor did she understand the tall gray-haired man in a dark suit who stood watching her from behind a big bay window on the second floor of DiMaggio's Restaurant that overlooks the pier.

He watched until she left, lost in the crowd of newly arrived tourists that had just come down the hill by cable car. Then he sat down again at the table in the restaurant, finishing his tea and lighting another cigarette, his fifth in the last half hour. It was 11:30 in the morning. None of the other tables was occupied, and the only sounds came from the bar, where a liquor salesman was laughing at something the headwaiter had said. But then the salesman, his briefcase under his arm, headed for the door, stopping briefly to peek into the dining room and call out, "See you later, Joe," Joe DiMaggio turned and waved at the salesman. Then the room was quiet again.

At 51, DiMaggio was a most distinguished-looking man, aging as gracefully as he had played on the ball field, impeccable in his tailoring, his nails manicured, his 6-foot-2 body seeming as lean and capable as when he posed for the portrait that hangs in the restaurant and shows him in Yankee Stadium, swinging from the heels at a pitch thrown 20 years ago. His gray hair was thinning at the crown, but just barely, and his face was lined in the right places, and his expression, once as sad and haunted as a matador's, was more in repose these days, though, as now, tension had returned and he chain-smoked and occasionally paced the floor and looked out the window at the people below. In the crowd was a man he did not wish to see.

The man had met DiMaggio in New York. This week he had come to San Francisco and had telephoned several times, but none of the calls had been returned because DiMaggio suspected that the man, who had said he was doing research on some vague sociological project, really wanted to delve into DiMaggio's private life and that of DiMaggio's former wife, Marilyn Monroe. DiMaggio would never tolerate this. The memory of her death is still very painful to him, and yet, because he keeps it to himself, some people are not sensitive to it. One night in a supper club, a woman who had been drinking approached his table, and when he did not ask her to join him, she snapped:

"All right, I guess I'm *not* Marilyn Monroe."

He ignored her remark, but when she repeated it, he replied, barely controlling his anger, "No—I wish you were, but you're not."

The tone of his voice softened her, and she asked, "Am I saying something wrong?"

"You already have," he said. "Now will you please leave me alone?"

His friends on the wharf, understanding him as they do, are very careful when discussing him with strangers, knowing that should they inadvertently betray a confidence, he will not denounce them but rather will never speak to them again; this comes from a sense of propriety not inconsistent in the man who also, after Marilyn Monroe's death, directed that fresh flowers be placed on her grave "forever."

Some of the older fishermen who have known DiMaggio all his life remember him as a small boy who helped clean his father's boat, and as a young man who sneaked away and used a broken oar as a bat on the sandlots nearby. His father, a small mustachioed man known as Zio Pepe, would become infuriated and call him *lagnuso*, lazy, *meschino*, good-for-nothing, but in 1936 Zio Pepe was among those who cheered when Joe DiMaggio returned to San Francisco after his first season with the New York Yankees and was carried along the wharf on the shoulders of the fishermen.

The fishermen also remember how, after his retirement in 1951, DiMaggio brought his second wife, Marilyn, to live near the wharf, and sometimes they would be seen early in the morning fishing off DiMaggio's boat, the *Yankee Clipper*, now docked quietly in the marina, and in the evening they would be sitting and talking on the pier. They had arguments, too, the fishermen knew, and one night Marilyn was seen running hysterically, crying, as she ran, along the road away from the pier, with Joe following. But the fishermen pretended they did not see this; it was none of their affair. They knew that Joe wanted her to stay in San Francisco and avoid the sharks in Hollywood, but she was confused and torn then—"She was a child," they said—and even today DiMaggio loathes Los Angeles and many of the people in it. He no longer speaks to his onetime friend, Frank Sinatra, who had befriended Marilyn in her final years, and he also is cool to Dean Martin and Peter Lawford and Lawford's former wife, Pat, who once gave a party at which she introduced Marilyn Monroe to Robert Kennedy, and the two of them danced often that night, Joe heard, and he did not take it well. He was possessive of her that year, his close friends say, because Marilyn and he had planned to remarry; but before they could she was dead, and DiMaggio banned the Lawfords and Sinatra and many Hollywood people from her funeral. When Marilyn Monroe's attorney complained that DiMaggio was keeping her friends away, DiMaggio answered coldly, "If it weren't for those friends persuading her to stay in Hollywood, she would still be alive."

Joe DiMaggio now spends most of the year in San Francisco, and each day tourists, noticing the name on the restaurant, ask the men on the wharf if they ever see him. Oh, yes, the men say, they see him nearly every day; they have not seen him yet this morning, they add, but he should be arriving shortly. So the tourists continue to walk along the piers past the crab vendors, under the circling sea gulls, past the fish-'n'-chip stands, sometimes stopping to watch a large vessel steaming toward the Golden Gate Bridge, which, to their dismay, is painted red. Then they visit the Wax Museum, where there is a life-size figure of DiMaggio in uniform, and walk across the street and spend a quarter to peer through the silver telescopes focused on the island of Alcatraz, which is no longer a federal prison. Then they return to ask the men if DiMaggio has been seen. Not yet, the men say, although they notice his blue Impala parked in the lot next to the restaurant. Sometimes tourists will walk into the restaurant and have lunch and will see him sitting calmly in a corner signing autographs and being extremely gracious with everyone. At other times, as on this particular morning when the man from New York chose to visit, DiMaggio was tense and suspicious.

When the man entered the restaurant from the side steps leading to the dining room, he saw DiMaggio standing near the window, talking with an elderly maître d' named Charles Friscia. Not wanting to walk in and risk intrusion, the man asked one of DiMaggio's nephews to inform Joe of his presence. When DiMaggio got the message, he quickly turned and left Friscia and disappeared through an exit leading down to the kitchen.

Astonished and confused, the visitor stood in the hall. A moment later Friscia appeared and the man asked, "Did Joe leave?"

"Joe who?" Friscia replied.

"Joe DiMaggio!"

"Haven't seen him," Friscia said.

"You haven't *seen* him! He was standing right next to you a second ago!"

"It wasn't me," Friscia said.

"You were standing next to him. I saw you. In the dining room."

"You must be mistaken," Friscia said, softly, seriously. "It wasn't me."

"You *must* be kidding," the man said angrily, turning and leaving the restaurant. Before he could get to his car, however, DiMaggio's nephew came running after him and said, "Joe wants to see you."

He returned, expecting to see DiMaggio waiting for him. Instead, he was handed a telephone. The voice was powerful and deep and so tense that the quick sentences ran together.

"You are invading my rights. I did not ask you to come. I assume you have a lawyer. You must have a lawyer, get your lawyer!"

"I came as a friend," the man interrupted.

"That's beside the point," DiMaggio said. "I have my privacy. I do not want it violated. You'd better get a lawyer. . . ." Then, pausing, DiMaggio asked, "Is my nephew there?"

He was not.

"Then wait where you are."

A moment later DiMaggio appeared, tall and red-faced, erect and beautifully dressed in his dark suit and white shirt with the gray silk tie and the gleaming silver cuff links. He moved with his big steps toward the man and handed him an airmail envelope unopened that the man had written from New York.

"Here," DiMaggio said. "This is yours."

Then DiMaggio sat down at a small table. He said nothing, just lit a cigarette and waited, legs crossed, his head held high and back so as to reveal the intricate construction of his nose, a fine sharp tip above the big nostrils and tiny bones built out from the bridge, a great nose.

"Look," DiMaggio said, more calmly, "I do not interfere with other people's lives. And I do not expect them to interfere with mine. There are things about my life, personal things, that I refuse to talk about. And even if you asked my brothers, they would be unable to tell you about them because they do not know. There are things about me, so many things, that they simply do not know. . . ."

"I don't want to cause trouble," the man said. "I think you're a great man, and . . ."

"I'm not great," DiMaggio cut in. "I'm not great," he repeated softly. "I'm just a man trying to get along."

Then DiMaggio, as if realizing that he was intruding upon his own privacy, abruptly stood up. He looked at his watch.

"I'm late," he said, very formal again. I'm 10 minutes late. You're making me late."

The man left the restaurant. He crossed the street and wandered over to the pier, briefly watching the fishermen hauling their nets and talking in the sun, seemingly very calm and contented. Then, after he turned and was headed back toward the parking lot, a blue Impala stopped in front of him and Joe DiMaggio leaned out the window and asked, "Do you have a car?" His voice was very gentle.

"Yes," the man said.

"Oh," DiMaggio said. "I would have given you a ride."

Joe DiMaggio was not born in San Francisco but in Martinez, a small fishing village 25 miles northeast of the Golden Gate. Zio Pepe had settled there after leaving Isola delle Femmine, an islet off Palermo where the DiMaggios had been fishermen for generations. But in 1915, hearing of the luckier waters off San Francisco's wharf, Zio Pepe left Martinez, packing his boat with furniture and family, including Joe, who was one year old.

San Francisco was placid and picturesque when the DiMaggios arrived, but there was a competitive undercurrent and struggle for power along the pier. At dawn the boats would sail out to where the bay meets the ocean and the sea is rough, and later the men would race back with their hauls, hoping to beat their fellow fishermen to shore and sell it while they could. Twenty or 30 boats would sometimes be trying to gain the channel shoreward at the same time, and a fisherman had to know every rock in the water, and later know every bargaining trick along the shore, because the dealers and restaurateurs would play one fisherman off against the other, keeping the prices down. Later the fishermen became wiser and organized, predetermining the maximum amount each fisherman would catch, but there were always some men who, like the fish, never learned, and so heads would sometimes be broken, nets slashed, gasoline poured onto their fish, flowers of warning placed outside their doors.

But these days were ending when Zio Pepe arrived, and he expected his five sons to succeed him as fishermen, and the first two, Tom and Michael, did; but a third, Vincent, wanted to sing. He sang with such magnificent power as a young man that he came to the attention of the great banker, A. P. Giannini, and there were plans to send him to Italy for tutoring and the opera. But there was hesitation around the DiMaggio household and

Vince never went; instead, he played ball with the San Francisco Seals and sports writers misspelled his name.

It was DiMaggio until Joe, at Vince's recommendation, joined the team and became a sensation, being followed later by the youngest brother, Dominic, who was also outstanding. All three later played in the big leagues, and some writers like to say that Joe was the best hitter, Dom the best fielder, Vince the best singer, and Casey Stengel once said: "Vince is the only player I ever saw who could strike out three times in one game and not be embarrassed. He'd walk into the clubhouse whistling. Everybody would be feeling sorry for him, but Vince always thought he was doing good."

After he retired from baseball Vince became a bartender, then a milkman, now a carpenter. He lives 40 miles north of San Francisco in a house he partly built, has been happily married for 34 years, has four grandchildren, has in the closet one of Joe's tailor-made suits that he has never had altered to fit, and when people ask him if envies Joe he always says, "No, maybe Joe would like to have what I have." The brother Vincent most admired was Michael, "a big earthy man, a dreamer, a fisherman who wanted things but didn't want to take from Joe, or to work in the restaurant. He wanted a bigger boat, but wanted to earn it on his own. He never got it." In 1953, at the age of 44, Michael fell from his boat and drowned.

Since Zio Pepe's death at 77 in 1949, Tom at 62, the oldest brother—two of his four sisters are older—has become nominal head of the family and manages the restaurant that was opened in 1937 as Joe DiMaggio's Grotto. Later Joe sold out his share, and now Tom is the co-owner with Dominic. Of all the brothers, Dominic, who was known as the "Little Professor" when he played with the Boston Red Sox, is the most successful in business. He lives in a fashionable Boston suburb with his wife and three children and is president of a firm that manufactures fiber cushion materials and grossed more than $3,500,000 last year.

Joe DiMaggio lives with his widowed sister, Marie, in a tan stone house on a quiet residential street not far from Fisherman's Wharf. He bought the house almost 30 years ago for his parents, and after their deaths he lived there with Marilyn Monroe. Now it is cared for by Marie, a slim and handsome dark-eyed woman who has an apartment on the second floor, Joe on the third. There are some baseball trophies and plaques in the small room off DiMaggio's bedroom, and on his dresser are photographs of

Marilyn Monroe, and in the living room downstairs is a small painting of her that DiMaggio likes very much; it reveals only her face and shoulders and she is wearing a wide-brimmed sun hat, and there is a soft, sweet smile on her lips, an innocent curiosity about her that is the way he saw her and the way he wanted her to be seen by others—a simple girl, "a warm, big-hearted girl," he once described her, "that everybody took advantage of."

The publicity photographs emphasizing her sex appeal often offended him, and a memorable moment for Billy Wilder, who directed her in *The Seven-Year Itch,* occurred when he spotted DiMaggio in a large crowd of people gathered on Lexington Avenue in New York to watch a scene in which Marilyn, standing over a subway grating to cool herself, had her skirts blown high by a sudden wind blow. "What the hell is going on here?" DiMaggio was overheard to have said in the crowd, and Wilder recalled, "I shall never forget the look of death on Joe's face."

He was then 39, she was 27. They had been married in January of that year, 1954, despite disharmony in temperament and time; he was tired of publicity, she was thriving on it; he was intolerant of tardiness, she was always late. During their honeymoon in Tokyo an American general had introduced himself and asked if, as a patriotic gesture, she would visit the troops in Korea. She looked at Joe. "It's your honeymoon," he said, shrugging, "go ahead if you want to."

She appeared on 10 occasions before 100,000 servicemen, and when she returned, she said, "It was so wonderful, Joe. You never heard such cheering."

"Yes, I have," he said.

Across from her portrait in the living room, on a coffee table in front of a sofa, is a sterling-silver humidor that was presented to him by his Yankee teammates at a time when he was the most talked-about man in America, and when Les Brown's band had recorded a hit that was heard day and night on the radio.

> *From Coast to Coast, that's all you hear*
> *Of Joe the One-Man Show.*
> *He's glorified the horsehide sphere,*
> *Jolting Joe DiMaggio . . .*
> *Joe . . . Joe . . . DiMaggio . . . we*
> *want you on our side . . .*

The year was 1941, and it began for DiMaggio in the middle of May after the Yankees had lost four games in a row, seven of their last nine, and were in fourth place, five and a half games

behind the leading Cleveland Indians. On May 15, DiMaggio hit
only a first-inning single in a game that New York lost to Chicago
13–1; he was barely hitting .300, and had greatly disappointed
the crowds that had seen him finish with a .352 average the year
before and .381 in 1939.

He got a hit in the next game, and the next, and the next. On
May 24, with the Yankees losing 6–5 to Boston, DiMaggio came
up with runners on second and third and singled them home,
winning the game, extending his streak to 10 games. But it went
largely unnoticed. Even DiMaggio was not conscious of it until it
had reached 29 games in mid-June. Then the newspapers began
to dramatize it, the public became aroused, they sent him good-
luck charms of every description, and DiMaggio kept hitting, and
radio announcers would interrupt programs to announce the
news, and then the song again: "Joe . . . Joe . . . DiMaggio
. . . we want you on our side . . ."

Sometimes DiMaggio would be hitless his first three times
up, the tension would build, it would appear that the game
would end without his getting another chance—but he always
would, and then he would hit the ball against the left-field wall,
or through the pitcher's legs, or between two leaping infielders.
In the forty-first game, the first of a doubleheader in Washington,
DiMaggio tied an American League record that George Sisler
had set in 1922. But before the second game began, a spectator
sneaked onto the field and into the Yankees' dugout and stole
DiMaggio's favorite bat. In the second game, using another of his
bats, DiMaggio lined out twice and flied out. But in the seventh
inning, borrowing one of his old bats that a teammate was using,
he singled and broke Sisler's record, and he was only three games
away from surpassing the major-league record of 44 set in 1897
by Willie Keeler while playing for Baltimore when it was a National League franchise.

An appeal for the missing bat was made through the newspapers. A man from Newark admitted the crime and returned it
with regrets. And on July 2 at Yankee Stadium, DiMaggio hit a
home run into the left-field stands. The record was broken.

He also got hits in the next 11 games, but on July 17 in
Cleveland, at a night game attended by 67,468, he failed against
two pitchers, Al Smith and Jim Bagby, Jr., although Cleveland's
hero was really its third baseman, Ken Keltner, who in the first
inning lunged to his right to make a spectacular backhanded stop
of a drive and, from the foul line behind third base, threw
DiMaggio out. DiMaggio received a walk in the fourth inning.

But in the seventh he again hit a hard shot at Keltner, who again stopped it and threw him out. DiMaggio hit sharply toward the shortstop in the eighth inning, the ball taking a bad hop, but Lou Boudreau speared it off his shoulder and threw to the second baseman to start a double play and DiMaggio's streak was stopped at 56 games. But the New York Yankees were on their way to winning the pennant by 17 games, and the World Series too, and so in August, in a hotel suite in Washington, the players threw a surprise party for DiMaggio and toasted him with champagne and presented him with his Tiffany silver humidor that is now in San Francisco in his living room. . . .

Marie was in the kitchen making toast and tea when DiMaggio came down for breakfast; his gray hair was uncombed but, since he wears it short, it was not untidy. He said good morning to Marie, sat down, and yawned. He lit a cigarette. He wore a blue wool bathrobe over his pajamas. It was 8:00 A.M. He had many things to do today and he seemed cheerful. He had a conference with the president of Continental Television, Inc., a large retail chain in California of which he is a partner and vice-president; later he had a golf date, and then a big banquet to attend, and, if that did not go on too long and if he were not too tired afterward, he might have a date.

Picking up the morning paper, not rushing to the sports page, DiMaggio read the front-page news, the people problems of 1966: Kwame Nkrumah was overthrown in Ghana, students were burning their draft cards (DiMaggio shook his head), the flu epidemic was spreading through the whole state of California. Then he flipped inside through the gossip columns, thankful they did not have him in there today—they had printed an item about his dating "an electrifying airline hostess" not long ago, and they also spotted him at dinner with Dori Lane, "the frantic frugger" in Whisky à Go Go's glass cage—and then he turned to the sports page and read a story about how the injured Mickey Mantle may never regain his form.

It happened all so quickly, the passing of Mantle, or so it seemed; he had succeeded DiMaggio, who had succeeded Ruth, but now there was no great young power hitter coming up, and the Yankee management, almost desperate, had talked Mantle out of retirement, and on September 18, 1965, they gave him a "day" in New York during which he received several thousand dollars' worth of gifts—an automobile, two quarter horses, free vacation trips to Rome, Nassau, Puerto Rico—and DiMaggio had

flown to New York to make the introduction before 50,000: it had
been a dramatic day, an almost holy day for the believers who
had jammed the grandstands early to witness the canonization of
a new stadium saint. Cardinal Spellman was on the committee,
President Johnson sent a telegram, the day was officially proclaimed by the Mayor of New York, an orchestra assembled in the
center field in front of the trinity of monuments to Ruth, Gehrig,
Huggins; and high in the grandstands, billowing in the breeze of
early autumn, were white banners that read: "Don't Quit, Mick,"
"We Love the Mick."

The banners had been held by hundreds of young boys
whose dreams had been fulfilled so often by Mantle, but also
seated in the grandstands were older men, paunchy and balding,
in whose middle-aged minds DiMaggio was still vivid and invincible, and some of them remembered how one month before,
during a pregame exhibition at Old-Timers' Day in Yankee
Stadium, DiMaggio had hit a pitch into the left-field seats, and
suddenly thousands of people had jumped wildly to their feet,
joyously screaming—the great DiMaggio had returned, they
were young again, it was yesterday.

But on this sunny September day at the stadium, the feast
day of Mickey Mantle, DiMaggio was not wearing No. 5 on his
back or a black cap to cover his graying hair; he was wearing a
black suit and white shirt and blue tie, and he stood in one
corner of the Yankees' dugout waiting to be introduced by Red
Barber, who was standing near home plate behind a silver
microphone. In the outfield Guy Lombardo's Royal Canadians
were playing soothing, soft music; and moving slowly back and
forth over the sprawling green grass between the left-field bullpen and the infield were two carts driven by grounds keepers and
containing dozens and dozens of large gifts for Mantle—a 6-foot,
100-pound Hebrew National salami, a Winchester rifle, a mink
coat for Mrs. Mantle, a set of Wilson golf clubs, year's supply of
Chunky Candy. DiMaggio smoked a cigarette, but cupped it in
his hands as if not wanting to be caught in the act by teen-aged
boys near enough to peek down into the dugout. Then, edging
forward a step, DiMaggio poked his head out and looked up. He
could see nothing above except the packed, towering green
grandstands that seemed a mile high and moving, and he could
see no clouds or blue sky, only a sky of faces. Then the announcer called out his name—"Joe DiMaggio!"—and suddenly
there was a blast of cheering that grew louder and louder,
echoing and reechoing within the big steel canyon, and Di-

Maggio stomped out his cigarette and climbed up the dugout steps and onto the soft green grass, the noise resounding in his ears, he could almost feel the breeze, the breath of 50,000 lungs upon him, 100,000 eyes watching his every move, and for the briefest instant as he walked he closed his eyes.

Then in his path he saw Mickey Mantle's mother, a smiling woman wearing an orchid, and he gently reached out for her elbow, holding it as he led her toward the microphone next to the other dignitaries lined up on the infield. Then he stood, very erect and without expression as the cheers softened and the stadium settled down.

Mantle was still in the dugout, in uniform, standing with one leg on the top step, and lined on both sides of him were the other Yankees who, when the ceremony was over, would play the Detroit Tigers. Then into the dugout, smiling, came Senator Robert Kennedy, accompanied by two tall curly-haired assistants with blue eyes, Fordham freckles. Jim Farley was the first on the field to notice the Senator, and Farley muttered, loud enough for others to hear, "Who the hell invited *him?*"

Toots Shor and some of the other committeemen standing near Farley looked into the dugout, and so did DiMaggio, his glance seeming cold, but he remained silent. Kennedy walked up and down within the dugout, shaking hands with the Yankees, but he did not walk onto the field.

"Senator," said Yankees' manager Johnny Keane, "why don't you sit down?" Kennedy quickly shook his head, smiled. He remained standing, and then one Yankee came over and asked about getting relatives out of Cuba, and Kennedy called over one of his aides to take down the details in a notebook.

On the infield the ceremony went on, Mantle's gifts continued to pile up—a Mobilette motorbike, a Sooner Schooner wagon barbecue, a year's supply of Chock Full O' Nuts coffee, a year's supply of Topps Chewing Gum—and the Yankee players watched, and Maris seemed glum.

"Hey, Rog," yelled a man with a tape recorder, Murray Olderman, "I want to do a 30-second tape with you."

Maris swore angrily, shook his head.

"Why don't you ask Richardson? He's a better talker than me."

"Yes, but the fact that it comes from you . . ."

Maris swore again. But finally he went over and said in an interview that Mantle was the finest player of his era, a great competitor, a great hitter.

Fifteen minutes later, standing behind the microphone at home plate, DiMaggio was telling the crowd, "I'm proud to introduce the man who succeeded me in center field in 1951," and from every corner of the stadium, the cheering, whistling, clapping came down. Mantle stepped forward. He stood with his wife and children, posed for the photographers kneeling in front. Then he thanked the crowd in a short speech, and, turning, shook hands with the dignitaries standing nearby. Among them now was Senator Kennedy, who had been spotted in the dugout five minutes before by Red Barber, and been called out and introduced. Kennedy posed with Mantle for a photographer, then shook hands with the Mantle children, and with Toots Shor and James Farley and others. DiMaggio saw him coming down the line and at the last second he backed away, casually, hardly anybody noticing it, and Kennedy seemed not to notice it either, just swept past, shaking more hands. . . .

Finishing his tea, putting aside the newspaper, DiMaggio went upstairs to dress, and soon he was waving good-bye to Marie and driving toward his business appointment in downtown San Francisco with his partners in the retail television business. DiMaggio, while not a millionaire, has invested wisely and has always had, since his retirement from baseball, executive positions with big companies that have paid him well. He also was among the organizers of the Fisherman's National Bank of San Francisco last year, and, though it never came about, he demonstrated an acuteness that impressed those businessmen who had thought of him only in terms of baseball. He has had offers to manage big-league baseball teams but always has rejected them, saying, "I have enough trouble taking care of my own problems without taking on the responsibilities of 25 ball players."

So his only contact with baseball these days, excluding public appearances, is his unsalaried job as a batting coach each spring in Florida with the New York Yankees, a trip he would make once again on the following Sunday, three days away, if he could accomplish what for him is always the dreaded responsibility of packing, a task made no easier by the fact that he lately had fallen into the habit of keeping his clothes in two places—some hang in his closet at home, some hang in the back room of a saloon called Reno's.

Reno's is a dimly lit bar in the center of San Francisco. A portrait of DiMaggio swinging a bat hangs on the wall, in addition to portraits of other star athletes, and the clientele consists mainly of the sporting crowd and newspapermen, people who know DiMaggio quite well and around whom he speaks freely on a number of subjects and relaxes as he can in few other places. The owner of the bar is Reno Barosocchini, a broad-shouldered and handsome man of 51 with graying wavy hair who began as a fiddler in Dago Mary's tavern 35 years ago. He later became a bartender there and elsewhere, including DiMaggio's Restaurant, and now he is probably DiMaggio's closest friend. He was the best man at the DiMaggio-Monroe wedding in 1954, and when they separated nine months later in Los Angeles, Reno rushed down to help DiMaggio with the packing and drove him back to San Francisco. Reno will never forget the day.

Hundreds of people were gathered around the Beverly Hills home that DiMaggio and Marilyn had rented, and photographers were perched in the trees watching the windows, and others stood on the lawn and behind the rose bushes waiting to snap pictures of anybody who walked out of the house. The newspapers that day played all the puns—"Joe Fanned on Jealousy"; "Marilyn and Joe—Out at Home"—and the Hollywood columnists, to whom DiMaggio was never an idol, never a gracious host, recounted instances of incompatibility, and Oscar Levant said it all proved that no man could be a success in two national pastimes. When Reno Barsocchini arrived, he had to push his way through the mob, then bang on the door for several minutes before being admitted. Marilyn Monroe was upstairs in bed. Joe DiMaggio was downstairs with his suitcases, tense and pale, his eyes bloodshot.

Reno took the suitcase and golf clubs out to DiMaggio's car, and then DiMaggio came out of the house, the reporters moving toward him, the lights flashing.

"Where are you going?" they yelled.

"I'm driving to San Francisco," he said, walking quickly.

"Is that going to be your home?"

"That is my home and always has been."

"Are you coming back?"

DiMaggio turned for a moment, looking up at the house.

"No," he said, "I'll never be back."

Reno Barsocchini, except for a brief falling-out over something he will not discuss, has been DiMaggio's trusted companion ever since, joining him whenever he can on the golf course or on the town, otherwise waiting for him in the bar with other middle-aged men. They may wait for hours sometimes, waiting and knowing that when he arrives he may wish to be alone; but it does not seem to matter, they are endlessly awed by him, moved by the mystique, he is a kind of male Garbo. They know that he can be warm and loyal if they are sensitive to his wishes, but they must never be late for an appointment to meet him. One man, unable to find a parking place, arrived a half hour late once, and DiMaggio did not talk to him again for three months. They know, too, when dining at night with DiMaggio, that he generally prefers male companions and occasionally one or two young women, but never wives; wives gossip, wives complain, wives are trouble, and men wishing to remain close to DiMaggio must keep their wives at home.

When DiMaggio strolls into Reno's bar, the men wave and call out his name and Reno Barsocchini smiles and announces, "Here's the Clipper!"—the "Yankee Clipper" being a nickname from his baseball days.

"Hey Clipper, Clipper," Reno had said two nights before, "where you been, Clipper? . . . Clipper, how 'bout a belt?"

DiMaggio refused the offer of a drink, ordering instead a pot of tea, which he prefers to all other beverages except before a date, when he will switch to vodka.

"Hey, Joe," a sports writer asked, a man researching a magazine piece on golf, "why is it that a golfer, when he starts getting older, loses his putting touch first? Like Snead and Hogan, they can still hit a ball well off the tee, but on the greens they lose the strokes."

"It's the pressure of age," DiMaggio said, turning around on his barstool. "With age you get jittery. It's true of golfers, it's true of any man when he gets into his 50s. He doesn't take chances like he used to. The younger golfer, on the greens, he'll stroke his putts better. The older man, he becomes hesitant. A little uncertain. Shaky. When it comes to taking chances, the younger man, even when driving a car, will take chances that the older man won't."

"Speaking of chances," another man said, one of the group that had gathered around DiMaggio, "did you see that guy on crutches in here last night?"

"Yeah, had his leg in a cast," a third said. "Skiing."

"I would never ski," DiMaggio said, "Men who ski must be doing it to impress a broad. You see these men, some of them 40, 50, getting onto skis. And later you see them all bandaged up, broken legs."

"But skiing's a very sexy sport, Joe. All the clothes, the tight pants, the fireplaces in the ski lodge, the bear rug—Christ nobody goes to ski. They just go out there to get it cold so they can warm it up."

"Maybe you're right," DiMaggio said. "I might be persuaded."

"Want a belt, Clipper?" Reno asked.

DiMaggio thought for a second, then said, "All right—first belt tonight."

Now it was noon, a warm sunny day. DiMaggio's business meeting with the television retailers had gone well; he had made a strong appeal to George Shahood, president of Continental Television, Inc., which has eight retail outlets in Northern California, to put prices on color television sets and increase the sales volume, and Shahood had conceded it was worth a try. Then DiMaggio called Reno's bar to see if there were any messages, and now he was in Lefty O'Doul's car being driven along Fisherman's Wharf toward the Golden Gate Bridge en route to a golf course 30 miles upstate. Lefty O'Doul was one of the great hitters in the National League in the early thirties, and later he managed the San Francisco Seals when DiMaggio was the shining star. Though O'Doul is now 69, 18 years older than DiMaggio, he nevertheless possesses great energy and spirit, is a hard-drinking, boisterous man with a big belly and roving eye; and when DiMaggio, as they drove along the highway toward the golf club, noticed a lovely blonde at the wheel of a car nearby and exclaimed, "Look at *that* tomato!" O'Doul's head suddenly spun around, he took his eyes off the road, and yelled, "Where, *where?*" O'Doul's golf game is less than what it was—he used to have a two-handicap—but he still shoots in the 80s, as does DiMaggio.

DiMaggio's drives range between 250 and 280 yards when he doesn't sky them, and his putting is good, but he is distracted by a bad back that both pains him and hinders the fullness of his swing. On the first hole, waiting to tee off, DiMaggio sat back watching a foursome of college boys ahead swinging with such freedom. "Oh," he said with a sigh, "to have *their* backs."

DiMaggio and O'Doul were accompanied around the golf course by Ernie Nevers, the former football star, and two brothers who are in the hotel and movie-distribution business. They moved quickly up and down the green hills in electric golf carts, and DiMaggio's game was exceptionally good for the first nine holes. But then he seemed distracted, perhaps tired, perhaps even reacting to a conversation of a few minutes before. One of the movie men was praising the film *Boeing, Boeing,* starring Tony Curtis and Jerry Lewis, and the man asked DiMaggio if he had seen it.

"No," DiMaggio said. Then he added, swiftly, "I haven't seen a film in eight years."

DiMaggio hooked a few shots, was in the woods. He took a No. 9 iron and tried to chip out. But O'Doul interrupted Di-Maggio's concentration to remind him to keep the face of the club closed. DiMaggio hit the ball. It caromed off the side of his club, went skipping like a rabbit through the high grass down toward a pond. DiMaggio rarely displays any emotion on a golf course, but now, without saying a word, he took his No. 9 iron and flung it into the air. The club landed in a tree and stayed up there.

"Well," O'Doul said casually, "there goes *that* set of clubs."

DiMaggio walked to the tree. Fortunately the club had slipped to the lower branch, and DiMaggio could stretch up on the cart and get it back.

"Every time I get advice," DiMaggio muttered to himself, shaking his head slowly and walking toward the pond, "I shank it."

Later, showered and dressed, DiMaggio and the others drove to a banquet about 10 miles from the golf course. Some-body had said it was going to be an elegant dinner, but when they arrived they could see it was more like a county fair; farmers were gathered outside a big barnlike building, a candi-date for sheriff was distributing leaflets at the front door, and a chorus of homely ladies was inside singing "You Are My Sun-shine."

"How did we get sucked into this?" DiMaggio asked, talking out of the side of his mouth, as they approached the building.

"O'Doul," one of the men said. "It's his fault. Damned O'Doul can't turn *anything* down."

"Go to hell," O'Doul said.

Soon DiMaggio and O'Doul and Ernie Nevers were sur-rounded by the crowd, and the woman who had been leading the chorus came rushing over and said, "Oh, Mr. DiMaggio, it certainly is a pleasure having you."

"It's a pleasure being here, ma'am," he said, forcing a smile.

"It's too bad you didn't arrive a moment sooner. You'd have heard our singing."

"Oh, I heard it," he said, "and I enjoyed it very much."

"Good, good," she said. "And how are your brothers, Dom and Vic?"

"Fine. Dom lives near Boston. Vince is in Pittsburgh."

"Why, *hello* there, Joe," interrupted a man with wine on his breath, patting DiMaggio on the back, feeling his arm. "Who's gonna take it this year, Joe?"

"Well, I have no idea," DiMaggio said.

"What about the Giants?"

"Your guess is as good as mine."

"Well, you can't count the Dodgers out," the man said.

"You sure can't," DiMaggio said.

"Not with all that pitching."

"Pitching is certainly important," DiMaggio said.

Everywhere he goes the question seems the same, as if he has some special vision into the future of new heroes, and everywhere he goes, too, older men grab his hand and feel his arm and predict that he could still go out there and hit one, and the smile on DiMaggio's face is genuine. He tries hard to remain as he was—he diets, he takes steambaths, he is careful; and flabby men in the locker rooms of golf clubs sometimes steal peeks at him when he steps out of the shower, observing the tight muscles across his chest, the flat stomach, the long sinewy legs. He has a young man's body, very pale and little hair; his face is dark and lined, however, parched by the sun of several seasons. Still he is always an impressive figure at banquets such as this—an "immortal" sports writers called him, and that is how they have written about him and others like him, rarely suggesting that such heroes might ever be prone to the ills of mortal men, carousing, drinking, scheming; to suggest this would destroy the myth, would disillusion small boys, would infuriate rich men who own ball clubs and to whom baseball is a business dedicated to profit and in pursuit of which they trade mediocre players' flesh as casually as boys trade players' pictures on bubble-gum cards. And so the baseball hero must always act the part, must preserve the myth, and none does it better than DiMaggio, none is more patient when drunken old men grab an arm and ask, "Who's gonna take it this year, Joe?"

Two hours later, dinner and the speeches over, DiMaggio was slumped in O'Doul's car headed back to San Francisco. He edged himself up, however, when O'Doul pulled into a gas station in which a pretty red-haired girl sat on a stool, legs crossed, filing her fingernails. She was about 22, wore a tight black skirt and tighter white blouse.

"Look at *that*," DiMaggio said.

"Yeah," O'Doul said.

O'Doul turned away when a young man approached, opened the gas tank, began wiping the windshield. The young man wore a greasy white uniform on the front of which was printed the name "Burt." DiMaggio kept looking at the girl, but she was not distracted from her fingernails. Then he looked at Burt, who did not recognize him. When the tank was full, O'Doul paid and drove off. Burt returned to his girl; DiMaggio slumped down in the front seat and did not open his eyes again until they arrived in San Francisco.

"Let's go see Reno," DiMaggio said.

"No, I gotta go see my old lady," O'Doul said. So he dropped DiMaggio off in front of the bar, and a moment later Reno's voice was announcing in the smoky room, "Hey, here's the Clipper!" The men waved and offered to buy him a drink. DiMaggio ordered a vodka and sat for an hour at the bar talking to a half-dozen men around him. Then a blonde girl who had been with friends at the other end of the bar came over, and somebody introduced her to DiMaggio. He bought her a drink, offered her a cigarette. Then he struck a match and held it. His hand was unsteady.

"Is that me that's shaking?" he asked.

"It must be," said the blonde. "I'm calm."

Two nights later, having collected his clothes out of Reno's back room, DiMaggio boarded a jet; he slept crossways on three seats, then came down the steps as the sun began to rise in Miami. He claimed his luggage and golf clubs, put them into the trunk of a waiting automobile, and less than an hour later he was being driven into Fort Lauderdale, past palm-lined streets, toward the Yankee Clipper Hotel.

"All my life it seems I've been on the road traveling," he said, squinting through the windshield into the sun. "I never get a sense of being in any one place."

Arriving at the Yankee Clipper Hotel, DiMaggio checked into the largest suite. People rushed through the lobby to shake hands with him, to ask for his autograph, to say, "Joe, you look great." And early the next morning, and for the next 30 mornings, DiMaggio arrived punctually at the baseball park and wore his uniform with the famous No. 5, and the tourists seated in the

sunny grandstands clapped when he first appeared on the field
each time, and then they watched with nostalgia as he picked up
a bat and played "pepper" with the younger Yankees, some of
whom were not even born when, 25 years ago this summer, he hit
in 56 straight games and became the most celebrated man in
America.

But the younger spectators in the Fort Lauderdale park, and
the sports writers, too, were more interested in Mantle and
Maris, and nearly every day there were news dispatches reporting how Mantle and Maris felt, what they did, what they said,
even though they said and did very little except walk around the
field frowning when photographers asked for another picture and
when sports writers asked how they felt.

After seven days of this, the big day arrived—Mantle and
Maris would swing a bat—and a dozen sports writers were gathered around the big batting cage that was situated beyond the
left-field fence; it was completely enclosed in wire, meaning
that no baseball could travel more than 30 or 40 feet before being
trapped in rope; still Mantle and Maris would be swinging, and
this, in spring, makes news.

Mantle stepped in first. He wore black gloves to help prevent
blisters. He hit right-handed against the pitching of a coach
named Vern Benson, and soon Mantle was swinging hard, smashing line drives against the nets, going *ahhh ahhh* as he followed
through with his mouth open.

Then Mantle, not wanting to overdo it on his first day,
dropped his bat in the dirt and walked out of the batting cage.
Roger Maris stepped in. He picked up Mantle's bat.

"This damn thing must be 38 ounces," Maris said. He threw
the bat down into the dirt, left the cage, and walked toward the
dugout on the other side of the field to get a lighter bat.

DiMaggio stood among the sports writers behind the cage,
then turned when Vern Benson, inside the cage, yelled, "Joe,
wanna hit some?"

"No chance," DiMaggio said.

"Com'on Joe," Benson said.

The reporters waited silently. Then DiMaggio walked slowly
into the cage and picked up Mantle's bat. He took his position at
the plate but obviously it was not the classic DiMaggio stance; he
was holding the bat about two inches from the knob, his feet
were not so far apart, and, when DiMaggio took a cut at Benson's
first pitch, fouling it, there was none of that ferocious follow-
through, the blurred bat did not come whipping all the way

around, the No. 5 was not stretched full across his broad back.

DiMaggio fouled Benson's second pitch, then he connected solidly with the third, the fourth, the fifth. He was just meeting the ball easily, however, not smashing it, and Benson called out, "I didn't know you were a choke hitter, Joe."

"I am now," DiMaggio said, getting ready for another pitch.

He hit three more squarely enough, and then he swung again and there was a hollow sound.

"Ohhh," DiMaggio yelled, dropping his bat, his fingers stung. "I was waiting for that one." He left the batting cage, rubbing his hands together. The reporters watched him. Nobody said anything. Then DiMaggio said to one of them, not in anger or in sadness, but merely as a simply stated fact, "There was a time when you couldn't get me out of there."

1967

THE TOUGHEST MAN IN PRO FOOTBALL

By Leonard Shecter

FROM ESQUIRE

Copyright © 1967, Esquire, Inc.

This readable story about Vince Lombardi, an unusual, though not complex individual who earned his high place in his small world of large men, is a finely documented piece with ample quotations from Lombardi's speeches to businessmen, stockholders, and players. The unemotional description goes right to the heart of an enigmatic phenomenon in the world of sports and is a fine analysis of a successful figure in athletics. Leonard Shecter, the author, who passed away as a comparatively young man, will be sorely missed by his many readers.

One of the favorite things of Vince Lombardi, coach, general manager, and spiritual leader of the world-champion Green Bay Packers, is the grass drill. He lets an assistant coach lead the bending and stretching exercises, the calisthenics, but he himself must run the part of the drill that turns grown behemoths into groveling, gasping, sweat-soaked, foamy-mouthed animals without breath enough left to complain. It is a simple drill, best conducted in the summer sun at brain-frying temperatures because sane men will not do it. The crazy men run in place, double time, as hard as they can, while Vince Lombardi shouts at them in his irritating, nasal, steel-wool-rubbing-over-grate voice. "C'mon, lift those legs, lift 'em. Higher, higher." Suddenly he yells, "Front!" and the players, who averaged $41,000 each for 14 football games last season (there also were two post-season games), many of them no longer boys, but men in their thirties with families to care for and paunches to battle, flop on their bellies, and as soon as they do, even while they are falling, Lombardi shouts, "Up!" and they must leap to their feet, running, running, faster, higher. "Front!" and they are down. "Back!" and they roll over on their backs. "Up!" Over and over, always that raucous voice, nagging, urging, demanding ever more from rebelling lungs and legs. "Move those damn legs. This is the worst-looking thing I ever saw. You're supposed to be moving those legs. Front! Up! C'mon, Caffey, move your legs. Keep them moving. C'mon, Willie Davis, you told me you were in shape. Front! Up! C'mon Crenshaw, get up. It takes you an hour to get up. Faster. Move those legs. Dammit, what the hell's the matter with you guys? You got a lot of dog in you. You're dogs, I tell you. A bunch of dogs. Let's move. Front! Up! For the love of Pete, Crenshaw, you're fat. Ten bucks a day for every pound you can't lose. Crenshaw! It's going to cost you 10 bucks a day. Lift those legs!"

The sound of their panting—70 men reduced to sodden football suits filled with quivering muscles—rising over them in a moist, squishy roar. As the drill goes on, the noises they make breathing almost drown out the sound of Lombardi's voice. The breathing becomes louder and somewhat wetter, until it sounds like the ocean when the last wave rolls up into the sucking sand. Finally, when they are beyond the point of humanity or sanity, Lombardi lets up. "All right!" he shouts. "Around the goalpost and back. Now run!"

"That's when you hate him," says Henry Jordan, bald at 32 and looking older. A defensive tackle, he has been with the Packers since 1959. He knows what Lombardi does to his players when they report in the summer, so for three weeks in advance he works out, hard, pushing himself. It is never enough. "He drives you until you know you can't go on. My legs just wouldn't come up anymore. When he walked by me, he hit them. He pushes you to the end of your endurance and then beyond it. If you have a reserve, he finds it."

Sometimes he bulls past the reserve. Leon Crenshaw, a graduate of Tuskegee, is an amiable young man who didn't mind being called Super Spook when he played minor-league football with the Lowell Giants last season. But he was met with enmity by Lombardi because he showed up with 315 pounds arranged paunchily over his 6-foot-6 frame. The coach said a pound a day or 10 dollars. Crenshaw opted the pound. That was Wednesday morning.

Thursday noon he is lying, semiconscious, moaning, on a bench outside the St. Norbert College cafeteria, where the team eats its meals during training. He has severe cramps and a doctor is rubbing ice over his ample middle while waiting for an ambulance. The other players, as they come out of the cafeteria, some of them sucking on toothpicks, avoid looking at him. It's as though he were lying in a doorway in the Bowery or had fallen, a victim of the plague, in a Bombay street. The diagnosis is heat prostration. But one of the players says he knows what it really is. "Starvation," he says. It doesn't matter which; Leon Crenshaw does not make the team. This is the Vince Lomardi process of natural selection. It's how you build a professional football dynasty.

Partly how.

It isn't enough to survive the tortures of the grass drills. One must enjoy them. So each time a fiendish new drill is announced, the players, college men every one, clap their hands in childish glee. They applaud. "Oh, yeah!" they shout. "All right. All ri-ght." And they applaud.

Jordan laughs. "It's like he says." He digs at a sore muscle in his back and grimaces when he finds the right one. "If you aren't fired with enthusiasm, you will be fired with enthusiasm."

Another way to get fired is to come late to meetings or practice. And arriving on time isn't enough. This would not show proper enthusiasm. So the Packers say there is Eastern Daylight Time and Central Standard Time and Greenwich Time and then there is Lombardi Time. "This is Lombardi Time," says Don Chandler, the elderly kicking specialist who has been in the league 11 years. He points to his wristwatch. It is set 15 minutes ahead. "If you come 10 minutes early, they've started without you." Or the bus is gone. Or practice has started.

The players have bent to Lombardi's will with a will and they have taken his Spartan attitude as their own. Says Dave Robinson, a large linebacker who wears a mean scowl most of the time, which is all right because he's that kind of football player: "If you come 10 minutes early, they make you feel like scum for holding them up."

Now Donny Anderson, a Viking type from Texas Tech who got, it is said, $600,000 as a bonus when he signed a year ago, whispers to a veteran player on the sidelines of the practice field: "Slip me some water." The veteran laughs. "There hasn't been any water around here in 11 years." Not true. There are perhaps six pints for the 70 huge players who will spend a violent two hours under a summer sun. But if Lombardi sees a player drinking water, he shouts, "Whaddaya want to get, a bellyache?"

Sometimes, during a scrimmage, one of the defensive units is allowed to come up for air. The players sit and watch Lombardi driving, driving, driving, and they talk about the kind of coach they would be. They agree tough is best. "I'd be a bitch," says Robinson. He thinks for a moment. "But that Wood." He shakes his head sadly, Willie Wood is a 5-foot-10 defensive halfback who plays football as though he had been shot out of a gun. "Wood," says Robinson, "he'd be a mother." The other players laugh.

The team has learned, too, to feel about injuries the way Lombardi wants them to. "Every week there are the injuries," Lombardi says. "It is foolish to think that, the way this game is played, you can escape them, but every week I feel that same annoyance."

Annoyance? Anger. Rage even. Players are afraid to get hurt. When they do, they try not to react to the pain. They pound the grass with a fist and say, "Oh, dammit, dammit." They react to being hurt, not to the hurt. They rail at fate, not at pain.

It began the first day in 1959 that Vince Lombardi, the man from the East with the odd New York accent and hot eyes the color of smoldering chestnuts, walked into the trainer's room after he had taken over the failing fortunes of the faltering Packers. There were, he remembers, 15 or 20 players waiting for the diathermy or the whirlpool or to be worked on by the trainer. "What the hell is this?" Lombardi roared, his big yellow teeth with the wide spaces between them making him look like an angry jungle animal. "You're going to have to live with pain," he told them. "If you play for me, you have to play with pain." Lombardi glared at the players, who looked like kids caught with their hands in the jam. Now they don't even like to talk about injuries. They sidle up to the trainer and, in whispers, ask for a muscle relaxer, a pain-killer. If Lombardi notices them taking a pill, he rasps, "What's the matter with you?"

"Not a thing, sir. Salt tablets."

Lombardi never stops trying to prevent injuries after they happen. On this ill-tempered summer day on the steamy practice field in Green Bay, Wisconsin—across the road from Lambeau Field, where the Packers play their games—Lombardi has been on his players hard. "C'mon, you lard asses!" Coach yells. (The players, most of them, call him that—Coach. Not the coach, but Coach, as in "Coach doesn't like anybody hanging around the ice bucket.") "What are you guys doing? For Crissakes, you look like you're playing mumblety-peg out there." The players are in full football regalia (making them all look like Boris Karloff in *Frankenstein*) under a relentless sun, and they are practicing pass patterns, which means it's offense against defense and the blocking on the line is serious. You can tell it from the slap of forearm pads as the defensive line whacks away and the strangled sounds that men make when others charge into their necks, football helmets first.

There is a pileup, and out of the bottom of the pile comes a cry that has been torn out of a man's throat, a shriek of agony. It's Jerry Moore, a rookie guard, who hasn't learned he is not supposed to cry his pain. The pile untangles and Moore is left writhing on the ground, his hands grabbing at a knee that is swelling so fast that in another minute the doctor will have to cut his pants leg to get at it. "Get up!" Lombardi bawls, the thick cords on his heavy, sun-browned neck standing out with the effort. "Get up! Get up off the ground." The sight has insulted him. He is outraged. "You're not hurt. You're not hurt."

Minutes later Marv Fleming, an end who has been with the Packers four years, has somebody fall on his arm and separate his shoulder from the rest of him. He knows enough not to make any noise. But he lies there for a moment summoning the courage to take the pain he knows will wash over him when he stands up. Lombardi is otherwise occupied for the moment, but the players get on him. "Get up, Fleming!" one yells. "Oh, poor Fleming," shouts another. "Stop·killing the grass, Fleming. Get up."

Ken Bowman, the center, three years with Green Bay, limps over to the trainer. "What you got for blisters?"

Lionel Aldridge, defensive end, four years a Packer, over-hears. He snorts. "Nothing," he says. "More blisters."

That is the spirit of the Green Bay packers. Lombardi instills it—relentlessly.

Jerry Kramer is 31 years old and is in his tenth season at Green Bay. Six-foot-3, 245 pounds, rated one of the best offensive guards in the business, he is handsome in a football-player way, not pretty like Frank Gifford, but handsome, with light eyes that glint with the amusement he finds in the ridiculous world around him. Through the years he has been battered and scarred, prob-ably more than most, and there is a line of angry hemstitching up the back of his neck and head, the result of an old spinal injury. The players are kind about it; they call him Zipper Head. "In 1962 I was banged up around the chest," Kramer remembers. "I was out for about two plays. I didn't know it at the time, but I had two broken ribs. I played anyway. The next week, all I can remember is Merle Olsen of the Rams making cleat marks up and down me all afternoon. After the game we took X rays and found out about the ribs. I went to Coach and told him I had been playing with two broken ribs and he said, 'No shit? Well, they don't hurt anymore, do they?' "

Elijah Pitts, who can run 100 yards in 9.6 seconds and can take a football through the hole in a needle: "I had a shoulder separation. In college I wouldn't have dreamed of putting my uniform on. Here I didn't dare tell him I had it. I was afraid to tell him. I played two games with it."

And Ray Nitschke. He is an odd-looking apple, a picture, a caricature of a fierce linebacker. His front teeth long since have been knocked out, and he plays without his removable bridge so that when he smiles he looks gummy and evil. He is only 30 years old, but he is bald, and when he pulls off his helmet, his fringe of wispy red hair stands straight up, like fur on a frightened cat. He is a bulky man and you understand, viscerally, that he would like to hurt you. Off the field, though, transformed. His teeth back in his mouth, his hair combed, eyeglasses—he looks like a college professor. He even talks like a college professor. Many football players do. Even if they majored in basket weaving (or, like the men on Syracuse's great teams, Canadian geography), they've been exposed to four years of college, often five. It rubs off on them. Nitschke is in his tiny room, his bulk almost filling it, at St. Norbert's Sensenbrenner Hall, the men's dorm in his little college that is tucked picturesquely into a bend of the beautiful Fox River. St. Norbert is in West DePere (pronounced, of course, "de peer"), six miles from the practice field and now, at 5:15, after a day of muscle busting, Nitshke is sprawled on one of the two narrow beds in the room, waiting for dinnertime and for the evening skull sessions in the basement. He tells about the time the tower fell on him.

There is a 20-foot tower in the center of the three fields the Packers practice on. It's for news photographers and, more important, Lombardi's own cameraman. Football people film everything, and Lombardi films everything plus one, including pass drills. He is said to have 16mm eyeballs. (When the assistant coach came back from his honeymoon, he was asked how it was. "I don't know," he said. "I haven't seen the films yet.") On this day a sudden gale came up and the tower tilted in the wind and then toppled. It pinned Nitschke. One of the bolts

crunched through his football helmet and he wonders what
would have happened had he not been wearing it. He was lying
under the twisted steel when Lombardi ran up. "Who is it?" he
asked. Nitschke. "Aw," said Coach, "he's all right."

Alex Hawkins, who was drafted by the Packers but cut
before the season began, and who has played with the Baltimore
Colts and the Atlanta Falcons, said: "No one went into the training room for the first couple of weeks Lombardi was there. If
anybody went, he wasn't a Packer long. I've seen some injuries
that would put players on other clubs into the hospital, but these
Packers wouldn't even ask for aspirin."

In his book *Run to Daylight!*, which was written in 1963
with W. C. Heinz, Lombardi says he got it all from his father,
Harry, an immigrant Italian butcher who settled first in Benson-
hurst, Brooklyn. Vince grew up in Sheepshead Bay, which must
have been as tough as his father. "No one is ever hurt," Vince
Lombardi says Harry Lombardi always said. "Hurt is in your
mind."

Perhaps it was Lombardi's father, too, who told him that
playing with pain builds mental toughness. Or is it mental toughness that enables you to play with pain? Either way, mental
toughness is one of Lombardi's little dogmas. He has others:

Winning isn't everything; it's the only thing.
If you can accept losing, you can't win.
You've got to be mentally tough.
Everything is "want" in this business. The man who wants to
play is the man I want.
If you can walk, you can run.
Fatigue makes you a coward.
There's no substitute for work in this business.
What the hell are you limping around for?
Dammit, get up, you're not hurt.

The players like to kid, gently, about his slogans. They tell
the story that once Lombardi said to his wife, Marie, "This damn
knee is acting up on me again," and his wife said, without a
blink, "You've got to be mentally tough." And they like to say
that Coach wouldn't talk to his wife for the rest of the week.

Whatever Lombardi means by mentally tough, a player has
to be it just to stand the abuse. There are coaches who cajole.
There are coaches who are fatherly. There are coaches who are
merely coldly professional and demand their players be the same.
Lombardi is hotly insulting. All the time. If a player can't take it,
if he doesn't respond with ever-increasing effort, Lombardi trades

him for a draft choice. Then he tests the new man. Henry Jordan:
"Coach is fair. He treats every man the same. He treats us all like
dogs."

On the practice field Lombardi says:

"You're stupid. How the hell did you get so stupid?"

"You missed that block. You missed the block. Do it over.
Do it again. You stay out here and do it all day."

"Where the hell is the blocking in the middle? What the hell
are you thinking there, Bowman?"

"What the hell are you limping about this morning, Williams? Get the hell out of here and don't come back until you can
run."

"For Crissakes, can't you block anybody?"

"Get in there, Mankins. Don't just stand there. Don't you
understand what I'm asking you to do? Are you that stupid?"

"Dammit, Williams, you're not running. I said into the hole,
not around end."

"You're not hitting. All you're doing is hitting and sliding. Go
into him."

"All right, Reed—after practice, you take two laps."

And seldom is heard an encouraging word.

Max McGee, the tall, also balding end who has played 11
years of professional football, who was 1A to Paul Hornung's 1 in
the pro football camp-follower's derby, and the man who helped
break up last January's Super Bowl game with a super catch:
"Sometimes I wonder about the way he pushes people. I really
wonder about it." He shakes his head and shrugs his shoulders.

Says Kramer: "Coach Lombardi is an intense, driving, striving perfectionist. He drives everybody—right down to the assistant trainer. I know he's got me brainwashed. Unless I have a
perfect day, I'm upset. He says to me, 'Boy, that stinks,' and I
say, 'Yes, it does.' I can't think of a football game in 10 years I've
been satisfied with. When he says you look like a dumb ass, you
feel he's right. I remember one year, '62, I was really busting ass.
And he tells me, 'We got the worst guards in the league.' I told
him he'd better draft some guards because I'd had it. He had me
all screwed up. He would call me an old cow and say I looked
like homemade horseshit. I really believed I was the worst football player in America. Then when the polls came out I was
voted All-Pro by the AP, All-Pro by the UPI, and then All-Star. I
couldn't believe it. I thought they were all crazy.

"Later on I got to talking to Jordan about it and what we
decided was this. Lombardi was a line coach. I'm on the line. He

was an offensive-line coach. I'm on offensive, when he played he was a guard. I'm a guard. Not only that, he was a right guard. He was on me more than he ever got on anybody."

Once in a while Lombardi goes far enough to upset his most pliant players. Such a time was before the Super Bowl, the first game between the champions of the National Football League, the Packers, and the upstart American Football League champions, the Kansas City Chiefs.

Lombardi has a standing roster of fines: breaking curfew, $500; late for meeting or practice, $10 a minute; anyone caught standing at a bar, $150. For the Super Bowl week in Los Angeles he did some adjusting. It was $2,500 for anyone who blew the 11:00 P.M. curfew and $5,000 for anyone caught with a woman in his room.

Obviously Lombardi wanted to win this one bad. So did the players. A winning share in the Super Bowl was worth $15,000. And the league prestige involved was of incalculable value. So it wasn't the enormity of the fines that bothered the players, but that Lombardi thought it necessary to institute them. "I just didn't think the rule had to be there," says McGee. "It was the biggest game of our life. If you didn't know how important it was, you wouldn't be in the Super Bowl. I'm a habitual rule breaker; so was Paul [Hornung]. But we were disappointed in Coach Lombardi. We knew how important it was. We were not about to break any rules."

Nor does Lombardi seem inclined to salve the wounded feelings of his Hessians with large salaries. He permitted Jim Taylor, a running back of long experience and such power that it is said of him that he could gain six yards against the U.S. Treasury Building, to take his services to New Orleans after a contract dispute. There is a tale told, too, that, before the 1964 season, an attorney presented himself to Lombardi and said, "I am here to negotiate the salary of Mr. James Ringo."

Ringo, an outstanding center, had long been a bulwark of Lombardi's offensive line and was considered a Green Bay fixture. Lombardi asked the lawyer to excuse him for a moment. He returned to his office 20 minutes later. "I believe you have come to the wrong city," he said. "Mr. James Ringo is now the property of the Philadelphia Eagles."

And when, after Sandy Koufax and Don Drysdale had banded together to extract huge salaries from the Los Angeles Dodgers, it was suggested to Lombardi that his players might do the same, the coach glowered. "If they come here in a group," he said, "they'll go out in a group." Since then, other teams, notably the Cleveland Browns, have had collective-bargaining problems. Lombardi has not. One doubts if he ever will.

"I've been told that the Packers are among the lowest-paying teams in the league," says Willie (he'd be a mother) Wood. "I don't know if that's true. [No comparison figures are available, but chances are it's not true. The Packers probably pay about the same as most, although Lombardi admittedly does not like "star" salaries. However, for a team that wins the title so much, one would expect the salaries to be higher than most. They are not.] If it was true, it would be a bad thing. I often think I can't possibly make enough money playing this game. That's how rough it is."

"In 1963 I had a hell of a contract fight," says Kramer. "It got to be kind of touchy. I got what I wanted, but it discouraged me from trying again the next year. You think for two or three thousand the hell with it. I suppose that's what he's after all the time."

As tight-fisted guardian of the exchequer, Lombardi did all he could to end the expensive war between the NFL and the AFL. At first he refused to pay any bonuses at all to closely contested-for talent and continued to win anyway. But two years ago he shelled out a reported $1,000,000 to get Anderson and Jim Grabowski, a fullback from the University of Illinois. This so shocked the little world of pro football that it was immediately speculated Lombardi had demanded—and received—financial help from the league. Not that he couldn't afford to handle the burden himself. Green Bay, with its tiny population (about 65,000), gets as much from television rights—$2,000,000 a year— as do New York and Los Angeles. Lombardi was influential in making this arrangement.

The financial and artistic success of the Packers (Lombardi took a team that had won eight games in three years and in eight years won five divisional titles, four championships and one Super Bowl) has surrounded him with an aura of infallibility he wears with pride and evident enjoyment. When Lombardi says, "I'm no miracle man," local people say he's lying in his teeth— and knows it. As a miracle man, however, Lombardi finds himself at odds with the press, which often does not accept miracle men with proper awe. He is impatient with reporters who ask probing questions and likes to put them off by taking the offensive. "Why don't you learn something about the game," he is likely to snarl at a questioner who displeases him.

"Lombardi meets each question like it was a stab into Packer territory and must be defended against," Glenn Miller of the *Wisconsin State Journal* once wrote. With the television boys, however, Lombardi is a pussycat. "Television spends a lot of money on this game," he says. "It's entitled to some privileges."

Lombardi likes to say that there are two things in the world he really understands—people and football. There's a third—money. At first he refused to be interviewed for this article, later relented somewhat, adding, "I have to be careful what I say to you. I'm getting $30,000 for an article from *Look*."

On Lombardi's practice field there is a chalked square around the camera tower, and reporters, by his edict, are imprisoned within it. This is to keep them as far from the football players as possible. It worked so well in Green Bay that when Norb Hecker, once an assistant to Lombardi, took over as head coach of the new Atlanta club, he installed the magic square there. When reporters walked off the field and said they would not cover the club, management apologized and Hecker had to back off. But the *Green Bay Press Gazette* is hardly the *Atlanta Constitution*.

The coach's most famous encounter with the press involved Taylor. It was an open secret that Taylor was playing out his option (a method by which a football player may release himself from contract peonage but which, in recent years, has become so difficult and expensive that few players attempt it). However, the story had not been printed, which is the sort of thing the sporting press is often guilty of. Finally, however, Ken Hartnett of The Associated Press wrote a story that told of Taylor's decision and said that he had been influenced by the enormous bonus young Grabowski had received. Lombardi was furious. He counted the story as a plot to cause dissension on his team. He promptly barred Hartnett from the Green Bay dressing room. At this point, though, he ran afoul of league commissioner Pete Rozelle, a public-relations-conscious man who understands the press's value to a sport. Rozelle said it was league policy to bar no accredited press man from the clubhouse. Lombardi had to relent. This summer during training, however, reporters were told not to enter the clubhouse because it was "too crowded." Nothing was heard from Rozelle.

Lombardi gets away with this sort of thing because he has enormous power in Green Bay. A New York reporter recounts with awe the time he got to a Green Bay barbershop at closing. Nothing closes more firmly than a Green Bay barbershop at dinnertime, so he was turned away. Lombardi, who was in one of the chairs, recognized the reporter and growled: "Cut his hair." The reporter got his haircut. "Now that," he says, "is power."

It's as coach and general manager of the Packers that Lombardi exerts his real power. He runs a sort of fiefdom in Green Bay, complete with automobile dealers who thrust free cars on him just so he will be seen driving them. The Packers are, theoretically, municipally owned. In fact they are an autocracy, run by Vince Lombardi.

In 1949, when the team was floundering financially, more than $125,000 was raised in a statewide campaign, citizens buying nondividend shares at $25 each. Last year the Packers made about $800,000 in profit after taxes, and the money was dropped into a fund and invested for contingencies. The club has already spent more than $2,000,000 modernizing the stadium, clubhouse, and offices and installing a heating system under the turf, and no one can foresee any contingencies. It does not take a CPA to calculate the speed with which that kind of money—and more like it each year—can grow. And who's in charge of all of it? Vince Lombardi, that's who.

There is a town board of directors that is supposed to meet with Lombardi and discuss progress of the team, finances, and related matters, but in recent years Lombardi has been so weighed down with his two hats of general manager and coach that he has not had time to attend the meetings.

For all of this Lombardi receives a huge salary. No one knows what it is, but some years ago he turned down an offer from Los Angeles that included $100,000 a year, a fully paid-for house, a $100,000 life-insurance policy, and a piece of an oil well.

Men of wealth and power often come under attack from those with less wealth and power, and Lombardi is no exception. "I've always thought the mark of a gentleman is how he treats people who can't do anything for him," says a man who once worked for Lombardi. "Coach, I'm afraid, is only interested in his own image and people who can help him."

The coach is accused of being frigidly aloof to local people (and too friendly with visiting New Yorkers); overly starchy in a town where summer formal dress consists of short-sleeve white shirt and tie; boorish with his employees ("Get me a drink." he says to people who have important jobs with the team, and neglects to add "please" or "thank you"); impolite even to his wife (at least once he bawled her out loudly on some frivolous matter—blocking his automobile with her own—in full view and hearing of a large group of local citizens); penurious with his help (he is said to run a tight ship in more ways than one—seems to enjoy pouncing noisily on an expense chit of $17 that he thinks should have been no more than $15); and autocratic with everybody around him ("Like him?" says eight-year-veteran Jordan. "I don't even know him").

Whatever it takes to be a successful professional football coach, however, Lombardi has. If he does not inspire love in his players, he does demand and receive their respect, even if this respect stems largely from the fact that he wins and that the two post-season championship games last season were worth $25,000 to each of his players.

Says Fuzzy Thurston, another of Lombardi's balding veterans of the football wars, an agile if somewhat lumpy offensive guard: "No one likes to be humiliated, but this is a totally dedicated man and somehow you don't mind it from him. He demands 125 percent from you and that's the way he gets 95 percent. He's always trying to reach perfection. I respect him and I feel I owe him a lot."

Says Wood: "The harder you work, the harder it is to accept defeat. This is what coaching is all about. If Coach is on you, it means he's giving you attention, he must think there's enough in you to make it worth hollering at you. I know if he doesn't keep on me, especially about my tackling, I develop bad habits. I'll tell you this: the man milks you. I've seen him take players we thought didn't have it and by the time he gets through with them they do a terrific job. They're afraid not to. He's the general and we're the privates. It has to be that way. You don't go over his head because you can't. There's nobody to go to."

Says Jordan: "When Coach got here, we were losers. He got us into superb condition. We couldn't believe how hard he was working us. But he was right. If you're in shape physically, you can be mentally tough, if I can coin one of Coach's phrases."

Says Robinson: "He's built pride into us. If you lose, you feel you've let down the town, your family, and Coach. If we go into the second half 14 points down, our defense will make a solemn oath not to let them score again, and the offense will make a solemn oath to score three times. And Coach is the catalyst. He puts you through hell, but what you feel afterward is that if you can go through that, you can go through anything."

Says Nitschke: "I'll tell you what he makes us feel. That the losing game is never long enough. We always feel if we had 10

more minutes we would have won. You go out there feeling you
have to win, but you know you don't do it just on Sunday. You
have to earn it. Each man has to feel this as a person. That's
Lombardi's singleness of purpose. He makes us unsatisfied because he's never satisfied. We've won 49–0, and he's not satisfied
because we didn't play a strong football game."

Says Kramer: "Let me tell you about Lombardi's Spartanism.
We had a guard, a fellow named Gale Gillingham. He was with
the College All-Stars, and when he broke his hand they dropped
him and he came to this camp. He got here and didn't miss a
scrimmage. He was treated as if this hand were perfectly normal.
It's like a baby bawling. If you don't pay attention, he'll go about
his business. Sympathize with him and he'll keep crying. Sure, he
treats us like children. But I think it's with good reason."

Says Willie Davis, 245-pound defensive end: "Whenever
there is enthusiasm, dedication, and pride, invariably you'll find a
dynamic individual who is communicating it. That's Lombardi.
Of course, he can be difficult. I've always felt it would be impossible to play under him if you didn't win. I don't think I could
take him. I used to feel you had to love a guy to work for him.
I'm no longer sold on this. The one thing that's a must—a coach
has to be able to reach the guys. And Coach is a great emotional
lecturer. He can get you aroused, really start the old adrenalin
flowing. Once, during the week after a bad game, I remember he
said, 'I just wish I had the chance to go out there and do it
myself.' Damn. I felt this man is so dedicated, so involved, that if
he could do it himself, it would get done and done well. And it's
too bad he has to depend on us. I felt, goddamn, the least I could
do was go out there and try.

"This man says things that challenge you. People think that a
pro just does a job, but there's a lot of emotion and desire involved. Money can't buy that emotion and desire."

Lombardi's most vocal admirer on the team is Bart Starr, the
first-string quarterback, who quietly and over a long period of
time had become recognized as one of the best of the highly
intelligent and talented group of NFL quarterbacks. The son of
an Army sergeant, Starr is a soft-spoken, self-effacing Alabaman
who keeps a Bible by his bed. He takes all of Lombardi's
commandments literally. He never goes near the water bucket.
He is almost never injured. (When he was injured at the beginning of this season, he played with great pain and so poorly that
finally his uniform had to be stripped from him.) "All our success
stems directly from Coach Lombardi," Starr says in his sincere

but somewhat marshmallowy way of speaking. "When he came
here, he changed our thinking from a negative attitude to a
positive attitude and from a losing attitude to a winning attitude.
This is the type of an attitude which you have to take into every
game, into every scrimmage, every encounter, every encounter of
life, as he puts it. He worked long and hard with us and showed
us not only how to do things but the why of it. In so doing, he
changed the entire complexion of the team."

Starr and Lombardi make an ideal combination in that the
quarterback's personality is properly recessive. When Starr is on
the field, it is as though he is an extension of Lombardi's overwhelming ego. This is a remarkable symbiosis, one that few
coaches attain, especially in a day when many plays are called
not in the huddle but on the line of scrimmage in order to foil
rapidly shifting defenses. "I like to feel that the job I'm doing on a
Sunday afternoon is the job that he would do if he were playing,"
Starr says. "I'm his representative. I want to call the ball game the
way he would want it called. That's what I'm striving to do all
the time, to do the job he wants me to do."

On appearance alone one would not think that Lombardi
could inspire this kind of fanatical devotion in a Bart Starr.
Vincent Thomas Lombardi, once alliteratively described by *Time*
as a bristling, brooding bear of a man, looks rather more like an
Italian papa than any other breed of cat or bear. Indeed, he looks
like an Italian papa whose feet hurt. (In fact they do, which is
why he wears those bulky soft-top shoes that are constructed
over casts of his feet and so appear to have been designed to
walk on water.) At 54 he has a bit of a weight problem and walks
with his belly sucked in and his chest extended, like a pigeon's.
Even so, the waistband of his beltless (but pleated) slacks sometimes folds over to show the lining—a problem of most middle-
aged men in a world where all clothing seems to have been
designed for Bobby Kennedy. His hair lies on his head in a series
of tight waves and is powdered with gray, as are his heavy
eyebrows. He appears to smile a lot, at least he often shows his
teeth in what seems a smile. But often as not it is a nervous
grimace. (Players on the Cleveland Browns have taken to calling
him The Jap.) He is 5-foot-10 and appears shorter in the company of the large young men whose fate he commands. When the
players look down on him, however, it's usually to say, "Yes, sir."
("The best thing to do when he is chewing you out," says one
player, "is just be still. Mighty still. And remember to say, 'yes,
sir,' when he's finished.")

If this sounds as though Lombardi runs a sort of paramilitary organization, it is only because he does. The man who had the single greatest influence on Lombardi's life was Colonel Red Blaik, one-time football coach at West Point. Lombardi worked six years under Blaik at the Point, and no doubt this is where he picked up his military bearing as well as a practice timetable that goes off with, well, military precision. This precision was enough, in the NFL, to earn Lombardi the reputation as an organizational genius.

"Red Blaik had a great deal to do with any success I've had," Lombardi says. "He not only was a great football coach, he was a great man. I had great respect for him. He was a man of great principle, a great organizer. I learned many things from Red Blaik."

What Lombardi also might have learned at West Point—and didn't—is the danger colleges face when they act as farm teams for professional football. He was at the Point in 1951 when 90 cadets, more than a third of them football players, were expelled in a cribbing scandal. Yet to this day he says, "A school without football is in danger of deteriorating into a medieval study hall."

Lombardi got to West Point by an indirect route. There was no football at Cathedral Prep Seminary in Brooklyn, which is the first step for those studying for the priesthood. (Ask what changed his mind and he says, "Oh, nothing.") He transferred to St. Francis Prep, also in Brooklyn, and as a senior played one year of football. Then it was Fordham University in the Bronx, where he became one of the Seven Blocks of Granite, the famous line of a famous football team, making up in ferocity what he lacked in poundage. After graduating from Fordham and deciding that he wasn't going to be an insurance investigator or a lawyer, Lombardi went to work as a high-school coach at St. Cecelia's in Englewood, New Jersey. There he achieved a measure of fame by taking his lads through 36 games without a defeat, although in eight years he never made more than $3,500 annually. His two kids know about being poor.

In 1947 Lombardi went back to Fordham as freshman coach. He stayed there more than a year, or long enough to see that football was dying at Fordham (and perhaps wonder why it wasn't becoming a medieval study hall). Then it was West Point under Blaik (who recently described Lombardi as being "a thoroughbred—with a vile temper"). Lombardi took the job as offensive-line coach with the Giants under Jim Lee Howell in 1954. He was slated to become a head coach when Howell retired, but Green Bay grabbed him and in 1959 the Giants tried to get Lombardi back, but he would have had a boss in New York. In Green Bay, he is it all.

At no point did Lombardi's early parochial training desert him. He still attends Mass every morning (and some players have noticed that it doesn't hurt them to be seen by Lombardi making that scene), and when he talks of important things in this world he puts it family, church, and football, in that order. Nor does he seem particularly out of place dropping to his knees in the clubhouse after a difficult victory and leading the team in an Our Father. "You wouldn't think a professional football coach could get by with anything like that," says a man who used to play for him. "But Lombardi does."

"I'm a religious man," Lombardi says. "I've got a great deal of faith in God, a great deal of dependency on God. I don't think I'd do anything without that dependency. We don't pray to win. I do think we pray to play the best we can and to keep us free from injury. And the prayer we say after the game is one of thanksgiving."

My conversation with Lombardi took place on a Sunday morning after I had been in Green Bay for a week, the coach taking little notice of me except to ask, from time to time, if I were getting enough "stuff," and to point out with great glee to his coaches that "there's a real New Yorker" when he spied me reading a newspaper subway fashion, folded into eighths, and finally to sic his young publicity man, Chuck Lane, on me to see if there couldn't be an arrangement whereby my quotes from the players could be inspected before publication. (There couldn't. The request, given the climate of professional football, was not so presumptuous as one might think. Bud Grant, the new coach of the Minnesota Vikings, issued the following manifesto to newspapermen this summer: "Questions regarding player performance—be it individual, teammate, or opponent—should be addressed to Coach Grant, not to players or assistant coaches. These are questions of evaluation and opinion and Coach Grant prefers to answer them himself." In other words, talk to the football players about anything but football.)

I was particularly anxious to talk to Lombardi about three things: his method of building a team in his own image; his reaction to being called a William Gladstone of professional football, conservative to the point of boredom; and an attitude he had expressed about individual freedom as opposed to respect for authority in an address before the American Management Association.

During this talk Lombardi, who, given other circumstances, could have been a tyrant only to his own family, got off lines like these: "Unfortunately, it had become too much of a custom to ridicule what is termed 'the company man' because he is dedicated to a principle he believes in. . . . Everywhere you look, there is a call for freedom, independence or whatever you wish to call it. But as much as these people want to be independent, they still want to be told what to do. And so few people who are capable of leading are ready and willing to lead. So few are ready. . . . We must gain respect for authority—no, let's say we must regain respect for authority. . . . We must learn again to respect authority because to disavow it is contrary to our individual natures." This is not out of the memoirs of some South American general, it's out of Vince Lombardi and he believes all of it.

Now, sitting in a little office in Sensenbrenner Hall, the birds making a racket in the trees outside, Lombardi was asked to explain. "I think the rights of the individual have been put above everything else," he said. "Which I don't think is right. The individual has to have respect for authority regardless of what that authority is. I think the individual has gone too far. I think 95 percent of the people, as much as they shout, would rather be led than lead."

That's what he said. It made me eager to change the subject to football.

The Lombardi method of football, he likes to say, is simple. It's blocking and tackling. The thick and complicated playbook that other teams' players lug around is not one of the Green Bay players' burdens. Lombardi likes to keep it simple. After the grass drill his favorite thing is the hole in the defensive line that his running back, digging in his cleats and churning up turf with an ankle-wrenching 90-degree cut, can slide through as smoothly as a piston into a cylinder. "Beautiful," Vince Lombardi will say of that hole in the line. "Just beautiful." He will push his blunt-fingered hands into the back pockets of the football pants without pads that he wears on the practice field, tilt his head back, and admire the hole as though he were standing in front of the Mona Lisa at the Louvre, and he will mumble, "Beautiful."

Give Lombardi a back who can make five yards on every try and he will five-yard you to death. He did it with Taylor and

Hornung; he was prepared this season to do it with Pitts, Anderson, and Grabowski. He has been using the forward pass more in recent years, but only because the defenses have forced him to. At heart he is still a block of granite.

"You know what that damn team is going to do on just about every play," says a rival coach. "But you can't stop them."

This tight, ball-control football has been winning. Nevertheless there are many who think it's dull football. One of these is Fran Tarkenton, the scrambling Minnesota quarterback who was traded to the New York Giants this season. Tarkenton said in *Sports Illustrated* not long ago: "The way to beat Green Bay is to play it at its own conservative, careful game. . . . In the last couple of years the Packers have raised their theory to the highest, emphasizing execution, sophistication, and discipline and there's nothing wrong with that. But there's also a place for imagination and verve and flair, for improvisation, for breaking out of there and turning a busted play into a long gain and trying everything. Furthermore, I'll go so far as to say that flexibility and mobility have NFL history on their side, and Green Bay's style is against the pattern of football history."

Lombardi's reaction to this is one of anger. "He's using words, that's all," Lombardi said, coming close to spluttering. "It's unfortunate they print things like that. Flexibility. Mobility. That's mumbojumbo. What does he mean? He's talking about running around in the backfield. That's not football, that's sandlot. There's no difference in our offense from that of any other team in the National Football League. I happen to get more enjoyment out of a well-excuted pass play. When I first came to the league, there was a great deal more passing than running. Now it's about 50–50 for all teams. I take a great deal of pride that people have thought we've done well enough to follow what we have done."

It's possible to call Lombardi's game something other than football. The word is "discipline." "Football is a discipline game," he says. "You have to have discipline to play it. Against what Tarkenton says, it's not mumbojumbo, flexibility, mobility. It's discipline." One could almost hear reveille being bugled at the Point.

Lombardi is so hung up on the discipline bit that he firmly believes that it counts more than talent. The talent in the league, he says, is almost even. The difference is in spirit and discipline. That's where the coach comes in and it's important to him, just as it's important to have the name on his office door read Mr.

Lombardi rather than Vince Lombardi, and to have a Scotch around that calls itself VL.

Most of his players agree with him. "He can take an average player and make a great one out of him," says Herb Adderly, who is rated a great defensive back. The older players point to the fact that the nucleus of men he ran to fame with were already on the losing team when he arrived. But others believe that his talent is more in trading for draft choices than anything else.

"I disagree when he says the only difference between teams in this league is the work they do," says Max McGee. "I honestly feel our personnel is better than everybody else's."

Probably it's a combination. Lombardi gets the good players, many of them by shrewd swapping of draft choices. Then the ones who can't stand his gaff, or who won't bust a ligament trying to avoid a Lombardi chewing out, are traded off for more draft choices. The result is a Lombardi kind of team, a winning team. They win or else.

Which is why Paul Hornung tells this story on the coach. One night after a long, cold, difficult day on the practice field and in front of the movie screen, Lombardi came home late and tumbled into bed. "God," his wife said, "your feet are cold."

And Lombardi answered, "Around the house, dear, you may call me Vince."

1968

IS THIS THE MAN TO SUCCEED PALMER?

By Nick Seitz

FROM GOLF DIGEST

Copyright © 1968, Golf Digest Magazine

Arnold Palmer was 39 and had been competing for 15 years as a top pro when this article appeared naming Tom Weiskopf as a future heir to the throne. It was a valid prognostication, confirmed as the years went by, but the value of the article is in the delineation of the young man as a winless competitor. He made some money but never came near a title in his first four years. The author's description of Weiskopf's moods, discouragements, apathy, and pressures makes the article a fine psychological piece.

The King is not dead—the King is alive and ensconced among the current leading money winners—but the King will be 39 this fall when he completes his fifteenth year as a touring pro. His children are nearly grown. He is passing up more and more tournaments, and soon Arnold Palmer's schedule will be only half what it once was.

To place a President of the United States in proper historical perspective might take several generations, but to evaluate the impact of Arnold Palmer on golf we need not wait. He has meant more to the game than anyone, ever, in virtually every conceivable way. His vibrant personality, aided by the world-shrinking capabilities of television, has made him the best-known athlete of this or any other age, and probably the most venerated. His gradual withdrawal poses a monumental challenge for the fur-lined world of professional golf. Professional Golfers' Association official Bob Gorham puts it succinctly. "We are going," he says somewhat dolefully, "to need a new hero."

252

Gorham is using that four-letter word in its strictest sense. Jack Nicklaus is quite likely the best golfer of all time, power-ful—which the populace finds appealing in any sport these days—and a nice fellow. But for all his victories and good manners, he hasn't been able to turn on the fans as Palmer can. He does not have the flair. Everyone agrees Nicklaus is a great player but no one looks on him as a hero.

"Jack doesn't have the sex appeal," says one pro, and no doubt sex appeal is a large part of Palmer's magnetism. This is not a phenomenon reserved to golfers; the owners of hockey teams will tell you they prosper or falter with their female ticket buyers, who bring to the arena dizzingly Freudian interpretations of what can be a simple game. Certainly as a sex symbol Arnold Palmer ranks right up there with Bobby Hull, or Paul Newman, for that matter. Observe the women in his galleries some time.

Tom Weiskopf has sex appeal. Granted it is a different brand. Where Palmer is older, outgoing, muscular, and hand-some in a rugged, outdoorsy fashion, Weiskopf is younger, rather shy, tall and slender and handsome in a smooth, semi-innocent manner. Where women daydream of being dominated by Palmer, they would rather mother the blond, dimple-chinned Weiskopf. (Often the same women are cast in both roles, for what its worth psychologically.) In real life Weiskopf is happily married to a former Miss Minnesota.

Weiskopf hits the ball prodigious distances. He plays ag-gressively, charging as fiercely as Palmer when victory is within reach. The expressions on his ax-handle face mirror his desires and frustrations for the galleries and let them identify with him; and he's a winner. After four years of trying he gained his first victory in the 1968 Andy Williams–San Diego Open, and zapped onto the year's best pre-Masters record, earning more than $70,000 in official and unofficial money. He was fourth in the Bob Hope Desert Classic, second in the Doral Open, and second in the Florida Citrus Open.

Close observers report that Weiskopf is attracting defectors from Arnie's Army, that he is clearly the second most popular player on the tour, and that his star is only starting on what should be a remarkable ascendancy. Tom Weiskopf, to hear his fellow pros tell it, is the next American golf hero, the man who at least will come close to filling the supervoid that will gape when Palmer puts his competitive game to rest.

Bert Yancey, a perceptive pro, says: "I think Tom'll go all the way. He has the game and the personality, and it's just a matter of time. All he has to do is continue to mature, and pace himself—take a week off now and then."

Weiskopf's first four years on the tour were by no means a lost cause. He made $125,000 and says you could not put a price on what he learned. But his failure to win was surprising in light of the expansive predictions that marked his first season.

Tony Lema said, "He's going to be a great one before you know it." Palmer proclaimed him the rookie most likely to succeed.

Probably Weiskopf's winless four years should be accepted as a natural adjustment period. Palmer won the Canadian Open his first year on the tour and added victories in each of the succeeding three years, but he was 25 when he turned pro. Weiskopf is 25 now.

His progress was slowed by an erratic attitude and a stomach ailment. Weiskopf is an oft-brooding perfectionist who wants to hit every shot precisely as he has planned it. No one does, of course, but it took him awhile to reconcile himself to the fact. His was not a Tommy Bolt–type temper, although he admits occasional pupil-teacher sessions with Bolt have been a hindrance as well as a help. Bolt's anger boils to the surface and results in club-throwing and loud curses. Bolt is apt to blame his misfortunes on others or on golf courses. Weiskopf's disgust is with Weiskopf. Bounding up the fairway with his long, splay-footed stride, he silently berates himself for a bad shot, his anger turning inward and gnawing at the lining of his stomach. In 1966 he lost 20 pounds and missed several tournaments due to a near-ulcerous affliction of the duodenum.

"I'm so darn moody," he says in an almost-tenor voice. "I can feel great one minute and sluggish the next. Gee whiz"—Weiskopf talks this way a lot—"it used to take me three holes to get over a poor shot. I got discouraged too quick. I hadn't had much experience in big amateur tournaments because I couldn't afford it, and I didn't have the patience and concentration to win out here." Now, for the most part, he does.

He calls a 66 he shot the final day at Orlando this year the finest round of his life. Yet he missed birdie putts of eight feet or less seven times. "Two years ago," he says, "I would have been so upset at missing those putts I'd never have broken 70."

Weiskopf diplomatically gives half the credit for his improved attitude to his effervescent brunette wife of 18 months. "Jeanne's wonderful. She doesn't know golf, but she knows me.

She's witty and has a little streak of sarcasm in her. She can jar me out of my bad moods. She'll come up to me on the course and tell me how silly I look pouting."

Says Jeanne, "Tom is basically a lonely person. He thinks most of the time. Now he thinks about the difference between being good and great. He sits and tries to recapture the exact state of mind he had when he was playing so well at San Diego, so he can repeat it. I do most of the talking, but he's changed a lot since we were married. He's more relaxed—he's really a lot of fun when he isn't worrying about golf."

Weiskopf says moodiness and lack of confidence are two different things, and that he never lacked confidence. As proof he points to his turning pro without a sponsor, an unheard-of move nowadays. "It wasn't because I had a lot of money; all I had to my name was the $2,500 the MacGregor-Brunswick people gave me to use their clubs, but I wanted to make it myself. I figured I'd learn more. If I had it to do over I probably would find a sponsor, but I'm proud that I made it on my own." He says winning, not making money, has always been his goal.

Weiskopf's ability to hit the long ball worked against him until recently. He was and is continually compared to the powerful Nicklaus, like Weiskopf, an ex-Ohio State student (Tom did not caddie for Jack at OSU, contrary to a popular folktale). Tom didn't want to disappoint the fans who came to see him clout the ball. "I'd get on the tee and hear some guy say, 'There's the kid who drives it farther than Nicklaus,'" Weiskopf remembers, "and I'd hit it as hard as I could." His yardage was often awesome, but his direction was often awful. Eventually he chose to forget the fans and swing easier, occasionally turning to a three wood or two iron off the tee to be sure of good position for his second shot.

He still rips into the ball, however. At San Diego he averaged 275 yards a whack on the two holes where drives were measured—best in the field. Nicklaus himself calls Weiskopf the longest hitter in golf.

"I don't mind," Weiskopf says. "I'm flattered by it. But I don't think it makes that much difference. The key is that I'm hitting 14 and 16 fairways a round. I guess around 350 yards is the farthest I've hit a drive, but the wind was blowing and the ground was hard."

Weiskopf is psychically attached to a new driver, although he says it is no different from his old one, which broke. He is a superstitious man, always marking his ball on the green with the

face of the coin down "so I don't get the yips" and being highly
partial to yellow shirts.

As much as Weiskopf has been likened to Nicklaus, their
swings are not very similar. The chunky Nicklaus generates more
of his power through his leg action, the rangy Weiskopf, through
his big shoulder turn. Weiskopf takes the club head away from
the ball on a path well inside the intended line of flight; Nicklaus
takes the club head away on as straight a line as he can, coming
back only about three-quarters as far as Weiskopf. "His body-
turn is more complete from the waist down," says Weiskopf.
"Mine is more complete from the waist up."

Weiskopf maintains that he is not particularly strong, that he
could press no more than 200 pounds weightlifting. He attrib-
utes his power to a big swing arc and the leverage it produces,
and good timing and rhythm. He says he tries to use his build (at
6-foot-3 and 180 he is known on tour as "The Knife") to
maximum advantage, and that he never copied anyone.

"I learned more from Bob Kepler, the coach at Ohio State
when I was there, than anyone else," he says. "Mainly on fundamentals." The Ohio State Scarlet Course remains his favorite.
Over 7,200 yards long, it is one reason the school has given the
tour such fence-busters as Nicklaus, Weiskopf, Tom Nieporte,
and Dick Rhyan.

Weiskopf considers the long and medium irons his best
clubs aside from his driver. He considers his short-iron play
adequate, his bunker play excellent, his putting good. "You
notice improvement fastest in your putting," he says. "I'm not
having many three-putt greens this year. I didn't have one at San
Diego, I'm not doing anything differently except putting the ball
in the hole more. I *am* doing *everything* a little more *boldly*,
because I don't have to worry about money the way I used to.
My pitching wedge is my worst club. I hit some real goofy-
looking shots with it sometimes. And I don't handle a chip-and-
run shot over 100 feet well. Actually, my fairway woods are the
worst part of my game, but I don't work on them much because I
can plan my shots so I don't need to hit them. Under pressure
you're going to rely on what you can do well anyway."

Under pressure the excitable Weiskopf has to watch his club
selection carefully. "That adrenalin gets flowing and I'll hit the
ball 15 to 25 yards farther than under normal conditions," he
says. "In the third round at Orlando I was near the lead and had
a 155-yard shot to the eighteenth green, and I knocked a nine
iron clear into the bleachers behind the green. At the Hope

tournament I kept hitting my tee shots over the par-3 holes when the pressure was on. In most other sports you want to get all fired up, but in golf you have to be in control of your emotions all the time." Disciplined imagination, says Weiskopf, is the essence of championship golf. By that he means the ability to consider all the possibilities for a shot and then to visualize it before hitting it. Ben Hogan, he believes, is the best at imagining a shot, then turning the actual execution over to muscle memory. He wishes Hogan were still traveling the tour so he could study the master.

Weiskopf's wife travels with Tom from tournament to tournament. The Weiskopfs met in the summer of 1966, and for Jeanne it was love at first sight. For Tom it was more like love at eleventh sight.

"I was Miss Minnesota Golf Classic," Jeanne says, "and was handing our invitations to the pro-am party. I thought it was pretty important—I learned later most of the players never go. I had seen Tom and thought he was quite handsome, and I was hoping to be introduced to him and maybe be asked for a date. Well, I handed him his invitation, and he thanked me and just walked away! I was crestfallen. But we ran into one another on the course later in the week, and he asked me if I'd like to do something that evening. He said he didn't have a car. I told him not to worry about that, I could get a courtesy car. I took him to the zoo—can you believe that? But he seemed to enjoy it. He seemed so lonesome. I was sure he didn't like me. I decided I would be like a sister to him—write him letters while he was traveling to cheer him up. We didn't see each other much until we were engaged later that summer, then Tom started commuting from the tour to St. Paul—I think he was pleading non-existent illnesses and deliberately missing the cut sometimes—and we were married in October, three months after we met."

Who can tell about marriages, but the Weiskopfs appear to be the all-American young couple living happily ever after. The frequent low-key kidding between them is stimulating and quickly broadened to take in an outsider. "Jeanne's just wonderful," Tom says."Of course, she isn't too domestic-minded," this last with a grin and wink toward Jeanne. "When we first got married, she washed my golf shirts with my underwear and everything came out pink."

From time to time Jeanne receives amorous suggestions from men who do not realize she is married. She has learned to take them lightly. One she took too lightly, however. This night she went to the motel ice machine, and an admirer, unbeknownst to her, was watching her from the other side of the machine. He followed her back to the Weiskopfs' room, and several minutes later the phone rang. Jeanne answered. It was her would-be suitor, who thought she was in the room alone. He said he had noticed her at the ice machine—a great line in its own right—and would like to buy her a drink. Jeanne knew Tom had been talking to fellow-pro Chuck Courtney. "Aha," she reasoned, "he put Chuck up to calling me." She affected her most alluring voice and told the caller she would like nothing better than to have a drink with him—in her room. "But don't wear orange, honey," she cooed. "It will clash with my nightie." The caller gasped at his good fortune. Jeanne hung up and giggled.

Moments later a knock at the door cut off the giggles. Tom answered it. It was the would-be Casanova, who stammered something about looking for the ice machine. "Downstairs and around the corner," replied Tom. Then Tom asked if the visitor had just called Jeanne. At that juncture the intruder did a remarkable imitation of Jesse Owens, and was gone into the night.

Jeanne plans to go around the country with her husband for four or five years. Her talent in beauty contests was interpretive jazz dancing, and she does her dancing exercises each morning, but more to maintain her figure than to prepare for a career. She revels in the tour life: the succession of trips, radio and television interviews, fashion shows, luncheons, and walks around golf courses—she walks every hole with Tom. "It's so exciting," she enthuses. "I'm only 21 and Tom's only 25. We have plenty of time to settle down and have children. We do things with Frank Beard and his wife and Bert Yancy and his wife and R. H. Sikes and his wife and some other young couples making the tour—go to the movies, play shuffleboard, play cards. I'm trying to learn to play bridge, which is an obsession with these golfers. I'm taking up golf, and Tom's a good teacher. Watching Tom improve is thrilling."

Weiskopf's goal? To win the Big Four—the U.S. and British Open, PGA, and Masters—an objective his newfound tranquillity and his penchant for playing well on difficult courses could well enable him to realize. Has he thought about becoming successor to Arnold Palmer? He has. "If it comes, fine," he says. "It would be tremendously exciting, but a hard life to lead. . . . I'm not going to change my personality, not going to tell jokes or wear flashy clothes. . . . I withdraw into myself more than Arnold does, but I *do* have good rapport with galleries. I react to a crowd. I like to hear the noise and be in contention. At times like that I lose my shyness. . . . Boy, Arnold can do some amazing things to win. I really admire him. . . . Under pressure you can concentrate so hard you forget to smile at the gallery, but I'm trying to smile and stuff like that.

"What the heck, I'm the leading money winner, and the only impression a lot of people will ever have of me is the one they take home from a golf tournament. . . . I'm far from reaching my peak. I learned a lot these last four years, and I expect to learn twice as much in the next eight. . . . It isn't a matter of beating Arnold as much as being as good as you can be. . . . It'd be something to be in his position, wouldn't it?"

1969

WILLIE MAYS, YESTERDAY AND TODAY
By Roger Kahn

FROM SPORT

*When Willie Mays walked off the baseball field in 1974
the news media could not give us enough of this great
player to try to make up for the loss. Perhaps this story
by Roger Kahn comes the closest to satisfying that need. It
received the first-place vote of the entire judging staff. This
absorbing story of the great Willie, on the field and most
rewardingly off the field, is written with affection and, as
one of our judges states, "shies away from sentimentality."*

He is sitting on the three-legged stool they give to ball players
and milkmaids, and he looks enormous and supple and strong.
He has a massive flat chest and bulging arms and shoulders and
the kind of muscled stomach I remember from comic-book
drawings of Tarzan. Still, he is 38 years old.

"What do you do to stay in shape, Will?" I say.

"Nothin' special," Willie May says. "I walk a lot and I play
golf now, 'stead of pool. And I don't eat too much, and I never
did drink, except three times, when we won pennants." A smile
lights the handsome brown face.

"Well, you look like you can go on forever."

"I won't lie to you," May says. "It gets to be work. Sometimes when I get tired and all that pressure, it gets to be work. I
knew when I was 16 years old I never did want to work for a
living." Again the smile.

"You want to manage?"

"Yeah, I think I'd like to."

"You're a manager," Willie says, "man, you get to hire help."

It is 11 o'clock the morning after a night game and Willie will play this afternoon. The team is not going well and last night in the ninth inning, with the count 3 to 2, he guessed curve. Then Ron Taylor of the Mets threw a fast ball by him. Willie is not playing for fun today, but from a sense of obligation. He has come out early so we can talk in an empty locker room, and the conversation sweeps across a broad range. We go back a way together and when Willie trusts you, he is warm and open and droll and humorously sly. Together, we consider divorce and alimony and child-raising and financial security and how time, the subtle thief of youth, steals from you, me, and even Willie Mays.

A spring, 15 years ago, comes back in a rush and I see again the wide, pellucid sky, the baked hills wanting grass, and the desert winds blowing whirls of sand. I hadn't wanted to come to Phoenix. I hadn't wanted to cover the Giants. For two previous years, I'd been assigned to the Dodgers. This nurtured a condition described in a general way by the late nonpareil of sports editors, Stanley Woodward. "Baseball writers," Woodward observed, "always develop a great attachment for the Brooklyn ball club if long exposed to it. We found it advisable to shift Brooklyn writers frequently. If we hadn't, we would have found that we had on our hands a member of the Brooklyn ball club rather than a newspaper reporter. You watch a Brooklyn writer for symptoms, and, before they become virulent, you must shift him to the Yankees or to tennis or golf." Woodward was gone from the *New York Herald Tribune* by 1954. I was shifted, under protest, to the Giants.

The ride from New York to Phoenix was interminable. We had to change trains in Chicago, wasting time, and somewhere near Liberal, Kansas, we stopped dead for 10 or 12 hours in a snowstorm.

Perhaps 50 hours after we had left New York, the train pulled into Phoenix and we stepped out into a cool and cloudless morning. Louis Effrat of the *New York Times* alighted with me and looked about the station. A few Indians were sleeping. In the distance lay brown hills. "Three thousand miles!" Effrat shouted. "I leave my wife, my daughter, my home and travel 3,000 miles." He inhaled before bellowing, "For what?" He was making a joke, but that was the way I felt.

My outlook did not improve immediately. The Giant manager, Honest Leo Durocher, offered me tidbits on his swelling romance with a post-virginal actress, but was more devious when asked about the club. The ball players were decent enough, but I didn't know them, or they me, and I was starting from scratch, building up confidences and new sources. And aside from that, the team bored me. I was used to the explosive Dodger atmosphere, with Jackie Robinson holding forth and Charlie Dressen orating and Roy Campanella philosophizing. The Giants seemed somber as vestrymen.

While I struggled and wrote a story a day, plus an extra for Sunday, Willie Howard Mays, Jr., was struggling with an Army team at Fort Eustis, Virginia, hitting, as he later put it, ".470, or something like that." They were all waiting for him. The Giants had won in 1951 with Mays. Without him in 1952 and 1953, they lost. Each day in the press room, one of the regular Giant writers or one of the officials would tell anecdotes in which Willie was always Superman. In exasperation, I sat down and wrote a story for the Sunday paper that began:

"Willie Mays is 10 feet 9 inches tall. His arms reach from 156th Street to 154th. . . . He caught everything, hit everything, done everything a center fielder can possibly do."

"Look," I told Charles Feeney, the Giant vice-president, amid the amber torrents of the Phoenix press bar. "There are a couple of other center fielders, too. Ever hear of Mickey Mantle or Duke Snider?"

Mr. Feeney erupted in song. "In six more days," he choired, to the tune of "Old Black Joe," "we're gonna have Willie Mays." He may have sung it "going to." He is a Dartmouth man.

Each day Feeney warbled, amending the lyrics cleverly enough, say changing the word "six" to the word "five." The song, like the sandy wind, became a bane.

M Day, as I came to call it, dawned like most other days, with a big bright sky. Durocher had scheduled an intrasquad game and was elaborately underplaying things. The post-virginal movie star was gone, making him somewhat irascible.

"Nothing unusual, Leo announced in the lobby of the Hotel Adams early M Day. "Just a little intrasquad game, boys, that's all." Then he walked off, barely able to keep his footing for his swagger.

The Phoenix ball park was typical medium minor league. Old stands extended part way down each foul line. A wood fence ringed the outfield. The players, Monty Irvin, Whitey Lockman, Alvin Dark, were in uniform and, as always in spring, it seemed odd to see great major-leaguers in a minor-league setting.

Willie was coming by plane, we all knew that, and in

Phoenix you can see great distances. Whenever an airplane appeared, one of the writers or Giant officials leaped up with a cry, "Willie's plane." Two Piper Cubs, four Beechcrafts and one World War I Spad were positively identified as the transcontinental Constellation bearing Mays.

"Feeney," I said, "this is ridiculous."

This time he chose the key of C-sharp minor.

"In no more days,
"We're going to have Willie Mays!"

The athletes were still playing catch, the intrasquad game had not started, when a trim figure in slacks and a dark open-collared shirt appeared in the dugout. He was blinking at the sunlight, mostly because he had not been to sleep, and seemed to be trying to hide, to be as unobtrusive as possible. "There's Willie!" someone cried in ecstasy, and the sports writers swarmed.

Mays stood next to Irvin, probably the closest friend he has had among ball players in a curiously lonely life. Irvin was very poised, very strong, very sensible.

"Hey, Willie!" someone shouted. "What you got in that bag?" He had dropped off his large suitcase, but clung to a smaller one.

"Not much," Willie said. "A couple of things."

"What?"

"Just my glove and my jock."

Durocher hugged him repeatedly for joy and for the news photographers. Monte, who felt like hugging him, shook his hand.

"He's shaking hands with the pennant," Barney Kremenko, one of the baseball writers, proclaimed.

"Hi, roomy," Irvin said.

"Hey, Monte."

Irvin smiled. "Roomy," he said, "how's your game?"

Willie shook his head. "What you mean my game, Monte? You talking about pool?"

"No, Willie," Irvin said. "I'm talking about your game, about baseball."

"Oh, yeah," Willie said, as if surprised there should be a question. "My baseball. I'm ready anytime."

A few minutes later, when the intrasquad game began, Mays remained on the bench. Durocher, with his sure sense of drama and his always brilliant sense of handling Willie, was letting the elements cook. The game proceeded without much excitement.

The most interesting thing at the Phoenix ball park was watching No. 24, striding back and forth, looking at Durocher, asking with his eyes, and being ignored.

Halfway through the game, he was sent in to hit. Willie sprang from the dugout. He ran to the batter's box. He took a tremendous swing at the first pitch. His form was flawed. There was a little lunge in the swing. But I don't believe I have ever seen anyone swing harder. Three swings, and mighty Willie had struck out.

"The thing about Snider," I told Kremenko in the press box, "is that his butt doesn't fly out of there when he swings."

"Now, listen," Kremenko began, as though I had assailed the family honor. And I suppose I had.

The first unusual thing that Willie did was snatch a sinking liner off the grass. The ball came out to center field low and hard and Willie charged it better than anyone else could have done and made a graceful somersault and caught the ball. "Nothing!" Kremenko shouted. "For Willie that's absolutely nothing."

The next time he came to bat, I resolved to look for specific flaws in his form. I was doing that when he hit a fast ball 420 feet and out of the park. An inning later, and with a man on first, someone hit a tremendous drive over Willie's head. He turned and fled and caught the ball and threw it 300 feet and doubled the runner. Pandemonium. The camp was alive. The team was alive. And Willie had gone through the delays of a discharge, then sat up all night in a plane. I conceded to Kremenko that, given a little rest, he might show me something.

Then I sat down and wrote an account that began, "This is not going to be a plausible story, but then no one ever accused Willie Mays of being a plausible ball player. This story is only the implausible truth." It ran quite long, and I had no idea whether the *Tribune* copy desk would eviscerate it, until a day later when a wire came from Red Smith in Florida. Red was the columnist for the *Tribune*, a thoughtful man, and his telegram, a personal gesture, was the first indication I'd had in a month that my stuff was getting printed and was syntactical.

That night Feeney, selecting the rather cheerful key of D-major, honored me with the final version of his aria.

"*Gone are the days,*
"*When we didn't have Willie Mays.*"

After Willie's debut and Red's wire, I was genuinely surprised to hear how much Feeney's voice had improved.

Willie conquered me. I had not come to praise him and sycophancy annoys me, but he brought to the game the outstanding collection of skills in our time and the deepest enthusiasm to play I've ever seen. He was the ultimate combination of the professional full of talent and the amateur, a word that traces to the Latin *amator*, "lover," and suggests one who brings a passion to what he does.

They used to play pepper games, Leo and Willie, sometimes with Monte Irvin as the straight man. Willie has what his father, Kitty-Kat Mays, described as oversized hands, and Durocher was one of the finest defensive shortstops. They'd stand quite close and Leo would hit hard smashes at Willie's toes, or knees, wherever. Mays' reflexes were such that he could field a hard line drive at 10 or 15 feet. And he liked to do it. He threw, and Leo slugged again. Once in a while Willie bobbled a ball. Then he owed Durocher a Coke. Durocher made great shows of cheating Willie. One morning he hit a hard smash on one hop, well to Willie's right, and Willie knocked the ball down with a prodigious lunge.

"Coke!" Leo roared. "That's six you owe."

"Ain' no Coke for that," Willie said. His voice piped high and plaintive. "That's a base hit."

"Six Cokes you owe," Leo insisted.

"Monte," Willie pleaded at Irvin. "What you say, roomy?"

"Six Cokes," Irvin said, solemnly. Willie's mobile face slumped into a pout. "I'm getting the short end," the expression said, "but I'll get you guys anyway."

Sometimes Irvin hit, and then there was added byplay. Not only did Durocher and Mays stab smashes, they worked to rattle each other. Durocher seized a line drive, wound up to throw to Irvin, and with a blur of elbows and hands tossed the ball to Mays at his left. Leo has the skills and inclinations of a juggler. Willie caught the toss, faked toward Irvin, and there was the ball floating down toward Leo. Durocher reached and Mays slapped a glove into his belly.

"Ooof," Leo grunted. Willie spun off, staggering through his own laughter. It wasn't long before people started coming to the ball park long before the game, just to watch the pepper. The clowning would have done honor to Chaplin.

Willie ran and threw and hit and made his astounding catches, and slowly that spring I began to get to know him. I was the youngest of the baseball writers and that helped. We had little conversations after the workouts and the exhibition games, and he always became very solemn and gave me serious answers. "Who suggested," I asked one day, "that you catch fly balls that way?" The technique is famous now: glove up, near the belt buckle.

"Nobody," Willie said. "I just started it one day. I get my throw away quicker."

"Nobody taught you?"

Willie's eyes, which sometimes dance, grew grave. "Nobody can teach you nothing," he said. "You got to learn for yourself."

On another afternoon we were talking, and Ruben Gomez, a pitcher from Puerto Rico, came up and said, "Willie. That man in New York. I forget the name. I sign a paper for him."

Willie mentioned a New York agent.

"That's him," Gomez said.

"You sign a paper," Willie said, "and you worried because you haven't got your money."

Gomez nodded.

"Well, don't worry," Willie said. "Long as you sure you signed. It may come soon, or it may come late, but long as you sign something, you'll get money." He looked at me. "Ain' that right?" I thought of leases, installment contracts, and overdue bank loans, but I said, "Yes." Maybe it would always be that way for Willie, spring and youth and plenty of cash and laughter. But it wasn't, not even that spring.

Along with the Cleveland Indians, a team wealthy with pitchers, the Giants flew to Las Vegas for an exhibition game late in March. The Giant management did not want the ball players spending a night in Las Vegas. The Stoneham regime is paternalistic and the idea of a troop of young ball players abroad among the gamblers and the bosoms of Vegas was disturbing. The team would play its game with the Indians. The players would be guests for dinner at one of the big hotels. They would watch a show and seek as much trouble as they could find up until 11:00 P.M. Then a bus would take them to the airport for a flight to Los Angeles, where two other exhibitions were scheduled. We wouldn't get much rest.

It was a gray, raw afternoon in Vegas, and Bob Feller pitched for the Indians. Sal Maglie opposed him. My scorebook is lost, but I believe the Giants won by one run. Afterward we wrote our stories and took a bus to the hotel that invited us all. We ate well, and I caught up with Willie in the hotel theater, where Robert Merrill, the baritone, was to sing. As I joined Willie's table, Merrill began "Vesti la Giubba," the famous aria from *Pagliacci* in which Canio, the clown, sings of having to make people laugh, although his own heart is breaking.

Merrill gave it full voice and all his passion. When he was done, Willie turned to me amid the cheering. "You know," he said, "that's a nice song."

An hour later, he was in a gambling room. He was standing quietly amid a group of people close to a dice table. Monte Irvin and Whitey Lockman were fighting a 10-cent one-armed bandit. Sal Maglie, looking like Il Patrone of Cosa Nostra, was losing a steady 50 cents a game at blackjack. I walked over to Willie. "How you doing?"

"Oh," Willie said, "I'm just learnin' the game." We both grinned.

I moved on. A stocky, gruff man grabbed me by the arm. "Hey," he said, "wait a minute."

I shook my arm free.

"That guy a friend of yours?" said the man. He pointed to Mays.

"I know him."

"Well, get him the hell away from the dice tables."

"What?"

"You heard me. We don't want him mixing with the white guests."

"Do you know who he is?"

"Yeah, I know who he is, and get that nigger away from the white guests."

If there was a good answer, except for the obvious short answer, I didn't come up with it. Very quickly I was appalled, unnerved, and angry. What unnerved me was the small, significant bulge on the man's left hip.

"Do you know that boy just got out of the Army?" I said.

"That don't mean nothing. I was in the Army myself."

"You bastards invited him down to your hotel."

"Who you calling a bastard?"

We were shouting and Gary Schumacher, the Giant's publicity director, suddenly loomed large and put a hand on my shoulder. "What's the trouble?" Gary said.

"This guy," the tough began.

"I asked him," Gary said, nodding at me.

I had a sensible moment. "No trouble, Gary," I said to Gary. I took my wallet out of a hip pocket and withdrew the press card. "This joker has just given me one helluva story for the Sunday *New York Herald Tribune*."

The hood retreated. I walked over to Irvin and told him what was happening. Lockman listened briefly and then, taking the conversation to be personal, stepped back. "Maybe Willie and I'll get on the bus," Irvin said. It was his way to avoid confrontations, but he was also worried lest Willie be shocked or hurt.

Now a hotel vice-president appeared, with a girl, hard-faced but trimly built. He asked if "my assistant and I can buy you a drink, Mr. Kahn."

We went to the bar and the man explained that he had nothing against a Negro like Irvin or Mays playing one-armed bandits. It was just that the dice table was a somewhat different thing. As far as he, the vice-president, was concerned, Negroes were as good as anybody, but he had to concern himself with customers. That was business.

"We're really in the South here," said the brunette.

"I thought the South was Alabama, Georgia, Texas."

"That's it," the brunette said. "We get a lot of customers from Texas." She glanced at the bartender, and I had another drink. "We're really a very liberal place," the girl said, "even though we are in the South. We not only book Lena Horne to sing here, but when she does, we let her live on the grounds. We're the only hotel that liberal." She leaned toward me, a hard, handsome woman, working.

"Why did you invite him if you were going to crap on him?" I said and got up and joined Monte and Will in the bus.

Later Irvin asked me not to write the story. He said he didn't know if it was a good idea to make Willie, at 21, the center of a racial storm. That was Monte's way and the Giants' way and Willie's way, and you had to respect it, even if dissenting. I never did write the story until now.

In the visitors' locker at Shea Stadium 15 years later, the headline on a folded newspaper cries out: "City College Torn by Black and White Strife." The times are different and I have heard a prominent black criticize Mays as self-centered. It was the job of every black to work for a free society, he said. To the militant—a Stokley Carmichael or a Rap Brown—Willie is the embodiment of the well-fed, declawed Tom.

"They want me to go out on some campus?" Willie says. "Why should I lie? I don't know nothin' about campuses. I never went to college. I wanted to play ball."

"Well, what about the whole black movement?"

"I help," Willie says. "I help in my way." His face becomes very serious. "I think I show some people some things. I do it my way." He is a good fellow, serious and responsible, never in trouble, never drunk, never in jail.

"Do you speak out?"

"Like what?"

"On schools, or full employment or whatever?"

He eyes me evenly. "I don't think I should. I don't know the full value of these things. I'm not the guy to get on the soapbox." He pauses, then announces with great assurance and pride, "I'm a ball player."

In the autumn of 1954, after Willie led the Giants to the pennant and a sweep over the Indians in the World Series, our paths crossed again. I was putting together a book featuring articles by All-Star ball players on the qualities that make one an All-Star. I sent questionnaires to many like Ted Kluszewski and Bob Lemon. I telephoned Stan Musial. I went to see Willie in the flesh. He had made his classic World Series catch, running, running, running, until he was 460 feet out and grabbing Vic Wertz's liner over his head. He had taken Manhattan, the Bronx, and Staten Island, too, and was in demand. At the Giants someone gave me the name of his agent.

After hearing that I could pay, the agent said Willie would let me have three to four minutes on a slow Tuesday afternoon, but while we talked, he might have to sign four endorsements, accept six speaking engagements, get his shoes shined, and telephone for a date. His business was being handled brusquely, although not, we were to learn, very well.

A few seconds before the appointed minute I appeared in the agent's office. Willie was in an anteroom, only signing endorsements. When I appeared he waved and smiled, relieved to see a familiar face. "Hey," he said, "Roger Kahn, is that you? I didn't know that was you. What you want to talk to me about?"

I explained.

"You writin' a book?" Willie said. "That's real good, you writin' a book."

Disturbed by gratuitous friendliness, the agent vanished and Willie held forth on playing center field. "The first thing," he said, "is you got to love the game. Otherwise you'll never learn to play good. Then, you know, don't drink, and get your sleep. Eight hours. You sleep more, you get to be lazy.

"Now in Trenton, where I played when I first signed, I was

nowhere near as good as I am now, but I have my way to learn things. People tell me, 'Willie, do like this, like that,' but that ain't the way."

He sat in a swivel chair, which he had tilted back. His considerable feet were on a desk. "Well, how do you learn?" I said.

"Some things maybe when you're real little, you got to be told. But mostly you got to be doing it yourself. Like once I was a pitcher and now I'm in the outfield. Watch me after I get off a good throw. I look sort of like a pitcher who has thrown.

"You got to be thinking, 'What am I doing wrong?' And then you look at the other two outfielders and think, 'What are they doing wrong?' And you're thinking and thinking and trying not to make the same mistake three times, or four at the most, and you're also thinking what you'll do if the ball comes to you. Understand?"

"Pretty much."

"You don't want to be surprised," Willie said with finality.

But on what Branch Rickey called the best catch in baseball history, Mays was indeed surprised. The Giants were playing in Pittsburgh, where center field runs 457 feet deep, a good stage for Willie. Rocky Nelson, a left-handed hitter, smashed a tremendous line drive and Willie, calculating at a glance, turned and sprinted for the wall. Nelson had hit the ball so hard that there was a hook to it. While Willie ran, the ball drifted slightly to the right.

At precisely the right instant, Willie looked. He had gotten back deep enough, a mini-miracle, but now the ball was to his right and sinking fast. He might have been able to reach across his body and glove the ball. Or he might not. We will never know. He simply stuck out his bare right hand and seized the liner at the level of his knees. Then he slowed and turned, his face a great, wide grin.

"Silent treatment," Durocher ordered in the dugout. "Nobody say nothing to him."

Willie touched his cap to acknowledge the crowd and ran down the three steps into the Forbes Field dugout. Everyone avoided Willie's eyes. Durocher was checking the lineup card. Bobby Thomson was pulling anthracite from his spikes. Hank Thompson was taking a very long drink. The silence was suffocating.

"Hey, Leo," Willie piped. "You don't have to say, 'Nice play, Willie.' I know that was a nice play."

A minute later a note from Rickey arrived. "That," Rickey

wrote, "was the finest catch I have ever seen and the finest catch I ever hope to see."

I finished the story by Willie with a comment that he offered in the agent's office. "You got to learn for yourself," he said, "and you got to do it in your own way and you got to become much improved. If you love the game enough, you can do it." It reads right after all the years, and true, but even as I was finishing I understood that no book was likely to help a young man play center field like Willie Mays.

In Shea, we start talking about the old times. "New York was a good town for center fielders," I say, "when you were here with Mantle and Snider."

"Yeah," he says, "Mick and I broke in together, but he had a real bad body. Legs."

"How do you feel being the only one left?"

"Proud. Proud that I'm still playing."

"Lonely?"

"There's more new faces, but . . ." He turns his palms up and shrugs. "That doesn't bother me none.

"I worry, though," he says. "I get worried now that I can't do the job. 'Course, I always was a worrier. I get the ball out, but I can't get it out as often as I used to."

"About old friends," I say.

"You know," Willie says, "I don't have many friends. People I know, people to say, 'Hi, Willie,' there's a million of them. My friends, I could count them on a few fingers."

I went calling in 1956, four days after Willie had taken a wife. Because he is handsome and country slick, and also because he is famous and well paid, he does not lack for feminine attention. Joe Black, the Dodger relief pitcher, told me Willie was getting married. We played winter basketball together and after one workout, Joe said he hoped Willie knew what he was getting into.

"I'm sure of that," I said.

"I mean I hope he doesn't get hurt."

"What's the girl like?" I said.

"The girl," Joe said, "is older than Willie and has been married twice before."

A number of people counseled Willie against getting married, but he doesn't like to be told how to run his life, and each bit of counsel was a shove toward the altar. Then, in February, he gathered Marghuerite Wendelle, stuffed her into his Lincoln, and set off for Elkton, Maryland, where one can marry in haste.

On the way, he picked up a $15 fine for driving 70 in a 60-mile zone.

He set up housekeeping in a tidy brick home not far from La Guardia Airport. East Elmhurst was one of the early colonies open to the black middle class and I remember the white taxi driver looking at the clean streets and detached houses in surprise. "Colored people live here?" he said.

Mrs. Mays received me with a cool hand, tipped with pointed fingernails. She was a beautiful woman who stared hard and knowingly when she said hello. It was midday, but Willie hadn't come downstairs. "Just go on up," Marguerite Mays said. "I have to go out to the beauty parlor."

I found Willie sitting in an enormous bed, gazing at morning television, a series starring Jackie Cooper and a talking dog. Willie was wearing tailored ivory pajamas. "Sit down," he said, indicating a chair. "What you doing now? How come you don't come around? You okay?"

I had left the newspaper business and gone to work as a sports writer for a newsmagazine. The salary was better and the researchers were pretty, but the magazine approached sports in an earnest, sodden way. One of the supervising editors had been a small-town sports writer once and then became a sports writer on the newsmagazine. The change of fortune downed poorly. He alternately tried to relate great events to his own experiences, perhaps covering a play-off game between Bridgeport and Pittsfield, or he demanded scientific analyses of the events and men. A great story on Mays, he told me, would explain in complete technical detail how Willie played center field.

In the bridal bedroom, I told Willie I was fine. I was wondering how to swing the conversation into a technical analysis. I asked what had made him decide to marry.

"Well," Willie said, "I figured that it's time for me to be settling down. I'm 24 years old."

"You figure being married will affect your play?"

"I dunno," Willie said. "How am I supposed to know? I hit 51 home runs last year. Man, if you come to me last spring and tell me I was gonna do that, I woulda told you you were crazy." Willie shook his head and sat straight up. "Man," he said, "that's a lot of home runs."

On top of the TV set rested three trophies. The largest was a yard-high wooden base for bright gilt figurines of ball players running, batting, and throwing. It bore a shiny plaque which read: "To Willie Mays, the most valuable player in baseball."

"What are you hoping to do this year?"

"I dunno," Willie said. He frowned. "Why you askin' questions like that?" he said.

I stopped and after a while we were talking about marriage. "You hear some people say they worried 'bout me and Marghuerite," Willie said. "Same people last summer was saying I was gonna marry this girl and that girl. But they was wrong then, like they're wrong now." He thumped his heart under the ivory pajamas. "I'm the only guy knows what's in there."

They didn't know what to make of my story at the newsmagazine. They cut out chunks of it, and devoted equal space to the picture of a 2-to-5 favorite winning a horse race. Willie's love song was not newsmagazine style.

The marriage went. I like to think they both tried. They adopted a son and named him Michael, but some years later they were divorced. "Foundered on the rocks off the Cape of Paradise" is how the actor Mickey Rooney likes to put it, but there is nothing funny about the failure of a marriage or having to move out from under the roof where lives your only son.

In Shea before the game against the Mets, Willie is talking about the boy. "He's with me, you know," Willie says.

"How come?"

"He was with Marghuerite, but when he started gettin' older I guess he missed me and we kind of worked something out.

"Michael is 10 years old," Willie says, "and there's a lady who keeps house and she looks after him when I'm away. A real nice boy. I send him to a private school, where they teach him, but they're not too hard with him."

I think of the ironworker's son with a boy in private school.

"I've made a deal with him," Willie says. "He needs a college degree in times like these, and the deal is I send him to good schools, put it all there for him, and after that it's up to him to take it."

"You think he will?"

"He's a real good boy."

Two men have come into the Mets' clubhouse to see Willie. Paul Sutton is a patent attorney and David Stern is a vice-president of Sports Satellite Corporation. Willie hopes that these men and a Salt Lake businessman named Ernie Psarras will build his fortune up to seven figures. For now Willie is concerned about filling the house he is building on an acre in Atherton, down peninsula from San Francisco. He stands to greet Sutton and Stern and says, "Hey, what about the furniture?"

"We're seeing about it," David Stern says.

"Man," Willie says, "I got to stay on you guys."

"Willie doesn't like to pay retail," Stern explains.

"I don't like to pay," Willie says, and he laughs.

Larry Jansen, a coach who pitched for the old Giants, approaches and asks Willie about a doctor or a dentist. Willie gives him a telephone number. Willie owns the keys to the kingdom in New York.

When the Giants moved to San Francisco after the 1957 season, I lost touch with Willie. I read he was having problems. He moved into a white neighborhood and a Californian threw a soda bottle through his living room window in protest. It was a good thing for the Californian that Willie didn't grab the bottle and throw it back. With that arm, he would have cut the man in half. Later, at least as we got word in New York, some San Francisco fans felt disappointed in Willie. They didn't appreciate him as we had; a number said they preferred Orlando Cepeda.

I was paying less attention to sports and writing more about other things, but I knew Willie was not disgracing himself. He kept appearing in All-Star games and driving homers into the high wind over Candlestick Park. But I wondered if the years and the franchise shift and the divorce had dampened the native ebullience.

It was 1964. Forces that would explode into Black Revolution were gathering and an editor asked me to spend a few months in Harlem, "a part of New York that white New Yorkers don't know."

"I don't know it," I said.

"You've been there," the editor said.

"Sure. Whenever I took a taxi to the Polo Grounds, I'd ride right through."

This time I got out of the taxi. I went from place to place on foot, trying to grasp the bar of music, the despair, the life and death, the sour poverty, the unquenchable hope of a black ghetto. It was different than living in a press box.

To shake off the gray ghetto despair, a man can stand a drink, and one evening I walked into Small's Paradise, with my new blonde wife on my arm. Across the bar a major-leaguer was drinking hard, although he had a girl with him. She was quite young, a soft off-tan, and wore an enormous round black hat. The athlete and I raised glasses to each other's ladies. Suddenly Willie walked in.

It was a cold day in January, but his stride was bouncy.

Willie wore a beautifully tailored topcoat of herringbone char-
coal. He has unusual peripheral vision and he covered the bar
with a glance. Then he bounced over with a smile.

"Buy you a Coke?" I said.

Willie shook his head. "How are you? You okay? Everything
all right? What you doing around here? Who's the girl over there
with . . ." And he mentioned the other major-leaguer's name.

"I don't know."

"You sure you okay, now?" Willie said.

"Fine." I introduced him to my wife.

Willie put an elbow on the bar and placed a hand against his
brow and fixed his gaze at the girl. "Who is that chick, man?"

None of us knows what happened next. Willie was around
the bar quickly, greeting the other ball player, talking very fast to
the girl. Then he bounced out of the bar, calling, "See ya, man."
Five minutes later the other major-leaguer was drunker and the
pretty girl in the big round hat was gone. "That," said the blonde
on my arm, "has to be the smoothest move I've seen."

You don't judge a man's vigor only by the way he pursues fly
balls.

Back at Shea, Willie is asking if he'd given me enough to
write an article and I tell him I think so.

I find his father sitting in the dugout. Kitty-Kat Mays has
his son's big grin and says sure, he'd like to talk about the boy.
Kitty-Kat is smaller than Willie. He has a round belly. He was a
semi-pro around Fairfield, near Birmingham, Alabama.

"I was down there, Mr. Mays, when Bull Connor was the
police commissioner."

"Things are a lot different now," Kitty-Kat says.

"You still live there?"

"No. I'm up here. I've got a good job."

The man knows baseball and I ask when it first struck him
that his son was going to be a superlative ball player. Kitty-Kat
screws up his face, and I can see that he is going backward in
time. He says, "Well, you know we lived right across from a ball
field, and when Willie was eight he had to play with older kids."

"I mean even before that."

"Soon as he started walking," Kitty-Kat says, "he's about a
year old, I bought him a big round ball. He'd hold that big round
ball and then he'd bounce it and he'd chase it, and if he ever
couldn't get the ball, he'd cry.

"I knew he'd be a good one, with those oversized hands."
Mr. Mays extends his own palms. "I was pretty good, but my

hands are regular size. Willie gets those big hands from his mother."

Willie emerges, taps his father's shoulder, and goes out for batting practice. He does not take a regular turn in rotation. He hits for three or four minutes, then sits down. That way is a little gentler on the legs.

He doesn't dominate the series. The Mets do. In one game Ron Swoboda hits a 430-foot home run to left center field. Willie sprints back, the way he can, but this is not the Polo Grounds. He had to pull up short. He is standing at the fence when the ball sails out. In his time and in his park, he would have flagged it.

Later, he crashes one single to left so hard that a runner at second couldn't score, and then he says he wished he'd hit it harder. He hits a long double to left that just misses carrying into the bullpen for a home run. He leads off the ninth inning of a close game with a liner to left that hangs just long enough to be caught. The Giants lose three straight and, in the way of losing teams, they look flat.

When we say good-bye in the clubhouse, Willie seems more annoyed than depressed. The last game ends with the intense frustration of a Giant pitcher fidgeting, scrambling, and walking in the winning run. "What can you do?" Willie says. "You got to play harder tomorrow."

For an aging ball player, he seems at peace with himself. He went through money wildly in the early days, borrowing from the team, spending August money by April. "You're really okay financially?" I say.

"Oh, yes," Willie says. "Very good." His face was serious. "I ought to be. I've been working a long time."

Back in the Arizona spring we wore Western string ties and we worried about flying DC-3s and we ate in a restaurant where a man dressed like a medieval knight rode a charger and pointed with his spear to show you where to park. Who would have thought then that the Giants would leave New York, and that my old newspaper would fold, and that in another spring, my hair showing gray, I would sit in a strange ball park and ask Willie Mays about legs, fatherhood, investments, and fatigue?

Driving home, while Willie flew to Montreal, the spring kept coming back. I saw in flashes a hit he made in Tucson, a throw he loosed in Beaumont, how Leo made him laugh, and I could hear how the laughter sounded. The racists were appalled that year. A Cleveland coach snapped at me for praising Mays and one writer insisted on betting me $20 Willie wouldn't hit .280. We made it, Willie and I, by 65 percentage points.

All this crossed my mind without sadness. Willie was a boy of overwhelming enthusiasm. He had become a man of vigorous pride. I don't say that Willie today is as exciting as Willie in 1954, but what he does now is immeasurably harder. Playing center field at 38 was beyond the powers of Willie's boyhood idol, DiMaggio, or his contemporary rival, Mantle. Willie stands up to time defiantly and with dignity, and one is fortunate to write baseball in his generation.

I guess I'll look him up again next trip.

1970

THE HOUSEBREAKER

By Bill Bousfield

FROM OUTDOOR LIFE

Copyright © 1970, Popular Science Publishing Co.

This memorable offbeat sports story is a conglomeration of exciting adventure, fun, and pity for a brave black bear and its compassionate pursuers. Red Smith said it was just a hell of a good adventure story with built-in excitement. Incidentally, this was the second hunting-magazine story that ever won a first prize in this annual anthology of sports stories.

The afternoon was cold but bright with sunshine when Percy King and I cranked up for the run to Mackenzie outpost, some 25 miles up the lake.,

It was late November, and winter had already set in with its snows and subzero temperatures. Scout Bay, the arm that connects our cove with the main body of Lac Seul, had been frozen over for more than a week. A test hole showed four inches of firm ice there. Scout Bay is sheltered, and we knew that we might encounter vastly different conditions before we reached our destination.

We were expecting a bit of trouble, but not the kind we found.

I'm an outfitter and guide. My wife, Judy, and I operate Onaway Lodge, a hunting and fishing resort on Lac Seul in northwestern Ontario. The main camp and winter headquarters are seven miles north of Perrault Falls, just of the Red Lake highway.

Percy King, an Ojibwa Indian, is our head guide, my right-hand man, a jack-of-all-trades, and, as you might expect, an accomplished outdoorsman in every respect. Percy should be relating this adventure, for it is his story. But Percy never had a formal education. In this part of Ontario the first public school—or a road to get to it—was not built until shortly before his eldest son was born.

Each year at the lodge, our last guests of the season are moose hunters. In previous years moose were legal game until Christmas. This late season was abused by some hunters, who would spot bulls from small aircraft and then land on a frozen lake nearby and make the kill. To prevent that practice, the last day of the 1969 nonresident season was set for November 15, before the lake ice is thick enough to support the weight of a plane on skis.

The resident season, however, continued until December 15. So after Percy and I had bade our last nonresident guest good-bye, we still had a month to bag our winter meat.

For this type of hunting, from the start of freeze-up in the fall until the season is over, we are well fixed for transportation. Ten years ago I built our first scoot—a waterproof metal cab powered by a 65-horsepower airplane engine—to transport my hunters between the lodge and hunting sites under almost any conditions of ice, snow slush, and open water.

With the scoot we can reach all of our outposts, which at certain times of the season would be inaccessible by any other means except helicopter. The scoot can go from ice to open water and back to ice again, taking both in stride. Its speed ranges from about 30 mph on open water to a supposed 100 mph on glare ice. I've never had the nerve to push the throttle that far.

As we crossed the Bay of Islands, the blanket of snow on the ice began to disappear. This portion of the lake had been open water during the snowstorm and had only begun to freeze up later. The ice was thin. Long cracks began to appear ahead of us and snake toward the distant shoreline. We could feel the ice begin to sag under the weight of the craft and could see the frozen surface belly up ahead.

"Hold on!" I yelled at Percy over the roar of the motor and the clank of frozen slush against the scoot's metal skin. "We'll ride her out on top as long as we can."

I hauled back on the throttle, and the guide wedged himself in for what he knew would be a rough ride. We skimmed past the mouth of Shanty Narrows and hit the big open area of Mackenzie Bay. There the ice was thicker and we could come out on top again. When we began to pick up snow cover on thicker ice, I throttled back to a more comfortable cruising speed.

The cabin at Mackenzie outpost would be our headquarters

for the moose hunt. It was owned by our friend and neighboring outfitter, Harry Yoachum, and sat on a clay bluff overlooking the lake. Along one side of the cabin was stacked an enormous pile of railroad ties, abandoned there years ago by a defunct lumber company. Percy pointed these out.

"Harry," he laughed, "use Ojibwa logic."

"How's that?" I asked.

"When firewood around house give out, Indian finds it easier to move house to new supply one time than to bring wood supply to old location many times."

I barely heard his words, for I had noticed something unusual about the cabin. Then I realized what it was. The door stood wide open. I distinctly recalled having checked the locked door when we had stopped by to pick up an empty gas drum just before freeze-up.

"Harry's got visitors," Percy said.

I cut the motor, and we coasted up to the dock. A black bear suddenly stood framed in the doorway. He was tall at the shoulders and looked to be a big one. I could tell by the guide's face that he was as surprised as I was. Earlier in the year, with the berry crop as short as it had been, we would have expected to find a bear looking for food around this or any other cabin. But now it was almost the dead of winter, and this creature should be tucked away somewhere in his hibernating hole, peacefully resting.

Percy didn't waste any time. While I maneuvered for a landing, he crammed shells into the clip of his semiautomatic .30/06. It was mutually understood that we were on a moose hunt, and neither of us wanted a bear. But a bruin walking around in a foot of snow at this time of year was either crazy or otherwise dangerous.

The bear stepped out of the doorway, stood broadside and studied us long enough for Percy to have put in a killing shot if we had wanted the animal. Then the bear retreated fast around the corner of the shack.

We found the cabin in a shambles. Apparently the bear was both hungry and impatient, for he had not stopped outside to reconnoiter. His tracks came straight up an old logging road, now overgrown to little more than a trail, and into the clearing. He had paused at the garbage pit long enough to dig up a few cans and had cut his foot on a broken bottle. From there he'd padded to the door of the cabin and, with raking blows, had ripped off the sign identifying the camp, plus the padlock and hasp and some pretty solid lumber to which it was attached.

Inside, a box of garbage was scattered from one end of the shack to the other, and utensils and food containers had been raked off the shelves and scattered about. A heavy bench was overturned, and the table was knocked askew. The only edibles left in the cabin were a four-pound can of sugar and another of peanut butter. Both bore teeth marks and were bent out of shape. Apparently we had interrupted the black's plan for lunch.

"Lucky we leave our own grub at Marty's," Percy said.

Marty Talgren is a commercial fisherman who lives alone at Shanty Narrows. In the warm months he operates by boat; occasionally in the winter he snowshoes the eight or 10 miles to Onaway Lodge. During the freeze-up and break-up periods, he is completely marooned.

Prior to freeze-up we had stored our groceries for this hunt at Marty's cabin. Though we had passed close by his place earlier in the afternoon, we were carrying about all the load our scoot would haul.

Speaking of grub," I said, "do you want to go back to Marty's for it, or shall I?"

Percy grinned.

"You go," he said. "I might have a talk with old bear while you gone. Besides, I got to nail door back together."

I parked the scoot on solid ice beside Marty's dock, and while we were having coffee I told him about the bear.

"Most unusual, most unusual," he said. "Something sure wrong there. Keep your eyes open, and don't let that old black get the drop on you."

Marty declined an invitation to hunt with us, stating that he had not yet fully recovered from his last trip to town.

I got back to Mackenzie outpost in late afternoon. Percy had the cabin livable again, wood split and stacked inside, and a fresh pail of hot coffee on the back of the tin cookstove.

We fixed supper and at about 8:30 put out the light for a good night's sleep. We'd be up at daybreak.

Most outposts are infested with deer mice, and Mackenzie is no exception. As soon as the lights go out, the mice usually get busy and often make quite a bit of noise for their size. In spite of all the activity, I was dozing off when a different kind of scratching sound came from the front of the cabin.

"You hear that?" I called softly.

"Pretty big mouse," Percy whispered. "I hear snow squeaking under his feet."

In cold weather we usually store our rifles in the scoot. Percy, however, must have had an idea that the bear would be back, for his loaded gun was within arm's length of his bunk.

Bear shooting by flashlight is a sport I would hesitate to recommend to my friends, but we held a whispered conversation and decided we'd better finish off our nocturnal visitor then and there. At that time of year perishable food must be left in the cabin, and we often encase it in our sleeping bags to keep it from freezing after the fire goes out. I could imagine what the bruin would do to our bags to get at the food.

The cabin has two windows, one on each side of the door. They are covered with a semiopaque plastic material that lets in some light, but you can't see much more than a shadow through it. The moon was full, and by sound and shadow we finally located the bear under the window farthest from the lake. He would be behind the door when it was opened.

Percy's rifle is equipped with a peep sight, which would make for tough shooting. But we decided to take the chance.

In my long johns and socked feet, I swung the door back and did some fast sidestepping to give Percy room to shoot. When I got the flashlight beam on the bruin's backside, he was going straight away, but then he wheeled to the right just short of the outhouse. Percy got off two fast shots before the bear disappeared into the woods. One shot grazed a foreleg, and the other went through the outhouse wall.

There wasn't any choice now; we'd have to go bear hunting in the morning.

We started out as soon as we had enough light to see the tracks. Percy followed the sign leading away from the cabin and I took the bear's back trail. An old Indian guide once told me that the best way to find a bear's den is to backtrack the critter. A black doesn't like to walk in snow any farther than it has to and will come from its den straight to where it thinks it can find food. Going home, however, the bear may wander all over the countryside to throw a pursuer off its trail.

After an hour of trailing I became convinced that this black did not have a home. I found several places where he had bedded down in the snow like a moose. The sign also told me that he was desperately hungry, for in his seemingly aimless wanderings through the woods, he had paused to dig up and eat dry grass and even the dead roots from upturned stumps.

The sun was clearing the tops of the tall spruce trees and I had turned back toward the cabin to get some coffee when I heard Percy shoot. I paused in midstride, stepped off the trail and stood for five minutes, looking and listening. I heard no more shots, so I assumed that the guide had caught up with our marauder and finished it off.

What really happened, however, was considerably more dramatic than one simple shot.

The bruin had bedded down less than 500 yards from the cabin, with the obvious intention of again investigating our grub supply at his first opportunity. His tracks seemed to indicate that he was not seriously wounded. He left a few drops of blood here and there, but that could have been from the foot he had cut on a broken bottle while digging in the garbage pit.

He had eased out of his bed ahead of Percy, for the trail was dead fresh. He obviously knew he was being followed, for he had picked his way through the densest spruce and balsam thickets instead of taking the easiest course around. Along much of the route lay two trails; one was made the night before, and it occasionally headed off on a tangent. Percy knew that his best bet was to stick with the fresh tracks, even though they led through dense thickets and blowdowns, which he often had to crawl through.

The guide had wormed his way through a brushy top and pulled himself upright to plow through a heavy thicket when the bear charged with a coughing roar. It had been lying in ambush only a few yards away. Percy had no time to aim. He swung the muzzle of his gun and shot from the hip, with the black barely a rifle length beyond the front sight. The animal came to a sudden halt, shaking its head with a jerky motion, but it did not go down. Percy pressed the trigger of his semiautomatic again but got only a click. Without taking his eye off the bear, he tried to work the action with his hand. But the rifle was hopelessly jammed.

Percy was familiar enough with bears to know he had to stand his ground. Moving slowly, he drew his hunting knife out of its sheath and held it ready, waiting for the black's next move. For several seconds the two stared at one another, only a few feet apart. The black was the first to yield. It turned and ran, and, as Percy related later, "I darn sure back up just about as fast the other way."

Percy's unaimed shot had hit the bear at the bridge of its nose and plowed out through the bottom of the throat. From my experience with blacks, I am convinced of two things. First, if that one shot had not given the bruin such a wallop and done so much damage, he most likely would have continued his attack. Second, if in those tense moments of confrontation Percy had shown any sign of fear, the result could have been disastrous.

Normally the black bear is a rather docile animal that will run from a man. Above all else, it is a big bluffer. Usually when threatened, it will turn and flee. There are, however, some notable exceptions.

Percy retreated a short distance before trying to clear the jammed cartridge case from his rifle. While he worked, he kept one eye peeled for the black, should it change its mind and come back looking for him. He couldn't pry the case loose. Finally he cut a stick, smoothed it down to caliber-.30 size, and punched out the empty hull from the front end of the barrel.

"After that," he said, "I was so damn mad with bear that I start to look him up a second time. But then I think, maybe gun jam again and bear won't be so polite second time. Better I go get boss."

I was at the cabin having coffee when Percy came in with his story. He flashed a wide grin as he finished it.

"I been trout guide, deer guide, and moose guide," he said. "Now take good look at chicken guide."

Percy downed his coffee, and then we set out. This time we had two guns instead of the one. Percy's legs are so long that even when he's walking slow he's hard to follow. A bull moose on a dead run would have been hard pressed to match his stride along the straight path he had made to the cabin from where he'd fixed his gun.

Again we took the bruin's trail, rifles at ready. Normally I do not hunt with my safety off, but it was off now. The blood trail was heavy, and I knew that the bear couldn't have gone far. We found one blood-soaked bed and then another. We proceeded cautiously, trying not to be taken by surprise. The tracks led into a dense thicket, and Percy stopped several yards behind to cover me while I made a tight circle of the brush clump.

I got less than halfway around the thicket when a roar and a crashing of brush told me that we had found our quarry. I swung aside, trying to get a glimpse for a shot, but the cover was too dense. Percy, 30 feet behind me, was in a position from which he could see the animal lunging at me. He put it down with one

When Percy stood in his tracks and pumped a second bullet into the dead bear, I gave him a questioning look.

"One for bear," he said, "and second to see if damn rifle works."

The first thing I noticed about the animal was its thinness. It was a big bear with long legs and feet like soup plates. I guessed the weight at no more than 200 pounds. In prime condition it would have gone over 450 pounds. Then we discovered the reason for the black's emaciation and strange behavior.

In my country we still have bounty hunting for wolves. Many of the wolves are snared by attaching a loop of cable, similar to that used in the controls of light aircraft, to the center of a drag pole and concealing the set in the runway of a wolf.

This big black bear, probably snuffing along, had blundered into one of those snares. We couldn't tell how far or how long he had dragged the log, but it was far enough for the wire to open a slit about two inches deep and two inches wide, completely around his neck. Probably he had been tied to the snare pole for several weeks without food, though he must have got some water. I would guess that he had broken the last strands of snare wire only days before we met him.

Without question, the bear had been hungry and had known instinctively that he could not survive hibernation. So he'd been out in the snow, trying to put on as many pounds as possible before his winter's nap.

The stench from the infected neck wound was horrible, and when I suggested to Percy that we skin out our trophy, he gave me one of those you-go-ahead-buddy-I'll-watch looks. But we planned to go back in the spring and bring out the skull. I was anxious to see how it would stack up against heads in the Boone and Crockett Club's book, *Records of North American Big Game*.

Our moose hunt, incidentally, was a success. Three days later I took a nice bull. Percy took me to the main camp and went back in the scoot with his son to bring out the meat. Both of them scored while they were there. The boy got a cow, and Percy knocked over a good bull, about the size of mine. Both bulls were in the 50-odd-inch class, which rates as a good trophy for the average hunter in our part of Ontario. We had our winter's meat, which was what we had gone after.

The highlight of the hunt, of course, was the bear. I'm sure we did the poor critter a favor and saved him a lot of suffering, for in his condition he could never have survived the winter.

1971

THE TRIUMPHANT TURNABOUT OF THE HARTSDALE HURRICANES

By Harry Waters

FROM NEW YORK MAGAZINE

Copyright © 1971, Harry F. Waters

Most Little-League articles are given over to the antics of the parents and coaches. The kids themselves are usually ignored. In "Turnabout" Mr. Waters tells about an integrated team from Hartsdale, New York, that was merged into the lily-white Scarsdale Recreation League. The camaraderie of combat and the efforts of the Hartsdale coach to fashion some kind of winning combination evoke a mixture of hilarity and sadness. But a number of heroes and hopes emerge that make for gratifying reading.

The first game of the season is only two minutes old, but already an all-too-familiar disaster confronts the Hartsdale Hurricanes. One hundred pounds of enemy fullback has burst through the Hurricanes' line and is shedding the secondary like a diminutive Jimmy Brown. Now all that stands between him and the goal is the Hurricanes' free safety—one P. Gregory McGlone, the son of the Hurricanes' coach and, at 11 years, 4-feet-8, and 75 pounds, the smallest player on the field.

"Get him, Greg . . . gettim, dammit!" shrieks one mother from the sidelines.

"Turn him out of bounds, boy!" bellows Greg's dad, almost dropping his clipboard as he races down the sideline with the play. Greg is game enough, God knows. He gets a good angle on the fullback and takes his best shot, but a stiff-arm cuts him

down and the fullback goes all the way in—exultantly slamming the ball to the ground just the way they do it on TV.

The Hurricanes' defensive team dejectedly troops off. The other Hartsdale dads look vaguely embarrassed, but Coach Mc-Glone knows when to be soothing. "It's okay, Greg . . . okay, Joe . . . don't get down, Davey . . . we'll whip these stiffs yet." This seems to have the properly galvanic effect on all of the Hurricanes but one. The team's most promising linebacker, an Afro-coifed black youth named Junior Jackson, has disgustedly hurled away his $10 "All-Pro" helmet. "This game is ovah," Junior announces as he pushes through the players. "This game is ooooohhh*vah!*"

Joe McGlone seems dumbstruck by the outburst. He has pleaded and cajoled for months to lure some of the neighborhood's black boys out for the squad and he's understandably proud that the Hurricanes are the only team in the Scarsdale Recreation League with a polychromatic composition.

McGlone catches up with Junior, who is now striding toward Central Avenue. "What do you mean this game is over?" he shouts at him. "We're going to *win* this game. You hear me? We're going to *win!*"

Junior pauses. He reflects. "Yeah?" he finally replies, ballooning his eyes like Flip Wilson. "Then how come we *losin'*?"

That particular question is one that Joe McGlone used to ask himself with traumatic regularity. Last season the Hurricanes lost every one of their seven games, and some members of the Hartsdale Dads' Club seemed to be having second thoughts about their choice of team mentor. Even Joe himself was beginning to doubt whether he really had the stuff of a Lombardi or an Allen. "At the time, no father could be found who would give the time to coach," recalls McGlone, who vaguely resembled Clark Ken (and by day channels his combative juices into his own a agency). "I was stuck with the job if we wanted to have a team Anyway, that was my rationalization. Actually, I had a fiendis desire to coach, to make up for the fact that in my freshman ye at Yale a hip injury had forced me to stop playing college foo ball. Somehow, through these kids, I would achieve my su limated goal of making All-Universe."

Somehow, however, Joe failed to get that message across the eight- and nine-year-olds who were carrying the ball. T Hurricanes played so pitifully last year that they even stomped by the Immaculate Heart of Mary Crusaders. Throug out it all, Joe behaved like any rookie coach with his contract

the line. He began pressing—oh, did he begin pressing. He would get out of bed at 3:00 A.M. and brood for hours over his Jiffy Jot notebook, designing peewee variations of the Crackback Crunch and the Wishbone Whomp. After each debacle he would relentlessly interrogate little Greg about what had gone wrong. "Was Jimmy getting his blocking signals crossed out there?" he would demand. "Has Kenny been getting my plays screwed up in the huddle?"

Greg himself grew so tense that he began wetting his bed on the eves of games. Joe's wife couldn't believe what was happening. Ellen McGlone had married the most congenitally rational human she had ever known, a man who could dissect the economy or resolve a domestic crisis with the wit and perspicacity of William Buckley, Jr. Suddenly she was living with a jock Jekyl.

Things finally came to a head on the morning of the last game of the season. Ellen was stopped by a policeman for speeding as she was driving Joe to the field. Joe, who was already late, simply got out of the Volkswagen, coldly informed the cop that his wife would handle the matter, and jogged off into the dawn. Ellen began crying. That evening, the conversation at 21 Rockledge Road resembled a scene from Edward Albee.

During that winter, however, Joe McGlone made two portentous discoveries. He learned that his son, Greg, who had hooked up with a neighborhood football team following the Hurricanes' Bay of Pigs, had emerged as a genuine mini-star under the tutelage of a wryly low-keyed coach who liked to do Don Adams impressions when things went amiss. That revelation plunged Joe into a long period of self-analysis. "I finally realized," he recalls, "that I was trying to live out my jock fantasies at the expense of the kids I was supposed to be teaching. Maybe I'm still doing that, but at least now I control my emotions. And maybe I still don't believe it myself, but I keep telling the Hurricanes that winning isn't everything."

Joe's second discovery was a book entitled *The Radar Defense for Winning Football*. It was by someone named Jules Yakapovich, who, according to the book's dust jacket, had coached the Kenmore West High School of Nyack, New York, to a magnificent 23-and-1 record over the past three years. "Now," blurbed the dust jacket, "the coach of THE NUMBER ONE HIGH SCHOOL FOOTBALL TEAM IN THE NATION reveals all the secrets of the unique defense that has made his squad invincible!"

Basically, the secret to Yakapovich's Radar Defense seemed

to lie in teaching one's linemen to run *away* from the opposition's blockers until one of them somehow managed to collide with the ball carrier they were supposed to be clearing a path for. That struck Joe as just loony enough to work for the Hurricanes. He thoroughly digested Yakapovich's book, transferred the more promising alignments of X's and O's to his own playbook, and then placed a call to the president of the Hartsdale Dads' Club. If the other fathers would have him, Joseph McGlone was willing to return as the Hurricanes' coach for the 1971 season.

Back at the Hurricanes' first game, the Radar Defense has suddenly closed off the opposition's offensive attack and Joe is starting to toss I-told-you-so looks at his three assistant coaches. Junior Jackson, who had agreed to return to the fray, is cutting down runners like an enraged Dick Butkus. Even Joey Burgos, who is so nearsighted he seems to play defensive tackle by Braille, has somehow begun colliding with enemy ball carriers— just as Yakapovich had predicted. And tiny Hiro Fujiyama, the Scarsdale Recreation League's only Japanese-American running back, has actually moved the Hurricanes past midfield—an achievement attained only twice all last season.

But when the second quarter ends (in this league they play eight-minute quarters), the Hurricanes are still trailing by 7–0. Joe calls the entire 35-member squad over to the parking lot for a half-time discussion. On the field, the Hurricanes' five nymphet cheerleaders—attired in blue pleated miniskirts and Ann-Margaret turtlenecks—are plaintively calling on the spectators to "Give me an H . . ." Joe stares at his sneakers until the final nose is blown. "I just want you to know that I'm damned proud of you," he says softly. "You're playing the best team in the league to a virtual standstill. You guys are finding out that we can hold our own with any team in the league. *Any* of them." Now his voice rises into a restrained but recognizable Rockne-esque exhortation. "The only way you will win this game is to *want* to win. You gotta *want* to beat them. *Want* it, *want* it, *want* it."

The team seems suitably stirred, but then Tommy Santini's mother punctures the spell, "Mister McGlone," she asks apologetically, "is there any place where Tommy can go to the bathroom?"

The Scarsdale Recreation League's regulations offer an interesting departure from those of similar operations in the nation. Any father of a slightly underdeveloped 10-year-old knows what's wrong—hell, what's downright unfair—about the U.S.'s system of little league competition. There is always one oversized boy (he invariably plays pitcher in baseball, center in basketball, and running back in football) who so overpowers his less physically precocious peers that the opposition is usually held scoreless. Child psychologists gnash their teeth over that sort of thing. They contend that undersized kids may carry their resentment against such Goliaths into adulthood and, through transference, become draft dodgers, homosexuals, Mark Rudds or—even worse—frustrated-jock patriarchs.

None of the dads who run the Scarsdale Recreation League seem overly conscious of such dismal possibilities, but they have worked out a complex rule system to even things up. The eligibility of every candidate for a league team is determined by a point system that takes into account height, weight, and age. Points are assigned for each category and, if a candidate comes out with more than the limit, he is ruled ineligible.

Even those boys accepted by the league are bound by certain egalitarian restrictions. A player who weighs more than a set limit (but still qualified under the point system) cannot be used in a position where he is likely to carry the ball. Even if he should intercept a pass or recover a fumble, the referee must rule the play dead at that point. To help referees recognize the restricted ones, all players who are ineligible ball carriers must wear a taped "X" of contrasting color on their helmets. The upshot of all this is that there has been only one serious injury (a broken leg) in the Scarsdale Recreation League during the past five years.

For their part, the Hartsdale Hurricanes comprise something of an anomaly in the traditionally lily-white league. While each of the league's seven other teams represents one of Scarsdale's élite elementary schools, the Hurricanes represent two school districts—one largely white and one largely black—that were merged two years ago amidst considerable furor. The Hartsdale kids are now bused around to different schools at varying grade levels. Thus Joe McGlone's interracial experiment. And in the Scarsdale Recreation League, where most of the other players have never met a poor black, much less tackled one, the Hurricanes' performance is viewed with considerable interest by the patriarchs on the other side of the field.

Coach McGlone is acutely mindful of this scrutiny and is determined that his team pass the test. In the beginning that wasn't easy. The first blacks to come out for the Hurricanes last season were a rough and ready-to-rumble lot that tended to settle physical issues within the rules of the projects where they lived.

During last season's first game, the team's black halfback got
kneed, accidentally, in the groin after a long gain. When he came
to his first words were not "Man, I hurt" but "Who got me? Who
did it? I'm going to get that mother after the game." Joe felt
obliged to mouth little homilies about sportsmanship before
every kickoff. "You don't curse at the other guy," he would say to
his charges. "And you don't try to beat him up if he tackles you
hard."

The black Hurricanes still like to look over the opposition
and then announce whom they're going to "get," but now they
invariably add the phrase, "strictly legal, of course." And Johnny
Copeland, the black halfback who was kneed last year, is usually
the first Hurricane to cross the field for some post-game hand-
shaking, and is the loudest participant in the traditional post-
game cheer for the other team (("Two-four-six-eight/Who do we
appreciate . . .")

The blacks' relationship with their white teammates has
undergone an equally salutary transformation. During the first
practice sessions, the same racial tensions that existed in the
community during the school-busing flap would occasionally surface on the gridiron off Central Avenue. But the camaraderie of
combat and Coach McGlone's watchful solicitude have managed
to change all that. A renowned sports pundit once described the
relationship between professional football teammates as "something very close to love." Among the integrated Hurricanes,
something very close to that emotion has taken hold.

Next season, the father of one of the black players will serve
as Joe's assistant coach. "When I played this game as a boy, it
was nothing like this," he recalled from the sideline last week.
"There'd be 25 kids with one leather helmet and a pair of beat-up
shoulder pads between us. But hell, this is great . . . absolutely
great."

With four minutes remaining in the second half, the referee
unravels a massive pileup on the opposition's 8-yard line and
discovers that Hartsdale tackle Tony Scappaticci has somehow
managed to steal the ball from the other team's quarterback. He
promptly signals first-and-goal for the Hurricanes. "Scappy did
it!" whoops McGlone from the sideline. "I've been trying to teach
him that trick. Way, Scappy, baybee . . ."

Enter an improbable hero. Last year Joel Masket was so
confused by it all that he would frequently leave his halfback
position and wander in puzzlement to other spots on the field,
beseeching his teammates for guidance. His father, a jocular type

who never missed a game, took to calling his son "the Wandering Jew." But today Joel's wandering takes exactly the right direction. He takes a perfect pitchout from Kenny Palmer, swings to the outside and suddenly finds himself in the end zone, inexplicably unmolested. A quarterback sneak notches the tying point, the ref blows the final whistle, and the Hartsdale Hurricanes have snapped the Scarsdale Recreation League's longest losing streak—albeit with a tie. Coach McGlone disappears beneath a writhing, exuberant mass of Hurricanes. (In subsequent games, the Hurricanes went on to chalk up two victories—a 2–0 squeaker over Immaculate Heart of Mary and a splendid 12–0 conquest of St. Pius.)

It is now later that afternoon. Mr. and Mrs. Joseph McGlone have just hosted a small but raucous party for one dozen Hurricanes, three studiously ignored cheerleaders, and a stray schnauzer. The party's *pièce de résistance* had been a large green cake, shaped like a football field and decorated with 22 tiny marzipan players. The cake has vanished now, as have all the guests but the schnauzer. The indefatigable Hurricanes are playing tackle football in the backyard.

Joe sprawls in his favorite easychair and begins to think about next Saturday. The Hurricanes are scheduled to play the only team in the league that employs a double-option, wing-T offense. Joe worriedly picks up his copy of *The Radar Defense for Winning Football.* Suddenly the doorbell chimes. It is little Hiro Fujiyama. "We need a quarterback," he tells Ellen. "Can Mister McGlone come out?" Ellen looks despairingly at her husband. There is a new rug to be laid and plans to be worked out for a Canadian vacation. "Go ahead, McGurk," she says resignedly. "But try to be in by dinner."

As Ellen begins loading the dishwasher, her husband's voice ebbs and flows through the open kitchen window. "Attaboy, Stevey, good cut . . . let's see you blitz like that next week, Davey . . . block with your helmet, Greg . . . Billy . . . Kenny . . . Hiro . . . Hermie . . . Joel . . . Artie . . ."

1972

THEY GET A GLASS OF BEER
... MAYBE

By Sandy Grady

FROM PHILADELPHIA BULLETIN

DISCOVER MAGAZINE

Copyright © 1972, Bulletin Co., Philadelphia

One of the judges who voted first place for this prize-winning article said that it was a story that he could hardly believe—guys playing football and getting their brains beat out for peanuts. Some had once played college or high-school football, others were dropouts. None quite made the big time. They became semipros. This brutal pastime, with all its attendant problems of seldom winning, hardly ever getting enough money even to pay for the trip, is a singularly touching and entertaining chronicle.

It is 5:30 on a Saturday evening. As usual, Larry Kozak is going to do something really crazy. For a 35-year-old man, his next act will be irrational, ridiculous, even atavistic.

Larry and his brother, Jimmy, own this bar. It is called the Captain's Table. It has a big color TV set that is inevitably tuned to some game. Behind the bottles are 16 sports trophies, gleaming. Larry picks up his bag and waves "So long" to Jimmy and the bar regulars, who understand his madness.

"Yeah, kill 'em tonight, kid," says Jimmy.

Then Larry gets in his car and rides up route 95 from New Castle, Delaware, to Aston, Pennsylvania. He's been doing this for 14 years. And for teams you've never heard of—the Swedesboro Red Devils, the Gloucester Vikings, the Delaware Clippers.

Tonight it will be the Aston Knights. Larry Kozak is the center. When it's over, his face will be chipped and bloody again. Larry Kozak is going to play a pro-football game for nothing.

Zilch. And he's humming as he turns into Sun Valley High
School. He can't wait.

"Face it," says Larry Kozak. "I'm crazy."

It's the magic moment for Tom and Butch, too. The field
lights just flicked on at 7:00 P.M.—those lights which are their
pride, because they put them up for a cheap $5,000. The green
autumn wetness of the field shimmers. The stands are empty in
shadows.

"We're all crazy," says Tom. "The players are crazy. Butch
and I are even crazier."

Tom Fisher owns Olympic Sporting Goods, which comes in
handy. He's 35 and was a catcher in the Philadelphia A's farm
system. Nick (Butch) Verrati is a paving contractor, a burly man
in a checked Mackinaw, benignly stoking a cigar. They are the
owners—blare of trumpets—of the Aston Knights of the Sea-
board Professional Football League. Tom and Butch are not to
be confused with the kind of pro owner who sips Scotch while he
cruises about in a helicopter guaranteeing a win each week from
his $16 million toy.

Not hardly. At this moment, Tom is (a) gulping down a
McDonald's Big Mac, (b) selling tickets, and (c) looking
amazedly at a kid who tells him three of the Aston Knights have
no shoes.

"Forget their shoes!" yelps Fisher, dashing off. "Did they
forget their heads? I'll run to the store."

Butch is worried too. The officials, who are costing him $200,
have not appeared. Neither have many paying ($2) customers.
Butch likes those lights, and the oom-pah-pah of the Sun Valley
Vanguard band, warming up. At least the tuba players will draw
a few mamas and papas.

"Oh, well, we're only five big ones in the hole so far," sighs
Butch, lighting his stogie. "Y'know, in four years, I've only missed
one game. Had tickets for the Saints-Eagles in New Orleans.
Whole game I kept worrying, 'I wonder how the Knights are
doing.' My wife thinks I'm pretty crazy."

The Hartford, Connecticut, team is doing pushups on the
field. Their "One-two-three!" floats across the empty stands.
Hartford looks huge and ominous in white jerseys. Butch growls
a little.

In the high-school locker rooms, the Aston Knights sit on the
concrete floor, smoking cigarets and muttering. The green shirts
look familiar—the Eagles wore them in the sixties, then the
Pottstown Firebirds, and Aston bought them for five bucks

apiece. The Aston coach, Fil Pompilii—a man with long yellow hair, aviator glasses, and a spectacular stomach beneath the blue windbreaker—looks gloomy.

Fil has a Quarterback Problem.

The Aston quarterback is John Waller, which would worry you on sight. You meet John Waller, you want to say, "Deliver the groceries at the rear, kid." Or, "No, sonny, I didn't order a singing telegram." John's a sixth-grade teacher in Ridley Park. He's 5-foot-7, 160 pounds, and says, "Sir," to any male over 15. But John was one of the hottest items at Temple U. since Bill Cosby. Temple has 14 all-time passing records and John still holds 14. Still, it worries you to discover John wears horn-rimmed glasses—when he plays.

"How you feelin', Johnny?" asks Fil Pomilii.

Classic pre-game confrontation between coach and quarterback, right? Just like George Allen and Sonny Jurgenson, right? After all, John Waller is so banged up, he's taped from knee to chest. He looks like an Egyptian mummy in horn-rims.

"I feel okay, Fil," says John Waller, "but I promised my wife I'd tell you—she doesn't want me to play."

Fil Pompilii looks heavenward through his big lavender glasses—an act he will repeat often before the night ends. You can hear his mind clicking: What would George Allen do if Sonny said his wife didn't want him to play?

Fil walks over to George Donald, a chunky, small-eyed man with a Chaplinesque mustache. Donald is 31, a toolmaker, three children, no college, 10 years of semipro ball (It's in my blood"). They say in the last Hartford game a lineman shattered a cast (and his arm) against Donald's head. Tough.

But he's never played a game at quarterback.

"You'll start," says Fil.

"I'm ready, Coach," says George.

Ah, immortal echoes. Did not Ronnie Reagan use those same words to Knute Rockne on the *Late Show?*

But nostalgia is the metier of the Aston Green Knights. An evening with them is a trip backward in the Time Machine. It is like flying in a 1928 Ford Trimotor—every creak and roar is the birth of the 727 jet. And the knights, these 1972 schoolteachers and salesmen and bar bouncers, playing for no reward but bruises, are beguiling ghosts. This is how it all began, before Dandy Don and Howard, before Willie Joe and plastic grass and Super Silliness.

No, the Aston Knights do not wear leather helmets and

baggy pants like an old Jim Thorpe movie (although that
wouldn't be a bad gimmick). But the mystique of town football,
played for blood, guts, and joy, is remarkably unchanged. It
began this way in the western Pennsylvania coal-and-steel vil-
lages of Latrobe, Greensburg, and Jeannette 70 years ago. Once
there were dozens of those town teams near Philadelphia, usually
centered around a mill. Then came the biggies of the 1920s—the
Frankford Yellow Jackets, Canton Bulldogs, Masillon Tigers,
Columbus Panhandles, Rock Island Independents. The Aston
Knights, who have changed names several times, are literally
pendants on that family tree. In the hardscrabble twenties—long
before Bert Bell invented pro TV—an owner got together a few
town toughs, a couple of college stars, a $100 fee, and collected
money in a cigar box.

Tom and Butch would have been right at home.

But Aston itself can prick the mood that you've been time-
shot into the 1920s. This is no hick village with a mill, feed store,
and blacksmith. It's a township in lower Delaware County that is
almost a cliché of suburbia. The franchise lights of the 7-11's,
Dunkin' Donuts, and Gino's wash against the split-level checker-
board. Driving up Concord Road, you're reminded of Gertrude
Stein's line about Los Angeles: "There is no there there." No, this
isn't your symbolic steel-and-football town. Sun Oil is still the big
employer—you didn't think they called it Sun Valley High because of the tropical climate, did your? So the Aston Knights are
strange antiques in all this plastic-and-neon moonscape. Guys
playing for nothin' and maybe a drink later at Capp's, when
Namath is getting $500,000 and all the Hollywood broads. Bring
back the mandolin and the Hupmobile.

So before the game I have some Dunkin' Donut coffee in a
plastic cup and think of Yeats' line: "A real tiger in an imaginary
garden." All those hoagie shops along Concord Road are fantasia.
The sweat of the Aston Knights is damn real.

You can see it in their eyes. The Aston Knights are worried.
The two high-school bands are tootling at midfield. The crowd (a
disappointing 1,700 paid) is coming to life. But Hartford looks
awesome. Everybody on their front four seems to be 6-foot-6, 260
pounds. The Aston linemen, relatively, seem to be punchy schoolteachers. Hartford has a 10–0 record and they have Tom Sherman
(ex-New York Giants) at quarterback, and Donnie Shanklin
(Kansas star, MVP in the Orange Bowl) at flanker, and a smashing black halfback named Cecil Bowens (Kentucky), who is the
best in the league. No, the night does not look easy.

Tom and Butch are already mad. Hartford is big time, they say. Pay their players $60 a game, plus $200 on construction jobs. Nineteen players are set for NFL camps next year. Why, Hartford can even afford motel stops on away games. (Aston hires a bus, has one $6-a-man meal, drives straight back from Portsmouth, Virginia, or Hagerstown, Maryland). Hartford draws 10,000 a game, Etcetera.

"Listen, it's all basics," Leo Levandowski is saying. "They're gonna run right, left, or pass. That's all."

You have to like Leo. You have to like a guy who lists Harvard as his school on the Aston program. Levandowski of Harvard? Leo has never even driven a cab in Cambridge. He came out of St. James High, played with Pottstown, got a job as a truck dispatcher, even had a trail with the Eagles until Joe Kuharich cut him because he was too short. ("Listen, Joe, this isn't basketball," said Leo).

Now Leo, 30, is going to play defense against these Connecticut Hessians for nothing. (A word about Aston salaries: John Waller is paid $50 a game, three others get $30, the rest zero unless there is a kitty after the season.) "It's just hitting," says Leo, resigned. "Not much polish or finesse in this league. We'll see. . . ."

But the Astons are worried about their quarterback, George Donald, the toolmaker, three kids, etc. John Waller keeps saying, "You'll do fine, just run the 42-trap, stay cool." Everybody is saying, "You'll be okay, George." But George is flicking his tongue, his eyes like two BB shots.

He is tremendously nervous. There are quick fumbles and Hartford goes in quickly, 14–0. On the sideline, John Waller tells Fil Pompilii, "Leave him in another series." The owners, Tom and Butch, are fidgeting. The crowd is getting quiet. An interception. In comes John Waller, limping, his glasses glinting in the lights. Another fumble. The defensive team comes off the field screaming.

"Goddamit, offense, hang onto the ball!"

"You're killin' us, offense!"

"C'mon, do something, offense, it's your turn!" MacPartland screams. "C'mon, we can't hold the bastards all night."

Waller turns. He seems to be lecturing his sixth-grade class in geography. "Do your job. We'll do ours," he says. "That's enough of that crap."

It is closest anyone has ever heard Waller, a darn-and-holy-cats type, descend to profanity. It drives the cornerback batty. Two linemen have to hold MacPartland back.

"Oh, ⸺ him! ⸺ him!" yells a defensive back. "You play your ass off and they give away the ball!"

Fil Pompilii rolls his eyes skyward behind the purple glasses. Two minutes later, Hartford is ahead 28–0. Half time, and Fil has to think of a half-time speech. What would Tom Landry say—if he knew that half of his team was angry enough to skip the second half and head for Cresmorr Bar?

Along the concrete floor, the Aston Knights loll sweatily, smoke, drink Cokes, and small-talk like a theater audience that knows it must endure the last half of a terrible play. Finally Fil gets atop a locker seat.

"All right, they're taking it to us on defense," Pompilii says. "They're picking up our blitz. You linemen, stay a yard off, they're using your momentum to beat you. Now, we gotta play as a team, lose or win. And I—don't—wanna—hear—any—more—bull—on the bench!"

Bodies and pads shift on the way out. Steve Maciolok, a sturdy, mustachioed tackle, interrupts. "Listen, we got our tails beat bad this year at Long Island," he says, voice high. "But that was away. This is our home crowd. We gotta save face. Let's show these people we've got some guts. Okay?"

The Astons shuffle down the dark macadam to the floodlit field. They are like people going to a dentist. Waller limps badly. "If I can get two quick scores, I'll stay in," says Waller. "Otherwise, I'll let George play. I can't blow the season on this."

They play bitterly for 10 minutes—the Astons looking like grim, snarling schoolteachers (a dozen of them are) against the Hartford studs. Then it hits 45–0, and everyone is embarrassed. Or restive. Or rebellious.

"We want Obey! We want Obey!" bellows a man from the stands, starting a mock chant for Wayne Obey, an injured split end. Then finally: "Aw, hell, Obey, if they threw it to you, you'd drop it!"

And the tackle, Maciolok, wanders over to Butch and Tom, to needle them: "Hey, if you guys weren't so cheap, you'd get us a running back. What stopped you from getting Woodeshick?"

"We didn't want to take the $50,000 out of your salary, Steve," said Tom Fisher. "You still want to get married?"

The tackle looks at the owner somberly.

"Right now, I'd like to pull down the shades and hide for a week," he says. "I'd like to get drunk and change my name."

The Astons have been slamming helmets and cursing. In the last minutes, they stare numbly. There could be a fight, probably, but the costs $35 and the next week's game. But it is a lesson: defeat burns 30-year-old men, no paycheck on the line, only ego. And something else: the violence in this bush league was as sporadically high as in any NFL game, with its highly paid gladiators. Don't pass this on to Pete Rozelle or Leonard Tose. But perhaps guys will hit as hard for machismo as for multi-year contracts. Have all our sports-page effluvia over $1,000,000 athletes distorted the old American virtues? Can we go back to 1910, guys huffing and puffing for pride?

"Nah," says one Aston player. "If we make the title game, I still figure to make $200."

It's all over. The Aston Knights walk slowly up the hill, through the shadows of the high-school parking lot. Now they are joined by wives and girl friends who hold hands. With a pang you sense it is a scene from the 1950s—and maybe that is why they do it, trying to hold back time, clutch their youth.

The girls are all pretty and consoling—talking to Walter Mittys who no longer hear a "pocketapocketa" dream. The team owners behave like—well owners. Butch has a pint of brandy. Tom says he's going to Capp's and ask for 18 beers. The coach sits in his pickup truck, one foot on the windowsill.

"They'd beat us three out of four times," says Fil. "But not like that."

John Waller walks up the hill with his wife, Sue. She wears a button on her sweater, "I Dig Football." John has to ask a friend to take off his shoes. He's hurting. He throws his stuff in the rear of his car. I asked how much longer he'd play semipro. Waller looks at Sue and grins.

"Our son is three," said Waller. "I'll play in this league until I can throw him a touchdown. Blanda is 40-something, isn't he? So I can do it, right, Sue?"

The coach looks at Waller, lidded, droll. He is only disturbed about one thing, says Fil Pompilii. In the last few minutes, Waller has been shouting across field at Frank Di-Maggio, another Temple quarterback, asking about his health.

"But he's my friend, Fil," says Waller.

"John, you yelled in my ear," says Pomilii wearily. "We were only down 45–0. I was ready to think of something brilliant. John, you upset my concentration."

The Aston placekicker, Noel Lemon, roars up in a black hardtop. Lemon had been a good pro soccer player in Belfast,

Ireland, where he had good and bad days for money. So it says
something of life with the Aston Knights: when Lemon missed a
21-yard field goal in the rain last year, he claims he cried for
three days.

Now Lemon leans out the car window.

"Hey, coach," yells Lemon, "forget the rest of it. You have to
admit my opening kickoff was spl-endid!"

Fil Pompilii looks toward heaven again.

Larry Kozak is driving back toward the Captain's Table, his
bar in New Castle. His legs feel okay; anyway, he's sick of the
talk that he can't play three or four more years. He's only 35. He
remembers some years he and Jimmy played 40 games under
different names, with different teams. This is easy.

"I'm not a dreamer," says Kozak. "I know I'll never make the
top now. Out of 40 of us, maybe one will—the kid at linebacker,
John Salk, he's got a big shot. I was always too slow in the 40. A
lot of us were close, Lee, Steve, Johnny, Harry Buzkirk, Jim Hall,
Frankie Ryan, who was so good at Duke . . . I mean, I keep
doing it because I didn't play in high school, I had only one
year at Michigan State . . . sounds stupid, but I keep proving to
myself I can play. Maybe we're all like that."

Kozak moves into the bar he owns, and people are quiet
about the 45–0. His face is nicked up, and his brother, Jimmy,
says, "Well, what the hell, kid, wait until next week."

"I'm going to the Super Bowl," Larry Kozak, 35, says suddenly. "I'm gonna watch the center and when he misses the first
block on the linebacker, I'm gonna boo that $60,000 sonavabitch."

In Larry's bar they laugh. The Aston Knights are a funny
team, sad funny. But real. There's no contest. You can have those
other 26 teams, those plastic, mechanical battalions who fill the
TV air between commercials. If there is ever a Reality Bowl, give
me the Aston Knights.

1973

PETER PAN'S UNEXPECTED BIRTHDAY

By David Klein

FROM THE NEWARK STAR-LEDGER

Copyright © 1973, *Star-Ledger, Newark, N.J.*

This is the story about the tennis match that attracted the greatest number of viewers—30,000 at the Houston Astrodome and millions over television—that ever saw a tennis match. In this respect the contest was a milestone, and undoubtedly it was one of the biggest betting events of the sports year.

David Klein, who has appeared in Best Sports Stories *often, does full justice to the bizarre event, catching, as he does, the circus atmosphere that preceded and followed it. But when the participants, Billie Jean King and Bobby Riggs, got down to serious tennis when the match actually was on, Klein, a fine sports reporter no matter what the sport, does full justice to it. It is one of the few actual coverage stories included in* Thirty Years of Best Sports Stories *and it stands up well.*

Peter Pan had an unexpected birthday last night. He suddenly turned 55, and he looked every year of it.

Thus did Bobby Riggs, the Master Hustler of Tennis, meet his humiliation in the ballyhooed Battle of the Sexes. He was trounced, soundly and decidedly, by 29-year-old Billie Jean King, who proved to be not only queen of women's tennis in this world but of 55-year-old hustlers as well.

The three-set victory was carved out in scores of 6–4, 6–3, and 6–3, as a crowd of 30,472 in the Astrodome first murmured, then chuckled in expectation, and finally raged and roared at the dramatic impact of the rout.

It was a winner-take-all challenge match for $100,000, which, of course, Billie Jean took gladly. But it was worth far more, both financially and in prestige.

Billie Jean, a lean, lancet-quick dancer on the court, won half of the ancillary rights, estimated at another $200,000. Equally valuable to her was the accomplishment of putting down Riggs, the self-proclaimed Male Chauvinist, before a national television audience and in the process avenging a Mother's Day defeat administered by Riggs to her comrade-in-arms, Margaret Court.

In defeat, however, Riggs might console himself with the near-$100,000 he will realize from his share of the ancillaries.

And it was entirely possible he placed a hefty bundle on Billie Jean, too—just in case.

He would have been well-advised to do just that. Billie Jean, who perhaps plays more like a man than any woman pro, was too much for him. He couldn't keep up with her speed and her footwork.

Her backhand returns, especially when the point was critical, were near-flawless. She was in on the net, which Court had not done, and she was able to put away several winners from there.

Riggs, whose stock in trade is "garbage" shots—spins, lobs, chops, and drops—was not able to make Billie Jean run. Indeed, he found himself going from side to side, chasing her marvelously well-placed shots, and his stamina—despite the 415 vitamin pills he so publicly takes daily—was obviously going fast.

The match began with lavish fanfare. Riggs presented Billie Jean, attired in a menthol-green tennis dress, with a huge "Sugar Daddy," which she immediately donated to a Houston orphanage. Then she clearly won this first battle of nerves by taking the cover off a live baby pig—her gift to the Male Chauvinist Pig dressed in yellow with red trim.

Finally, they began to play tennis, and through the first four games both held their service. But in the fifth game Billie Jean weakened and Bobby broke through to take a 3–2 lead. It was to deuce twice before she blew an overhead smash.

Yet Riggs, with an opportunity to simply hold on, immediately saw Billie break his service, double-faulting the decisive point to tie it again, 3–3 in games.

Billie Jean held her service, Riggs held his, and at 4–4 she won hers 40-love and then broke his, as he again double-faulted on set point.

Billie Jean had the old man running now and as the second set began she fell behind as he broke through her service. But again she immediately turned the tables and tied it at 1–1, and then went up 2–1.

The fourth game, longest of the night, went 24 points before Bobby won it, but it was costly in that he might have spent the final reserves of energy. They were at deuce 10 times before Billie Jean hit the tape on a backhand return and then was long with a service return.

But she won her serve to move ahead 3–2, lost the lead when he won his serve, and then played out to win the set 6–3 and go up 2–0.

The third and final set went to 3–2 King when she broke Riggs' service in the fifth game on four straight points. She made it 4–2, he rallied once more to cut it to 4–3, and then she rode in to her stunning victory.

The last game went to three match points and five deuces before Billie Jean did it. Riggs was serving. He went into the net on his first offering—indeed, he had had trouble all night on his first services—and then sent her return weakly into the net. It was over, and he used his final bit of energy to hurdle the net and shake her hand.

Afterwards, in a mob-scene press conference that saw several skirmishes erupt between reporters and TV cameramen, King was kind to her victim—"Roberta Riggs," as she called him.

"I feel Margaret had one of the worst days of her life when she played him, otherwise she might have beaten him, too," said the queen of the Kings. "She helped me a lot. She told me to attack his backhand, because he can't roll off it. I'll tell you, I feel this is the culmination of 19 years of tennis. It's different from winning the Wimbledon and U.S. Open titles, but it's just as important."

King said she felt confident after winning the first set. "I hadn't known what to expect," she explained, "but when I won that first one and saw what he was doing, I felt if I just held my services, I couldn't lose."

Billie Jean's backhand, tremendously strong, seemed to be tailor-made last night. "His style of play hits to my backhand," she said, "and I wasn't going to argue with that. It's my strong point, and I feel my backhand, as well as my game at the net and my mobility beat him."

She said she has played "lots of men" who are better than Riggs, but added that "none of those matches made this kind of money. Now I'd love to go and drink some beer."

Then Riggs arrived, looking disheveled and worn. "I just feel

I have to have a return match to make it right for the guys again," he said. "But she was much too quick for me. I don't know how I'd be able to play her any differently. She was too good tonight, too good.

"She won and Women's Lib won and that's that. But I'll be looking and hoping for a rematch."

A smiling Billie, sitting at his elbow, said about the rematch request:

"Give me 24 hours and a beer—and I'll think about it."

Riggs was a crestfallen figure after the match in the air-conditioned arena which is a world showplace of sports.

"I'm going to the bridge," he said.

Billie added charitably:

"Be sure and get a parachute first."

Riggs had boasted in one of his public appearances that if he didn't beat Billie Jean, the five-time Wimbledon champion, in their ballyhooed spectacular, he would jump off Pasadena's "Suicide Bridge."

Billie, who called Bobby a "creep" before the match, had said that she would insist that he carry out his vow.

Billie was ecstatic.

"This is a culmination of 19 years of tennis for me," she said. "I've wanted to change the sport and tonight a lot of non-tennis people saw the sport for the first time."

She said she was inspired by the boisterous, cheering crowd, the blaring bands and circuslike atmosphere surrounding the match.

"This was a dream come true," she said. "I've always wanted people to scream at matches."

"I have to eat a lot of crow," Riggs said. "I was wrong and I'll have to be the biggest bum of all time. I have to take it and I will, but I want a return match."

At the close of the news conference, photographers wanted Riggs to give Mrs. King a victory kiss. Riggs accommodated, but some photographers didn't get the shot and asked them to repeat, which they did, after which Riggs told Mrs. King: "You better be careful, I'm going to turn you on."

Who's Who
in Thirty Years of
OF BEST SPORTS STORIES

The Writers

GERALD ASTOR ("Mickey Mantle: Oklahoma to Olympus") broke in with the now defunct *Look* magazine and then became an editor of *National Affairs*, from where he moved to the *Saturday Evening Post* and then to the *Ladies' Home Journal* and *Sports Illustrated*. In 1963 he rejoined *Look* as a senior editor. He makes his home in Scarsdale, New York.

BILL BOUSFIELD ("The Housebreaker") was born in Ontario, Canada. After a series of business adventures, he moved with his wife and two children into the forest area of Lac Seul and established a hunting lodge in the virgin bush. His business stationery reads "Lac Seul, Onaway Lodge: The Home of Record Northerns and Excellent Walleyes." He has earned citations for catches in deep-sea fishing.

BOB COLE ("The Methuselah of Bowling") was the associate editor of the *Alumni Bulletin* at Lehigh University while working toward a Ph.D. in English. His undergraduate work was done at Marshall University, and he received his M.A. from Wake Forest. His newspaper background includes stints with *The Huntington* (West Virginia) *Herald Dispatch* and the *Winston-Salem Journal*. He has been given sports-writing awards by the American Bowling Congress, American Alumni Council, and the North Carolina Press Association.

BILL CONLIN ("A Bad Day for Conservatives") is a Temple University graduate and had been with the *Philadelphia Bulletin* covering mainly basketball and football. At college he edited the undergraduate newspaper and was the outstanding journalism graduate in his class at Temple. Mr. Conlin has lately joined the *Philadelphia Daily News*.

KYLE CRICHTON ("Hot Tamale Circuit") was a magazine and newspaper writer of wide experience. He was also an associate editor of *Collier's* and other magazines and the author of several novels, including *The Proud People*. He won the *Best Sports Stories* magazine award in 1946 with his two-part article that appeared in *Collier's*. Kyle Crichton died in 1960. His son, Andy, is a senior editor of *Sports Illustrated*.

TOMMY DEVINE ("Michigan State Construction Job") graduated from the University of Dayton. After his graduation he served an apprenticeship with the *Dayton Journal,* then worked in the UP office at Columbus, at the *Columbus Citizen* and in the Chicago UP bureau. He went on the *Detroit Free Press* and later became a freelance writer.

STANLEY FRANK ("Brooklyn's Brainiest Bum") is a native-born New Yorker who was both a newspaperman and magazine writer before he left the business to enter the public-relations field. He worked for the *New York Post* as a sports columnist and as a foreign correspondent in Europe. On his return from abroad he left the *Post* to freelance and his work appeared in nearly all of the top magazines. His fine writing has merited many inclusions in the *Best Sports Stories* anthologies.

ERNEST (SANDY) GRADY ("They Get a Glass of Beer . . . Maybe") won the magazine award in *Best Sports Stories*—*1973* with the story included here, after winning a news-coverage prize in 1967 with his article on the Joey Archer–Emile Griffith fight. He has been sports columnist for the *Philadelphia Bulletin* since 1959 and before that he worked for the *Charlotte News,* the *Gastonia* (North Carolina) *Gazette,* the *Waynesville* (North Carolina) *Mountaineer,* and the *Philadelphia Daily News.* He entered the newspaper business after attending Catawba College and the University of North Carolina.

W. C. (BILL) HEINZ ("Brockton's Boy") is a novelist and freelance magazine writer who received his newspaper training on the old *New York Sun* and who won the magazine award in the *Best Sports Stories* competition four and a half times (he shared it in 1952). He has written three novels: *The Professional, The Surgeon* and *Emergency,* which was published last May. With Vince Lombardi he also wrote *Run to Daylight.* He now resides in Dorset, Vermont.

AL HIRSHBERG ("Roommate: Bob Cousy") became one of this country's most prolific sports writers before his sudden death in 1973. He had written over 25 sports books and his biggest success, *Fear Srikes Out,* the story of Jimmy Pearsall, was made into a movie. He also wrote many juveniles and was published in most major magazines. He did most of his newspaper writing with the *Boston Post* before he turned to freelancing.

ROGER KAHN ("Willie Mays, Yesterday and Today") is a native
New Yorker. He attended New York University and began his
newspaper career as a copy boy for the *New York Herald
Tribune*. He was later promoted to the sports staff of that newspaper, covering, among other assignments, the Brooklyn
Dodgers. He left the *Tribune* to become sports editor of *Newsweek* and then a senior editor of the *Saturday Evening Post*
before he turned exclusively to freelance writing. The author of
several books, two of which, *The Passionate People* and *The Boys
of Summer,* made the best-seller lists, he is engaged in writing a
novel.

DAVID KLEIN ("Peter Pan's Unexpected Birthday") was the winner
of the *Best Sports Stories—1974* news-coverage award with this
story. A sports columnist for the *Star-Ledger* of Newark, New
Jersey, and associated Newhouse newspapers, he is the author of
14 books, including *The New York Giants, Yesterday, Today and
Tomorrow*. He has also contributed to the nation's top periodicals. He attended the University of Oklahoma and Fairleigh
Dickinson University.

AL LANEY ("Ching, Ching, Chinaman") is hereby introduced as
the very first winner. (There was only one winner in the 1944
anthology.) Today there are three for each book—one in news
coverage, one in features, and one in magazine writing. His
article in the 1944 volume was "A Dark Man Laughs." Laney was
born in Pensacola, Florida, in 1896 and after doing all kinds of
reporting chores, joined the *New York Herald Tribune* in 1935.
Since its demise he has been freelancing.

JOHN LARDNER ("Mr. Henderson and the Cooperstown Myth")
wrote some of the liveliest sports commentary in the nation
before he died suddenly in the late 1960's. A son of the late
beloved Ring Lardner, his magazine articles for *Newsweek* and
other periodicals (the story reprinted in the current volume originally appeared in *True*) presented a fresh slant on the sports
scene and his book *It Beats Working* received critical accolades.
Before he turned to magazine writing he was a member of the
staff of the *New York Herald Tribune.*

ED LINN ("The Sad End of Big Daddy") is one of the most
talented freelance writers in the business, author or co-author of
four nonfiction books and a novel as well as numerous magazine

articles on a variety of subjects, not all of them sports. A Bostonian by birth and a graduate of Boston University, he was a member of the State Department's press section and a member of the staff of Macfadden Publications before he turned to freelancing. He is co-author with Bill Veeck of three books and he also collaborated with Sandy Koufax on the latter's autobiography. His novel, *The Adversaries,* was published in January, 1974, by Saturday Review Press.

JACK MANN ("20 Seconds from Home + a Few Inches") at 31 years of age held the title of National Sports Editor of his paper, *Newsday* on Long Island. He originally started as an assistant city editor and in 1956 he joined the sports staff. A few years ago he left *Newsday* and moved to the *Washington Daily News.* He has also done considerable freelancing.

JACK MURPHY ("The Mongoose") has been the sports editor of the San Diego Union for over two decades. This fine writer was formerly employed by the *Tulsa World Star-Telegram* and the *Daily Oklahoman and Times.* He was born in Tulsa, saw combat service in Okinawa, served a stint as a war correspondent, and has had his articles published in many of the better national magazines. He has merited many honors for his work, including the National Headline Award as a columnist.

ELWYN (BUD) MYERS ("Ten Terrible Days"), after spending three years in the Marine Corps, returned to Central Michigan University to get his degree. He later attended the University of Louisville Dental School and married the "girl in the offing" mentioned in his hunting story.

JERRY MASON ("Mad Marathon") is a three-time winner of the news-coverage award in the *Best Sports Stories* series. Although football is his first love, he has covered every sport in the books for the *Boston Globe,* of which he was executive sports editor before he retired last year. The *Globe,* which he joined in 1931 as a sports cartoonist, has been his only paper.

MURRAY OLDERMAN ("The Man Behind the Muscles") was a cartoonist and sports editor of the Newspaper Enterprise Association, stationed in New York City, before he was lured to the West Coast and San Francisco, where he now makes his home. He is a former president of the Football Writers Association of

America and his work appears in 500 papers around the country. Prior to joining NEA, he worked for the McClatchy Newspapers of California and the *Minneapolis Star-Tribune*. He attended Missouri, Stanford, and Northwestern universities.

TOM O'REILLY ("Pie in the Sky"), now deceased, was a native of Lancaster, Pennsylvania, and started his newspaper career there in 1925. He was a member of the sports staff of the *New York World-Telegram* for 10 years, was with *PM* for five, and also with the *Morning Telegraph*, before joining the staff of the *New York Herald Tribune*, for which he covered horse racing and wrote a sports column. He also wrote a column for *The New Yorker* on horse shows and hunts. During World War II, he served in the merchant marine and wrote a book, *Purser's Progress*, on his experiences.

JOE H. PALMER ("Notes on the Gay Science") was born in Lexington, Kentucky, and was graduated from the University of Kentucky. After graduation, he was with *Blood Horse* as an associate editor, later becoming the executive secretary of the American Trainers' Association. In 1946 he joined the *New York Herald Tribune*. He also contributed occasional pieces to periodicals. His books included *Names in Pedigree, Blue Grass*, and the *American Race Horses* annuals since 1944. He passed away shortly after writing the article reprinted in this book.

BILL RIVES ("Football Family") won the news-feature award in 1951. He was the sports editor of the *Dallas News* for many years and also served as a lieutenant colonel in the public-relations section of the United States Strategic Air Forces. At present he is president of News-Texan, Inc., a group of suburban dailies in the Dallas–Fort Worth area, owned by the same corporation which controls the *Dallas Morning News*.

HAROLD ROSENTHAL ("Return of the 'Verce'") became a member of the sports staff of the *New York Herald Tribune* in 1941 and subsequently joined the United States Army Air Command. During his stint as a buck sergeant he turned to magazine writing as a diversion. After his return to the sports desk at the *Herald Tribune* his assignments were mostly in the major sports. On the demise of that paper he became the public-relations advisor for the American Football League, where he holds forth today.

NICK SEITZ ("Is This the Man to Succeed Palmer?") is a graduate of the University of Oklahoma, where he majored in philosophy. He was named editor of the *Norman* (Oklahoma) *Transcript* at the age of 22 and later became sports editor of the *Oklahoma Journal*. He is now associate editor of *Golf Digest* magazine and freelances for other periodicals, including *Golf* and *Parents Magazine*. He has won numerous prizes in golf and basketball writers' competitions.

LEONARD SHECTER ("The Toughest Man in Pro Football"), now deceased, won the *Best Sports Stories—1968* magazine award with the story reprinted here. Born in New York City, he attended New York University and began his newspaper career as a copy boy with the *New York Post*. He became successively a reporter, night editor, and sports columnist for that newspaper. He was also the sports commentator for Westinghouse Broadcasting. After 20 years in the newspaper business, he became a freelance writer exclusively and his work appeared in the leading magazines.

WALTER W. (RED) SMITH ("Gaelic Disaster") made his first appearance in *Best Sports Stories* in 1944. He attended the University of Notre Dame and since then he has had a long and successful career with papers in Philadelphia, St. Louis, and New York City. He now is a columnist for the *New York Times* and also one of the three judges for this series.

GAY TALESE ("The Silent Season of a Hero") won a *Best Sports Story* magazine award with this article. A former newspaperman (with the *New York Times*) he is a freelance writer who devotes himself to books (he is now working on a book on sex in America) and magazine articles, notably for *Esquire*. Born in Ocean City, New Jersey, he attended the University of Alabama, graduating, he says, by the skin of his teeth. He lives in Manhattan with his wife and daughter.

HARRY WATERS ("The Triumphant Turnabout of the Hartsdale Hurricanes") is a graduate of Columbia University and the Columbia School of Journalism, which he attended on a Daily News–Frank J. Hause Scholarship. He worked for the Associated Press and the *Stamford* (Connecticut) *Advocate* and then, in 1962, joined *Newsweek*. At that magazine he now conducts the Media Department, having previously written the Life and Leisure, TV, and Cities departments. He won the J. C. Penney–University of Missouri Award for magazine journalism in 1971.

STANLEY WOODWARD ("One Strike Is Out") was one of America's most highly regarded sports writers. He was born in Worcester, Massachusetts, and became the sports editor of the *New York Herald Tribune* in 1937. He served for a time with Miami and Newark papers and as general sports editor of the Newhouse chain. He edited the Dell football annual and authored a book on sports writing entitled *Sports Page* as well as an autobiography, *Paper Tiger*. He died in 1965.

The Photographers

ERNEST ANHEUSER ("Heads Up") was a student at the Chicago Art Institute before turning to photography as a profession during World War II. He is now on the staff of the *Milwaukee Journal* and is a member of both the National and Wisconsin Press Photographers Associations.

JOHN E. BIEVER ("Confrontation of the Giants") is a recent graduate of Wisconsin University and has won many honors, including the action shot award in *Best Sports Stories—1973*. He works with his father, John Biever, who has appeared many times in this anthology.

BOB CAMPBELL ("Glasses for the Umpire") was with the *San Francisco Chronicle* as a distinguished photographer in all areas before he passed away in 1968.

PAUL J. CONNELL ("Double Duty") is a two-time winner in *Best Sports Stories*. He has to his credit over 80 awards in various categories and was named as the New England "Best Photographer" three years in a row. He started in with the *Boston Globe* in 1937 as an errand boy and became a *Globe* staffer in photography in 1941.

PAUL DE MARIA ("The Battery Is Fully Charged") first studied photography in high school and went to work for the *New York Daily News* as a copy boy. In 1962 he became a full-fledged photographer and since then he has earned many honors for his work.

JOE DENARIE ("Terpsichore in Triplicate") had his photo in our first book, in 1944. After years of meritorious service with the *San Francisco Examiner* he struck out on his own as a real-estate man. He now lives in San Rafael, California.

BOB DOTY ("I'm Having a Ball") joined the *Dayton Journal* in 1938 and became one of the winningest photographers in this series, with three firsts. His shots were usually in the feature division. He broke in as an AP wirephoto man and then went to

314

the *Dayton Journal Herald.* He retired from active service several years ago.

NAT FEIN ("No. 3"), who was with the *New York Herald Tribune* as a photographer for many years, became a freelancer after his paper's demise.

JACK FRANK ("The Old School Try") was with the *New York Herald Tribune* and was primarily a sports photographer. He retired to Florida after his paper ceased publication. He died about six years ago.

CARL E. FRANKS ("Death Takes a Winner") was one of our earliest contributors (1948) in *Best Sports Stories*. He is still snapping the lens for his paper, the *Cedar Rapids* (Iowa) *Gazette,* and has earned a wide following and many citations.

LARRY C. GRAFF ("A Lunge to Victory"), a photographer for the Chicago *Sun-Times* for the past five years, has won several photo awards, mostly in sports. Before joining the *Sun-Times* he was photo chief of a 10-paper chain of semi-weeklies covering suburbs north of Chicago. While there he was named national Suburban Photographer of the Year for 1967–1968.

HARRY HARRIS ("The Catch") has been with the Associated Press since 1928, first as a messenger, then as a printer and then as a photographer. In 1934 he made one of the first aerial photos while covering the burning at sea of the *S.S. Morro Castle.* He also worked in the New Haven and Louisville bureaus of the AP and in the latter post photographed the Kentucky Derby.

CHARLES HOFF ("Sock Treatment") has won three prizes, all in the action category, in the *Best Sports Stories* series. In 1928 he began work with the *New York Daily Mirror;* five years later he joined the *New York Daily News.* His most famous picture is of the burning of the dirigible *Hindenburg* at Lakehurst, New Jersey. He died a few years ago.

FRANK HURLEY ("Out by a Foot") joined the *New York Daily News* over 30 years ago and is still active as a photographer. His career started with the trial of Bruno Hauptmann for the murder of the Lindbergh baby. He has had many shots in *Best Sports Stories* and won the action award in 1961.

TED KELL ("American Beauty") worked for the *New York Herald Tribune* and won many honors, particularly with his yachting pictures. At present he is freelancing on Long Island, New York.

JAMES R. KILPATRICK ("A Stick-to-It-iveness") has been with the *Detroit News* over 40 years. Since 1950 he has been a sports photographer exclusively and he has received numerous honors.

JOE KORDICK ("Pro-Amateur Miss"), who died early in 1974, was with the *Chicago Sun-Times* photographic staff for over 30 years. For most of that time he specialized in sports photography and his work appeared in *Best Sports Stories* many times. A son is also a photographer.

NEILS LAURITIEN ("Head Hunter") was with the *Milwaukee Sentinel* for over 30 years and his fine work has merited many appearances in this sports anthology. He was one of the most highly regarded photographers of the Midwest until his untimely death a few years ago in an automobile accident.

HARRY LEDER ("Beginning of the End") is chief photographer of United Press International and completed 33 years with the photo agency early in 1974. Before going to UPI, he worked for *Newsweek* magazine and the Associated Press. During World War II he served in the Navy as a member of a combat photo unit. Harry Leder has covered political conventions as well as sports.

ANDREW LOPEZ ("The Bitter End") has been a staff photographer for UPI for 34 years and also worked for the *New York Times* and the Associated Press. In World War II he served overseas as a war correspondent in the European theater and covered the landings in Normandy. He has won many photo contests.

PAUL MAGUIRE ("The Laurel Fits") has been regaling the readers of the *Boston Globe* for over 40 years with his splendid photographic work. A Holy Cross graduate, he pioneered in sending photographs to his newspaper by portable transmitter.

CHARLES L. PUGH ("Catch as Catch Can") started his career with the *Johnson City* (Tennessee) *Press Chronicle* and in 1956 joined the *Atlanta Journal-Constitution*, where he still is. He has many awards to his credit, including a number of first places in the Associated Press Photo Contest and the action shot award for this photo in *Best Sports Stories—1969*.

BOB RAY ("When the Cheering Stopped") joined the *Nashville Banner* in 1956 and is still with the same paper. He won the photo feature prize in *Best Sports Stories—1967* and is active in all phases of press photography.

ARTHUR RICKERBY ("That's My Pop"), deceased, was one of the pioneers in 35mm photography. A graduate of Duke University, he worked for UPI and then *Life* magazine. He shot the famous picture of Don Larsen's last pitch in his perfect World Series game in 1956.

JERRY RIFE ("Expos' Last Stand") has won over 25 annual photographic awards from the National, California, and Press Photographers' Associations. He received a degree in education from San Diego College in 1964 and is now on the staff of the *San Diego Union and Tribune*. His photo won first prize in the action category in this anthology in 1971.

KEN ROSS ("Flying High") is at present with the *Memphis Press-Scimtar*, where he has established himself as one of the fine photographers of the Southeastern sporting scene.

BILL SERNE ("Innocent Bystander") won the action photo award with this photo in *Best Sports Stories—1974*. Twenty-five years old and a graduate of Kent State, he went to work for the *Tampa Tribune* in 1972 immediately after graduation and is still with that paper.

PAUL SIEGEL ("Dirt Eater") was with the *Minneapolis Star and Tribune* for many years. After leaving the *Star and Tribune* he continued active as a freelance photographer.

BARNEY STEIN ("After the Ball Was Over") was with the *New York Post* for almost half a century and was acknowledged as one of Manhattan's best photographers. He retired about five years ago, but his creative restlessness put him right back to work for the *Sarasota* (Florida) *Herald-Tribune-Journal*, where he is on the photographic staff and still as busy as ever.

HOWARD SWIFT ("Football Ballet") was a photographer for the *Des Moines Register and Tribune* when this picture was taken, but now he is director of photography for Dow Chemical Company in its Midland, Michigan, branch. He was with the *Register* for 10 years and left to go to Dow 12 years ago.